Chamber Music

Chamber Music

AN ESSENTIAL HISTORY

Mark A. Radice

The University of Michigan Press • *Ann Arbor*

Published in the United States of America by
The University of Michigan Press
Manufactured in the United States of America
∞ Printed on acid-free paper

2015 2014 2013 2012 4 3 2

A CIP catalog record for this book is available from the British Library.

Library of Congress Cataloging-in-Publication Data

Radice, Mark A.
Chamber music : an essential history / Mark A. Radice.
p. cm.
Includes bibliographical references and index.
ISBN 978-0-472-07165-4 (cloth : alk. paper) —
ISBN 978-0-472-05165-6 (pbk. : alk. paper) —
1. Chamber music—History and criticism. I. Title.
ML1100.R34 2012
785.009—dc23

2011037284

ISBN 978-0-472-02811-5 (e-book)

To My Mom and Dad—Always there, always ready

Contents

Introduction

The term *chamber music* was introduced in the seventeenth century by the theorist Marco Scacchi. For him, chamber music was one of three contexts in which music was ordinarily found; these were *musica ecclesiastica* (church music), *musica theatralis* (theater music), and *musica cubicularis* (chamber music). These categories had nothing to do with the number of players, the number and sequence of movements, or the formal design of individual movements. Indeed, details of the actual compositions could not be deduced on the basis of Scacchi's three classifications. The designation *chamber music* indicated only that a particular composition was intended to be performed in a private residence rather than in a church or in a theater. Many works that were initially performed in private residences hardly seem to be chamber music to the present-day music lover: The *Brandenburg Concertos* of Johann Sebastian Bach, for example, and Beethoven's Fourth Symphony were first heard in aristocratic homes.

There are several reasons why the *Brandenburg Concertos* might seem to us poor examples of chamber music. Since they are concertos, we expect a contrast between the ensemble of soloists and the orchestral tutti. Also, it is quite likely that the harpsichord player would have led the performance from the keyboard. These factors are at odds with our contemporary notion of chamber music, which typically presumes a work requiring more than a single performer, but having only one player per part. In addition, most chamber music is performed without a conductor.

With the demise of western European aristocracy during the late eighteenth and early nineteenth centuries, courtly ensembles were replaced by domestic gatherings, often of amateur musicians. Domestic ensembles tended to be smaller and to play music of only moderate difficulty. It was during this time that the principal genres of chamber music became standardized: the sonata for keyboard and one or more melody instruments, the string quartet, and the piano trio. Music of this sort became a highly marketable commodity. Music publishing shops opened throughout Europe, and magazines and other periodicals commonly published multimovement chamber pieces in installments. Soon, however, musicians in duos, trios, and quartets who performed together on a regular basis became specialists in the repertoire for their particular group. Composers—who were often members of such ensembles—responded by writing music of a more demanding nature. Franz Joseph Haydn and Wolfgang Amadeus Mozart, for example, wrote some of their finest chamber works for ensembles of which they were members. In so doing, they gradually pushed chamber music repertoire out of the reach of typical amateur groups.

Nineteenth-century Europe and America witnessed dramatic changes in demographics. In general, rural populations declined, and urban populations grew. Two extreme cases are seen in the instances of London and New York City. The population of London jumped from one million in 1800 to 6.7 million at the end of the century. For most of the nineteenth century, it was the most populous city in the world. In New York City, the population jumped from 49, 487 in 1790 to 2,581,541 in 1890.[1] In order to accommodate these larger populations, buildings intended for music performance changed dramatically during that century. Whereas the typical concert hall of the eighteenth century accommodated an audience of approximately 550 people, the average nineteenth-century hall was designed for an audience of approximately 2,400.[2] These gargantuan halls were suited to the high-profile genres of the day, such as operas, concertos, oratorios, and symphonies, but they were hardly congenial to the intimacy of chamber music. Many of the Romantic century's leading composers cared little—if at all—for composing chamber music. Hector Berlioz, Franz Liszt, Richard Wagner, Anton Bruckner, and Richard Strauss are just a few of the composers who might be cited as examples. Those composers who did write chamber music were often fascinated with music history—like Felix Mendelssohn and Robert Schumann—or, believed that they were upholding standards that had been established by the giants of the late eighteenth century. Working in Vienna, where the music critic Eduard Hanslick guarded the city's musical heritage, Johannes Brahms felt a special responsibility to uphold the chamber-music tradition that virtually originated there during the Classical era.

With the transformation of tonality that took place at the close of the nineteenth century and the beginning of the twentieth, chamber music ensembles provided the ideal venue for experimentation with new and often difficult idioms. Many of these experimental styles rejected traditional harmony, melody, and meter. At the same time, timbre, register, and rhythm assumed greater importance; consequently, composers turned to ad hoc chamber ensembles, often with unusual instrumentation. Debussy, for example, thoroughly reconstituted the traditional trio for piano, violin, and cello with one consisting of flute, viola, and harp. Chamber ensembles thus became a testing ground for progressive ideas and novel sonorities. Contemporary chamber ensembles are remarkable equally for the types of music they play and for the fact that they are not chamber music ensembles at all—at least, not in the sense that Scacchi had imagined when he coined the term. Instead, they are concert artists who specialize in the performance of recent repertoire. Ensembles such as Earplay, the Kronos Quartet, and the Verdehr Trio are just a few outstanding examples of groups that specialize in contemporary chamber music.

The instrumentations of chamber ensembles became still more diverse with the advent of academic programs in ethnomusicology. Traditional instruments of China, Japan, Korea, and many other nations began to appear with Western instruments in chamber ensembles. In some cases, too, Asian composers write for Western instruments in the manner of traditional Asian instruments. Composers such as Chou Wen-chung, Chen Yi, and Zhou Long have made great accomplishments in combining Asian artistic concepts with Western musical materials. The "non-Western" curiosities of the 1950s have now yielded to masterpieces that draw their musical materials from global resources.

In the pages that follow, the turning points briefly outlined here will be considered in greater detail. This study examines the personalities involved with the creation, dissemination, and performance of chamber music as well as representative compositions, considered both as autonomous musical structures and as mirrors of the societies in which they came into being.

Musical examples occasionally call attention to distinctive features of a particular piece, but since music students and professionals will necessarily procure complete scores and recordings of those works that strike their fancy, examples are concise. Access to scores has become much easier owing to recent electronic sources, such as the following:

Alexander Street Press Classical Scores Library (http://alexanderstreet.com/)
International Music Score Project (http://imslp.org/)

ScorSer (http://www.scorser.com/)
Digital Scores from the Eastman School of Music
(https://urresearch.rochester.edu/viewInstitutionalCollection.action?collectionId=63)
Variations Project, University of Indiana
(http://www.dlib.indiana.edu/variations/scores/)

Readers should also consult the University of Michigan Press home page for listings of related links.

Listening resources available on line have also burgeoned during the past several years, and now Classical.com (www.classical.com), the Naxos Music Library (http://www.naxos.com/), and other online sources put repertoire at our disposal with ease. Indeed, one can even find many works in live performances on YouTube (http://www.youtube.com/).

I have kept detailed, theoretical discussions to a minimum, preferring instead to focus on the cultural, aesthetic, and philosophical circumstances that led composers to their particular artistic visions. The Table of Compositions According to Ensemble Size will be useful primarily for practical musicians looking for repertoire for actual performance situations. Throughout the text, pitches are given as capital letters. Pitches in the octave of middle C are indicated simply as C, D, E, and so forth. Octaves above the middle-C octave are designated with capital letters and superscript numbers (e.g., C^1, C^2, etc.); octaves below with subscripts (e.g., C_1, C_2, etc.).

ONE

The Nature of Early Chamber Music

Haut and *Bas* Instruments

Music for domestic performance—chamber music—is the focus of this book. Aristocratic homes of medieval Europe often had rather expansive music rooms, but these spaces were generally smaller than a church or theater. Less volume was required to fill them with sounds, and ensembles tended to be smaller.

Early musical instruments were classified either as *haut* (i.e., high-volume) or *bas* (low-volume). The high-volume instruments included the trumpet, trombone, shawm, buisine, and so forth. The low-volume instruments included the viol, lute, bandora, chitarrone, and the violin family (which came into common use only in the early seventeenth century), as well as the more subtle wind instruments, such as the recorder and transverse flute.

Instrumentation in the Music of the Late Medieval Era and the Renaissance

Idiomatic instrumental and vocal styles came into being during the early Baroque. Older repertoire was constructed according to the laws of voice-leading without regard to instrumentation. This abstract approach to composition led to a singular style that was used both for voices and for instruments. Compositions from this era can often be found in multiple versions, some with texts, others without. Almost any late medieval or Renaissance score could be converted into a piece of instrumental chamber music simply by performing it on *bas* instruments with suitable ranges for the particular musical lines.

EARLY MUSICAL INSTRUMENTS

Instruments of the medieval and Renaissance fell out of use during the Classic and Romantic eras, but instrument builders and early music ensembles have stimulated interest in these antiques. Some of the most important early instruments are described in the following list.[1]

Early Musical Instruments

bandora Plucked stringed instrument, similar in construction to the lute but tuned differently, having six or seven courses.

buisine Brass instrument constructed like the ancient tuba, but with a long slim pipe curved round and terminating in a funnel-shaped bell.

chitarrone *See* **lute.**

cittern Small stringed instrument having a pear shape, flat back, six courses and frets; the cittern was usually strung with wire and played with a plectrum.

clavichord Keyboard instrument in which the string was activated by a tangent attached directly to the key; tone was subtle in the extreme, but the instrument was capable of producing graduated dynamics.

cornetto Curved woodwind instrument with finger holes front and back; conical bore; played with a mouthpiece similar to that of a trumpet, but made of wood and more shallow; available in consort; bass instrument of this sort was curved into the shape of an S to provide access to the finger holes and was therefore called a "serpent."

crumhorn Family of capped double-reed instruments; cylindrical bore; finger holes front and back; shaped like the letter J; literally "bent horn."

curtel Family of double-reed instruments with two parallel conical bores joined at the bottom. The bore often terminated in a small bell. The bass version of the instrument was the ancestor of the modern bassoon. The name is a corruption of the word "curtail."

dulcian *See* **curtel.**

dulcimer Stringed instrument with flat soundboard; strings usually activated by striking with hand-held hammers.

harpsichord Keyboard instrument often with multiple sets of strings; the strings were activated by a plectrum that plucked the strings when the key was depressed.

lute Stringed instrument with rounded back and shaped like a halved pear; often with eleven strings in six courses; flat fingerboard with gut frets; smaller instruments of this type called mandola; related to modern mandolin; construction varied widely, especially as regards length of fingerboard as related to body. The chitarrone, a large bass lute, was especially popular during the sixteenth and seventeenth centuries as a continuo instrument.

nackers Type of kettledrum usually used in pairs and struck with mallets.

pandora *See* **bandora.**

panpipes Wind instrument consisting of a number of tuned pipes of different sizes bound together with glue; pipes are typically stopped at one end and blown across the top; also known as "vertical flutes."

psaltry Similar in construction to dulcimer, but strings were activated by plucking with the fingers or with a plectrum.

racket Family of double-reed instruments in which the tube is continuously doubled back on itself in order to form nine verticals alternately joined at top and bottom with U-shaped crooks to yield one continuous column of air. This design was devised to keep the instrument compact.

recorder Most popular type of fipple flute (i.e., end-blown); cylindrical bore; finger holes front and back; available in full consort.

regal A small pipe organ constructed with reed pipes exclusively.

sackbut Ancestor of the modern trombone; distinctive features included a U-shaped slide for changing pitch and a flared bell.

shawm Family of double-reed instrument; ancestor of the modern oboe; finger holes front and back; reed was held directly in the player's lips.

slide trumpet Early brass instrument with the characteristics of a trumpet but without valves or pistons; some flexibility in pitches played was achieved by equipping the instrument with a slide; design proved impractical, consequently the instrument was not widely used.

sordune Family of instruments constructed, like the dulcian, with the tube doubled back on itself. It differed from the dulcian in that it had a cylindrical rather than a conical bore. This feature gave it a somewhat more gentle, mellow sound.

vihuela Stringed instrument with flat front and back; ancestor of modern guitar; flat fingerboard with frets; often as "vihuela *da mano.*"

viol Family of stringed instrument; flat back; fretted fingerboard; typically had six strings; bowed with an underhanded grip (as many present-day double bass players can be seen using). The bow was shaped as a gentle curve, and the tension on the bow hairs was regulated by the player's finger.

virginal English or Italian type of harpsichord constructed in a rectangular case with strings running at right angles to the keys; activated by a plectrum, like the harpsichord.

OPTIONAL SCORING

With the advent of music publishing in the early sixteenth century, optional scoring became increasingly desirable since it resulted in a wider market for printed compositions. Ottaviano de Petrucci issued the *Odhecaton*, the earliest example of printed music, in 1501. Although the majority of these compositions were originally vocal pieces, the absence of complete texts suggests that they may have been performed by instrumental ensembles.[2]

Similarly confusing cases exist in manuscript sources of the period. In an early sixteenth-century manuscript prepared for King Henry VIII, twenty-four instrumental consort pieces and six puzzle canons are sandwiched among numerous texted part songs.[3] An even dozen of the consorts were written by Henry himself; one each came from the pens of William Cornish and Thomas Farthing. The remaining ten are of unknown authorship. The pieces are about equally divided into works in three and four voices. Most pieces are in duple meter, but triple meter also appears. Imitation appears in most of the consorts.

In published works of the period, optional scoring is often invited by the composer and/or publisher. Paul Hofhaimer (1459–1537), who was active at the court of the Emperor Maximilian, issued his *Harmoniæ poeticæ* in the year 1539. On the title page, we read: "*Harmoniæ poeticæ* . . . most excellently suited for voices as well as for instruments." Similar flexibility is apparent in Orlando Gibbons's *First Set of Madrigals and Mottets of 5 Parts: Apt for Viols and Voyces* (London, 1612).[4] In both cases, voices and instruments might have been mixed depending upon the resources at hand. In his collection of dance music published in 1599, Anthony Holborne (ca. 1560–1602) indicates that the volume contains "Pavans, galliards, almains and other short æirs both grave, and light, in five parts for viols, violins, or other musicall winde instruments." Optional scoring was common until the late Baroque era. The autograph manuscript of the "Benedictus" of Bach's *B-minor Mass*, for example, does not specify the obbligato instrument.

THE BROKEN AND FULL CONSORTS

Instrumental ensembles of the Renaissance are frequently described with the words "broken" or "full." A broken consort combined instruments of different types.[5] Conversely, the full consort used instruments from a single family. Broken consorts were used more often than full consorts during the Renaissance.

The instrumentation of a broken consort was not standardized, but one of the more common combinations included flute, lute, treble viol, cittern, bass viol, and bandora, the ensemble specified by Thomas Morley (ca. 1557–1602) in his two volumes of Consort Lessons (1599, 1611).

The repertoire for full consort was limited almost exclusively to stringed instruments, especially the viol.[6] From the late sixteenth century to the last quarter of the seventeenth century, the viol family enjoyed great prestige and popularity, particularly in England. The polyphonic chamber music for full viol consort was often written in six parts and required two treble viols, two mean (i.e., middle-range) viols, and two bass viols. A set of six constituted a "chest of viols" because the instruments were stored in "chests" specifically designed as protective cases.

PAIRED DANCES AND SUITES

Both broken and full consorts were used throughout the Renaissance for playing dance music. Dances varied from one country to the next, but in most countries it was common to find them in pairs: the first in a slow duple meter, the second in a faster triple or compound meter. In France and England, the most common pair of dances was the pavane and the galliard. In Italy the passamezzo and the saltarello were comparable. In Germany the *Tanz* and *Proportz* were a common pairing.

Dance music was nothing new in the sixteenth century, but its availability in printed editions was. Publishers like Tylman Susato (ca. 1500–ca. 1564) in Antwerp, Pierre Attaingnant (ca. 1494–1552) in Paris, Jacques Moderne (ca. 1495–ca. 1562) in Lyons, and Thomas Morley (1557–1602) in London were at the forefront of this enterprise, and their publications preserve hundreds of samples from this repertoire.

During the seventeenth century, newer dances were added to the conventional pairs. The particular dances added depended upon regional trends and preferences. In France, for example, the minuet became very popular; or, in English scores, one might find the hornpipe. Dances assembled into groups are commonly called "suites."

CHAMBER MUSIC BASED ON IMITATIVE POLYPHONY: THE *Canzona*

Some of the most fascinating music written during the late Renaissance and the early Baroque achieves its structural unity by treating a particular motif in imitation. The imitation may be free or strict. From the closing decades of the fifteenth century until the beginning of the eighteenth, the most important genre using free imitation was the *canzona.*

The word *canzona* means "song," but most canzonas are instrumental pieces. The explanation for this disparity actually reveals the origin and typical stylistic features of the canzona. During the high Renaissance period, Josquin des Pres (ca. 1440–1521), Pierre de la Rue (ca. 1460–1518), Loyset Compère (ca. 1445–1518), and other Flemish composers wrote secular part songs called *chansons*, which employed motivic imitation in some sections but free counterpoint or homophony in others.

The *chanson* had no predetermined form, and the music of its various sections was freely invented to accord with the poetry being set. These secular part songs quickly became popular in Italy, sometimes with their French texts, but more often without them. The Italians referred to a piece of this sort as a *canzona francese*, or "French song."

In many cases, these "songs" were performed on instruments rather than sung. Italian composers soon began writing canzonas that had no texts at all; instead, these canzonas simply reproduced the characteristic interplay of voices, the lively rhythms, and the contrasting sections that characterized the French *chanson.*[7]

Florentio Maschera (ca. 1540–ca. 1584) and his teacher, Claudio Merulo (1533–1604), played an important role in the history of the canzona. Merulo's organ canzonas served as the compositional models for Maschera, but it was Maschera who first published a set of canzonas written especially for an instrumental ensemble. His volume entitled *Libro primo de canzoni da sonare a quattro voce* (First book of canzonas to be played in four parts) was the first of hundreds that used the designation *da sonare* to specify instrumental performance.[8]

The Italian word *sonare* means "to sound" in the sense of producing sound from an instrument. In Renaissance and Baroque scores, the word is used in contrast to *cantare*, "to sing"; hence, instrumental music carried the instruction *da sonare*, and vocal music was designated as repertoire *da cantare.* Eventually the cumbersome designation *canzona da sonare* was shortened to the more familiar word *sonata.*

The hundreds of composers who contributed to the canzona repertoire cannot be discussed here, but many fascinating examples of the genre can be found in collections like the *Canzoni alla Francese a quattro voci per sonare* of Adriano Banchieri (1568–1634), the *Canzoni da sonare a quattro, et otto voci* of Florio Canale (ca. 1550–ca. 1603), *Il primo libro delle canzoni a quattro voci per sonare con ogni sorte de stromenti musicali* by Tarquinio Merula (ca. 1594–1665), and the *Canzoni a 3: doi violini, e violone, col suo basso continuo* of

Canzona ottava: La Banchierina

Adriano Banchieri

Canzona subject

Maurizio Cazzati (ca. 1620–1666). Cazzati's collection was later reprinted as *Canzoni da sonare a tre.*[9]

These canzonas reveal a growing distinction between vocal and instrumental music, which led ultimately to idiomatic styles of writing suited to specific instruments and voice types. This stylistic refinement was one of the major achievements of the Baroque era.

In their musical settings, many of the *chanson* texts were fitted to a dactylic rhythm in duple meter. This rhythm and meter came to be a characteristic feature of the earliest instrumental canzonas. The eleven canzonas contained in Banchieri's 1596 collection, for example, are uniformly in common meter. Canzona subjects are energetic, often beginning with a dactylic rhythm.

Duple meter was predominant in the earliest canzonas, but later examples of the genre frequently introduced contrasting sections in triple or compound meter. Very often, sections were set off one from another by dynamic contrasts or by varied tempo indications. Imitative sections tended to be in lively tempos, whereas passages in free counterpoint or homophony were at a slower pace. Precise instrumentation was seldom indicated in the scores of canzonas *da sonar.*

Formal designs within canzonas were as varied and numerous as were the composers. In Banchieri's canzonas, two or three sections may be related thematically and call for repeats. Other pieces consist of continuous manipulation of a single motif. Ordinarily, a single voice states the primary motif, which then appears at regular intervals in the imitating voices. Contrapuntal sections in which all voices commence simultaneously are rare. A distinctive feature of Banchieri's collection is his use of titles for each canzona.

In most canzonas, little continuity is apparent from one section to the next. Within the context of the original, vocal *chansons,* the text held the compositions together. As instrumental music, the free-form canzona was less effective. Composers experimented with various techniques in order to achieve coherence. Some canzonas conclude with a return to the opening thematic material. Others involve a systematic alternation between imitative and homophonic sections. The most ingenious structures appear in a type of canzona known as the *variation canzona,* in which imitative portions are built on thematic variants of the opening motif.

CHAMBER MUSIC BASED ON IMITATIVE POLYPHONY: *Ricercar*-TYPE PIECES

The high Renaissance motet exerted a powerful impact on contemporaneous instrumental music based on strict counterpoint. In Italy, the terms *ricercar* or *capriccio* were commonly used to designate motet-like instrumental pieces. In Spain, *tiento* or *fantasia* was the more typical designation. In England, the customary labels for such pieces were *fancy*, *fantasia*, or *fantasy*. The word *ricercar* is derived from *cercare:* to search. Exactly what the search (or "research," in this case) entailed differed at various times in the history of the genre. The earliest pieces bearing the label *ricercar* were intended to test the tuning of strings and the placement of the frets on the lute. Ricercari of this sort can be found mainly in the early sixteenth-century works of composers like Francesco Spinacino and Joan Ambrosio Dalza, whose ricercari appear in Petrucci's 1507 publication of the *Intabolatura de lauto*. In its more common application, the term *ricercar* designates a piece exploring the possibilities of elaborating a subject or series of subjects. The typical ricercar subject is "abstract in character and well fitted for its function of displaying contrapuntal artifice."[10]

A "monothematic" ricercar is based on one single motif, whereas the "polythematic" ricercar employs a variety of subjects. In either case, the composer will present a musical motif, called the *dux*, or "lead voice," which will then be imitated in the remaining voices. When an imitating voice enters at a tonal level other than the tonic, it is called an answer, or *comes*. The answer is described either as a "real" or a "tonal" answer. If the intervallic content of the *dux* is reproduced exactly in a strict transposition, then the answer is "real." If any of the intervals of the *dux* is changed in the *comes*, the answer is described as "tonal." A special type of answer that is sometimes found in music of the seventeenth century is the so-called *inganno*, a permutation of the original subject obtained by using its solmization syllables rather than its intervallic content.[11]

Imitative works of the eighteenth and nineteenth centuries typically alternate between the tonic and dominant levels or, perhaps, the tonic and subdominant. This regular alternation of tonal planes was by no means standardized in the fifteenth and sixteenth centuries. Variable also is the length of time between the initial statement of the motif and its successive imitations. Some composers, like the Venetian Gioseffe Zarlino (1517–1590), advocated widely spaced entries of the principal motif in order to permit the greatest possible diversity and imagination in the construction of the musical subject. Other composers, like Thomas Morley

Fantasia of Foure Parts

Orlando Gibbons

Ricercar theme

(ca. 1557–1602), preferred short themes in close imitations so that performers and listeners could more easily follow the subjects.

Spacings between entries of the subject can also have a dramatic effect. As a piece nears its conclusion, the composer may shorten the gap between the subject and its answer so that entries are stacked one upon the other in rapid succession. This device is called *stretto*—the Italian word for "pressure" or "stress."

The leading masters of the Italian ricercar were Adriano Willaert and Girolamo Frescobaldi. Willaert's ricercari appeared in two mid-sixteenth-century collections of *Fantasie et recerchari.* He generally preferred the polythematic ricercar. Frescobaldi wrote his ricercari a bit later. They are landmarks of the early Baroque style, especially since the subjects are highly expressive, and the harmonies are often daringly chromatic.

The seventeenth-century *capriccio* was a special type of ricercar that displayed some unpredictable behavior—for example, extensive chromaticism, or irregular resolutions of dissonances.

Most Italian composers who wrote ricercar-type pieces were church organists, and the repertoire that they produced were pieces *da chiesa* (for church) rather than *da camera* (for chamber), but in England imitative polyphony made its way into the domestic music-making of amateurs. The ensemble most often used to this music was a full consort of viols.

Viol playing had become popular in England by the close of the sixteenth century. Publishers cultivated the amateur viol player by issuing instruction books on "how to play the viol." Christopher Simpson's *The Division-Violist* appeared in London in 1659. Thomas Mace's compendium, *Musick's Monument,* was published there in 1676. *Musick's Monument* contains three sections. The last is entitled "The Generous Viol, in Its Rightest Use."

The popularity of the viol fantasia evoked scores from the pens of leading composers like William Byrd, Giovanni Coprario (ca. 1575–1626), Alfonso Ferrabosco (ca. 1575–1628), Orlando Gibbons (1583–1625), John Jenkins (1592–1678), and William Lawes (1602–1645). Their combined works form a genuine treasure trove of chamber music for strings.

Owing to the growing market for chamber compositions, music publishing flourished in sixteenth- and seventeenth-century England. William Byrd, who had been granted a patent for music publishing in 1575 by Queen Elizabeth, was a key figure in the dissemination of this repertoire. The three collections of fantasies by Orlando Gibbons are also important to the history of music publishing since one of these collections, the *Fantasies of Three Parts* (London, n.d.), was "cut in copper." Copper-plate engraving—a fast, accurate, and relatively cheap way of producing scores—became the most common way to print music during the eighteenth century. At the time of Gibbons's publication, though, it was a process that, as the title page states, was "not heretofore extant."

THE *In Nomine*

A type of piece cultivated exclusively by English composers was the *In nomine*. These were secular, instrumental consort pieces; however, they all used the Sarum rite plainchant for the text *Gloria tibi Trinitas æqualis* in one way or another.

The pieces were called *In nomine* because the plainchant melody was known to composers of the era in the context of John Taverner's *Missa Gloria tibi Trinitas,* which states the full melody in the mean voice at the appearance of the words *in nomine Domine* at the close of the *Sanctus.*[12]

Many composers contributed settings of the *In nomine* tune: John Bull (ca. 1562–1628), William Byrd, Alfonso Ferrabosco, Orlando Gibbons, Robert Parsons (ca. 1530–1570), Thomas Weelkes (1576–1623), and many others. Despite their churchly origin, some pieces based on the *In nomine* are humorous. Christopher Tye (1505–1573), for instance, composed a setting (known as "In nominee Crye") in which cries of London street vendors hawking their goods are woven around the plainchant. The *In nomine* remained an important genre of English instrumental music until the time of Henry Purcell (1659–1695), who contributed a number of outstanding examples.

The early-music revival has resulted in the use of this tune in several contemporary works. Peter Maxwell Davies (b. 1934) has written two elegant orchestral fantasies based on it, and between 1963 and 1965, he composed seven settings for chamber ensembles.

THE EARLY BAROQUE SONATA

To a musician of the Baroque era, the term *sonata* designated a piece to be "sounded" (*suonare*) rather than sung (*cantare*). The most important sonata

"In nomine" plainchant

literature of the Baroque era consists of the so-called solo and trio sonatas. These terms are confusing. The "solo" sonata often required two or three players: the "solo" violinist and the accompanying basso continuo group consisting of the bass line instrument (cello possibly with violone) and the chord-playing instrument (a harpsichord, lute, harp, or guitar in secular works; or, an organ in church works).[13] For a "trio" sonata, three or four players were needed: two equal, treble instruments (usually violins), and the basso continuo group.

THE SONATA *da Chiesa*

Depending upon whether the pieces were intended as service music for church or music for amusement at home, the sonatas were described as being either *da chiesa* (for church) or *da camera* (for chamber). The *da chiesa* sonata typically has three or more movements in contrasting tempos.[14] Tempos are indicated by Italian words such as *grave* (i.e., serious), *allegro* (i.e., happy), *vivace* (i.e., lively) and so forth. These words indicated moods, but they in no way had the specificity of metronome markings. Sonatas often had a succession of four movements in the tempos slow-fast-slow-fast; but this pattern was not universal. Even within the four-movement plan, Archangelo Corelli (1653–1713) and his contemporaries frequently introduced contrasting subsections within movements. Sonatas *da chiesa* often contain movements in contrapuntal texture as well as occasional movements in closely related keys. Since organ was available in Italian churches at the time, it was generally part of the continuo group in church sonatas; however, other chord-playing instruments may have been added.

Starting in the mid-sixteenth century, the art of violin building flourished in Italy. The trade was usually passed from fathers to sons in families. Some of the most important families were the Amati, Guarneri, Stradivari, and Guadagnini. Many of these builders were active in the tiny north-Italian town of Cremona, which is about twenty-five miles southwest of Brescia and seventy-five miles northwest of Bologna. These two music centers kept the Cremonese string builders productive during the heyday of the Baroque era.[15]

Perhaps the most important composer of Baroque string sonatas was Corelli, whose orderly publications became for historians the paradigms of the genre. Corelli was highly regarded during his own lifetime and became a model for many other Baroque composers, including John Ravenscroft (d. ca. 1708), Francesco Geminiani (1687–1762), George Frideric Handel (1685–1759), and Johann Sebastian Bach (1685–1750). In contrast to most musicians, Corelli died a rich man with considerable cash assets as well as a fine collection of paintings.

Little is known about Corelli's early life and training. We do know that between 1666 and 1670, he was active in Bologna. By 1675, he had settled in Rome, where he found willing benefactors in Queen Christiana of Sweden and Cardinal Pamphili. From 1690 until his death, Cardinal Pietro Ottoboni was also among Corelli's patrons.

Corelli's output consisted of six sets of instrumental organized as table 1 shows.

Corelli's music reflects the state of the art of Italian instrumental music at the turn of the century. Functional harmony, major and minor mode, sequences and suspensions, and respect for the role of the leading tone had been firmly established in practice, though theoretical explanation of these structures did not appear until Jean-Philippe Rameau's *Traité de l'harmonie* (1722).[16]

Corelli's melodies often use thematic transformations like those we find in the variation canzona repertoire. For instance, the principal themes of the first and second Allegro movements in the Sonata in G minor, Op. 1, No. 10, are closely related in their pitch content; however, whereas the former theme appears in common time, it is transformed in the second Allegro by its use within 6/8 meter.

Corelli's melodies tend to be derived from persistent rhythmic figures and pitch configurations (such as sequences). Melodies exhibiting this con-

TABLE 1. Publications of the Works of Arcangelo Corelli

Op. 1	1681	12 trio sonatas *da chiesa*
Op. 2	1685	12 trio sonatas *da camera*
Op. 3	1689	12 trio sonatas *da chiesa*
Op. 4	1694	12 trio sonatas *da camera*
Op. 5	1700	11 solo sonatas *da chiesa* and *da camera;* variations of *La folia d'Espagne*
Op. 6	1714	8 concertos *da chiesa,* 4 concertos *da camera*

tinuous forward motion are said to employ *Fortspinnung*, which may be translated as "spinning forth." In Corelli's trio sonatas, neither the first violin nor the second violin can be said to dominate. Voice crossings are very common, and the music appearing in the first violin part is frequently transferred later to the second violin and vice versa. Key signatures of pieces in the minor mode typically omit that status of scale degree six since the theoretical model for Corelli and his contemporaries was Dorian mode rather than our diatonic natural minor with lowered third, sixth, and seventh scale degrees.

THE SONATA *da Camera*

The sonata *da camera* consisted of a suite of dances. The names of the dances were sufficient to suggest appropriate tempos; thus, there was no need for Italian tempo words. Harpsichord, lute, guitar, or harp was normally used in the continuo group. Little emphasis was placed on scholarly, contrapuntal writing. The core dances of the typical sonata *da camera*, along with their characteristic meters and tempos, are shown in table 2.

These dances are in binary form. Each half of the structure (e.g., I–V : ‖ V–I : ‖ in major, or i–III : ‖ III–i : ‖ in minor) is to be repeated with improvised ornamentation.

With the exception of the sarabanda, these dances normally began with an anacrusis, or "pickup" beat. This feature was inherited from functional dances in which the foot was lifted to begin the choreography; however, most sonatas *da camera* were clearly not intended for practical use on the dance floor.

Sonatas of the sort that we have described began to appear in the early seventeenth century in the works of Salomone Rossi (1570–ca. 1630), Giovanni Paolo Cima (fl. 1610–1622), and Giovanni Battista Buonamente (late 1500s–1642). They spread throughout Europe, and important contribu-

TABLE 2. Characteristic Dances, Meters, and Tempos in Sonatas *da Camera*

Allemanda	duple	moderate
Corrente	triple, frequently with hemiola	fast
Sarabanda	triple	usually slow, but sometimes *allegro* or *presto* in Corelli; agogic accent on second beat
Gavotta	duple	moderate to fast
Giga	duple compound or triple, frequently with hemiola	fast

tions to the repertoire were made in England by Henry Purcell (1659–1695), in France by Francois Couperin (1668–1733), and in Germany by J. S. Bach (1685–1750). They remained in vogue until the late eighteenth-century works of Francesco Maria Veracini (1698–1768). Sonatas of the late Baroque display an astounding mixture of elements including polyphony, double stops, bariolage, *scordatura* (i.e., irregular tunings), and special types of bowing.

THE CONCERTO *da Camera*

Early chamber concertos were distinguished from church concertos because, like the sonatas *da camera*, the chamber concertos were based upon a series of dances. Three types of concertos were cultivated during the Baroque era: the solo concerto, the concerto grosso, and the ripieno concerto.

The solo concerto featured a single soloist who was alternately accompanied by or pitted against the orchestral tutti. The solo concerto provided opportunities for the featured player to extemporize brilliant passage work. As the emphasis on virtuosic playing grew, the solo concerto became correspondingly popular. The concerto *grosso* utilized several soloists, most often, the two violins and cello of the trio sonata. Additional players were added on each voice of the trio-sonata texture to create contrasting groups: the *concertino* of soloists, and the *ripieno* of multiple players. The *ripieno* concerto achieved variety and contrast by juxtaposing the various orchestral choirs of strings, woodwinds, and brass instruments. Instruments could also be grouped according to dynamic level or by range.

THE KEYBOARD PART IN BAROQUE SONATAS

Baroque sonatas contain either of two distinctly different types of keyboard. In the continuo sonata, the keyboard part is a figured bass. The keyboard player would have filled in harmonies based upon the intervals above the bass line indicated by the composer. In sonatas of this sort, the obbligato instrument(s) carry the main thematic elements of the composition. The continuo bass line may imitate important motives from time to time; however, the thematic involvement of the basso continuo is not essential. The texture of a sonata for obbligato soloist(s) and continuo, therefore, is generally homophonic.

In other sonatas, the keyboard part is fully written out on two staffs. Aside from the typical sorts of ornamentation that might have been supplied by any eighteenth-century keyboard player, nothing is left to the performer's invention. The texture in this type of sonata is different from that of the continuo sonata because the keyboard part is equally important as the instrumental part. Both performers are responsible for the presentation and development of themes.

In the sonatas with obbligato keyboard parts, no bass-line instrument is needed for performance. The texture of a sonata for solo instrument with obbligato keyboard usually consists of three real parts: the bass line and one of the treble lines to be played on the keyboard instrument, and another treble line to be played by a melody instrument, usually a violin or flute. This texture derived from the conventional trio sonata. One sonata by J. S. Bach exists in two versions. One version is the four-movement Trio Sonata in G major for Two Flutes and Continuo, BWV 1039. The other, BWV 1027, distributes the same musical lines between a viola da gamba and a harpsichord. Fully written-out keyboard parts became increasingly common as the eighteenth century progressed. Of the instrumental chamber sonatas composed by Bach, those with obbligato keyboard parts outnumber those with basso continuo parts by approximately two to one.[17]

VOCAL CHAMBER MUSIC: THE CANTATA

Just as the term *sonata* designates any composition performed as instrumental music, the designation *cantata* specifies a piece involving voices. In seventeenth-century Italy, the cantata was typically a secular piece for a vocal soloist with basso continuo and one or more obbligato instruments. The texts for these vocal chamber pieces were often the work of aristocratic amateurs or literati, such as clergy and lawyers. Performances typically took place in the palaces of ruling families or high-ranking clergy in the Roman Catholic Church—Queen Christiana of Sweden, Cardinal Ottoboni, and Cardinal Pamphili, for instance. The poems typically included passages with lines of seven or eleven syllables (and suitable for recitatives), in alternation with strophic, rhymed lines with a consistent syllable count (and suitable for arias). Cantatas of a more elaborate nature, including a variety of recitatives, arias, ariosos, and perhaps even instrumental introductions, interludes, and codas are often called *arie di più parte* (arias with multiple sections).

Alessandro Stradella (1639–1682) ranks high among the early cantata composers. We are not certain of the origin of all of his works, but those cantatas with texts by poets active in Rome were almost certainly composed by late January 1677, since he left for Venice at the beginning of February of that year.[18] Most of these pieces are for a single or several vocalists with accompaniment of basso continuo with one or more obbligato instruments. Because many of these pieces were composed for special occasions and performed for family and friends at private, evening entertainments, they are sometimes called "serenatas." Stradella's tale of the two jealous lovers Tirsi (bass) and Licori (soprano) has a modest ensemble of two violins and basso continuo. The piece, "Lasciate ch'io respiri, ombre gradite" G. 1.4–12, opens with a sinfonia in two movements for instruments, and continues with five arias and two duets. The chamber ensemble of violins and basso continuo accompany the voices throughout. The instrumental parts are all quite easy and can be managed with minimal rehearsal.

Of the seventeenth-century Roman composers of cantatas, Alessandro Scarlatti (1660–1725) was the most prolific. The texts of his cantatas deal not only with men and women in love and the associated issues, but also with history and mythology. Scarlatti, who was also a prolific opera composer, sometimes used *da capo* structures in his cantata arias. In some cantatas, such as *Su le sponde del Tebro,* Scarlatti augments the ensemble of two violin parts and basso continuo with virtuosic solo trumpet to pair with the solo vocalist. When this is the case, several players should be assigned to each of the first and second violin parts.

Though the Italians generally preferred secular cantatas, the composers of Lutheran Germany almost invariably chose spiritual texts. In his three volumes of *Symphoniae sacrae* (sacred ensemble pieces; 1629, 1647, 1650), Heinrich Schütz used the techniques he had learned during his two trips to Italy in 1609 and 1628 to study with Giovanni Gabrieli and Claudio Monteverdi respectively. The "few-voiced concertato" pieces of the Italians were especially important during Schütz's second Venetian trip, and he examined this repertoire carefully. Although Alessandro Grandi had left Venice only a few months before Schütz's arrival there in 1628, his music was still easily accessible to Schütz.[19] In fact, Schütz's "O Jesu süß, wer dein gedenkt," SWV 406, is an arrangement of Grandi's "Lilia convallium." By September 1629, Schütz had compiled his first volume of *Symphoniae sacrae*—all with Latin texts, incidentally—for publication by the Venetian firm of Gardano.[20] Of the twenty pieces in the first volume, some must have been composed before Schütz left Germany. Because wind instruments played a lesser role in Venetian music-making than in German ensembles, the pieces featuring winds are most likely those that Schütz brought along for inclusion in volume 1. Among those pieces with winds is the stunning "Fili mi, Absalon," for basso, four trombones, and basso continuo. The text, from 2 Samuel 19:1, recounts the reaction of King David to the news of the death. The piece is in four sections. The solemn opening for trombones and continuo only makes it clear that the message we are about to hear is a gravely serious one. At the same time, it demonstrates Schütz's magisterial command of counterpoint. The first vocal section declaims the text with basso continuo only before repeating the text within the context of dense counterpoint including the trombones. King David's opening statement is followed by another purely instrumental segment written in the imitative contrapuntal style of the Italian canzona. The concluding section again delivers the text sung without trombones. The final section combines voice with the full instrumental ensemble while repeating text that has already been clearly heard.

The unusual instrumentation for bass soloist, four trombones, and basso continuo is identical to that of Schütz's "Attendite, popule meus," SWV 270, which has a comparable, multisectional design alternating contrapuntal segments for instruments only, passages for voice and continuo only, and others utilizing the voice as one strand within the contrapuntal fabric of the piece. Other interesting combinations of instruments in volume 1 appear in "In te, Domine, speravi," SWV 259, for alto, violin, bassoon, and continuo; "Anima mea liquefacta est," SWV 263–64, for two tenors, two cornettos, and continuo; "Domine, labia mea aperies," SWV 271, for soprano, tenor, cornetto, trombone, bassoon, and continuo; "Jubilate Deo omnis terra," SWV 262, for bass, two recorders, and continuo; and "In lectulo per noctes," SWV 272–73, for soprano, alto, three bassoons, and continuo.

This type of "few-voiced concertato" based on sacred texts provided the foundation for German cantatas of the later Baroque. Dieterich Buxtehude (ca. 1637–1707) wrote several secular cantatas, both in Italian and German, but the vast majority of his cantatas with obbligato instruments are on spiritual themes. His texts for the sacred works are mostly German, but a handful of pieces are in Latin. The scoring is usually for solo soprano voice with one to four solo string players plus basso continuo. Ironically, Buxtehude never worked in a church situation that would have required any of these sacred vocal compositions, and none of them is genuine "liturgical" music for the Lutheran church.[21] His cantata *Singet dem Herrn ein neues Lied*, BuxWV 98, for violin, soprano, and basso continuo is a fine example of his work that shows features of the *arie di più parte*. The eight sections of the piece include three for instruments only as well as different tempos and meters for the various sections. In this cantata, an exuberant setting of the words "singet, rühmet, und lobet" (sing, glorify, and praise) brings the piece to its conclusion. In other cantatas, Buxtehude applies similar treatment to the words "Amen" or "alleluia."

In his *O dulcis Jesu*, BuxWV 83, for two sopranos, two violins, and basso continuo, Buxtehude sets the prose passages in a free recitativo or arioso style, whereas the poetic passages assume the character of an aria. Structurally, this design parallels the secular cantatas of the Italians. It has been suggested that Buxtehude composed this piece for an Italian castrato visiting the Marienkirche.[22]

It is well known that J. S. Bach knew and admired the music of Buxtehude. From mid-October 1705 until early February 1706, he was absent from his post at the Neue Kirche in Arnstadt, having gone to Lübeck for the purpose of attending Buxtehude's famous *Abendmusiken* (evening music) at the Marienkirche. These programs would have included some of these cantatas or similar ones. The impact of Bach's experience was both immediate and long-range: Within weeks of his return to Arnstadt, the Consistory of the Neue Kirche complained about his outlandish and extravagant harmonizations of the traditional Lutheran chorale tunes. These, they contended, confused the congregation and disrupted the services. Years later, when Bach was cantor of the Lutheran churches of Leipzig, he wrote five cycles of cantatas for the liturgical year. Among the surviving cantatas are some real gems for solo vocalist, obbligato instrument, strings, and continuo.

The original version of Cantata 82, *Ich habe genug*, dates from 2 February 1727. It was composed for the feast of the Purification. The scriptural impetus for the libretto (authorship unknown) is the Song of Simeon (Luke 2:29–32), the text of the "Nunc dimittis," customarily used at Vespers services. In its original version, bass soloist is paired with oboe solo against the backdrop of strings and continuo. In one of the subsequent versions (1731), Bach gave the vocal solo to a soprano, the obbligato part to a flute, and changed the key to E minor. Another (1735) uses a mezzo-soprano and changes the key to C minor. In still other versions (1745/1748), the oboe *da caccia* (oboe "of the hunt," an oboe with a brass bell) is a curious addition to the score.

The formal design of the aria "Schlummert ein" is an interesting expansion of a conventional five-section da capo aria plan whereby two additional reprises of the ritornello result in a rondo-like form, a design that was also used from time to time by George Frideric Handel.

That Bach was fond of this cantata is apparent from the fact that portions of it appear in the Anna Magdalena Klavierbüchlein (begun 1725);

however, it is clear that the "transcription was made *from* the cantata *into* the little keyboard book—not vice versa."[23]

Cantata 51, *Jauchzet Gott in allen Landen,* is another of Bach's Leipzig cantatas, probably composed for 17 September 1730, *after* Bach completed his five cycles of cantatas for every Sunday of the church year. The designation "In ogni Tempo" (at any time [of the church year]) probably indicates that Bach was less strict in linking the text of this cantata to the scripture readings of a particular occasion.

The cantata is a showpiece for the two soloists, soprano and trumpeter. (Incidentally, a version of the piece by Bach's son Wilhelm Friedemann adds a second trumpet and timpani to his father's original score.) This instrumentation is most curious in German, Lutheran repertoire; however, it is common enough in Italian, secular cantatas of the time, such as Alessandro Scarlatti's previously discussed *Sul le sponde del Tebro.* Because those Italian pieces were secular compositions, women would have sung the vocal portions. But what about Bach's sacred, Lutheran cantata? Could he have had a woman in mind? A leading Bach scholar claims that "in conservative Leipzig, to think of a female soprano would be utterly out of the question."[24]

Concerning the trumpeter, we are on firm ground: The part would have been taken by Gottfried Reiche (1667–1734), the leading *clarino* player in the Leipzig, municipal wind players.

Despite its modest duration, Cantata 51 is remarkable for its compositional diversity. It employs "five characteristic formal designs of the Baroque: concerto (movement 1), monody (movement 2), ostinato variations (movement 3), chorale [trio sonata] (movement 4), and fugue (movement 5)."[25]

TWO

The Crystallization of Genres during the Golden Age of Chamber Music

TUNING, TEMPERAMENT, AND FORM

Important changes took place in the art of music around the end of the first quarter of the eighteenth century. One of the most significant was the introduction of well-tempered tuning for keyboard instruments. With the advent of well-tempered tuning, all twenty-four major and minor keys became available to composers. The first volume of Sebastian Bach's *Well-Tempered Clavier* appeared in 1722. In this same year, Rameau's groundbreaking *Traité de l'harmonie* appeared in print.

The availability of all led to the creation of new musical forms based on the contrast between stable and unstable structural components. This contrast became the basis of the pattern forms used throughout western Europe in what is now generally called the Classical style.

With the advent of well-tempered tuning, it became possible to expand the simple binary forms of the early eighteenth century by introducing numerous tonalities, often quite remote from the original tonic, at the beginning of the second half of the binary plan. Initially, this tonal freedom was exploited in an almost childlike fashion. One scholar has observed that: "Pre-Classic composers and writers seem to have taken special pleasure in modulations for their own sake. The empfindsam composers used them for their shock value as they indulged in one "sea of modulations" after another (to use Burney's term for Emanuel Bach's improvisations)."[1] By the last quarter of the eighteenth century, composers had learned to utilize shifting tonalities for purposes of form and expression. Ultimately, the broadened harmonic palette made possible by equal temperament led to an expansion of all of the tonally unstable components within the binary form, including the modulatory transition section in the first half, as well as the development section, and the retransition section in the second half.

The advances made by the end of the first quarter of the eighteenth century in tuning and temperament not only provided composers with a more diverse harmonic vocabulary, but also enabled them to expand considerably the dimensions of an individual movement while maintaining its structural integrity. Similar tonal and architectonic expansion can be seen in the rondos and other harmonic forms of the later eighteenth century.

In multimovement works, the rondo is often placed as the concluding movement to balance in energy and complexity with the opening, expanded binary form movement. Internal movements generally are points of relative repose, and, therefore, tend to make fewer demands of the listener's harmonic consciousness. The formal designs of inner movements are quite diverse, but some of the more commonly encountered ones include theme and variations, minuet and trio, scherzo and trio, or song form.

THE ADVENT OF THE PIANOFORTE

Though Bartolomeo Cristofori (1655–1731) had already built pianos in the opening decade of the eighteenth century, the instrument did not come into popular use until after the midcentury. Accordingly, many keyboard compositions of the later eighteenth century appeared with titles like the one we find in the Sonatas, Op. 3 of Leopold Kotzeluch: *Trois sonatas pour le clavecin ou le forte-piano avec accompagnement d'un violon et violoncelle* (Three sonatas for the harpsichord or the fortepiano with accompaniment of a violin and violoncello).[2]

The question invariably arises: Do the scores of these works "for the harpsichord or the fortepiano" betray any stylistic features that would make them more suitable for one instrument than the other? In many cases, the decision is easily made. The prominence of echo passages, for example, would suggest that the music was conceived for harpsichord, since that instrument typically possessed two manuals that could be set in advance with stops that would produce contrasting dynamic terraces. Similarly, the presence of graduated dynamics would indicate that the music was intended for the fortepiano. Unfortunately, not all cases are so clear-cut. Title pages were often written with one eye on musical aesthetics, while the other was fixed steadfastly upon the commercial market.

MUSIC FOR THE BOURGEOISIE

The rise of the bourgeoisie during the second half of the eighteenth century accounted for the increased importance of chamber music. Music making became a pastime for amateurs. Many compositions appeared with title pages indicating that the works were suitable "especially for music loving amateurs." Some composers, Carl Philipp Emanuel Bach (1714–1788) for example, attempted to appeal to the dilettante and the professional musician alike by titles like that of his famous *Sonaten für Kenner und Liebhaber* (Sonatas for connoisseurs and amateurs). A booming music-publishing industry came into being, and everything from solo sonatas for harp to multimovement symphonies became available to the general public. Popular magazines of the day included scores that appeared one movement at a time over a series of several issues. Music instruction manuals became absolutely commonplace. C. P. E. Bach set the standard with his famous *Versuch über die wahre Art das Klavier zu spielen* (Essay on the true art of playing keyboard instruments; 1753–62).[3] Other treatises of the period include Johann Joachim Quantz's *Versuch einer Anweisung die Flöte traversiere zu spielen* (Essay of instruction for playing the transverse flute; Berlin, 1752),[4] and Leopold Mozart's *Versuch einer gründlichen Violinschule* (Essay on fundamental violin technique; Augsburg 1756).[5] Later eighteenth-century tutors of note are Daniel Gottlob Türk's *Clavierschule* (Keyboard tutor; 1789) and Muzio Clementi's *Introduction to the Art of Playing on the Piano Forte* (London, 1801). To this short list, dozens of other titles could be added.

The increasing importance attached to the amateur player accounted in large part for the proliferation of chamber music genres. It also accounted for the characteristic style that came to be associated with chamber music of the mid-eighteenth century, a style that was light, pleasant, and agreeable.

This phase of midcentury chamber music is well documented in the writings of contemporary theorists. Johann Adolph Scheibe (1708–1776), for example, wrote: "The ultimate purpose of the chamber style is above all to delight and enliven the listener. He is thus brought to splendor, to joy, and to laughter. . . . From this can be determined the general character of chamber music. It must above all be lively and penetrating."[6]

MUSIC PUBLISHERS OF THE EIGHTEENTH CENTURY

The growing popularity of chamber music during the later eighteenth century was due in large part to technological progress. The use of mass media for the dissemination of musical scores contributed directly to the expanding number of amateur musicians. Increased demand for reasonably priced scores led to further advances in the printing process. Perhaps the most important development in late eighteenth-century music printing was the invention of lithography by Aloys Senefelder (1771–1834). This technique, which was used for the printing of Haydn's sonatas Hob. XVI/40–42 in 1797, enabled publishers to produce scores in large numbers, quickly, and with high quality.[7] Many composers—even the heros of our musical heritage, like Haydn and Beethoven—deliberately modified their musical styles for the purpose of increasing the market for their works.[8]

Among the music publishing firms came into being during the mid-eighteenth century, several merit discussion here. Johann Gottlob Immanuel Breitkopf took over his father's meager business in 1745 and turned it into the most progressive music-publishing enterprise in Germany. Breitkopf sold the firm to Christoph Härtel in 1796. Equally important was the publishing company opened in Vienna in the fall of 1778 by Domenico Artaria. He and his brothers became the publishers for Franz Joseph Haydn, Wolfgang Amadeus Mozart, Ludwig van Beethoven, Antonio Salieri, Muzio Clementi, and many other luminaries of the later eighteenth century. Another important Viennese publisher was Johann André, whose third son, Johann Anton, took over the firm after his father's death and greatly expanded it. Johann Anton was also responsible for the purchase from Constanze Mozart of her husband's unpublished manuscripts in the year 1800.

In France, the firms of Boyer, Bailleux, Huberty, and Pleyel catered to the increasing demand for accessible music at reasonable prices. Huberty was one of the primary publishers for the repertoire of the Mannheim school. He relocated in Vienna in 1777. Ignaz Pleyel's shop, which operated during the years from 1796 to 1834, issued the first complete edition of Haydn's string quartets in 1802. Haydn had been Pleyel's composition teacher, and so, these editions are of particular historical importance.

In London, the firm of Longman and Broderip opened in 1767. Muzio Clementi also operated a music-publishing house there beginning in 1798. The enterprise was successful, and he began manufacturing musical instruments—his pianos are perhaps the finest that were available at that time.

Even small towns like Augsburg and Nuremberg enjoyed the benefits of a local music publisher. Listing all of the music publishers of the late eighteenth century would fill an entire volume, but several other firms that should at least be mentioned include those of Franz Anton Hoffmeister

(1754–1812), Tranquillo Mollo (1772–?), and Christoph Torricella (1715–1798) in Vienna.

Hoffmeister published some of Mozart's most important works: His Quartet in D minor, K. 499, known as the *Hoffmeister Quartet,* is only one product of the congenial relationship that existed between the composer and this publisher. Mollo had once been a member of the firm of Artaria, but opened his own company in the summer of 1798. The publishing house of Torricella saw its heyday during the 1770s and early 1780s. Its publications included works by Haydn, Mozart, J. C. Bach, Leopold Kotzeluch, Franz Anton Hoffmeister, and others. Torricella also acted as a distributor for Antoine Huberty. Torricella's plates—all of engraved copper—were acquired by Artaria in the summer of 1786. The catalogs of these firms present in detail the changing tastes of the music-loving public and the evolution of chamber music and its principal genres during the late Classical era.

ENSEMBLE SONATAS OF THE LATER EIGHTEENTH CENTURY

Some of the most typical fare to be found in the average later eighteenth-century music shop was the sonata repertoire for keyboard (i.e., harpsichord, clavichord, piano, or organ) with the accompaniment of one or more instruments. The vogue for such works was inaugurated in Paris by Jean-Joseph Cassanéa de Mondonville (1711–1772), who published his *Pieces de clavecin en sonatas* in 1734. Some years later, Johann Schobert (ca. 1735–1767) made his career in that same city by writing such works. His Op. 1 was a set of two *Sonatas pour le clavecin qui peuvent jouer avec l'accompagnement de violon* (Sonatas for the harpsichord that may be played with the accompaniment of a violin).[9] Schobert's title invites performance either with or without the violin, but he was not alone in allowing such flexibility: Leopold Kotzeluch (1747–1818), Jan Ladislav Dussek (1760–1812), and many others published pieces with indefinite scoring.

Some eighteenth-century collections of sonatas combine pieces for keyboard alone with others including added instruments. Marie-Emmanuelle Bayon's collection of *Six sonates pour le clavecin ou le piano forte dont trois avec accompagnement de violon obligé, œuvre 1* (Six sonatas for harpsichord or piano forte, three with obligatory violin accompaniment, Op. 1), which were published in the late 1760s, is a good example of a mixed collection.[10]

Titles sometimes involve a single melody instrument—usually a violin or a flute. At other times, two instruments are mentioned—normally one treble and one bass instrument. Either or both parts may be described as accompanimental, obbligato, or *ad libitum.*

In this sonata repertoire, it is impossible to differentiate between solos, duets, and trios.[11] The performance of any given sonata depended mainly upon the instrumentalists at hand and their respective skills at sight reading or improvising parts, and the relationship of instruments in this repertoire is variable. In some pieces, the keyboard part is clearly the primary one, and it carries the main melodies and harmonies. On the other hand, the titles of some works suggest a fully developed, concertante sonata for keyboard and melody instrument. For example, a set of three sonatas by Jacopo Gotifredo Ferrari (1763–1842) contains the designation: *Trois sonates pour clavecin ou forte-piano avec violon obligé et basse ad libitum . . . œuvre IIm.*[12] (Three sonatas for harpsichord or fortepiano with obbligato violin and bass ad libitum, Op. 2.)

It is a mistake to assume that the interaction of the instruments in these ensemble sonatas became more complex and highly integrated as the genre progressed historically. In fact, "There is not a direct line of 'progress' from an early optionally-accompanied style to the fully developed concertante sonata of Mozart and Beethoven. Rather, the two styles existed side by side from mid-century and even beyond the turn of the century."[13] The accompanied style sonata persisted even in the very latest works by Mozart.

For the sake of clarity, sonatas with real, obbligato parts for melody line instruments will be referred to as *duo keyboard sonatas,* whereas those written in the optionally accompanied style will be called *accompanied keyboard sonatas.* The neutral designation *ensemble keyboard sonatas* will be used in general references to both types of pieces simultaneously.[14]

The Schobert sonatas of Op. 2 are representative of the ensemble sonata with keyboard during the midcentury. The overall plan normally included several movements. Two-movement and three-movement formats were about equally popular.[15] In two-movement sonatas, both movements were ordinarily in the same key, though a change in mode was possible. A contrast in tempo is also to be expected, but the precise tempo of each of the two movements was never standardized. Three-movement sonatas were typically arranged with the inner movement in the subdominant, relative minor, dominant, or (less frequently) the relative major. The tempo sequence of the various movements was not regulated, although three-movement sonatas in the order fast-slow-fast are common.

Schobert's sonatas are remarkably dramatic and expressive; the young Mozart realized that when he first encountered them during the sojourn he made to Paris with his family in 1764. Mozart was not alone in his admiration for this type of writing, and "Schobert's works became immensely popular and continued to be reprinted throughout the century."[16]

In the later eighteenth-century sonata repertoire, a harp was sometimes substituted for the keyboard instrument. Gotifredo Jacopo Ferrari's works, for instance, include the *Trois grandes sonates pour harpe avec accompagnement de violon et basse,* Op. 18.[17] Antonín Kammel (1730–1787) is more liberal in permitting any of three possibilities in the instrumentation of his *Six sonates for the piano forte, harpsichord, or harp with accompaniments for a violin and violoncello,* opera IX.

Though some of these titles suggest a trio of two melody instruments with some chord-playing instrument, very few examples of this texture are present in the scores of the mid-eighteenth century. In many cases, the bass line instrument simply doubles the lowest part of the harpsichord, piano, or harp.

Among the earliest chamber pieces to include an obbligato treble instrument, a written-out keyboard part, and an independent string bass part was Jean-Philippe Rameau's *Pieces de clavecin en concert, avec un violon ou une flûte, et une viole ou un deuxieme violon* (Harpsichord pieces in ensemble with violin or flute and viol or cello), published in Paris in 1741.[18] Even here, though, some pieces can actually be played—with Rameau's full approval—as solo harpsichord works.

MOZART'S SONATAS FOR VIOLIN AND PIANO

In the course of his brief career, Wolfgang Amadeus Mozart (1756–1791) wrote more than forty sonatas for piano and violin.[19] The earliest of these were youthful works during the grand family tour of Europe undertaken from June 1763 until November 1766. In the index of Wolfgang's compositions that was assembled by his father in 1768, the first entry is: *Sonates pour le clavecin avec l'accompagnement de violon dediées a Madame Victoire de France par Wolfgang Mozart agé de sept ans. A Paris. œuvre I.* His last such work, the Sonata in F major, was composed in Vienna during the summer of 1788, the summer that witnessed the composition of his last three symphonies.

The fact that Mozart's father, Leopold (1719–1787), was himself a fine violinist ensured that as a young composer, Wolfgang came into contact with important repertoire for that instrument—and probably some unimportant repertoire as well.[20] If not by his father's doing, then, at least, as a result of his travels between 1762 and 1779, Mozart was thoroughly familiar with stylistic developments taking place in western Europe during the mid-eighteenth century. One scholar has assembled a list of important musical centers that Mozart visited during these years. That list includes Munich, Vienna, Pressburg, Augsburg, Schwetzingen, Mainz, Frankfurt, Coblenz, Aachen, Brussels, Paris, London, den Hagg, Amsterdam, Utrecht, Malines (= Mechelen), Dijon, Lyons, Geneva, Lausanne, Berne, Zurich, Schaffhausen, Donaueschingen, Biberach, Innsbruck, Rovereto, Verona, Milan, Parma, Bologna, Florence, Cremona, Mantua, Lodi, Rome, Naples, Venice, Turin, Padua, Vicenza, Mannheim, Nancy, and Strasbourg.[21] This tally does not include recurrent visits that took place during the course of Mozart's numerous tours.

Despite the ascendancy of the music-publishing industry during the mid-eighteenth century, musical styles at the time were still largely regional affairs involving distinctive musical practices.[22] These journeys provided Mozart with comprehensive and firsthand knowledge of later eighteenth-century styles. Notorious but often vaguely defined styles like the *style galant*, the *Empfindsamer Stil*, and the rococo, were, for Mozart, part of a living musical culture. In all probability, he would have been aware of still other musical dialects that never made their way into the history books.

Like his father, Mozart was a skilled violinist. As a leading pianist of the era, though, Wolfgang brought to this repertoire the insight of the keyboard player and that of the violinist simultaneously. Accordingly, Mozart's steady production of ensemble sonatas from the early 1760s until the summer of 1788 can be traced as a guide through that literature in the later eighteenth century.[23]

Most of Mozart's sonatas for piano and violin begin with movements in duple meter; only about one-fifth of them are in triple meter; there are two sonatas, K. 305 and 526, with opening movements in duple compound meter. Major mode is used for most opening movements; only three sonatas, K. 59, 60, and 304, begin in the minor mode. They may have two or three movements, and some commence with slow introductions. Perhaps the best known of these is the Largo opening of the Sonata in B-flat major, K. 454, which Mozart wrote in 1784 and performed with the twenty-year-old Italian violinist Regina Strinasacchi, who was making her concert debut in Vienna.

The duo Sonata in C major, K. 296, was written in Mannheim during the month of March in the eventful year 1778. At the time, Mozart had grown weary of the Salzburg court and was looking for a new position. He composed the C-major Sonata for Therese Pierron Serrarius, who was the teenage daughter of one of the Mannheim court dignitaries and a pianist of some skill. The piece was intended as a gesture of gratitude for accommodations that the family had provided for Mozart and his mother; hence, the overall mood of each of the three movements in the sonata is cheerful, poised, and refined. The opening Allegro combines duple and triple subdivisions of the beat, a characteristic rhythmic feature of the *style galant*. The violin part is idiomatic to be sure. It begins with a full, C-major triad and continues with rich writing with more triads and double stops.

In this sonata, it would be impossible to eliminate the violin: The imitations of the principal motif that appear in measures 9 to 14 of the exposition and in the corresponding passage in the recapitulation and countless other details of the score could not be condensed into a single part for piano solo. The concluding movement of the sonata, a modified rondo form, was subsequently revised and expanded to become the finale of the Concerto for Flute and Harp, K. 299.

Later compositions, such as the accompanied Sonata in F major, K. 547, confirm that there is no evolutionary line that leads from one ensemble keyboard sonata to the next. This sonata is "a small keyboard sonata for beginners, with a violin." Although the first movement contains some interesting interplay between the keyboard and violin, the violin has a paltry role in the concluding, third movement, a set of variations that Mozart later arranged for keyboard solo (K. 547b).

Despite the fact that the Sonata in F major was written ten years after the Sonata in C major, the interplay of the two instruments in the earlier sonata is far more complex and effective. For that matter, even early works, like the Sonata in C major, K. 10, contain passages such as those in the minuet "in the manner of a carillon," where the violin is an essential partner in a duo texture. Throughout his career, Mozart produced both duo keyboard sonatas and accompanied keyboard sonatas, but it is clear that the choice fell to the one or the other as a result of circumstances rather than stylistic or technical evolution.

CHAMBER MUSIC WITHOUT KEYBOARD

Figured-bass keyboard parts persisted throughout the eighteenth century in theatrical and orchestral music, but they rapidly disappeared in chamber works. Terminology is not always helpful in determining what type of piece we are looking at. During the mid-eighteenth century, what we call a "string quartet" could have been labeled a *sonata a quattro*, *sonate en quatuor*, *concerto*, *concertino*, *sinfonia*, *divertimento*, *cassation*, *serenade*, or *notturno a quattro*. It may be helpful to note the following guideposts in addressing such issues:

> In Viennese ensemble music from 1750 to 1780, *Divertimento* was the title of preference for every nonorchestral scoring. Before ca. 1760, the title *Partita* also served the same function. The alternate titles *Cassation, Notturno, Serenade,* and *Concertino* designated "light" music in various scorings from 1750 on. The titles *Quartet* and *Quintet* occurred infrequently before ca. 1770 and supplanted *Divertimento* as customary designations for "serious" chamber music only after 1780. . . . Each of the five principal genres of Viennese chamber music in this period—the sonata for melodies and bass; the Classical string trio, quartet, and quintet; the Classical scorings with an obbligato wind instrument; the cassation for mixed ensemble with two horns; and the partita for winds—is transmitted under the title *Divertimento* as well as more specialized ones. Thus *Divertimento* did not designate a genre at all; it was a general title for nonorchestral instrumental music.[24]

In addition to the confusion of genres, ensembles, and forms, stylistic trends were also numerous and not entirely distinct. To think that we are any more certain today about these stylistic distinctions than the musicians of the eighteenth century would be a mistake. Our present-day terminology includes a befuddling array of terms that have been applied in such diverse ways that they have lost whatever meaning they may have had. Consider, for example, the words *rococo, Empfindsamkeit, Sturm und Drang,* and *style galant.*[25] No decisive termination of Baroque style is evidenced in the repertoire per se. Some Baroque genres were carried into the later eighteenth century with little or no modification; others were discontinued altogether and only appear as curiosities in the works of the most atavistic composers; and some genres came into being as a reaction against or as a synthesis of existing genres of the early eighteenth century.

THE STRING TRIO

The two violins and string bass of the Baroque trio sonata did remain as the typical ensemble in the midcentury string trio without keyboard: Of the twenty-one authenticated string trios written by Franz Joseph Haydn during the 1760s, this scoring is used in all save one; nevertheless, this combination seems to have had limited appeal during the eighteenth century or since then. The removal of the basso continuo resulted in an awkward void between the high violins and the bass line.

The limited repertoire for string trio from the later eighteenth century includes a few interesting pieces. One of them is Haydn's *Echo Sonata,* Hob. II/39, which requires two string trios seated in different rooms. The nickname of this piece is an apt one, since the two ensembles play nearly identical phrases antiphonally and only combine to form a sextet at elided cadence points.[26]

Only one of the authenticated trios, Hob. V/8, is scored for violin, viola, and cello. Among the works of questionable authenticity, only Hob. V/D6, V/E-flat 1, and V/G7 indicate a scoring for treble, alto, and bass stringed instruments. The String Trios, Op. 53 are arrangements of two-movement sonatas for keyboard solo that Haydn had composed between 1782 and 1784 and dedicated to Princess Marie Esterházy.

Mozart's only important example of the string trio is K. 563, the Divertimento in E-flat. Beethoven contributed to this genre with his Opp. 3 and 9, but not as richly as did Luigi Boccherini, for whom the medium had a particular appeal. Ultimately, the string trio was superseded by the string quartet, the most important medium for Classical chamber music.[27]

THE STRING QUARTET

There is no single parent source for the Classical string quartet. Though isolated works like Gregorio Allegri's *Symphonia* for two violins, viola, and bass (1650) and Alessandro Scarlatti's four *Sonate a quattro per due violini, violetta e violoncello senza cembalo* (ca. 1715–25) appear well in advance of the midcentury, these were isolated rather than the origin of the genre.[28] In orchestral writing of the Baroque, four-part string texture was common. Many orchestral works could have been "string quartets" if performed with one player per part without continuo. The symphony, sinfonia, overture, and concerto all contributed something of their formal and stylistic features to the evolving quartet, as did the diverse compositions that were called divertimento, notturno, serenade, and cassation, but this repertoire was usually predicated two-part counterpoint of the outer voices with harmonic filler in the inner parts. Within this two-voice texture, doubling was common, and the viola often duplicated the violin melody an octave below, or the bass line an octave above, while the cello was normally doubled at the octave below by the double bass.

Different instruments often play from the same written line even though the doubling instrument might be in a different octave. Usually the instruction *colla parte* (with the part) was simply written at the beginning of the part along with an indication of the intended doubling instrument. This type of writing, commonplace throughout the century, was essentially orchestral in conception; consequently, not all scores that have two treble clefs, an alto clef, and a bass clef are necessarily genuine string quartets.

The principal challenge of quartet writing was finding a way to promote equality among all voices. This texture—known in late eighteenth-century French sources as the *quatuor concertant*—posed difficulties not only for the composers but for the performers as well since, in such a piece, each voice of the musical fabric is essential.

The title of J. B. Feray's *Quatuor de petits airs, variés et dialogués pour deux violons, alto et basse, œuvre 1er* (Quartet of little songs, varied and set in dialogue for two violins, viola, and bass, Op. 1) makes it clear that the "little songs" were intended to be familiar, easily accessible, and appealing. Quartets made up of familiar songs were actually a French specialty that went under the designation *quatuor d'airs connus* (i.e., quartet of familiar airs). Quartet arrangements of this sort remained popular in France well into the nineteenth century. Richard Wagner (1813–1883), during his poverty-stricken years in Paris, agreed to arrange favorite tunes from Fromental Halévy's opera *La reine de Chypre* (1841) for string quartet.[29] Perhaps it was this distasteful task that turned him for ever against the string quartet as a genre!

The quartet of popular tunes was complemented in France by the *quatuor brillant*, in which the first violin played virtuosic passages while the other three players provided a simple accompaniment. Such quartets persisted well into the nineteenth century.

Both the quartet of popular tunes and the quartet of brilliance exerted an undeniable influence on the writing of later quartet composers, but neither provided the foundation for the string quartet as a genre. The repertoire of the Classical era depended fundamentally upon formal integrity, harmonic interest, and thematic vitality in all four parts. String quartets based on sonata form seem to have originated in the works of Italian composers including Boccherini, Cambini, and their contemporaries. In their quartets, the influence of the opera sinfonia is apparent: Its three-movement plan and the formal designs of those movements correspond precisely to the structure of the earliest Italian string quartets. The four-movement was largely the work of the Viennese Classicists, Haydn, Mozart, and Beethoven; but even in their works, many examples that depart from the four-movement design can be found.

Much obscure repertoire will have to be examined before the definitive history of the string quartet can be written. The pages of the *Einzeldrücke vor 1800* of RISM list hundreds of midcentury quartets that have neither been accounted for in scholarly literature to date nor been issued in modern editions.[30] Until we have a more comprehensive view of the earliest quartet literature, we must accept the traditional view that Franz Joseph

Haydn and his colleagues in and around Vienna were the composers who established the Classical string quartet.[31]

Among this group of Viennese composers, Franz Aspelmayr (1728–1786) played an important role. He was a violinist, and he performed some of Haydn's quartets in 1782—perhaps those of Op. 33. He also knew both Leopold and Wolfgang Mozart personally. Aspelmayr published two sets of quartets, Op. 2 and Op. 6, with six in each set. These were his only quartets that appeared in print during his lifetime.

Frantisek Xavier Dusek (1731–1799), a close friend of Wolfgang Mozart and his wife, Constanza, also wrote string quartets. The immensely prolific Jan Vaňhal (1739–1813) wrote approximately one hundred quartets. He also performed quartet literature with Haydn, Mozart, and Karl Ditter von Dittersdorf (1739–1799), and so he must have known at least some of Haydn's and Mozart's quartets, and they must have known some of his.

Dittersdorf published a set of six quartets with Artaria in 1788. He also wrote an isolated Quartet in E-flat major. Important too are the works of Carlos Ordonez (1734–1786), who, despite his Spanish name, was a native of Vienna. His Op. 1 was a set of six quartets published around 1775; Op. 2 was another set of six quartets. He wrote many other quartets that survive only in manuscript copies. Wenzel Pichl (1741–1805) was absent from Vienna during the years Mozart lived there, but he had been active at the Viennese court theater from around 1770 until 1777. Pichl wrote a great deal of solo violin music, violin concertos, and dozens of chamber pieces that Mozart, as a violinist himself, might well have known. Pichl returned to Vienna in 1796. Whether Haydn knew his music is difficult to say, but given Pichl's productivity and notoriety, it would have been hard for him to avoid it.

FRANZ JOSEPH HAYDN'S STRING QUARTETS THROUGH OP. 33

Haydn's earliest string quartets to appear in print were those of Opp. 1 and 2 (with six quartets in each set), which were published in 1764 by Chevardiere and in 1765 by Hummel. The fifth and sixth quartets of Op. 1 were actually flute quartets by Karl Joseph Toeschi (1731–1788), a Mannheim composer and flutist. Haydn's Op. 2 also contains bogus quartets, the third and fifth (i.e., Hob. III/9 and III/11). Both pieces were originally for an ensemble including double bass and two horns (see Hob. II/21 and II/22). In these early quartets, there are usually five movements in the tempo sequence fast, moderate, slow, moderate, fast. The moderate tempo movements are typically minuets with a trio.

The first quartets exhibiting the four-movement plan that became customary in Haydn's mature quartets are the set of six in Op. 3 (Hob. III/13–18); however, Alan Tyson and H. C. Robbins Landon have pointed out that "the evidence for Haydn's authorship [of Op. 3] is in fact somewhat flimsy." The principal reason for counting these six among the traditional total of Haydn's eighty-three string quartets derives from "their inclusion in the thematic catalogue which Haydn approved and which prefaced Pleyel's collection. . . . But it is easy to give too much weight to the fact that the elderly Haydn . . . acknowledged the thematic list *in toto*."[32] Apparently, these pieces were actually the work of Romanus Hoffstetter (1742–1812), a monk active at the monastery of Amorbach. "There was a very good reason for a publisher's removing Hofstetter's name from a work and replacing it by Haydn's: Haydn's quartets were in greater demand."[33] Antoine Bailleux, who issued the set in 1777, hoped to improve sales by associating the quartets with Haydn. This ruse must have been successful, since "Bailleux . . . two years after issuing the [Op. 3] edition . . . published as Haydn's 'Op. 28' six more quartets—all spurious."[34]

Haydn's next authenticated quartets, those of Op. 9 (Hob. III/19–24) use the four-movement plan, but with the minuet and trio as the second movement and the slow movement in third place. The quartets of Op. 9 were probably composed during the closing years of the 1760s.[35] The quartets of Op. 17 (Hob. III/25–30), which were completed by 1771, have a feature in common with the quartets of Op. 9 insofar as both sets exploit the playing of Luigi Tomasini (1741–1808), the first-chair player in Haydn's orchestra at Esterháza. Tomasini's brilliant technique inspired the style of the first movement of Op. 17, No. 2 in F major with its frequent double stopping and almost concerto-like flare.

The twelve chamber pieces in Opp. 9 and 17 not only establish the four-movement plan in Haydn's quartets, but also, they "were conceived by Haydn as sets, and, as he was to do in all his later collections of quartets and symphonies, he used a different key for each work. . . . Both sets also include, for the first time in Haydn's output, a quartet in the minor mode: op. 9 No. 4 . . . and op. 17 No. 4."[36] Beethoven later used this same plan in his quartets of Op. 18, where the one minor quartet is No. 4 in C minor.

Donald Francis Tovey was the first to point out that in the quartets of Op. 20, written in 1772, Haydn finally achieved equality among all four instruments. As he puts it, "Haydn's imagination has now awakened to the tone of the cello as something more than a mere amenable bass to the harmony. This awakening . . . freshens the tone-colour of all four instruments from now onwards."[37] The quartets of Op. 20, also known as the *Sun Quartets*, exhibit more varied textures than the earlier sets. Particularly striking is the importance of counterpoint.

Though the preferred texture in the second half of the eighteenth century was homophony, polyphony is an important element in almost all of Haydn's scores. Mozart and Beethoven also imbued their compositions with substantial contrapuntal passages. As a young man, Haydn learned the art of counterpoint by studying the *Gradus ad Parnassum* (Vienna, 1725) of Johann Joseph Fux (ca. 1660–1741).[38]

Fux's treatise was widely disseminated, and it was studied by many of Haydn's colleagues including Leopold Mozart, Michael Haydn, Nicolo Piccini, Luigi Cherubini, Johann Georg Albrechtsberger, Wolfgang Amadeus Mozart, Abbé Vogler, Johann Joachim Quantz, Karl Ditter von Dittersdorf, Ignaz Holzbauer, and Ludwig van Beethoven—to name a few. The text was so dear to Beethoven that, shortly before his death, he earmarked his personal, annotated copy of it for his young friend, Ferdinand Piringer.[39] Thus Fux's *Gradus* was the most important link between the contrapuntal art of the high Renaissance and the mature Classical style.

Of the six quartets in Op. 20, three have fugal final movements. Each of the fugues is based upon a specified number of subjects (*soggetti*); however, these are concise motifs rather than fugue subjects of the Baroque manner. Counterpoint enabled Haydn to achieve equality among all four instruments; however, that goal was achieved at the expense of other elements of quartet composition. When the subjects are combined, a dense musical web results. Smaller groupings of several measures with clear phraseology—a characteristic feature of the *style galant*—are virtually absent from the score. The pieces show Haydn's skill at serious writing: Learned devices such as stretto, pedal points, and retrograde statements of themes appear on every page. Haydn was justifiably proud of these compositional details, and he even pointed some of them out with prose labels in the scores.

Haydn was not alone in turning to counterpoint as a means of achieving equality among voices. Franz Xavier Richter (1709–1789), one of the most important composers of the Mannheim school, wrote string quartets with similar complexities. Although Richter and Haydn worked independently, both faced the same challenges and experimented with similar solutions.

The quartets of Op. 20 are intended for the connoisseur. Some modern critics even maintain that these *Sun Quartets* are only partially successful from a musical point of view.[40] Though the style of the Op. 20 Quartets is

not the one that came to be typical of Haydn's later works, frequent study of these scores will reveal many charms and ingenious details that are not apparent at first hearing.

The fugue subjects from Op. 20, No. 6 demonstrate—in embryonic form—the characteristics that Haydn seized upon in his later quartets. Of the three subjects, the third is the least like a fugue subject. It is the most concise and clearly motivic; it lends itself to repetition, transposition, and variation. This terse construction afforded Haydn the flexibility that enabled him to create long, interlocking, contrapuntal lines, on the one hand, and, on the other hand, to weave the fragments freely among the voices. To hear this complex interplay of subjects is difficult. In his later quartets, Haydn used even more concise motifs and took greater advantage of the flexibility they offered.

One flaw that might be claimed in Haydn's finales has to do with dramatic balance. The tension generated by these fugues—all at lively tempos—must be dissipated. Haydn attempted to do this by uniting the four instruments in unison statements of the fugue subjects, but the sudden shift from polyphony to monophony is jolting. The interesting harmonies and rhythmic interplay of voices suddenly evaporate.

After the completion of the Op. 20 Quartets, Haydn was utterly silent as a quartet composer for almost ten years. The six quartets of Op. 33 appeared in 1781. The Op. 33 Quartets are known by two different nicknames: They are called *Gli scherzi* since, for the first time, Haydn replaced the minuet and trio with movements bearing the designation *scherzo* or *scherzando*. The set is also known as the *Russian Quartets* because they are dedicated to Grand Duke Paul Petrovich, who heard them in 1781 while visiting Vienna.

The *Russian Quartets* represent a turning point in Haydn's development as a composer of chamber music:

> Haydn's opus 33 is the masterwork of this epoch in which the Classical string quartet found its first realization. . . . It is classic not only in the sense of a ripe, mature style whose evolution can be traced with singular regularity from the first quartet-divertimenti onwards, but it is also classic in concrete musical detail: in the forging of exceptional clarity of form with abundance and versatility of detail, in individual deployment of voices within the basically homophonic framework of the movements, in subtle manipulation of musical materials and bewilderingly simple musical effect, in cyclic interlocking of structural forms and structural character, and in development of individualistic movement forms and movement characteristics.[41]

According to Haydn himself, these quartets were written "in an entirely new and particular manner." Some dismiss this remark, which appears in Haydn's letters soliciting subscribers for manuscript copies of the *Russian Quartets*, as a mere advertising gimmick. True, Haydn was an astute businessman; but as a businessman, Haydn knew that disappointed customers would not return to be disappointed again. There are, indeed, new elements in Op. 33.

In leafing through the *Russian Quartets*, a feature that strikes the eye is their generally thinner and more variable textures, particularly in the finales, which tend to be sonata-rondos or rondo-variations.[42] The new texture in the Op. 33 is not really equal-voiced in the old, Baroque sense. It has been noted that "over the course of a movement, Haydn gives each line equal opportunity to carry melodies, motives, or purely accompanimental figures; at any one moment, however, he distinguishes melody from accompaniment."[43] Furthermore, freedom in motivic manipulation is not limited to transitional passages and developmental sections, as in the repertoire of the 1760s and 1770s. Instead, "The new texture may appear anywhere . . . and thus affects the interaction of virtually all melody and accompaniment, whether or not the latter imitates the former or utilizes motives."[44]

In Op. 33, Haydn uses periodic structure to amuse, delight, and surprise. In light of Haydn's publishing activities at the time, the new tone of these pieces makes sense. His first publication with Artaria was his Pianoforte Sonatas, Op. 30, published in 1780.[45] At this point, he was concerned with the commercial market for his music and hoped to establish a long-term relationship with the firm. In a letter to Artaria, Haydn wrote: "Should they [Op. 30] have a good sale, this will encourage me to further efforts in the future, and to serve you diligently at all times in preference to all others."[46] In the case of the *Russian Quartets*, Haydn's artistic outlook

was tempered by the healthy influence of popular appeal. In them, he accommodated the tastes of the music-loving public while preserving musical craftsmanship and artistry.

Haydn's periodic structures seldom use pairings of four-measure phrases that move from tonic to dominant and then from dominant back to tonic. Instead, Haydn changes some feature of this construction and eludes our expectations. This tension between anticipated events and actual events gives the music its vitality and humor. In the finale of Op. 33, No. 3, for instance, there is no harmonic motion at all in the first four measures. In the second group of four measures, the harmony finally moves to the dominant. Although the construction is perfectly symmetrical, the lack of harmonic motion in the opening four measures results in our being in the wrong place, harmonically speaking, at the conclusion of the eight-measure "period."

An equally amusing example appears in the finale of Op. 33, No. 2, the quartet that has come to be known as the *Joke.* In this instance, the harmonic progression is what we might expect: motion from tonic to dominant in the first four measures and the return to tonic in the second group of four; however, the period is not constructed of two four-measure segments, but rather, of four two-measure groups. To underscore this arrangement, Haydn isolates each two-measure fragment at the close of the movement (see meas. 152–72). The teasing pauses between phrase fragments are a humorous twist, but Haydn has another trick in store: Since the first, two-measure phrase fragment comes to rest on the tonic triad, it is added after an extended pause as a codettina to the full statement of the period. This phraseological chicanery is so confounding that, unless one is following a score, the actual ending of the piece is unclear; hence the "joke."

The long-range forms of individual movements in Haydn's *Russian Quartets* mirror the witty cleverness of the periodic structure. In Op. 33, Haydn uses two movement types that came to be specialties of his: the sonata-rondo and the rondo-variation. Both forms combine elements of common pattern forms of the later eighteenth century. In both instances, the unpredictable modifications that Haydn makes to these pattern forms add an intriguing charm that sets his music in a class of its own.

The style that Haydn perfected in Op. 33 opened new vistas to him as a composer. The sparkle and spontaneity of every page, the unlimited flexibility in transferring motivic interest from one voice to another, the cunning use of periodic structure, and the masterful control of form were now confirmed. Listeners react to such music instinctively. How fortunate for Haydn that, as of 1782, Wolfgang Amadeus Mozart was a resident of Vienna as well as a close personal friend! The satisfaction of approval, whether silent or spoken, from such a knowledgeable composer would have been ample reward for Haydn; but the relationship between these two was a profound one of mutual affection and professional respect. What will be of greater interest to the chamber music enthusiast is the interaction that took place between these two men as each responded to the other's ingenuity.

THE STRING QUARTETS OF WOLFGANG AMADEUS MOZART THROUGH OP. 10

Mozart's first string quartets were written in Italy during his childhood visits there in the final months of 1772 and the first several of 1773. At that time, the quartet was a relatively new genre.[47] Although the First String Quartet, K. 80, was originally in three movements, Mozart later added the Gavotte-en-rondeau that serves as the present finale. This change was probably made late in 1773 during a trip to Vienna that Mozart made with his father. Quartets Two through Seven are also in the three-movement plan commonly used in Italy at the time.

A fairly regular tempo sequence of movements is apparent in these early works. In its four-movement form, K. 80 uses a layout reminiscent of the old sonata *da chiesa*—in this case, slow, fast, moderate, fast. The first movement, in binary form, opens with a melody that anticipates the Countess's aria "Porgi, amor, qualche ristoro" in act 2 of *Le nozze di Figaro*. The second movement is an energetic sonata-allegro form that sounds more like a typical opening movement. The minuet and trio that forms the present third movement is in the customary A-B-A design.

Five of the six subsequent three-movement quartets follow the plan fast, slow, fast or fast, slow, moderate. K. 159 contains three movements in the sequence Andante, Allegro, and Allegro grazioso.

The tonal relationships of movements in the early quartets are highly regulated. In the First Quartet, all four movements are in G major. In five of the next six quartets, the central movements are in related keys: the relative minor (K. 156, 159), the dominant (K. 155), a third-related key (K. 158), and the subdominant (K. 160). The central movement of K. 157 does not change key; Mozart achieves harmonic variety by using the resources of the parallel minor.

Mozart wrote K. 158 in F major in Milan, while composing the opera *Lucio Silla*. The first movement is a terse sonata form. The principal theme exploits the alternation between duple and triple subdivision of the beat that was characteristic of the *style galant*. The exposition of the principal themes is largely the responsibility of the first violin; however, salient motifs frequently drift into the second violin part and even into the viola and cello parts. When the second violin is not sharing in thematic development, it fills out harmonies with Alberti figuration. Unison passages are important, and one such passage (m. 10) effects the transition to the dominant key in less than half a measure. The development section is initiated by another unison passage in which staccato articulation and sudden dynamic accents set it in contrast with the preceding material. The recapitulation (meas. 74–118) is a literal one with the customary transpositions, and a codetta brings the movement to a close.

The second movement, in A minor, bears the tempo indication Andante un poco allegretto. This binary form movement is a canonic elaboration of an Alberti figure. Here Mozart achieves a perfect synthesis of melody and accompaniment: In reality, the melody is the accompaniment and the accompaniment is the melody. The distinction between the two only becomes apparent as a result of delicate figuration, the interplay of duple and triple subdivisions of the beat, and in the adaptation of the canonic imitations to the demands of binary form.

The last movement is a minuet exploiting duple and triple division of the beat, stock ornamental figures, and unison passages. K. 158 is the most cohesive of the youthful quartets and gives a glimpse of Mozart's later quartets. As a group, the seven Italian quartets generally exhibit homophonic texture, whereas counterpoint is limited and largely coloristic. Sometimes transitions from homophonic to contrapuntal textures are awkward. Texture, periodic structure, harmonic rhythm, and harmonic progression are effective yet predictable. In these four parameters, Mozart's maturation as a composer can be traced. In his later quartets, greater compositional skill is wedded with a corresponding growth in the originality of his invention.

The next six quartets, K. 168 through K. 173, were all composed in Vienna during the month of August in the year 1773. Wolfgang and Leopold had gone there as part of the retinue of the Prince Archbishop of Salzburg, Hieronymus Colloredo. Presumably, Mozart hoped to publish the pieces in Vienna, but they were not published until 1801, when they were issued by Johann Anton André as Op. 94. In these quartets Mozart uses the four-movement plan that came to be the norm in his formal chamber pieces, including the late string quartets and quintets.

In the four-movement scheme, Mozart's preferred tempo sequence is fast, slow, moderate, fast. The moderate movement is ordinarily a minuet. Exceptions are K. 170, which has the sequence Andante, Menuetto, Poco Adagio, and Allegro [rondo]; and K. 171, with its unique design, Adagio-allegro-adagio, Menuetto, Andante, Allegro assai. Both quartets reverse the internal movements and place the minuet in second position.

The tonal arrangement of movements remains variable in these four-movement quartets, but in three of them, the slow movement is in the key of the subdominant. Of the remaining quartets, two, K. 168 and 173, have all movements in the same key with a change of mode in the slow movement. In K. 168, the shift is from F major to F minor; in the latter, three movements are in D minor with a shift to D major in the second movement. The Andante of K. 171 (third movement) is in C minor, the relative minor of the principal tonality, E-flat major.

These six Viennese quartets contain some impressive writing, such as the canonic Andante (*con sordini*) of K. 168 and the fugal finale of that same quartet. The rich texture of the Andante of K. 169 results from frequent double stops in the second violin and viola. This movement represents a true chamber music style, since double stops are virtually nonexistent in the orchestral writing of the period. The opening movement of K. 170, a theme with five variations, is the first example of this form in Mozart's compositions for string quartet. The finale of K. 173 is a remarkable fugue based on a chromatically descending subject. The spirit and detail of this fugue, though, relate it more closely to the Baroque tradition than to the increasingly motivic fugues of Haydn's Op. 20 Quartets.

After these thirteen youthful quartets, Mozart wrote none for almost ten years. In 1782, his interest in the genre was renewed as a result of his acquaintance with Haydn's recently completed quartets of Op. 33. Mozart's knowledge of Haydn's Op. 33 must have been an in-depth one: He played the viola in a quartet with Haydn, Dittersdorf, and Vahal (who played first violin, second violin, and cello respectively); thus, Wolfgang came to know these pieces with their composer at his elbow.

Mozart usually wrote quickly and with great facility; but the six quartets of Op. 10 were labors of love that occupied him for several years. In December 1782, Mozart completed the first one, the G-major Quartet, K. 387. In 1783, he added the D-minor Quartet, K. 421, and the E-flat-major Quartet, K. 428. A fourth quartet, the Quartet in B-flat major, K. 458, was completed in 1784. The fifth and sixth quartets in this set, K. 464 in A major and K. 465 in C major, were completed in January 1785. This was dedicated to Haydn, to whom Mozart expressed his esteem in the elegant dedication that he wrote for the first edition, which was published by Artaria in 1785.

> To my dear Friend Haydn
>
> A father who had decided to send his children out into the great world felt that it was his responsibility to confide them to the protection and guidance of a very celebrated man, especially when the latter by good fortune was at the same time his best friend. Here they are then, O great man and dearest friend, these six children of mine. They are, it is true, the fruit of a long and laborious effort, yet the hope raised in me by some friends that it may be at least partly compensated encourages me, and I flatter myself that this offspring will serve to afford me some solace one day. You yourself, dearest friend, during your last visit to this capital, demonstrated to me your satisfaction with them. It is this indulgence above all that urges me to commend them to you and encourages me to hope that they will not seem to you altogether unworthy of your favor. May it please you to receive them in a kindly way and be their father, guide, and friend. From this moment, I cede to you all of my rights in them, begging you, however, to look indulgently upon the defects that the partial eye of a father may have concealed from me, and in spite of them, to continue in your generous

friendship for him who so greatly values it, in expectation of which I am, with all my heart,

To my dearest friend
From your most sincere friend,
Vienna, 1 September 1785
W. A. Mozart

The proportions of the Op. 10 quartets are roughly double the lengths of Mozart's earlier quartets. More significant is their greater musical density. The motivic interplay of voices is thorough; texture changes constantly, the harmonic idiom is more complex; and formal designs are more extensive. The demands upon listeners and upon the players, particularly the cellist, are increased too.

The compositional daring of Op. 10 must have intrigued Haydn. The harmonies in the opening of the C-major Quartet, K. 465, for example, were so bold that eighteenth-century publishers "corrected" what they believed to be mistakes. These striking sonorities resulted in the nickname by which this piece is still known: the *Dissonance Quartet.* The opening twenty-two measures use the key of C in its major and minor form simultaneously. A-flats grind against A-naturals and B-flats against B-naturals, but within the context of the individual lines, each of the chromatic forms of the sixth and seventh scale degrees is necessitated by Mozart's exacting voice leading. Note the astonishing precision in specification of phrasing, articulation, and dynamics; almost every single note is accompanied by some instruction.

In this introductory passage, Mozart integrates ornament and structure. The principal theme, stated in the viola in the first measure, is a turn figure that is imitated in the second violin part a fifth higher on E-flat, then in the first violin part a tritone higher on A-natural. The cello line combines variant scale degrees of the ascending and descending minor scale in its chromatic descent from C to G, the root of the dominant half cadence on which the introduction comes to rest. Interesting, too, is the reversal of this chromatic movement, which appears in the cello part in measure 13. This ornamental condensation of the larger, bar-by-bar descent occurs in the midst of a voice exchange that delays the arrival at the dominant.

This concentration and intensification of musical events gives some indication of the intricacies of these quartets. Haydn realized this: During Leopold Mozart's 1785 visit to Vienna, he met with Haydn, who told him: "Before God and as a honest man, I tell you that your son is the greatest composer known to me in person or by name."

K. 465
W. A. Mozart

Haydn's reaction to Mozart's Quartets of Op. 10 went beyond praise. In his six Quartets, Op. 50, completed in 1787 and dedicated to King Friedrich Wilhelm II of Prussia, the influence of Mozart's ingenious chromaticism is clear. Within the first seventeen measures of Op. 50, No. 5, for example, Haydn has introduced two chromatic alterations, C-sharp (meas. 5, 13) and E-flat (m. 17). These pitches give colorful departures from the prevailing tonality, but as the quartet progresses, they assume more than local significance. In the first twelve measures of the development, we return to E-flat, but now it is temporarily tonicized (meas. 77ff.). Similarly, when C-sharp appears in the recapitulation, it is respelled as a D-flat in the retransition, and acts as a Neapolitan of the dominant in the key of F major. What initially appeared as local ornamentation has now assumed structural significance.

By the early 1780s, both Haydn and Mozart were producing quartet masterpieces in the Classical style. The consolidation of the string quartet as a genre seems to have taken place at the precise moment that the fully developed manner of Viennese Classicism came into being; thus, the string quartet might well be viewed as the quintessential genre of the era.

MOZART'S LATE STRING QUARTETS

Mozart wrote four quartets after Op. 10. These are the *Hoffmeister Quartet*, K. 499 in D major, and the three *Prussian Quartets.*

The *Hoffmeister Quartet*, named after Franz Anton Hoffmeister, who published the first edition of the piece, marks a new direction in Mozart's use of form. Generally, Mozart's stable tonal areas—in sonata forms, particularly the tonic and secondary key areas of the exposition and the corresponding portions of the recapitulation—contain a great diversity of themes and motifs. In the first movement of the *Hoffmeister Quartet*, though, Mozart uses the same theme in the tonic and dominant. The first theme is not a single idea but actually a series of distinctive motifs. In the secondary key area, Mozart uses the same motifs, but their application is so different that the absence of a new theme is hardly noticed. Furthermore, the contrapuntal ingenuity with which he handles his material never fails to hold the listener's interest. The *Hoffmeister Quartet* was completed in 1786 (on 19 August), one of the most happy and productive years in Mozart's life.

The first movement of K. 499, with its downward skipping theme, is cast in sonata form, but the tempo indication, Allegretto, gives the movement a more relaxed mood than is customary in Mozart's first movements. The ensuing minuet begins conventionally, but in the second strain of the A section, imitations appear in syncopated rhythms. The third movement, though conforming to prevailing tastes in its generally relaxed tone, is nevertheless a sonata form without the repeats. The finale is another sonata form.

Mozart's C-minor Adagio and Fugue for strings, K. 546 dates from 1788, but the fugue, originally for two pianos (K. 426) was probably composed in 1783, when he was investigating various scores by Bach and Handel in the collection of Baron Gottfried van Swieten. The piece, which was published by Hoffmeister, is usually played by string quartet even though the original sources for the fugue suggest that it was probably intended to be performed orchestrally with multiple players and double basses. The fugue shows that Mozart had fully absorbed the influence of J. S. Bach's contrapuntal art, for in it, he treats the subject in canon, inversion, and stretto. Despite its archaic style, this fugue, like the double fugue based on a theme of Handel's that Mozart wrote as the "Kyrie" of the Requiem Mass, K. 626, is powerful music.

The so-called *Prussian Quartets* were intended for King Friedrich Wilhelm II, an amateur cellist. (Beethoven later wrote the two Sonatas Op. 5 for cello and piano for him.) The history of the *Prussian Quartets* begins in April 1789, when Mozart set out with Prince Karl Lichnowsky for Berlin. Mozart appeared at the court in Potsdam on 26 May. It is conceivable that the idea of his writing some quartets for King Friedrich was suggested at this time. Composition probably began immediately. The D-major String Quartet, K. 575, and the B-flat Quartet, K. 589, were the first two completed, but the third of the quartets, K. 590 in F major, was not finished until June 1790. When the set of three appeared in print, the edition contained no mention of Friedrich Wilhelm II, and Mozart was already dead.

The tonal levels in the first movement of the D-major Quartet are delineated by contrasting themes, the second of which is stated by the cello.

The ensuing Andante and minuet movements lead to a remarkable finale in which a transformation of the principal theme of the first movement serves as the basis of a sonata-rondo design. In 1789, cyclic recollection of themes was still a rarity, and so this quartet stands out for historical as well as musical reasons.

The prominence of the cello is not much apparent in K. 589; however, the first movement of K. 590 showcases the monarch's instrument. Note, too, that a thematic transformation of the first movement's main theme becomes the basis of the second theme.

MOZART'S STRING QUINTETS

Mozart composed six string quintets, all requiring two violins, two violas, and one cello. Recordings frequently feature all six pieces as a set; however, Mozart neither wrote them at the same time, nor intended them as a group. The quintets exhibit disparate styles: The earliest, K. 174 of 1773, shows Mozart as a gifted but not yet brilliant composer. Another of the quintets, K. 406 in C minor, is actually a transcription of the Serenade K. 388 of 1782, which Mozart apparently felt was too good to let pass by the wayside after only a few hearings. Indeed, the version for string quintet is so thoroughly convincing that one must question whether, perhaps, Mozart envisioned the string quintet scoring of the piece even as he wrote the serenade version. The formal complexity of the score and its contrapuntal richness—exceptional in music for wind ensembles at the time—would certainly suggest this view.[48] The pair of quintets, K. 515 in C major and K. 516 in G minor, were completed respectively on 19 April 1787 and 16 May 1787. This year witnessed changes in Mozart's life. At the time he wrote the quintet in G minor, "It must have been obvious to Mozart that, at least with the Viennese, he had failed as a composer."[49] Family heartaches compounded Mozart's difficulties: "His father, Leopold, . . . was ill and, in fact, died less than two weeks after the Quintet was finished."[50]

The G-minor Quintet is suffused with a tension and profound despair that are rarely encountered in Mozart's works. The details of Wolfgang's relationship with Leopold are, by now, well known. It will be sufficient to note that virtually all of Wolfgang's education—both musical and academic in the broader sense—was Leopold's doing. Wolfgang's letters to his family reflect not only a deep-rooted respect for his father's judgement, but even a certain dependence upon him for approval.[51] The turmoil of the G-minor Quintet parallels Wolfgang's psychological state in face of his father's impending death. Still, this passionate music had a specific function within

Mozart's artistic vision: The quintets K. 515 in C major, K. 406 in C minor, and K. 516 in G minor were apparently intended to be published as a set of three. The former work is typical of Mozart's music in C major: It is powerful, dynamic, and exhilarating. The C-minor and G-minor quintets are counterparts as well as complements within the context of the set of three.

The opening of the C-major Quintet is almost orchestral in its style. The principal theme is essentially a "Mannheim Rocket"; similarly, the lower strings employ a *temolando* figuration that was common in symphonies of the Mannheim school. What is not typical of midcentury style, though, is the complexity of this music. The self-assured C-major rocket is quickly transformed into a minor version. Chromatic alterations of all sorts intrude upon the typical simplicity of this favorite key of beginning musicians. Formal plans are extended—the exposition alone is 151 measures—but, nevertheless, clear. In the first movement, tonal levels are delineated by sharply contrasting thematic ideas. The repeated-note figure of the second theme sets it apart from the opening rocket. The closing theme is the only one that uses syncopation.

The publication of the piece by Artaria placed the Minuet and trio in second place followed by the Andante, but recent scholarly editions have reversed the movements in order to restore what were apparently Mozart's intentions.

The G-minor Quintet opens with an expansive sonata whose principal theme is a highly chromatic line with an equally chromatic harmonization. The third movement, Adagio ma non troppo, calls throughout for muted strings. Mozart chose a third-related key, E-flat major, for this movement. The lovely melody sung by the violin in the central section is soon taken up in imitation. Its off-beat accompaniment gives it a degree of melancholy sweetness and charm achieved rarely even by Mozart. The finale is prefaced by a doleful arioso for violin played at an adagio tempo. Hardly an "introduction," this exquisite passage constitutes somewhat more than one-fourth of the whole finale. The ensuing rondo, flowing and elegant, rescues the quintet from utter despair, and sends the listener away contented.

Of the remaining quintets, we should note the Quintet in E-flat major (K. 614, of 1791). This was Mozart's final work for chamber ensemble.

HAYDN'S LATE QUARTETS

Haydn's later string quartets include the sets issued as Opp. 51, 54, 55, 64 (those of Opp. 54, 55, 64 generally known as the *Tost Quartets*), 71, 74 (these two known as the *Apponyi Quartets*), 76 (*Erdödy Quartets*), and the last two completed quartets, those of Op. 77 (*Lobkowitz Quartets*). In all these, he used many of the musical devices that he had established in his early quartets, but certain of the quartet groups are more serious—along the lines of Op. 20—while others show a more genial tone—reminiscent of Op. 33.

The quartets of Op. 51 originated as orchestral pieces to be played between the meditations on the Seven Last Words of Christ on the Cross. They were commissioned by the Cathedral of Cádiz in southern Spain in 1785. To these seven adagio movements, Haydn added an Introduzione and Terremoto (introduction and earthquake). In 1787, he revised them for string quartet. The movements are monothematic and supposedly use themes inspired by their corresponding Latin texts. (Haydn later made a choral arrangement, so the correspondence of words and melodies can be verified.)

The twelve quartets of Opp. 54 (three), 55 (three), and 64 (six) were composed between 1788 and 1790 for Johann Tost, who, after serving as violinist in the Esterhaza orchestra, became a wealthy merchant. The first violin part is designed to highlight Tost's playing; thus, the quartets are representative of the *quatuor brillant* manner. Op. 64, No. 5 in D, nicknamed the *Lark*, because of its frequent, soaring, arpeggiated first-violin melodies, has emerged as a favorite from these twelve. The second movement, Adagio cantabile, shows Haydn's finest lyrical manner. Here and there, it is reminiscent of the slow introduction to the finale of Mozart's G-minor Quintet, K. 516. Interesting, too, is the chromatic trio of the Minuet.

Opp. 71 and 74 contain three quartets each. They are known collectively as the *Apponyi Quartets* after Count Anton Apponyi (1751–1817) to whom they are dedicated. Haydn and Count Apponyi were personal friends, and the count had been Haydn's sponsor when he sought admission to the Masonic lodge "Zur wahren Eintracht" (Genuine concord). Although Count Apponyi was himself a violinist, Haydn's quartets were composed for performance at the London concerts of Johann Peter Salomon (1745–1815) during the 1794 concert season. Salomon, who specialized in the performance of chamber music, gave the premiere of these quartets at the Hanover Square Public Rooms.

Haydn first visited London in 1791. He heard Salomon's playing during that sojourn—perhaps in a performance of the recently completed quartets of Op. 64. When Haydn wrote the *Apponyi Quartets*, Salomon was well known to him, as were the concert hall in which the performances took place and the tastes of the audiences there. Haydn was fascinated by England, by British customs, and by its society and concert. Apparently the gentry of the city were equally fascinated by him.[52] The public concerts that Salomon sponsored had been a great success. The set of six *London Symphonies* that Haydn composed for the first visit were greeted with warm applause, and Haydn became somewhat of a hero in the eyes of English music lovers. For his second journey, he wrote another set of six symphonies as well as these two sets of quartets. The B-flat major and D-major quartets, the first two in Op. 71, were probably composed in the closing months of 1792; the remaining quartets were composed in Vienna during 1793.

The six *Apponyi Quartets* are not "domestic" music; they are for the concert hall; thus, they mark the transition to our contemporary understanding of "chamber music." The challenge to Haydn was a new one, but he was already familiar with most of the practical considerations of public music-making. The first concern was to quiet the audience and attract their attention. In the E-flat and C-major quartets, Op. 71, No. 3 and Op. 74, No. 1 respectively, this objective was achieved with only a few chords marked with fermatas and sounded at a *forte* dynamic. (Perhaps performers may hold these chords until their purpose is accomplished.) In the first quartet of Op. 71, the Quartet in B-flat major, a striking succession of chords achieves the same objective. The Quartet Op. 71, No. 2 in D major commences with an introductory Adagio. Each quartet begins with a gesture that grabs attention, yet the ideas are well suited to the medium of the string quartet.

Harmonies are unusual; the Quartet in E-flat, Op. 71, No. 3, contains music in the key of F-double-flat! Virtuosity both in the use of counterpoint as well as in performance techniques complements Haydn's remarkable harmonic manner. Formal designs, such as the pairing in the finale of Op. 71, No. 2 of an Allegretto with an Allegro based on a transformation of the theme of the former, also contribute to the diversity found in this fascinating group of quartets.

Among the late quartets, Op. 76, No. 3 in C major (1796) is undoubtedly the best known, its second movement being the set of four variations on Haydn's hymn "Gott erhalte Franz den Kaiser" (God protect Emperor Franz), a tune that served later for the national anthems of Germany and Austria, as well as the popular hymn "Glorious Things of Thee Are Spoken."[53]

HAYDN'S SIGNIFICANCE IN THE HISTORY OF THE STRING QUARTET

Haydn was one of the first composers to achieve a compelling style of quartet composition. The public recognized him during his own lifetime as a formidable voice in the field of chamber music. Haydn's influence on Mozart, particularly in this difficult, new genre, is equally clear; but Mozart was one of many composers who learned from Haydn, either as a result of personal contact or through knowledge of his compositions. Ignaz Joseph Pleyel (1757–1831), a prolific composer, a pupil of Haydn's, and an instrument manufacturer, was also an important music publisher. During the years 1801–2, he published eighty-three Haydn quartets (up to Op. 76 and including the misattributed Op. 3) as the *Collection complette des quatuors d'Haydn dédiée au Premier Consul Bonaparte.* Finally, Haydn acted as Beethoven's mentor from the of his arrival in Vienna in 1792 until Haydn's departure for his second London visit. Beethoven took the techniques that Haydn had developed in his quartets and transformed them to serve his needs in the first Romantic works for that medium.

The string quartet was the most important type of chamber music during the Classical era. The sheer number of them bears witness to its role in the musical culture of the time. Of greater significance is the fact that the string quartet was the genre in which composers tended to express their most profound ideas; nevertheless, to limit our understanding of later eighteenth-century chamber music to the string quartet would be to exclude a vast and significant body of repertoire. Our discussion of Beethoven's music must therefore be put aside until we have investigated the chamber music of the Classical era that involved wind instruments.

THREE

Classical Chamber Music with Wind Instruments

CHAMBER MUSIC FOR WINDS WITH STRINGS

Many scores by Haydn, Mozart, and their contemporaries throughout Europe have come down to us bearing the designation *divertimento.* Other pieces are called *notturno, serenata, cassation,* or *Nachtmusik.* Whereas *divertimento* denoted performance by one player per part, these other designations did not necessarily indicate nonorchestral scorings.[1] The serenade literature of the later eighteenth century can only be understood as chamber music insofar as no conductor would have been needed, and, in some cases, the performance would have had one player per part; nevertheless, some of the repertoire encompassed by these designations was not chamber music at all since it would have been played out-of-doors. In that context, the performers usually stood during concerts.

The cello had a rather short peg during the eighteenth century; consequently, it could not easily be played in a standing position. The double bass, on the other hand, had a longer peg as well as a strap to be used for suspending the instrument around the player's shoulder. With this information in mind, the significance of the term *basso* in designating the lowest part of the divertimento/serenade literature becomes apparent. The labeling of the lowest string part as either *basso* or *violoncello* in late eighteenth-century scores is also helpful in distinguishing actual string quartet literature from divertimento/serenade repertoire. When chamber music for strings was performed indoors, the bass line was usually played by the violoncello; on the other hand, repertoire performed *al fresco* more commonly used the double bass on the bass line.

This modified instrumentation had significant consequences. The eighteenth-century double bass was different from the present-day instrument in that its tone was lighter, more transparent, and blended more easily with the stringed instruments in the higher registers. The serenade double bass was also unusual in that it was a

> five-string model . . . and its lowest string was normally tuned to contra F'—not to E', and certainly not to contra C'. Hence we hypothesize that any bass part in soloistic chamber music which consistently goes below notated F, especially one that exploits notated low C frequently or in exposed contexts, is written for cello. Conversely, if in a full-scale multimovement work the bass never goes below notated F, it may well reckon with solo double bass.[2]

The pitches that we find in the scores of string bass parts of serenades, cassations, nocturnes, and some divertimenti would actually have sounded an octave lower than written. The disparity in register between viola and double bass was resolved by the addition of pairs of winds—often horns—to fill in this range.[3]

Mozart's Divertimento in F major, K. 247, composed in June 1776 for the name day of Countess Antonia Lodron, the sister of Archbishop Hieronymus Colloredo, is a good example of his essays in this genre. The ensemble consists of four-part strings with a pair of horns. The first movement is a bristling Allegro in common time with the primary melodic motifs in the first violin part. The second violin often reinforces the melody at the third or octave below, or at the unison. The terse phraseology in all seven movements places this work by the twenty-year-old Mozart squarely in the tradition of the *style galant.* The concise harmonic and melodic building blocks are repeated liberally, but each time, Mozart enlivens the repetition with some modification of dynamics, phrasing, or articulation.

The first movement is a conventional sonata. The secondary theme, in the dominant key, contains some interesting chromatic color tones as it moves on to the closing thematic group. The opening theme is truncated in the recapitulation, but Mozart compensates by replacing the deleted material in an eight-measure codetta.

A triple-meter Andante and a first Minuetto lead to an Adagio movement in the subdominant. With a practical eye to the endurance of the brass players, Mozart reduces the scoring in the Adagio to two violins, viola, and *basso.* Here Mozart makes much more extensive use of double stops in the second violin and viola parts than in any of the preceding movements, presumably owing to the absence of the horns.

The remainder of this divertimento consists of three movements: a second Minuetto, a diminutive Andante, and a concluding Allegro, which balance and round out the piece. The architecture of the work is quite carefully conceived—including a Trio in B-flat major that acts as a counterpart to the excursion to that key in the Adagio movement.

The New Mozart Edition of the Divertimento in F major, K. 247, is prefaced by a March, K. 248, in the same key.[4] Almost invariably, a march would have been included in outdoors performances. "These marches served, as all authorities confirm, as the entry- and exit-musics before and after the program, and they indicate that the performance of the Divertimento proper would have taken place in the fresh air."[5]

MOZART'S OCCASIONAL WORKS FOR WINDS AND STRINGS

As we return indoors, we find other works for mixed chamber ensembles of winds and strings. Among Mozart's simplest pieces of this type are the quartets for flute and strings, K. 285 in D major (1777), K. 285a in G major (1778), K. 285b in C major (1781), and K. 298 in A major (1786–87). The first two quartets were apparently the result of a commission from a Dutch amateur named in Mozart's letters as "De Jean." Some suppose him to have been Villem van Britten Dejong, while others suggest that he was Ferdinand Dejean, a surgeon by trade.[6]

The flute quartets resemble the ensemble sonatas and popular French quartets of the period insofar as the basic texture consists of a singing melody with straightforward accompaniment. The strings generally provide harmonic support for the flute part, which varies in interest from one quartet to the next and from one movement to the next. Another similarity with the ensemble sonata literature can be seen in the format of movements, which may number two or three. K. 285, generally considered the best of the four flute quartets, follows a three-movement plan. The central movement, an expressive Adagio, shifts to the relative minor key.

K. 298 has traditionally been assigned to the Paris journey of 1778.[7] Einstein long ago noted that K. 298 was a humorous, musical hodgepodge including parodies of works by Cambini and Paisiello.[8] Subsequently, the name of Franz Anton Hoffmeister was added to the roster.[9] Of particular interest, though, is the fact that the citation of "Chi mi mostra, chi m'addita dove sta il mio dolce amore," from Paisiello's opera *Le gare generose* (1786), renders the date of 1778 impossible.

On a different level from the flute quartets is the three-movement Quartet in F major for oboe, violin, viola, and cello, K. 368b. Mozart composed this piece for Friedrich Ramm (1744–1811), then the leading oboe player of the Mannheim orchestra. Mozart had formed a friendship with Ramm during a brief stay in Mannheim en route to France in 1778. In 1780, the Elector Karl Theodore of Mannheim became Elector of the Palatinate and consequently moved with many of his staff, including Ramm, to Munich. There, in the closing months of that year and January and February 1781, Mozart composed the second and third acts of *Idomeneo,* K. 366, and supervised its rehearsal and production. Ramm's presence in the orchestra is reflected by the beauty and craftsmanship of the writing for his instrument in Mozart's score. That Mozart, already fully occupied with work on the opera, made time to compose this chamber work for Ramm speaks volumes about his skills as a performer.

The oboe part is impressive, but the strings are far more than accompaniment. Detailed motivic work and important thematic ideas enliven all of the string parts, and the shift of the leading role to a string is sometimes used to articulate important moments in the unfolding structure—such as the statement of the secondary theme in the exposition of the first movement. The second movement is pure lyricism, while, the third movement, a bubbling rondo in 6/8 time, anticipates the brilliant writing in the finale of the Clarinet Concerto, K. 622. The rhythmic independence of the oboe from the strings, especially in the episode preceding the final statement of the rondo theme, is so extensive that we may well apply the term *polymetric* to this remarkable passage.

The three-movement quintet K. 386c for horn and four stringed instruments dates from Mozart's first season in Vienna, the fall of 1782. The work, written for Joseph Ignatz Leutgeb (1732–1811), calls for one violin, two violas, and a fourth instrument to play the bass line. That line bore the designation *basso* in the first edition; the term *violoncello* appeared in a later edition by André. It is therefore possible that the piece may actually have been intended for performance with double bass.[10]

Leutgeb was the artist who also elicited three of the four horn concertos from Mozart's pen. As a child in Salzburg, Wolfgang knew Leutgeb, and when Mozart settled in Vienna in 1781, he was pleased to renew his acquaintance with the horn virtuoso, who had moved there in 1777.

Mozart wrote quartets with a single wind instrument and three stringed instruments during his Salzburg years, but his Viennese chamber music uses an ensemble of four strings and one wind. Mozart's last piece using the combination of four strings and one wind was the Clarinet Quintet, K. 581, for Paul Anton Stadler (1753–1812), one of the most interesting figures among the virtuosos of the later eighteenth century. He was born in Bruck, the same town where Haydn was born. Paul Anton and his brother Johann began presenting clarinet concerts in Vienna as early as 1773, and both were employed in Emperor Joseph II's wind band in 1782. Anton was a man of vision, and he drew up a plan addressing general considerations of music education (*Musik Plan* of 1800). He also extended the range of the clarinet, thereby creating the so-called basset clarinet, the instrument for which the Clarinet Quintet of 1789 and the Clarinet Concerto, K. 622 of 1791 were conceived. Unfortunately, the original score of the quintet has not survived, and the differences between it and the version for conventional clarinet must remain a matter of conjecture.[11] In all likelihood, Mozart also had Stadler in mind when he wrote the Quintet in E-flat for piano, oboe, clarinet, bassoon, and horn, K. 452.[12]

Mozart viewed the Clarinet Quintet as an exceptional work. It is the only example among his occasional chamber works for winds and strings that utilizes the four-movement plan. The opening movement is a sonata; however, in the recapitulation, Mozart transfers some passages originally assigned to the clarinet to the first violin. The recapitulation also contains triplet subdivisions that were not present in the exposition as well as an elaboration in the clarinet part (meas. 182–84) of a figure consisting of a trill with a *Nachschlag* that had appeared as a stock cadential figure in the first violin part in measure 6 of the exposition.

The Larghetto is an elegant movement written as a duet between the clarinet and the first violin with lower strings accompanying. It is unclear whether the indication *con sordino* in the score applies to all strings or excludes the first violin. Even with muted first violin, the clarinet is capable of providing an appropriately subtle dynamic level to balance well; however, the mute eliminates much of the brightness of the violin tone and seems to me less satisfactory in achieving the effect of an accompanied duo. The minuet is extended by the insertion of a second trio section, a formal plan that Beethoven later used. The finale is an Allegretto with six variations, the third of which is in the parallel minor key.

CHAMBER MUSIC FOR WINDS ONLY: *Harmoniemusik*

Small ensembles of mixed wind instruments often played in the open air at social and civic functions. The advantage of these modest wind bands consisted in their constitution by instruments that were easily portable and that could produce a suitable dynamic level for the intended performance environment. Wind ensembles commonly ranged from five to thirteen instruments. Sometimes the scorings included exotic instruments, such as English horn and serpent, though the most typical *Harmoniemusik* ensemble of the later eighteenth century consisted of pairs each of oboes, clarinets, horns, and bassoons.

Both Haydn and Mozart made significant contributions to this medium. Most of the authenticated Haydn repertoire was composed during the 1760s, whereas Mozart's compositions generally date from the following decade. Among the many works attributed to Haydn, standard *Harmoniemusik* scoring appears in Hob. II/41, 42, 43, and F7. Three other of Haydn's wind ensembles, Hob. II/44, 45, and 46, require a pair each of oboes and horns, with three bassoons and a serpent.[13] The best known of this latter group is undoubtedly Hob. II/46, which includes the "St. Anthony Chorale" that was used by Johannes Brahms as the basis of his *Variations on a Theme of Haydn*, Op. 56a and b. The *St. Anthony Partita* is in four movements, *Allegro con spirito, Chorale St. Anthoni, Menuetto,* and *Rondo-allegretto.* The concluding rondo uses a thematic variant of the chorale melody heard in the second movement. Probably the five-bar phrases of the chorale rather than the instrumentation attracted Brahms to Haydn's melody.

Most of Mozart's music for small wind ensembles was composed during his early years in Salzburg. The instrumentation is normally limited to pairs of oboes, horns, and bassoons, since the Salzburg court orchestra did not include clarinets. Any of Mozart's works with a pair of clarinets is suspect: Either it was composed after the year 1781, when Mozart moved to Vienna where clarinets would have been available, or that particular piece was written for use outside of Salzburg. The Divertimento, K. 113, for example, was composed in 1771, but its inclusion of a pair of clarinets reflects the fact that it was composed for use in Milan. It is also possible that works scored with clarinet are revisions of earlier pieces that did not originally include that instrument.

Mozart's outdoors chamber music differs in one important respect from the actual chamber music compositions: The periodic structure of the indoor music is interesting, ingenious, and often quite complex, whereas the outdoors pieces tend to be straightforward, as is their texture.

Mozart's divertimentos for winds, more than any other of his compositions, exhibit the characteristics of the *style galant* that was fashionable during the 1760s and 1770s. Mozart would have experienced the *galant* manner firsthand during his childhood sojourns to Augsburg, Leopold Mozart's birthplace and a center for the cultivation of that midcentury style. These simple and direct structures are characteristic not only in Mozart's scores, but in those by his contemporaries as well. It was in this repertoire that the stereotype of the light and accessible divertimento had its origin.

FOUR

The Chamber Music of Beethoven

The most important chamber works by Ludwig van Beethoven (1770–1827) are his string quartets. His earliest, begun in 1798, eventually became the set of six string Quartets, Op. 18. His middle period quartets are the three *Razumovsky Quartets*, Op. 59, the *Harp Quartet*, Op. 74, and the *Quartetto serioso*, Op. 95. The late quartets include Opp. 127, 132, 130, 131, and 135. Along with these sixteen quartets, we possess the *Grosse Fuge* (grand fugue) for string quartet, Op. 133, which was originally the finale of Op. 130.[1]

THE EARLY QUARTETS

Beethoven dedicated his six quartets, Op. 18, to Joseph Franz Maximilian Prince of Lobkowitz. They were composed between 1798 and 1800. The published order of these quartets (i.e., F major, G major, D major, C minor, A major, B-flat major) does not reflect the chronology of their composition. Beethoven commented about the edition published by Tranquillo Mollo in 1801: He wrote to Franz Anton Hoffmeister that Mollo's edition was "full of mistakes and errata—on a large scale and on a small scale. They swarm like little fishes in water, that is to say, ad infinitum. . . . My skin is full of pricks and scratches—thanks to the beautiful edition of my Quartets."[2] Unfortunately, the autograph manuscripts of these quartets have all been lost.

The Op. 18 quartets are conservative: All are in four movements with fast outer movements. Sonata form movements are conventional, as is Beethoven's inclusion of six quartets in the set. The melodic style relies on terse motifs of the *galant* sort, and the principal themes are often standard ornamental figures.

The turn figure is the fundamental melodic idea in the first movement of the F-major Quartet, Op. 18, No. 1, and it forms the basis of both the opening theme and the secondary theme. The full quartet plays this motif in unison at the opening, but in the secondary key area, it is stated in reduced note values (i.e., diminution), and it forms the basis of a dialogue between the outer voices. Though the quartet exhibits an unprecedented singularity in its melodic continuity, the motivic transformations are always so ingenious that listeners hardly notice the movement's monothematic design. Similar thematic unity can be seen in the first movement of the G-major Quartet, Op. 18, No. 2, which also uses a typical ornamental flourish as its main theme.

Beethoven's first set of variations to appear within the context of a string quartet occurs in the Andante cantabile of the A-major String Quartet, Op. 18, No. 5. The movement is positioned in third place following a Minuet and trio in the principal tonality of A major. All five variations are in the subdominant, D major. These are strict variations in which the original theme is preserved in its essentials. The theme is remarkable for its syncopations and melodic retardations that make the metrical shape and harmonic progress somewhat confusing upon first hearing. Phrase endings are obscured by tied values, and weak-beat cadences delay arrivals at pivotal harmonies where these are expected. From this theme, Beethoven was able to elicit a wide range of emotions. In the first variation, he develops the tune in imitative counterpoint. The first violin dominates, as in *quatuor brillant* texture, in the second variation. The third is devoted to the lower strings, which play the tune and fragmented motifs derived from it beneath a repeated figure in the first violin. The ostinato pattern of the first violin gives way in the fourth variation to an essentially harmonic treatment of the melody. Chromatic alterations within secondary dominants produce striking harmonic shifts. The fifth variation is a raucous, military march reminiscent of some eighteenth-century patriotic celebration. The march, which is the final numbered variation, leads to a sixth, unnumbered variation that is free and figural. Presumably, Beethoven eschewed the assignment of a number for this variation because of its structural function as a coda.

Of the twenty-four movements in Op. 18, the finale of the B-flat-major String Quartet, Op. 18, No. 6, is the most bizarre and original. Beethoven gave this movement the subtitle *La malinconia.* He also wrote the instruction that *Questa pezzo si deve trattare colla piu gran delicatezza* (This piece should be rendered with the greatest delicacy). The harmonic idiom of this movement is intriguing. In many ways, it is Beethoven's equivalent of Mozart's introduction to the famous *Dissonance Quartet*, K. 465.[3]

A progressive feature of this movement is the structural significance of the fully-diminished-seventh chord. The first four measures present a peaceful series of parallel sixths in the first and second violin parts; in the next four measures, this is echoed an octave lower by the second violin and the viola. The affection is that of absolute tranquility; but, the tranquility is disrupted by the fully-diminished-seventh chord (m. 9). The sonority is further emphasized by its repetition on pause chords (mm. 13 through 16). The pause chords are placed in bold relief by dramatic alternations between *piano* and *forte* dynamics.

Beethoven's use of diminished sonorities anticipates the harmonic idiom of mature German romanticism: The mysterious progressions in von Weber's *Der Freischütz* (1821) and Wagner's endless melody both depend on the diminished-seventh chord rather than the dominant-seventh chord, and composers of the Romantic era took full advantage of the tonal mobility that this sonority provided. Equally important is the dramatic function of this chord. Since it consists of two interlocking tritones, it is a volatile, unstable sonority—particularly when placed in such a grand and rhetorical manner as we find it in *La malinconia.* This concluding movement of Op. 18 must have made a powerful impression on listeners of the early nineteenth century.

When we clear away the smoke and shadows from *La malinconia,* we find that this curious passage that begins the finale of the quartet is actually a slow introduction to fairly tradition movement. In its closing measure, the adagio introduction is poised (with *fermata*) on a dominant triad that leads without break into the Allegretto. This "introduction" reappears several times in the course of the movement, thereby assuming structural significance.

QUARTETS OF THE MIDDLE PERIOD

Beethoven's Op. 59, generally known as the *Razumovsky Quartets* (1806), contains only three quartets. They were dedicated to Count Andrei Kyrillovich Razumovsky, the representative of the Russian czar at the Habsburg court in Vienna. As Paul Griffiths has pointed out,

> In the winter of 1804–05 Ignaz Shuppanzigh [sic], already thoroughly familiar to Beethoven as the outstanding quartet leader in Vienna of his day, began to give subscription concerts of quartets, and in 1808, the year of the publication of the "Razumovsky" quartets, Shuppanzigh's ensemble was to receive a salaried appointment to the household of Count Razumovsky [until 1814]. It was certainly for Shuppanzigh that Beethoven wrote op. 59 (as he did all his later quartets), and in doing so he was writing for a violinist who . . . was primarily a quartet player. Thus op. 59 presumes not merely brilliance, though on occasion the three works do require that of the first violin, but also dedication and understanding.[4]

Schuppanzigh's technique and refined playing would have made an impression on Count Razumovsky since he was himself a keen quartet player.

Each of the *Razumovsky Quartets* is longer by a third or even a half than those of Op. 18. The first movement of Op. 59, No. 1, the String Quartet in F major, is one of the longest sonata-form movements in all of Beethoven's chamber music. This extraordinary length is achieved without the customary repetitions of the halves of the binary form. Instead, passages with unstable harmonies (i.e., those passages often called "transition sections") are expanded. Likewise, the coda is enlisted for further development rather than being limited to the customary confirmation of tonic harmony.

Similar expansion takes place in the third movement of the string quartet Op. 59, No. 2, the String Quartet in E minor. In its Allegretto, we find a formal plan that was to become a favorite of Beethoven's: the double scherzo and trio. Here Beethoven enlarges the typical tripartite form of the minuet and trio (or scherzo and trio) by adding a repetition of the trio and a third statement of the minuet (or scherzo) *da capo*. In this instance, the repetition is merited: the trio section, customarily an easygoing point of repose within a larger movement, is actually a double fugue using a tuneful melody as the principal subject and a more active countersubject full of intricate figuration. As the subjects and answers of both themes speed by, the listener is engulfed in scintillating, fourth-species counterpoint that is both technically impressive and characteristic of the contrapuntal style preferred by composers working in traditionally Roman Catholic countries.

This is an ironic bit of music, since the songlike subject is actually a Russian folk melody, one of several that Beethoven used in the *Razumovsky Quartets*. Russian themes also appear in the fourth movement of the First *Razumovsky Quartet*. In each movement, Beethoven points out the folk

String Quartet Op. 59, No. 2, 3d movement

Ludwig van Beethoven

song with the designation "Theme russe." Contrary to Romantic lore, there is no evidence that Razumovsky taught Beethoven these melodies. He actually took them from a collection published by Johann Gottfried Pratsch in 1790.

Beethoven composed two additional string quartets during his middle period; these were the so-called *Harp Quartet,* Op. 74, in E-flat major, and the *Quartetto serioso,* Op. 95, in F minor. These were written in 1809 and 1810 respectively. The nickname of the former piece stems from the fact that the first movement contains passages for pizzicato strings playing arpeggios that suggest the sound of the harp. In the third movement, Beethoven replaced the typical minuet/scherzo and trio with a double scherzo and trio; however, its form differs from the Scherzo of Op. 59, No. 2 insofar as the repetitions of Op. 74 are notated in full. Beethoven extended the final statement of the C-minor scherzo section with a forty-five-measure codetta that comes to rest the dominant of E-flat major, the key to which we return in the final Allegretto con Variazioni movement. Beethoven indicates an *attacca* in moving from the Scherzo to the closing movement.

The *Quartetto serioso* takes its nickname from the tempo indication of the scherzo movement, *Allegro assai vivace ma serioso.* The most striking features of this quartet are the connection of movements without pause and the use of introductions to obscure the customary four-movement plan. Departures from pattern forms within movements are also interesting.

In the first movement of Op. 95, measures 3 through 17 contain gestures suggesting that the key of C major will emerge as the secondary tonal area. The gestures of a movement to C are always thwarted, though, by the addition of the tone B-flat, which forms the dominant-seventh chord of F and returns us to that key. The true secondary key turns out to be the submediant (meas. 43ff.), an indicator of Beethoven's growing predilection for third-related keys. This tendency to replace the tonic-dominant axis with two or more keys related by thirds became characteristic of the nineteenth-century style in general. As in the case of the first *Razumovsky Quartet,* the sonata form in the first movement of the *Quartetto serioso* dispenses with the clear division into binary halves with a double-bar line. The recapitulation is also irregular insofar as measures 3 through 17—the flirtation with the key of C—are dropped. This structural alteration to the recapitulation, coupled with the choice of minor mode, affects the balance of the movement as a whole. Whereas sonata recapitulations traditionally affirm balance, this truncated reprise creates a nervousness that stands in contrast to the tranquil contrapuntal lines of the second movement.

The double scherzo and trio also appears as the third movement in the *Quartetto serioso.* The F-minor scherzo section follows the preceding Allegretto ma non troppo without break. The trio is in D major, a third-related key. The reprise of the trio is substantially rewritten and leads to a condensed version of the opening scherzo material.

In both the *Harp Quartet* and the *Quartetto serioso,* the double scherzo and trio is significantly more complex than that in Op. 59, No. 2. Whereas that *Razumovsky Quartet* simply incorporated literal repetitions of harmonically closed material, both of these latter quartets employ true, five-section designs.

A similar modification of the traditional balance of components can be seen in the sonata-form finale of Op. 95. There is no central development section in this sonata; however, harmonic, thematic, and rhythmic development is not abandoned, but merely transferred to the coda.

> The phenomenon that has occurred here is an actual fusion of the recapitulation and development sections, for part two contains both, as in the normal sonata form, but delays the development, inserting it in the middle of the recapitulation. Looked at another way, the form is a mixture of the sonatina and the sonata forms. Like the sonatina, part two begins with the restatement of part one. Yet it does not give up the sonata form's development section. For this reason the scheme is sometimes referred to as the "enlarged sonatina."[5]

Other remarkable features of the finale include the transformation of motifs drawn from the scherzo movement in the introductory Larghetto espressivo as well as the whimsical coda (Allegro–molto leggieramente) in which the seriousness of all the preceding movement is forgotten in a vigorous flurry of activity in the tonic major. This final change of mode from minor to major is suggested in the opening two measures of the first movement, where the strings arrive at the tone F as the goal of the ascending melodic-minor scale.[6]

The formal flexibility of the *Quartetto serioso* must be viewed within the context of the standards that had been established for the string quartet as a genre during the course of the Classical era. The quartet contains sonata-form movements, scherzos and trios, and, indeed, the typical four-movement plan. At the same time, the work is representative of Beethoven's middle period masterpieces in that constructive means are applied to new ends—ends that are decidedly *un*-Classical in character.

THE LATE QUARTETS

In 1822, Beethoven began testing the commercial market for string quartets by an offer to the Leipzig publisher C. F. Peters for a new quartet, after almost a dozen years of silence in that genre.[7] By chance, Beethoven received a commission shortly afterward for "one, two, or three new quartets" from Prince Nicholay Borisovich Galitzin, an amateur cellist who played in a string quartet in St. Petersburg. Beethoven did not get to work on the commission until two years later.

The period between 1822 and 1824 was one of great productivity: Beethoven completed both the *Missa solemnis* and the Ninth Symphony. Then, in 1824 and 1825, he composed three monumental quartets in rapid succession. The three quartets that Beethoven wrote for and dedicated to Galitzin were Opp. 127, 132, and 130. The Quartet in E-flat, Op. 127, was composed between May 1824 and February 1825; the completion of the Quartet in A minor, Op. 132, followed in July; the third, the Quartet in B-flat, Op. 130, occupied the composer from August to November.[8] Op. 127 was published by B. Schott's Söhne (Mainz) in 1826; it was the last of Beethoven's compositions to be published during his lifetime. In 1827, Schlesinger (Berlin and Paris) issued Op. 132, and Artaria printed Op. 130.[9] The original finale of Op. 130 was not to Artaria's liking; thus, they asked Beethoven for a new one. Artaria issued the original finale as the *Grosse Fuge*, Op. 133. Beethoven supplied a new finale for Op. 130; this movement was his last completed composition.

The remaining quartets, Opp. 131 and 135, were issued by Schott and Schlesinger respectively. We should point out that in 1825 Schlesinger had hoped to print both Op. 132 and Op. 130. Beethoven's decision to give the Op. 130 quartet to Artaria apparently caused Schlesinger some consternation. In the hopes of setting this situation right, Beethoven wrote the F-major Quartet, Op. 135, which Schlesinger published in 1827.

The preceding information should clarify the chronology of Beethoven's late quartets, but more significantly, the fact that the composer was writing these pieces with practical considerations in mind. His letter of inquiry of 1822 to Peters, the subsequent commission from Prince Galitzin, his willingness to remove entire movements and replace them with new music, and his dealings with various publishing houses all confirm that he intended these pieces to appeal to a broad audience. Beethoven took equal pains with the final step in presenting these quartets to the world: their premieres.

Beethoven was concerned about the public's reception of his new quartets. In an appeal to the members of the ensemble entrusted with the premiere of the Quartet in E-flat, Op. 127, Beethoven wrote:

> Best Ones!
>
> Each one is herewith given his part and is bound by oath and indeed pledged on his honor to do his best, to distinguish himself and to vie each with the other in excellence.
>
> Each one who takes part in the affair in question is to sign this sheet.
>
> Beethoven
>
> Schuppanzigh
> Weiß
> Linke
> The grand master's accursed violoncello.
> Holz
> The last, but only in signing. Schindler secretarius[10]

The premiere by Schuppanzigh went poorly; accordingly, Beethoven asked Joseph Böhm, who led another professional quartet in Vienna, to give the "official" premiere of the piece. Böhm wrote the following account of the incident:

> The affair did not come off well. Schuppanzigh, who played first violin, was weary from much rehearsing, there was no finish in the performance, the quartet did not appeal to him, he was not well disposed towards the performance and the quartet did not please. Few were moved; it was a weak *succes d'estime*.
>
> When Beethoven learned of this—for he was not present at the performance—he became furious and let both performers and the public in for some harsh words. Beethoven could have no peace until the disgrace was wiped off. He sent for me first thing in the morning—In his usual curt way, he said to me. "You must play my quartet"—and the thing was settled.—Neither objections nor doubts could prevail; what Beethoven wanted had to take place, so I undertook the difficult task.—It was studied industriously and rehearsed frequently under Beethoven's own eyes: I said Beethoven's *eyes* intentionally, for the unhappy man was so deaf that he could no longer hear the heavenly sound of his compositions. And yet rehearsing in his presence was not easy. With close attention his eyes followed the bows and therefore he was able to judge the smallest fluctuations in tempo or rhythm and correct them immediately. At the close of the last movement of this quartet there occurred a *meno vi-*

vace, which seemed to me to weaken the general effect. At the rehearsal, therefore, I advised that the original tempo be maintained, which was done, to the betterment of the effect.

Beethoven, crouched in a corner, heard nothing, but watched with strained attention. After the last stroke of the bows he said, laconically, "Let it remain so," went to the desks and crossed out the *meno vivace* in the four parts.[11]

FORMAL ASPECTS OF THE LATE QUARTETS

The figure of Beethoven looms great in the history of music. In particular, the aura that musicologists have painted around these late chamber works may lead some to believe that this music is incomprehensible, save to an elite few; but the several documents cited here indicate that this is not the general impression that the composer intended; nevertheless, they do make unprecedented challenges to the listeners and performers alike. Difficulties arise in conjunction with formal orientation because the four-movement plan is either drastically modified or abandoned altogether. Similarly, the formal construction within individual movements is linked only in the most tenuous way with the pattern forms of earlier literature. Tonal relationships among movements exhibit greater variety, and frequent tempo changes within the various movements obscure formal boundaries of movements. In Op. 131, the composer indicates seven consecutive "numbers" into which he casts his highly dramatic music. The design of this quartet, coupled with its highly charged emotion, suggests an affiliation with the operatic stage.

Though it would be tempting to devote the remainder of this chapter to an examination of each of the five late Beethoven quartets, the ensuing discussion will be confined to the Quartet in A minor, Op. 132, one of Beethoven's most deeply felt compositions. Its sincerity and profundity have touched the creative spirits of numerous artists since its composition. In his novel *Point Counter Point*, Aldous Huxley (1894–1963) uses this movement as an image to represent all that is good. Huxley wrote this novel in 1928 during the heyday of Benito Mussolini's dictatorship. In chapter 37 of the novel, the central movement of the quartet (a hymn of acceptance and praise in the Lydian mode) becomes the focal point of a lengthy and detailed discussion between two important characters.[12]

In similar fashion to Huxley's novel, the central movement of Béla Bartók's Third Piano Concerto takes this same movement, the *Heiliger Dankgesang eines Genesenen an die Gottheit*, as its model.[13] Not only the spiritual character and tone of Beethoven's movement, but also its formal and structural features are taken over in Bartók's concerto.

The serenely intense beauty of Beethoven's *Dankgesang* is undeniable; however, the impression created by the movement depends upon its placement within the five-movement quartet as a whole. The time span of this quartet is similar to that of the three *Razumovsky Quartets*—about double the length of one of the Op. 18 quartets.

A slow passage (Assai sostenuto) introduces the first movement (Allegro); an expanded scherzo-trio (Allegro ma non tanto) follows here as the second movement; the *Dankgesang* acts as the slow movement; and a march (Alla Marcia, assai vivace), in fourth place, gives way to dramatic transitional passages that introduce the intense finale (Allegro appassionato). The added movement in this case accounts for rather little of the piece as a whole. Really, the expansion takes place within the context of the four conventional movements.

In the first movement, Beethoven's introduction is derived from a germinal motif consisting of four tones: G-sharp, A, F, E. The intervals that these tones form in their first statement in the cello are an ascending half-step, the upward leap of a minor sixth, and a descending half-step, but subsequent intervallic configurations change constantly in compositional permutations like transposition, inversion, fragmentation, and so on. This same motif appears in two other quartets, Opp. 130 and 131. Joseph Kerman makes the following remarks about the significance of the pervasiveness of this motif.

> There is a persistent conception or misconception about the late quartets which derives some small support from the chronology of composition, and which turns up in one form or another in almost all the literature. This is the view of the three middle quartets (in A minor, Bb and C# minor) as a specially unified group. For the fact is that one thematic configuration, stated most simply at the beginning of the A-minor Quartet as G#-A-F-E, occurs prominently in all three. The configuration dominates the Great Fugue; and it follows that critics who make the most of this view of the late quartets tend also to be partisans of the Great Fugue, which they prefer as the finale of the Quartet in Bb over the piece later substituted for it.
>
> The thematic parallels among the quartets are quite unmistakable. The question is what to make of them (the familiar crux of analysis and criticism—what æsthetic sense to make out of observed or "analyzed" fact). Is there an interrelationship among the three works on an actual

> level of æsthetic response? This seems to me the very heart of the matter, but it is not something that most writers on the late quartets treat at all squarely.

In the closing paragraph of his discussion, Kerman concludes:

> As for the "threads" crossing lines of demarcation, their meaning seems to me no greater than that of parallels that can be drawn among Beethoven's compositions at any period. Such parallels have been drawn very many times in the course of this study; as didactic aids they help focus on the individual qualities of the works under consideration. But in themselves the "threads" contribute nothing to the æsthetic weave. Granted also that the "style of the late quartets" has a certain synoptic beauty of its own, and that an appreciation of this is even necessary as a context for response to the individual members. So it is with the "Razumovsky" Quartets and the neighboring compositions of 1803–6. But once again, this is a different and (crucially) a more abstract matter than the direct æsthetic experience of particular works of art. It is not enough to allow the late quartets "a certain 'wholeness' "; each of them provides us with a separate paradigm for wholeness. What truer criterion could be found for individuality in works of art is hard to know.[14]

The thematic links among these quartets do not compel us to understand them as a "trilogy." We have seen the care that Beethoven devoted to the publication and first performances of his final works. If, indeed, these quartets were planned as a cycle, then Beethoven would have stated that specifically.

The four-note constellation of pitches that Beethoven works over in these late compositions is admittedly fascinating. The tones of the germinal motif in Op. 132 form the second four-note segment of the harmonic minor scale. In stepwise order, E, F, G-sharp, A, they produce pairs of ascending half-steps separated by an augmented step (enharmonically, a minor third). The pairs of half steps play an important role in the themes of the first key area of the sonata. Taken in a different sequence, the four tones produce a pair of major thirds (E, G-sharp, and F, A). One of the unusual features of this sonata is the fact that its secondary key area (meas. 48ff.) is F major, related, of course, by a major third to the central tonality of A. Whereas the first theme was rich in half-step motion and minor thirds, the secondary theme is concerned with major thirds and diatonic whole-steps; however, Beethoven maintains a close relationship with the germinal motif in spite of the bold contrasts of mood, key, and musical character. The concern with the four pitches E, F, G (natural in this case), and A continues. The cello part in measure 57 and later the first violin part in measure 58 contain a new permutation of the original idea.

Though the source of Beethoven's pitch content in this movement is, as we have shown, the second four-note segment of the harmonic-minor scale, the intervals that Beethoven uses in stating these four tones in the opening cello line are an ascending half-step, an upward leap of a minor sixth, and a descending half-step (G-sharp, A, F, E). This ordering of tones is a permutation of the harmonic-minor segment. As we study this segment, we begin to discover, as Beethoven did, hundreds of motivic variants. The germinal cell multiplies geometrically, it seems, and we find a sort of thematic transformation that anticipates the compositional style of César Franck.

Closely aligned with the intervallic features of this eight-measure opening is the dynamic design. The only specified dynamic—and that twelve times—is *pianissimo. Crescendo* instructions appear in the closing two measures of the Assai sostenuto in the transition to the Allegro tempo and *forte* dynamic. The reappearance of the *pianissimo* dynamic in the course of the movement establishes a link with the introduction. In some cases, references to the introduction are more easily recognized by the return of the dynamic level than by motivic content.

The scherzo appears in Op. 132 as the second movement. Its thematic connection with the first movement is made clear within the first two measures, where we find the pair of half steps again, but separated in this case by a major third (i.e., A to C-sharp), the inversion of the minor sixth that had split the pair of half steps in the first movement. The trio section of this movement is one of the most charming that Beethoven ever wrote in any medium. The main theme is put forth by the first violin doubled at the tenth in the second violin against a drone on the tone A. The drone later migrates to the viola and cello parts. The sounds suggest the pastoral bagpipe music that became so popular during the reigns of Louis XIV and XV, and in the pastorale idioms of the *style galant*.

The third movement (Molto adagio) of this quartet is one of the best-known movements in all of the chamber music literature. It was this movement, the *Heiliger Dankgesang*, that sparked Huxley's imagination and Bartók's too. In part, the fascination with the movement results from familiarity with biographical details of Beethoven's life. At the time of composition, the composer was in a state of turmoil owing to the suicide attempt of his nephew, Karl, of whom Beethoven had custody at the time. Beethoven was also terminally ill with liver and stomach ailments.

In no other music do we so clearly see Beethoven in the tradition of Viennese Roman Catholicism. The movement is identified as a song of thanksgiving "to the Godhead." The use of the Lydian mode as the basis of the opening contrapuntal melodies is a deliberate abstraction; it is consciously archaic.

In striking contrast to the Lydian polyphony of the first thirty measures is the diatonic D-major scale that dominates the section with the designation *Neue Kraft fühlend* (feeling new strength). The movement contains five sections in all, each, in alternation, is a variant of the Lydian and D-major materials respectively.

In the case of Op. 132, the march is the added movement. By the time Beethoven composed the Op. 132 quartet, the Viennese march was essentially an easygoing affair for regimental bandmasters. Even during the height of the Classical era, the march was a standard element in the cassation and the divertimento. In his chamber music, Beethoven's marches tend to be of this genial, Viennese type. The march in Op. 132 is in a straightforward binary form. With each half repeated, the movement remains a modest affair of only forty-eight measures. The second half proceeds without break into the Più allegro and Presto sections that are actually introductory to the fifth and final movement. In the penultimate measure of the march (meas. 23), the germinal motif reappears; in this case, the pitches are E, F-sharp, G-sharp, A. The four-note segment of the harmonic minor scale (E, F, G-sharp, A) plays an important role as a cyclic theme in the finale. The motif first appears in the last movement in the first violin part in measures 20 and 21 of the introduction.[15] Less obvious than this unaccompanied statement of the motif is the absolute barrage of permutations that appears in measures 105 to 111; the first violin part in measures 105 and 106 even contains the motif in its original form (i.e., G-sharp, A, F, E). Not only does Beethoven reproduce the exact pitch pattern of the motif that we heard in the first movement, but he reproduces the *pianissimo* dynamic as well.

A striking moment in the finale is the reference to the *Heiliger Dankgesang* in measure 265 and following. The *pianissimo* dynamic, the quarter-note motion, the strict, contrapuntal style, and the motivic structure of the *Dankgesang* are recalled in a most astounding manner. The subject of the finale is an inverted form of that appearing at the opening of the *Dankgesang*, but this is not the only "inversion" that takes place; comparison of the parallel passages in each movement shows that the order of entries is also inverted. (First violin descending through the successive instruments to the cello in the *Dankgesang* becomes cello ascending through first violin in the finale.)

The relationship between the third and fifth movements is unmistakable. Equally clear is the fact that Beethoven had intended a symmetrical design for the entire quartet. In comparing the first and fifth movements, we find concordances of thematic material, dynamic structure, contrapuntal textures, and so forth. At the same time, the third movement presents an extended contrast to the outer movements.

The innovative aspects of the finale are balanced by Beethoven's use of traditional rondo form for that movement. The rondo refrain returns in measures 112, 186, and 302. The first episode (meas. 73–111) returns in modified form (meas. 230–65). The central section (meas. 145–85) is the axis of the rondo. The refrain always returns to the tonic, but it is never exactly the same as in its first appearance; thus, the varied reprises produce a rondo-variation form.

BEETHOVEN AND THE EVOLUTION OF THE PIANO TRIO AS A GENRE

Though the string quartets form the most formidable and voluminous portion of Beethoven's chamber music (approximately seventy published movements), he chose to make his formal debut as a composer with the three Piano Trios, Op. 1, published in 1795. In them, Beethoven uses the standard scoring of violin, piano, and cello; however, other works from roughly the same time often contain alternate instruments.[16] Among the more important alternative scorings, we should note Mozart's *Kegelstatt Trio* in E-flat, K. 498, for clarinet, viola, and piano, and Beethoven's Trio, Op. 11, for clarinet, cello, and piano.

In early piano trios, the keyboard was featured; the violin part—often devised by the performer *ad libitum*—was generated by the right-hand keyboard part; and the cello doubled the bass line of the keyboard in the old-fashioned, basso continuo style. Attempts at a more substantial collaboration among the three players were particularly difficult in this genre, however, owing to the widely differing timbres of the individual instruments.

The secondary role of the strings is apparent in Mozart's first chamber work for piano trio, K. 254, which was composed in Salzburg in 1776. He designated this three-movement piece as a "divertimento." Mozart did not use this instrumental combination again until ten years later, when he composed the Piano Trio in G major, K. 496, and another in B-flat-major, K. 502. His remaining trios, K. 542 in E-flat major, K. 548 in C major, and K. 564 in G major, date from 1788. These later works were given the designation "terzett" rather than divertimento.

Most of Haydn's piano trios—approximately forty-five in number—also date from the 1780s and 1790s. The increased importance of the genre late in the careers of Haydn and Mozart, and Beethoven's treatment of it in Op. 1, suggest that this medium was essentially a product of the late Classical period. Indeed, the most important chamber music for piano trio—such as Beethoven's *Archduke Trio* and the trios of Schubert and Mendelssohn—are early examples of romanticism.

The number and sequence of movements in the piano trio of the late eighteenth century were variable. Two- and three-movement trios appear regularly in the works of Haydn and Mozart. The four-movement plan does not appear in Mozart's trios; it is rare in Haydn's (Hob. XV/41, for example).

The formal designs of movements in piano trios of the late Classical era were largely those same pattern forms encountered in compositions for solo keyboard or string quartet, specifically, sonatas, minuets and trios, themes with variations, and rondos. In general, the treatment of these forms in trios written before approximately 1780 tended to be less complex than the same patterns in the contemporaneous string quartets. Whereas variations and minuets were generally restricted to inner-movement status in the string quartet, piano trios admitted opening movements in variation form—such as Haydn's D-major Trio, Hob. XV/7, and concluding minuets—for example, Hob. XV/6 (1784) and Hob. XV/8 (1785). Furthermore, the technical demands upon the performers were held in check.

K. 502 is Mozart's first composition for this medium that begins to take in hand the distinctive characteristics of each instrument. *Concertato* writing is prominent throughout the piece, and the last of its three movements employs counterpoint to a considerable extent.

Just as the style of Mozart's ensemble sonatas did not reveal a continuous, chronological evolution, his piano trios likewise show returns to the older, more simple textures in which violin and cello play secondary roles. In fact, A. Hyatt King concluded that the last two trios show a disappointing decline of the standard of their predecessors.[17] Another scholar, at pains to explain this evolutionary embarrassment in the case of K. 548, suggests that in the piece, "Mozart denies himself any personal expression. . . . It clearly identifies itself as chamber music for the amateur."[18] Regarding the Trio, K. 564, Einstein states unequivocally that it "was conceived purely as a piano sonata," which, he says, was "obviously intended for beginners."[19] An analogous case of movements from solo keyboard sonatas being revised as a trio can be found in Haydn's F-major Trio, Hob. XV/39.

The straightforward style of the string parts in piano trios of the late eighteenth century accounts to a great extent for their neglect in contemporary concert life. "Professional cellists and violinists tend to regard the performance of a Haydn trio as an insult to their talents, while amateurs often consider it (mistakenly) as not ambitious enough."[20]

The composer primarily responsible for transforming the ensemble sonata into a distinguished medium was Beethoven, who published eight compositions for piano trio ensemble during his career. These works were the three Trios, Op. 1, issued by the firm of Artaria in 1795; the set of fourteen Variations on an Original Theme, Op. 44, which were sketched in the years 1791–92, completed by 1800, and published by Hoffmeister and Kühnel (later C. F. Peters) in 1804; the two Trios of Op. 70, which were composed in 1808 and published by Breitkopf und Härtel in 1809; the single Trio, Op. 97, known as the *Archduke Trio*, which was sketched during 1810–11 and published by Steiner in 1816; and the Variations on "Ich bin der Schneider Kakadu," a song from Wenzel Müller's comic opera *Die Schwestern von Prag* (1794). In 1824, Steiner published the Variations as Op. 121a.

Though published last, the Variations, Op. 121a, were probably Beethoven's earliest work for piano trio, perhaps dating from 1794, when Müller's opera first appeared on the stage. The eleven variations in the piece present a mixed collection of serious and light, accessible and complex music. Beethoven begins with a variation of the theme—an ominous bit of work in the minor mode. After several more minor-mode variations, the familiar tune finally emerges in the major mode, cheerful and in keeping with the general tone of accompanied sonata literature. The major mode statement of the theme is followed by a variation for violin solo with piano, and that by one for cello and piano. The remaining variations are remarkable for their use of imitative counterpoint and frequent fluctuations from major to minor mode. The ninth variation (adagio) already suggests some of the more intense writing that appears in the Op. 1 Trios. The finale, a galloping, hunting-style variation, brings the set to an ebullient conclusion.

Beethoven's conception of the piano trio was essentially different from either Haydn's or Mozart's. This is apparent in several of the variations on "Ich bin der Schneider Kakadu," but it is clear throughout the Trios of Op. 1. Beethoven viewed the piano trio "as a substantial piece of music requiring the balance of four movements, like a string quartet or a symphony."[21] At the premiere of these trios, Haydn was puzzled by Beethoven's treatment of the genre. The following account by Ferdinand Ries, a pupil of Beethoven's between 1801 and 1805, explains.

> Beethoven's three Trios, Op. 1, were to be introduced to the musical world at a soirée at Prince Lichnowsky's. Most of Vienna's artists and music lovers had been invited, in particular Haydn, whose verdict all were eager to hear. The trios were played and at once made an extraordinary impression. Haydn, too, said many fine things about them, but advised Beethoven not to publish the third one, in C minor. This surprised Beethoven greatly, for he thought it the best, and, in fact, to this day it is the one which always makes the greatest impression. Haydn's remark, therefore, made a bad impression on Beethoven, and left implanted in his mind the idea that Haydn was envious and jealous and wished him ill. I must admit that when Beethoven told me the story I did not put much faith in it. So I took occasion to ask Haydn himself about it. His answer, however, confirmed what Beethoven had said, for he told me he had not imagined that the trio would be so rapidly and easily grasped, and so favorably taken up by the public.[22]

In spite of Haydn's advice, Beethoven included the controversial Trio in C minor in the publication of Op. 1.

The scherzo is used in the first two trios in the set, and the minuet only in the last of the three. The tonal arrangement of movements within each trio is generally conservative; however, the second movement of the G-major Trio (Largo con espressione) is in the key of E major. Though Beethoven used third-related keys regularly, they were decidedly uncommon in the scores of the 1790s save in the case of shifts in tonal focus from major to relative minor or the reverse. Just such a shift can be seen in the C-minor Trio in which the slow set of five variations (Andante cantabile con variazioni) is in the key of E-flat. Variations of the Classical era were typically unified by a consistent tonality but included an excursion into the parallel mode. In this case, the fourth variation ventures into E-flat minor—at the time, an exotic key to be sure. The second Trio is the single one in this set to include a slow introduction (Adagio).

The relationship of instruments in Beethoven's trios is novel. Violin and cello generally do not double keyboard voices. Instead, a concerto-like contrast dominates the writing. The strings very often function as a unit, and are set against the piano in call-and-response gestures. At other times, they provide the main motivic ideas while the piano functions as accompaniment or vice versa. Occasionally, the whole ensemble joins in unison statements in order to achieve a bold, orchestral effect. Such unison passages abound in the finale (Prestissimo) of the C-minor Trio, Op. 1, No. 3, as well as in the opening movement (Allegro vivace e con brio) of the D-major Trio, Op. 70, No. 1. This latter is generally known by its nickname, the *Ghost,* because its second movement (Largo assai e espressivo) makes extensive use of murky bass figuration and fully diminished sonorities. Indeed, one would be hard pressed to find a piece before Weber's overture to *Der Freischütz* that utilizes the diminished sonority so extensively and expressively as Beethoven does in this movement. The *Ghost Trio* is Beethoven's only piano trio in three movements. The Trio in E-flat major returns to Beethoven's conventional four-movement scheme, but its second movement (Allegretto) constantly fluctuates between C major and C minor, and moves among third-related keys. The chain of third-related tonalities continues in the third movement (Allegretto ma non troppo), which is in A-flat major. Though Haydn and Mozart typically had only a single movement in a secondary key area, Beethoven here has two.

The Trio in E-flat contains striking features of its own. The first movement begins with a slow passage (Poco sostenuto) based on a subject treated in imitation. The cello leads, is imitated by the violin, and then the subject appears in the piano. The subject actually falls into two brief segments. The first segment consists of a falling third beginning on the tonic. The second segment begins on the supertonic, falls through a fifth to the dominant, and then ascends by step to return to the tonic. When the two segments appear in the piano part, however, they are not heard in succession, but simultaneously with the falling-third motif forming the right-hand part and the falling fifth constituting the left-hand part. The sonata form that follows the introduction includes a reprise of the introductory material as the coda, but the repetition is not literal. The order of entries has been reversed so that the piano leads; furthermore, the two segments of the motif are now successive rather than simultaneous.

Similar intricacies permeate the piece, but the finale is one of Beethoven's most complex movements. Formally, it suggests a synthesis of sonata and rondo procedures. Stylistically, the rapid changeover of themes, harmonies, textures, dynamics, and phrase lengths all recall the *Empfindsamer* compositions of Carl Phillip Emmanuel Bach (1714–1788), whose music Beethoven is known to have admired. The likelihood of Bach's influence is confirmed by the fact that when Beethoven was assembling instructional materials for Archduke Rudolph, he included selections from C. P. E. Bach's *Essay on the True Art of Playing Keyboard Instruments.*[23] Beethoven was compiling these theoretical items at precisely the same time that he was composing the Op. 70 Trios.[24]

The archduke became a pupil of Beethoven's sometime late in 1803 or early in 1804. In 1809, Rudolph joined with Prince Lobkowitz and Prince Kinsky in granting to Beethoven a fixed stipend of 4,000 florins per year so that "the necessaries of life shall not cause him embarrassment or clog his powerful genius."[25] The list of Beethoven's works written for Rudolph includes the Triple Concerto, Op. 56 (which uses a piano trio for its solo ensemble), the *Les adieux Sonata,* Op. 81a, the Sonata for Violin and Piano, Op. 96, the *Missa solemnis,* Op. 122, the *Archduke Trio,* Op. 97, and the Piano Sonata, Op. 111.

The *Archduke Trio* is one of Beethoven's more formal works. It consists of the customary four movements. The first, in sonata form, opens with a bold, almost orchestral theme in B-flat major and proceeds with a third-related secondary theme in the key of G major. The recapitulation is substantially rewritten, but the most curious feature about it is the transformation of the broad opening theme into a glittering, delicate affair marked *dolce.* The second movement is a lively scherzo, but the movement has many unexpected harmonic twists, and the customary *da capo* is abandoned in favor of fully-notated and varied restatement. The third movement (Andante cantabile ma però con moto) moves to another third-related key, D major. The movement consists of a theme and five variations, each in a more complex rhythmic setting. The first variation introduces triplet subdivision of the quarter-note theme; the second variation moves in sixteenth notes; the third in alternating duplets and triplets with frequent ties to confuse the issue; the fourth (Poco più adagio) in thirty-second notes; and the final variation back in the original tempo and quarter-note motion of the theme. The movement leads without break into the finale (Allegro moderato).

BEETHOVEN AT THE END OF AN ERA

Beethoven was, at once, the last great composer of the Classical era and the first great composer of the Romantic era. His debt to the Classical style is most clearly seen in his use of pattern forms and traditional genres. What made Beethoven's music unique was the idiosyncratic manner in which he used ordinary formal designs and the intensity of the message that he uttered through these conventional vehicles. The genres in which Beethoven expressed his musical genius were also conventional: symphonies, concertos, solo and ensemble sonatas, piano trios, and string quartets were clearly prevalent; but the application of the genres by Beethoven was distinctive. Though vestiges of Classicism remain, the number and sequence of movements are often unorthodox. Quartets of the late period exceed the four-movement norm; piano trios are elevated on a par with four-movement string quartets; and demands upon the performer—both technical and musical—are far beyond those encountered in music for the bourgeoisie.

As an individual, too, Beethoven left the restraint of Classicism behind. His acquaintances were noble gentlemen and ladies. If he deemed them worthy, some—like Lichnowsky, Kinsky, and Rudolf—were admitted to Beethoven's circle of friends. Finally, the ongoing, personal tragedy of his life made it inevitable that his music should reflect his anger, frustration, resolve, resignation, and serenity. Beethoven's musical genius necessarily ruptured the boundaries of polite, late eighteenth-century society.

FIVE

The Emergence of the Wind Quintet

The combination of pairs of oboes, horns, and bassoons to form a wind sextet was common enough during the Classical era. When the clarinet arrived upon the scene, the sextet was expanded to the traditional eight-instrument assembly associated with *Harmoniemusik.* Pairs of flutes, basset horns, and other wind instruments were often added to the ensemble, particularly in later repertoire. These wind bands were maintained by wealthy courts "for performing serenades and divertimenti during dinner or as a background to conversation." In general, the music for these ensembles went under the designation *partita.* Furthermore, the repertoire often "included transcriptions of operas."[1] This music was casual stuff intended for ease of execution and comprehension. Neither Mozart nor Beethoven escaped such corruption of their works; excerpts from Mozart's Singspiel *Die Entführung aus dem Serail,* and Beethoven's well-known rescue opera, *Fidelio,* were widely circulated even during the composers' lifetimes.

The instrumentation of *Harmoniemusik* betrayed its origins: It was simply the wind section of an orchestral ensemble. Both the character of the repertoire and the constitution of the wind ensemble belied the simple fact that *Harmoniemusik* really stood apart from the mainstream of chamber music literature.

The first composer who sought to elevate wind-ensemble music to the level that had been achieved in the string quartet literature of the eighteenth century was Giuseppe Maria Gioacchino Cambini (1746–1825), whose set of *Trois quintetti, Livre 1,* was published by Sieber in Paris in the year 1802. Cambini was a violinist, and he was well acquainted with serious chamber music for strings. After relocating in Paris in the 1770s, he wrote hundreds of string quartets, quintets, and chamber works for other combinations of instruments. His wind quintets show him as a virtuosic composer capable not only of interesting ideas, but of highly idiomatic ones as well.

Cambini's first step in the transformation of music for winds—and perhaps the most important one—was to eliminate the pairings of identical instruments that had been and remains customary in orchestral writing. The wind ensemble that resulted consisted of solo flute, oboe, clarinet, horn, and bassoon. None of these instruments was new; nevertheless, their construction changed significantly during the late eighteenth and early nineteenth centuries.

CONSTRUCTION OF WIND INSTRUMENTS IN EARLY NINETEENTH-CENTURY FRANCE

To an extent, Cambini's achievements in wind quintet writing were the result of a united effort by many people. Solo winds had generally not been practical before Cambini's time. Problems in construction resulted in difficulties with intonation, dynamic control, and nuance. These deficiencies became the focus of instrument builders' attention in the early stages of the Romantic era, largely because of the more complex harmonic idiom that contemporaneous scores required. As Anthony Baines informs us,

> Nineteenth-century woodwind history is an action story of brilliant, dominating individuals—performers or craftsmen, sometimes both—and of their patented inventions through which the elegantly simple instruments of the past were transformed into the complicated tools of the woodwind section today.
>
> First there came a period of some twenty-five years which saw the development of the basic "simple systems." With these, each instrument came to be provided with a set of simple closed keys following the example already set by the later eighteenth-century flute-makers. These gave an accurately-tuned keyed note for every semitone that had previously been unsatisfactory as a cross-fingering. Ten years after the *Eroica*, Beethoven's Seventh and Eighth Symphonies would have been introduced with eight-keyed flutes and eight- to twelve-keyed clarinets. Oboes and bassoons, on which chromatic cross-fingerings on the whole worked the best, were still mainly classical in design, but another ten years later, when the Ninth Symphony was produced [i.e., 1824], these instruments too had become available with extra keys.

Baines cites some of the most important instrument builders active during the early part of the nineteenth century and refers to

> "new inventions" [such as] . . . [Jospeh] Sellner's full simple-system oboe (newly introduced by the maker [Stefan] Koch in Vienna), the [Iwan] Müller clarinet (first devised in about 1810, in Paris), and . . . [Carl] Almenraeder's newly remodelled bassoon.[2]

We know, too, that Anton Joseph Hampel (ca. 1710–1771) had devised a method of hand stopping that enabled the player to produce tones that were not otherwise possible on the natural horn. Equally important was his use of crooks, which were extensions of the horn's tubing inserted into the body of the instrument rather that at the mouthpiece; this was the so-called *Inventionshorn*. By 1815, builders had developed the valved horn, the instrument used for most of the literature discussed in this chapter.

Paris was the center for the cultivation of improved or new wind instruments. One figure in particular, Bernard Sarrette, played a crucial role in this development. As a young officer in the National Guard in post-Revolutionary France, he organized National Guard bands. Sarrette's bands were significantly larger than older French military bands, "sometimes more than forty-five players strong."[3] In 1793, Sarrette founded a training school that two years later became the Conservatoire National Supérieur de Musique.

> The wind and brass [instruments], previously associated with the monarch, were now publicly extolling the government of the people. . . . They were at times . . . reinforced by newly constructed instruments modelled after depictions from Ancient Rome: the *buccin*, a kind of straight trumpet, and the lower-pitched *tuba curva*, said to make the sound of six serpents.[4]

In this atmosphere, Charles-Joseph Sax (1791–1865) and his son Adolphe (1814–1894) made their improved flutes, clarinets, and bassoons. During the 1840s, Adophe developed new instruments like the saxhorns, saxtrombas, and saxophones, and by 1845, he had established a hefty market supplying instruments for the French military bands.

Cambini's quintets were untimely; had they been written several decades later, they would have marked the beginning of a burgeoning literature for the wind quintet. The three pieces, intended as a set with the first in B major, the second in D minor, and the third in F major, contain three movements in the tempo sequence fast-slow-fast. The first and third quintets conclude with rondos. Each one is written with exquisite craftsmanship, and more frequent performances of them would be welcome.[5]

With the reconstituted and improved ensemble of five solo winds, the demands upon the individual players were increased. Though advances in design and construction facilitated, skilled soloists were, nevertheless, required on each of the five parts.

The composers primarily responsible for the establishment of the wind quintet as a standard ensemble in the early nineteenth century were Anton Reicha (1770–1836) and Franz Danzi (1763–1826).[6]

ANTON REICHA

Anton Reicha was the first composer who achieved popular acclaim with his wind quintets. He was born in the same year as Beethoven. Though a Czech, he relocated in Wallersen, in the Swabian region of Germany, so that he could study with his uncle Joseph Reicha. When Joseph was engaged as a cellist in Maximilian's court at Bonn, Anton went along and played second flute in the orchestra. In 1785, Reicha met Beethoven, who played the violin in the same ensemble. The two became fast friends, and Reicha remarked that during the fourteen years they spent together in Bonn, they were "united in a bond like that of Orestes and Pylades, and were continually side by side. . . . After a separation of eight years we saw each other again in Vienna, and exchanged confidences concerning our experiences."[7] Throughout his career, Reicha held Beethoven in high esteem.

Reicha resided in various cities in Germany and Austria, relocating frequently owing to the turmoil caused by the Napoleonic wars. In the course of his travels, Reicha chanced to meet many of Europe's leading musicians, including Johann Georg Albrechtsberger, Antonio Salieri, and Prince Louis Ferdinand of Prussia, who offered him a position as Kapellmeister (which Reicha declined). From 1818 until his death, Reicha was professor of counterpoint at the Paris Conservatory, were his students included George Onslow, Hector Berlioz, Adolphe Adam, Jean-Georges Kastner, Franz Liszt, and César Franck.

Among his acquaintances Reicha counted a wide variety of outstanding performers: the flautist Joseph Guillou, the oboist August-Gustave Vogt, the clarinettist Jacques-Jules Bouffil, the hornist Louis-François Dauprat, and the bassoonist Antoine-Nicola Henry.[8] It was for them that Reicha wrote his first set of wind quintets, and they presented the premiere of them in 1815.[9]

Reicha's wind quintets were issued between the years 1811 and 1820. In all, he published two dozen quintets in four sets of six: these were Op. 88, printed in Paris by [Pierre-Honoré] Janet et [Alexandre] Cotelle, Opp. 91, 99, and 100, which were all issued in Paris by Costallat. Op. 100 was also released in Mainz by Schott.

From a stylistic point of view, Reicha's pieces for wind ensemble stood apart from earlier essays for that ensemble.

> Reicha differed from his predecessors inasmuch as he abandoned the rather loose sequence of serenade-like movements, which he replaced by the stricter four-movement pattern of the sonata form. In other words, he shifted his quintets from the lighter divertimento genre into the more serious one of chamber music. In workmanship and effectiveness, his wind quintets were compared to the string quartets by Haydn.[10]

Reicha's quintets are colorful pieces. As a flute player himself, he was aware of the limitations and potentials of winds. Whereas string ensembles provide a homogeneous sound, the wind quintet is a heterogeneous ensemble of one woodwind, two double-reeds, one single-reed, and one brass instrument. Louis Spohr noted that Reicha's music for winds often exhibits a disconcerting diffusion of materials.

> I found the composition of these two new quintets . . . rich in interesting sequences of harmony, correct throughout in the management of the voices, and full of effect in the use made of the tone and character of the different wind-instruments, but on the other hand, frequently defective in the form. Mr. *Reicha* is not economical enough of his ideas, and at the very commencement of his pieces he frequently gives from four to five themes, each of which concludes in the tonic. Were he less rich, he would be richer. His periods also are frequently badly connected and sound as though he had written one yesterday and the other today. Yet the minuets and scherzi, as short pieces, are less open to this objection, and some of them are real masterpieces in form and contents. A German soundness of science and capacity are the greatest ornaments of this master. The execution in the rapid subjects was again wonderfully correct, but somewhat less so in the slow ones.[11]

This thematic diversity resulted, at least in part, from the nature of the instruments at hand. It is far more difficult to transfer a motivic figure from a flute to a horn, for example, than from a violin to a viola. Reicha's themes for wind instruments had to be tailored for the characteristics and capabilities of each instrument; thus, the medium had a direct impact on the nature of the material that the composer invented.

FRANZ DANZI

Franz Danzi, who followed Reicha as the principal cultivator of music for wind quintet, was more successful in managing formal considerations. Danzi and his forebears were associated with the progressive court of Carl Theodore at Mannheim. A student of Abbé Vogler, Danzi played stringed instruments and keyboard, but he also had a thorough training in voice, and was interested in opera. He composed several works for the lyric theater and was personally acquainted with Carl Maria von Weber.

Danzi composed three sets of wind quintets, Opp. 56, 67, and 68, with three pieces in each. Though Danzi was the older man, he clearly took his lead from Reicha, to whom his first set of three wind quintets is dedicated. Danzi's nine chamber pieces for wind quintet were probably composed between 1820 and 1824.[12] Op. 56 was issued under the title *Trois quintetti pour flute, hautbois (ou clarinette en ut) clarinette, cor et basson.* The edition appeared simultaneously from the presses of Janet et Cotelle, in Paris, and Schlesinger in Berlin. Both Op. 67 and Op. 68 were printed by Jean André with the title *Trois quintetti pour flute, hautbois, clarinette, cor & bassoon.*

In his wind quintets, Danzi reflects Reicha's concern with writing serious chamber music in the Classical tradition. The four-movement plan is utilized consistently. First movements are ordinarily in sonata form; however, details of the structure are sometimes modified. In the first movement of Op. 56, No. 1, the Quintet in B-flat major, for example, the recapitulation dispenses with the opening theme since it had been extensively worked out in the course of the development section. The secondary theme, which begins at measure 37 of the exposition and reappears at measure 115 of the recapitulation, is stated in the exposition by the horn, but is given in the recapitulation to the clarinet. Although the essential gestures and contours are preserved, Danzi's switch from the mellow tone of the horn to the more piercing, single-reed sonority of the clarinet gives the theme an entirely new character. As we survey the scores of Danzi's nine quintets, we find that, almost invariably, parallel passages are subjected to modifications in instrumentation. Although this procedure can also be found in chamber music for strings, varied instrumentation in wind ensembles is much more easily perceived.

Danzi consistently places his slow movements in second place and minuets in third place. Some of the minuets—particularly those that use syncopation or irregular metrical accentuation—have the character of a scherzo; the minuet of the Quintet in G minor, Op. 56, No. 2, is a good example. Final movements are rondos, sonatas, or the synthetic sonata-rondo that had become common by this time. Tonal relationships among movements are precisely those of the string quartet: Outer movements stress the tonic, while second movements are in closely related keys, such as the subdominant or relative key, while third movements return to the principal tonality. For each set, two quintets are in the major mode, one in the minor. Slow introductions appear only before first movements, and they are used only in the final quintet of each set. Danzi's periodic structures are usually regular. Perhaps he, too, found that Reicha's phrase structures distracted from the music's overall impact.

SIX

Schubert and Musical Aesthetics of the Early Romantic Era

Beethoven died in 1827, only a single year before Franz Peter Schubert (1797–1828). Both spent their most productive years in Vienna; however, their respective styles are light years apart.

Schubert's radical departure from the Classical style cannot be attributed to any unfamiliarity with the standard repertoire of the period. We know that he played string quartets with his father and two brothers as a child. We know, too, that, from the time he entered the Stadtkonvikt in 1808, he was immersed in the music of Haydn, Mozart, and lesser masters such as Leopold Kotzeluch and Franz Krommer.[1] Similarly, Schubert received his musical training from Antonio Salieri (1750–1825), who, despite popular notions to the contrary, was a composer of distinction.

Given Schubert's intimacy with the scores of late eighteenth-century masters, it is hard to understand the unorthodox character of many of his works—particularly the early works. Among his twenty string quartets, the First, the String Quartet in B-flat, D. 18 (1812), is one of the most daring. The first movement opens with a plaintive introduction in C minor. The principal tempo arrives in the key of G minor, and a sonata-allegro form unfolds in that key. The last movement, however, is in the relative major, B-flat. The idea of beginning a piece in one key and ending in some other tonality—generally called "directional tonality"—was new.[2] The First Quartet is filled with distinctive melodies, intensity of feeling, textural variety, and genuine musical inspiration. The first movement includes effective sections of contrapuntal imitation placed as contrast to passages in which Schubert's characteristic melodies are featured in a homophonic texture against a backdrop of nervously repeating chords in the lower stings.

A similarly novel approach can also be seen in the well-known Piano Quintet in A major, Op. 114, known as the *Trout Quintet* (1819). The scoring is unusual, since it includes the double bass, an instrument that Schubert later included in his Octet in F major, D. 803 (1824) for clarinet, horn, bassoon, two violins, viola, cello, and bass. The presence of this instrument in the Quintet had important consequences for the piano part, which consists much of the time of a single line played by both hands in octaves. Furthermore, these melodies are generally pitched very high in the compass of the instrument. Schubert probably realized that the bass part was already amply covered by the cello and bass, and that he would be compelled to use the piano in an unorthodox manner in order to make his strange ensemble effective.

The *Trout Quintet* is one of the first, fully revealing examples of Schubert's chamber music. The name of the piece derives from the fact that the fourth movement is a series of variations on Schubert's song of 1817, "Die Forelle" (The trout). Schubert frequently used his own songs within chamber works: "Sei mir gegrüßt" (I greet thee) appears in the Fantasy for Violin and Piano, and the song "Der Tod und das Mädchen" (Death and the maiden) gives its name to the String Quartet in D minor, D 810. Clearly, lyrical melodies occupy a crucial role in all of Schubert's music.

The compositional draft of Schubert's song cycle *Die Winterreise* (1827) reveals his compositional procedure: The two layers of ink (sepia and black) show that Schubert wrote the melodies first and the accompaniment afterward. Though motivic interplay among voices appears, it does so within the context of an essentially melodic conception.

As a consequence Schubert's orientation towards melody, the role of harmony is significantly altered. While melodic content may often be repeated with little or no modification, harmonies supporting the melodies are constantly changing. Two devices were important in enabled Schubert to achieve such great harmonic freedom: the structural interchange of parallel major and minor modes, and the arrangement of tonalities within formal structures in chains of thirds.

The first movement of the *Trout Quintet* contains an example of a typical, Schubertian modification to Classical pattern forms. The structure is a sonata-allegro plan. The exposition contains the standard duality of themes (here accentuated by the fact that the secondary theme is introduced by piano solo—to compensate for the curious keyboard writing earlier mentioned). Tonal relationships are similarly conservative: the first theme, with its lilting, triplet figuration, is in the key of A major; the second theme is in E major. In the recapitulation, however, the first theme returns in the key of D major. A retransition section follows, and it modulates up a fifth to the tonic key of A major. This type of recapitulation is often called a subdominant recapitulation, but since the formal principle may be applied at other tonal levels, the procedure might be more general designated as a nontonic recapitulation.

The questions must invariably arise: is recapitulation a harmonic or a melodic process? Furthermore, what is the purpose of this procedure, if not simply to save the composer time in writing the recapitulation of a sonata? The answer to the first question returns us to our initial comments about Schubert as an innovator of the early Romantic era. Melody assumes an increased importance in his music. It is not surprising that this phenomenon should be apparent in the formal level as well as in the localized context. Another important consideration to bear in mind is the role of the retransition section of Classical sonatas. Since tonic is reached by the time the first theme reappears, the retransition section does not achieve any harmonic motion. Though motivic ideas from the transition section of the expositions are customarily used, they must be rewritten within their new harmonic role. In Schubert's subdominant recapitulations, the role of the retransition section is greatly enhanced: True harmonic motion takes place, and melodies from the exposition can be preserved in transpositions of their original forms. In Schubert's music, melody is elevated to a form-generating role, a role that becomes increasingly important in later nineteenth-century and twentieth-century music.

SCHUBERT'S CHAMBER WORKS WITH PIANO

Though he was himself a pianist, Schubert wrote only a handful of compositions for piano with obbligato instruments. In addition to the *Trout Quintet*, there are the Adagio and Rondo Concertante, D. 487, for piano with strings, and the two late piano trios, Op. 100 in E-flat major, and Op. 99 in B-flat major. More copious are his scores of four-hand piano music.

In assessing the repertoire requiring two pianists, we must distinguish between "duo pianism" and "piano duet." The former term refers to music for two pianists, each at his own instrument.[3] This repertoire is not chamber music. When two pianos are required, the expectation is for performances in public concerts halls. Music for piano duet, on the other hand, is true chamber music.[4]

Many of Schubert's finest piano duets were written during his visits to

Zselis, Hungary, where he acted during the summers of 1818 and 1824 as music tutor for the children of Count Esterházy (the same Esterházy family that had employed Haydn). Other piano duets were composed at various times throughout his career.

Schubert's four-hand piano pieces are quite variable in form and content. Variations were in very great demand among amateur musicians of the period. Schubert wrote several important examples of this genre including his first published work for piano duet, the eight *Variationen über ein Franzosisches Lied*, Op. 10, D. 624 (1818). Lightweight dance music was also much in vogue; accordingly, we have a number of Polonaises, such as the four composed in 1818 and published as Op. 75, D. 599 and the six that, though dating from 1824, were published as Op. 61, D. 824. Among the "dance" music of the period, marches occupied an important place. To this genre, Schubert contributed the three *Marches heroïques*, of Op. 27, D. 602 (1818), the six *Grandes marches*, Op. 40, D. 819 (1825), the three *Marches militaires*, Op. 51, D. 733 (1822), the *Grande marche funebrè*, Op. 55, D. 859 (1826), the *Grande marche heroïque*, Op. 66, D. 885 (1826), and the two *Marches characteristiques*, Op. 121, D. 886.

In addition to these popular works for piano duet, Schubert also wrote serious pieces, such as the Sonata in B-flat major, Op. 30, D. 617 (1818?), another in C major, Op. 140, D. 812 (1824), the Rondo in A major, Op. 107, D 951 (1828), and the magnificent Fantasie in F minor, Op. 103, D. 940 (1828).

Schubert's use of the word *fantasy* to describe the last piece is misleading. Within the context of this single continuous movement, the four-movement plan used by the Viennese Classicists for their more complex scores is still apparent.

The first movement is in sonatina form, and the tonal planes of the exposition are the third-related keys, F minor, D-flat minor, and A minor. Schubert dispenses with the development section typical of the complete sonata form and proceeds directly to a brief recapitulation of the opening melody in the principal key.

The relationship between Schubert's main theme for the first movement and Mozart's opening theme in the Symphony No. 40 in G minor has already been observed in the scholarly literature devoted to Schubert's Fantasie.[5] Striking though the relationship is, Schubert's manner of treating the theme is quite different from Mozart's. Distinctive in Schubert's movement is his extensive use of the parallel major key; the appearance of the main theme in the key of F major is both striking and poignant.

The second movement, in the key of F-sharp, contains dotted rhythms in its more assertive sections as well as in its lyrical interlude in the key of F-sharp major. The scherzo movement commences with the tempo indication Allegro vivace; this movement is a playful delight that should not be missed by any chamber pianists.

Schubert's final movement is one of the most serious and complex of his compositions. Structurally, the finale is an extended fugue in F minor culminating in a powerful coda. We know that during the summer of 1824, Schubert had a copy of Bach's *Well-tempered Clavier* at Zselis. The fugue of the F-minor Fantasy gives us certain evidence that he must have studied Bach's contrapuntal manner in detail.

By his last several years, Schubert had achieved some reputation as a composer. The firm of Artaria established professional relationships with him at precisely this time.[6] They commissioned the Rondo in A major, Op 107, but by the time they published it, Schubert had been dead for a month. It is one of his most convincing scores, but it is also one of his most conventional pieces. The beauty of the thematic material and the fascinating treatment of the melodies are typically Schubertian. The structure of the work conforms precisely to the rondo formula. Tonal relationships are also conventional, but fluctuations between major and parallel minor constantly bring new aspects of the melody to light.

SCHUBERT'S VOCAL CHAMBER MUSIC

Schubert sometimes used solo voices in his chamber music. Two important works of this sort are the songs *Auf dem Strom*, Op. 119, D. 943, for soprano solo, horn, and piano and *Der Hirt auf dem Felsen*, Op. 129, D. 965, for soprano solo, clarinet, and piano (both 1828). The former piece is based on a text by Ludwig Rellstab. The latter, generally known in English as "The Shepherd on the Rock," combines of verses by Wilhelm Mülller and Wilhelmine von Chezy.

Schubert composed *Der Hirt auf dem Felsen* for Pauline Anna Milder-Hauptmann (1785–1835), the soprano he hoped would create the leading role in his opera *Der Graf von Gleichen*.[7] Milder-Hauptmann had a formidable reputation. Her voice came first to the attention of Emmanuel Schikaneder. She subsequently studied with Salieri. She created the parts of Leonore in Beethoven's *Fidelio* and Giunone in Franz Xavier Süßmeyer's *Specchio d'Arcadia*, and was known for her rendition of many roles in the operas of Luigi Cherubini and Christoph Willibald Gluck. Napoleon was among her admirers. Milder-Hauptmann was familiar with

Schubert's music prior to the composition of *Der Hirt auf dem Felsen*. (She was largely responsible for the popularization of *Erlkönig*.)

A versatile and dramatic singer, she nevertheless possessed a flexible voice of which Schubert took full advantage in *Der Hirt auf dem Felsen*. The text, based on one of Müller's *Ländliche Lieder* with alterations by von Chezy, begins with a pastoral atmosphere, progresses to one of sadness, and concludes in a mood of hopeful anticipation of the return of spring—and happiness along with it. The text and translation are given below.

Wenn auf dem höchsten Fels ich steh',
In's tiefe Thal herniederseh',
Und singe, und singe,
Fern aus dem tiefen dunkeln Thal
Schwingt sich empor der Wiederhall,
Der Wiederhall der Klüfte.

Je weiter meine Stimme dringt,
Je heller sie mir wiederklingt
Von unten, von unten.
Mein Liebchen wohnt so weit von mir,
Drum seh'n ich mich so heiss nach ihr
Hinüber, hinüber.

In tiefem Gram verzehr' ich mich,
Mir ist die Freude hin,
Auf Erden mir di Hoffnung wich,
Ich hier so einsam bin.
So sehnend klang im Wald das Lied,
So sehnend klang es durch die Nacht,
Die Herzen es zum Himmel zieht
Mit wunderbarer Macht.

Der Frühling will kommen,
Der Frühling meine Freud',
Nun mach' ich mich fertig,
Zum Wandern berteit.

(When high upon the crag I stand,
And look forth to the vale below,
And sing, and sing,
Far from out the deep, dark vale,
Then echo forth resounding tones,
Resounding tones from chasms.

The longer that my voice resound,
The brighter to me it rebounds
From down below, from down below.
My darling is so far away,
I yearn to go now to her side!
To her side! To her side!

By deepest woe I am o'ercome,
Joy from my path has fled,
On earth for me all hope is lost,
I stand here, desolate.
Thus yearing sounds through woods my song,
Thus yearning sounds it through the night,
It draws two hearts t'ward heaven in rapture.

The springtime will arrive,
The springtime of my joy,
Now be my soul preparèd,
For wand'ring prepar'd.)

Schubert's setting of the poem falls into three large sections that reflect the mood shifts in the poetic text. The piano accompaniment, though interesting harmonically, remains essentially subservient to the duet texture of the soprano and clarinet soloists. The themes of the duet are quite evenly distributed between the clarinet and the vocalist. Again, we must remark that Schubert has reacted to circumstances in a most sensitive and musical way. The poetic images of echoing sounds resulted in clarinet and voice parts designed largely in call-and-response fashion.

Schubert's wish of having Milder-Hauptmann sing this remarkable piece was ultimately realized; however, by the time she gave the premiere performance in 1830, Schubert had already been dead for two years.

SCHUBERT'S PIANO TRIOS

Schubert's final works for piano duet, and the late vocal chamber music repertoire as well, attest to the fact that he had reached the zenith of his creative powers by about the year 1822—the year in which he composed the two movements that we now know as the *Unfinished Symphony.* It was during this period that he also composed his finest string quartets and the two piano trios.

The Trio in E-flat, Op. 100, D. 929, dates from November 1827, as the inscription in the upper right-hand corner of the composer's manuscript shows. Other primary sources document its history: Early in 1828, the publishing house of B. Schott's Söhne, Mainz, wrote to Schubert requesting some pieces. Not long before, the violinist Ignaz Schuppanzigh had joined forces with the cellist Joseph Linke and the youthful pianist Carl Maria von Bocklet in the first performance of the Trio in E-flat. Schauppanzigh played regularly with Linke, and the gifted Bocklet apparently joined in with ease. The premiere on 26 December 1827 was a great success. A second performance followed on 28 January 1828 at the home of Josef von Spaun. Encouraged by the favorable reception of the piece, Schubert offered it to Schott. As it turned out, however, Schott decided that the piece was too long; thus, unsuitable for publication. This view was shared by Schubert's friend, Leopold von Sonnleitner, who insisted that "one cannot deny the fact that the Trio *is too long* and that it has only gained in effect through the cuts which have been tried out in recent times."[8]

The cuts to which Sonnleitner refers are those in the fourth movement of the edition of Heinrich Albert Probst. This Leipzig publisher had approached Schubert at the same time as Schott, and when Schott declined to publish the Trio, Schubert sent the abridged version to Probst. This edition was not available in Vienna until December 1828, almost a month after the composer's death. The original, unabridged version has been preserved, and it is included in the *New Schubert Edition.*[9]

Two curiosities of the E-flat Trio should be mentioned: First, it presents another example of Schubert's using a preexistent tune as the basis of an instrumental chamber piece. Sonnleitner is our source on this point. In his account of Schubert's life, he says, "Here I will provide you with some further information about the origin of the Trio: the well-known singer Josef Siboni, who was director of the Conservatory in Copenhagen at the time, had a pupil, [Isaak Albert] Berg, a young tenor of remarkable talent. . . . He sang Swedish folk songs very well, and Schubert . . . was quite taken up with these Swedish songs. He asked for a copy of them and used the best of them as themes for the E-flat Trio."[10]

The second point is that in the fourth movement, Schubert recalls thematic material from the second movement, and—in the climax of the piece—presents the principal themes of the second and fourth movements simultaneously. This passage, unusual for Schubert since he rarely attempted to integrate movements of a larger work in this fashion, was omitted in the shortened version.

Robert Schumann praised this work highly, and Johannes Brahms owned Schubert's handwritten score of it.

We know little about the B-flat Trio, D. 898, save that Diabelli published it in 1836 as Schubert's Op. 99. It was probably not performed during the composer's lifetime. Because of its opus number, musicologists have assumed that this work predates the E-flat Trio, but this is not necessarily so. The manuscript was not part of Schubert's estate at the time of his death. In all likelihood, Schubert himself disposed of it earlier. It may be that Schubert, encouraged by the success of the E-flat Trio, composed the B-flat Trio in hopes of repeating the triumph. Consequently, it is possible that the B-flat Trio was composed *after* the E-flat Trio. The fact that Schubert offered the E-flat Trio to both Schott and Probst in the early part of 1828 would seem to verify this hypothesis, since, if he had had two unpublished trios on hand, he would have offered one to Schott and the other to Probst.

As Schumann points out in his discussion of these two pieces, "They bear little resemblance to each other." He viewed the E-flat Trio "active, masculine, and dramatic" and the B-flat Trio as "passive, feminine, and lyrical."[11] Regarding the Andante of this trio Schumann observed that "it is a happy dream, a rising and falling of genuine feeling." Here, as in the F-minor Fantasie, Schubert's gift for combining pure lyricism with contrapuntal imagination is impressive: Note how the theme is treated at length by each of the instruments of the ensemble.

SCHUBERT'S FINAL STRING QUARTETS

Schubert composed fourteen quartets. In addition, he left isolated movements, presumably intended as part of multimovement pieces. We have already discussed the peculiar features of the First String Quartet, D. 18. The next nine quartets (D. 32, 36, 46, 68, 74, 94, 112, 173, 87) were all composed between 1812 and 1816 for performance by Schubert's immediate family.

In his history of the string quartet, Paul Griffiths has called the single quartet movement of 1820 in C minor, D. 703, "the majestic stepping stone to the mature Schubert quartet."[12] The movement is in 6/8 meter and bears the tempo indication Allegro assai. The movement is in sonata-allegro form, and the principal themes are organized in third-related keys. The recapitulation is not simply a tonally adjusted version of the exposition. Instead, the liberties taken in the second part of the sonata reveal most clearly Schubert's progressive ideas. The movement in C minor is followed in the manuscript, which was once owned by Brahms, by a fragment of a triple-meter Andante.

It is difficult to understand why Schubert abandoned this quartet. The first movement is convincing enough. What we do know is that during the late teens and early 1820s, Schubert experienced some sort of compositional block. From the year 1818, for example, we have the sketch of a symphony in D. From 1821, there survive drafts of a symphony in E, a work in four movements that was known to Mendelssohn and Sir George Grove. Best known, of course, is the pair of movements written in 1822, known commonly as the *Unfinished Symphony*, D. 799.

Schubert's next completed string quartet was the A-minor Quartet, D. 804, of 1824. This piece was to have been one of three quartets in a projected Op. 29. The A-minor Quartet was published as Op. 29, No. 1 by the Viennese firm Sauer & Leidesdorf in 1824. (They later published his song cycle *Die schöne Müllerin.*) The other two quartets that would have completed the set are those in D minor, D. 810, and G major, D. 887, which were composed between 1824 and 1826.

Of these, the D-minor Quartet, generally called *Death and the Maiden*, is the best known. All three quartets are equally impressive, but the D-minor Quartet has become popular because of its nickname, which stems from Schubert's use of his song of 1817 "Der Tod und das Mädchen," D. 531, as the basis of the variations in the second movement (Andante con moto). The original poem was the work of Matthias Claudius, whose "simplicity of form and piety of thought" have endeared him to generations of readers. His verses "combine childlike naiveté with a rare depth and purity of feeling, which gave some of his poems the true ring of a folk song."[13]

Vorüber, ach vorüber,
Geh wilder Knochenmann!
Ich bin noch jung,
Geh Lieber und rühre mich nicht an.

Gib deine Hand, du schöne und zart Gebild,
Bin Freund und komme nicht zu strafen.
Sei gutes Muts! Ich bin nicht wild,
Sollst sanft in meinem Armen schlafen.

(Pass by, Oh pass by
Go on, you wild skeleton!
I am yet young;
Go, dear, and touch me not.

Give your hand, you beautiful and charming apparition;
I am a friend and have not come to chastize.
Be of good courage! I am not wild,
Gently shall you sleep in my arms.)

For his variations, Schubert quotes only the music related to the character of Death. Self-quotation in Schubert's last quartet series is not unique to the D-minor Quartet; in the A-minor Quartet, Op. 29, No. 1, D 804, he cites the Entr'acte following act 3 from *Rosamunde, Fürsten von Cypern*, D. 797.

Within the D-minor Quartet Schubert establishes thematic interdependence among its movements with a four-note figure that appears in the first violin part of the first movement in measure 15. This figure, a note ornamented with upper- and lower-neighbor tones, appears again and again, and in guises too numerous to count.

The first movement begins with a gripping introductory gesture that features intense dynamics and homorhythmic statement of the theme. Throughout the first segment of the exposition, triplet rhythm within the context of common time is of utmost importance. The exposition ends in the key of A minor. This is one of the few instances we can point to as evidence for a structural *minor* dominant function in tonal music. The recapitulation (meas. 198) is unmistakable, but everything is entirely rewritten; even the opening gesture is modified in the first violin part by a transposition of the theme an octave higher. The codetta (meas. 311) makes brilliant use of motivic imitation and tempo contrasts.

The second movement shows the influence of Beethoven; the characteristic dactylic rhythm of the theme, the bland character of the melody, the formal design—based at least in part on the variation principle—and the harmonic peculiarities all mirror similar ideas in the Allegretto of Beethoven's Seventh Symphony. The boldness of the third variation with its rich chords in first violin and cello, its diminution of the dactylic rhythm, and many other details show the mature master at work. The delicacy of the fourth variation and its shift from G minor to G major are also characteristic of Schubert's nuance. The intensity resulting both from the return to minor mode and the deliberate confusion of the beat by persistent triplet figures in the cello part of the fifth variation are Romantic rather than Classic gestures.

The Scherzo (Allegro molto) returns to the key of D minor. Formally, this movement is conservative. Beethoven's influence can be perceived in its driving rhythms and syncopations. Even more striking, and relating again particularly to the Allegretto of the Seventh Symphony, is the use of the second inversion sonority at the opening of the second strain of the scherzo.

The finale, a synthesis of sonata and rondo forms, is a powerful Presto in 6/8 time. The germinal motif appears at various points, as it had in the

Scherzo, to lend unity to the four-movement cycle. The coda that rounds the movement off takes the tempo up a notch to Prestissimo and looks forward to the manner of Felix Mendelssohn.

We have an account from Franz Lachner, who tells us in his memoir of Schubert (1881) about the premiere performance of the *Death and the Maiden* quartet, which took place in his own apartment in Vienna. He observes that

> this latter quartet, which nowadays delights everybody and is counted among the grandest creations of its kind, by no means met with undivided approval. The first violin, Sch., who, on account of his great age, was admittedly not equal to such a task, declared to the composer, after playing it through, "My dear fellow, this is no good, leave it alone; you stick to your songs!", whereupon Schubert silently packed up the sheets of music and shut them away in his desk for ever.[14]

Ludwig Speidel clarifies the identity of "Sch." in his account:

> One day Schubert took his newly completed String Quartet in D minor to Schuppanzigh, in his day a very famous quartet player, with the request that he would play it to him. The members of the quartet put out the parts and began to play, but after several bad mistakes they came to a stop in the middle of the first movement, and abandoned the others, Schuppanzigh declaring that this was not quartet writing and was not playable at all. Franz Schubert, silent and smiling, put the parts together and behaved as if nothing had happened.[15]

On the basis of these accounts, it is difficult to say exactly what happened when Schuppanzigh's ensemble played Schubert's new piece. Parts may have been faulty; in 1826, Schuppanzigh (b. 1776) was sixty years old—hardly what one would refer to as "great age." It would be unfair both to Schubert and Schuppanzigh to propose any hypothesis. All that can be said with certainty is that Schuppanzigh had devoted his entire career to the advancement of art music—and particularly chamber music; that Schubert had thought enough of him to dedicate his Quartet in A-minor, Op. 29, No. 1 to him; and that, despite the initially negative reaction to the boldness of the D-minor Quartet, it has become one of the cornerstones of chamber music literature.

SEVEN

Prince Louis Ferdinand and Louis Spohr

PRINCE LOUIS FERDINAND: A MUSICAL AMATEUR

Frederick the Great's nephew, Friedrich Christian Ludwig (1772–1806), Prince of Prussia—known as Louis Ferdinand—shared his uncle's enthusiasm for music. Gifted with enormous talents, Louis was active both as a performer and as a composer. He always remained an amateur musician, but he certainly had the capability to have become a professional.

Though he composed a great deal of fine chamber music, his works remain largely unknown. The reasons for this neglect are easily discovered: his name is associated first and foremost with the powerful Prussian aristocracy of the late eighteenth and early nineteenth centuries; consequently, he himself, in a sense, overshadowed his works as a creative artist. Furthermore Louis, like Schubert, had the bad fortune of dying before he reached the age of forty. He was killed in combat with Napoleon's army at the Battle of Saalfeld on 10 October 1806.

Louis had been surrounded with fine music since his early childhood. He was acquainted with the works of Mozart, Dittersdorf, Beethoven, and other Viennese Classicists, Cramer, Gluck, composers of the Berlin song school, and also music of J. S. Bach, which was preserved in the library of Princess Amalia. Louis Ferdinand knew many of the leading composers of his own age firsthand. He met Jan Ladislav Dussek (1760–1812) in 1803 at Magdeburg. Subsequently, Dussek often advised him concerning both piano technique and composition. He first met Beethoven in Berlin in 1796, then they met again in Vienna in 1804. Beethoven dedicated his Third Piano Concerto in C minor, Op. 37, to the prince, whose virtuosity at the keyboard was widely respected. As a composer, too, Louis Ferdinand was recognized as a formidable talent. Robert Schumann once called him "the Romanticist of the Classical period."[1] Other musicians who expressed admiration for Louis Ferdinand's abilities include Johann Friedrich Reichardt, Louis Spohr, Carl Maria von Weber, and Franz Liszt. Liszt did this by using themes of the prince's music in an Elegy that he composed in 1842 and dedicated to Princess Augusta of Prussia.

The principal chamber works of Louis Ferdinand include the Quintet in C minor for Piano and Strings, Op. 1, which was issued in Paris by Erard in 1803; the Piano Trio in A-flat major, Op. 2; a second Piano Trio in E-flat major, Op. 3; and a Quartet for Piano and Strings in E-flat major, Op. 5, all published in Leipzig by Breitkopf und Härtel in 1806; a second Piano Quartet in F minor, Op. 6, printed in the following year by Breitkopf und Härtel; and a "Grand Trio" in E-flat major, Op. 10, which was published in Berlin by Werckmeister in 1806.[2] In that same year, Breitkopf und Härtel began publishing his works in cooperation with Dussek. The prince did not live to see his music in print, nor did he have the opportunity to make corrections of the proofs.

The Quintet in C minor for Piano and Strings, Op. 1, is remarkable; it is the earliest example of the piano quintet (piano with string quartet), a chamber ensemble that subsequently became one of the standard chamber ensembles.[3] The Quintet is an impressive work in four movements dedicated to Friedrich Heinrich Himmel (1765–1814), himself a prolific composer and virtuoso pianist.

The first movement, in sonata form, treats the ensemble in the manner of a concerto with the piano contrasting with the string quartet. Virtuosic aspects of the piano part include extended arpeggios, rapid scalar passages, and scales in parallel thirds. The first appearance of these scales in thirds presents little problem to a competent pianist since the right hand can take the upper note and the left hand the lower note; however, the corresponding passage in the recapitulation actually has scales in parallel thirds in both the right- and left-hand parts.

The structure of the movement is absolutely clear. Each of the three themes—the opening theme, the subordinate theme, and the closing theme—is highly profiled and distinctive. The powerful, upward leaping minor sixth is the conspicuous feature of the opening theme.

The secondary theme, an expressive melody in E-flat major, is stated initially by the piano with doublings here and there in the string parts to enrich the sonority and add splashes of color. After its statement, the string

Piano Quintet, Op. 1

Prince Louis Ferdinand

ensemble takes up the theme, and the piano accompanies. Occasionally, the strings join with the piano for statements of grandiose character. The concerto influence is apparent in the frequent articulation of structural elements by tonic $^{6}_{4}$ chords, and by trills in the solo piano part that lead to a reentry of the strings.

The second movement, a minuet and trio, is conspicuous for its "wrong-note" theme that anticipates the sarcastic tone of later Romantic scores by composers like Gustav Mahler. The third movement, a set of variations on an original theme, exhibits fluid rhythms and flexible subdivision of the beat. This sort of subdivision—in which five, six, or more tones are combined under a slur with a numerical tally—is common in the music of Chopin and his successors; however, Louis Ferdinand's compositions are among the earliest to use such fluid rhythms. Interesting harmonies and extensive chromaticism pervade this movement. The finale is the most conventional movement of the four, and it wraps up the piece with a good-natured display of virtuosic writing for the piano. Robert Schumann knew and admired the prince's music, and this score doubtless served as Schumann's model when he came to write his own piano quintet.

The four-movement Piano Quartet in F-minor, Op. 6, opens with an Allegro moderato in an extended sonata form with an expressive coda.[4] The minuet, placed as the second movement, has two trios. The minuet sections resemble scherzos because they are riddled with syncopations and sudden dynamic accents, while the contrasting trios flow along smoothly. The slow third movement bears the tempo indication Adagio lento e amoroso. Virtuosic passages for the piano, extensive use of Classical *rubato* (i.e., one hand is delayed by an eighth- or sixteenth-note rest from the other), dramatic shifts from major to minor mode, and an elaborate cadenza all form a movement that is expressive yet balanced. The final movement, Allegro ma moderato, is a theme with variations. The layout of the movement is such that there is a fairly regular alternation between minor and major tonalities. A highly flexible melodic style results from the frequent use of irregular subdivisions of the beat, as we have already observed in the slow movement of the C-minor Quintet.

Throughout the four movements, the various instruments are maintained on an equal footing. The judicious distribution of melodies and motifs throughout this score is a good indication of Louis Ferdinand's skill as a composer of chamber music. The violin virtuoso and composer Henri Vieuxtemps (1820–1881) revived this work for concert performance in 1848.

Louis Ferdinand also wrote a number of light, occasional pieces, such as the Andante with Variations for Piano Quartet, Op. 4 (1806); the *Notturno* (1808) for obbligato piano, flute, violin, viola, and cello with optional parts for two horns; and a Larghetto variée for piano, violin, viola, cello, and bass. Pieces of this sort were written in great number for the musical salons of well-to-do families.

LOUIS SPOHR: A PROFESSIONAL MUSICIAN

The music of German-born Louis Spohr (1784–1859) was much admired during his lifetime, and he had an extraordinarily active career as a concert artist and conductor. In his extensive travels, which are recounted in his autobiography, he visited the principal music centers of Austria, Belgium, Czechoslovakia, England, France, Germany, Holland, Italy, Russia, and Switzerland.[5]

Spohr's contributions to chamber music literature include sixteen duos for two violins, thirty-four string quartets, seven string quintets, a string sextet, four double-quartets for strings, twenty-one duos for violin and piano, five piano trios, two piano quintets with strings, a quintet for piano and winds, four sonatas for violin and harp, a septet, an octet, and a nonet.[6] These last three pieces are all for mixed ensembles. In addition to these serious pieces, he wrote a number of works calculated to be crowd-pleasers. Three such pieces, all written early in Spohr's career, are scored for violin solo with the accompaniment of violin, viola, and cello, but Spohr did not use the designation *string quartet* for these pieces; hence, they are not counted in the tally given above.

The number and sequence of movements in the various chamber music genres cultivated by Spohr can be traced to the Viennese Classicists. Serious chamber works in three movements are generally called "sonata." For the five piano trios, the three piano quintets, the Octet, Op. 32, the Nonet, Op. 31, the four double-quartets, and his string quartets, Spohr adhered to the traditional, four-movement plan. In his quartets featuring the first violin as soloist (examples of the *quatuor brillant*), Spohr prefered the three-movement plan of the concerto. Slow introductions are used infrequently and only to preface first movements. When they do appear, introductions are brief—generally in the range of two-dozen measures. The Adagio opening of Op. 32, only eight measures long, is the shortest. Other works with introductions include the string quartets Op. 45, No. 3, and Op. 152 and the double quartet Op. 87.

Spohr felt most at home writing in the genres that were familiar to him from his own performance experiences. As a young man, he won the good favor of Duke Carl Wilhelm Ferdinand, a nephew of Frederick the Great, who ruled over the Duchy of Brunswick.[7] Eventually, Spohr became the concertmaster at Brunswick, the preferred soloist in concertos, and the featured player in chamber music concerts.

> In the Brunswick quartet circles that Spohr frequented, his imagination was fired by the chamber music of Haydn and Mozart and, shortly after their publication in 1801, by Beethoven's op. 18 string quartets. Contact with music of this order helped to sharpen his sense of style and spurred him on. . . . At these private gatherings his playing was also stimulated by encounters with visiting violinists such as Carl August Seidler and the young Friedrich Wilhelm Pixis.[8]

Spohr began using a Tourte bow in 1802, and he played a Guarneri violin during the years 1803 and 1804; however, when the instrument was stolen, he replaced it with one by Guadagnini.[9] This violin was probably the work of Giovanni Battista Guadagnini (ca. 1711–1786), a builder noted particularly for the full, rich, and powerful timbre of his instruments.

Contemporary writings by and about Spohr tell us a good deal concerning his bowing, phrasing, and articulation: He liked to play as many notes as possible under one bow stroke; he used portamento extensively (particularly in slow movements); and he disapproved of the French practice at that time of accenting the last note of a phrase.

SPOHR'S DUOS FOR VIOLIN

Spohr's chamber music from the early part of his career is almost exclusively for strings. His first published chamber work was a set of three Duos for Violins, Op. 3 (1802). By the time Spohr wrote these pieces, the violin duo as a genre already had an impressive history, both as a medium for pedagogy and for display of virtuosity. Early nineteenth-century virtuosi, such as Giovanni Battista Viotti (1755–1824), Pierre Marie François de Sales Baillot (1771–1842), Pierre Rode (1774–1830), Emmanuel Guérin (1779–after 1824), and François Antoine Habeneck (1781–1849), had contributed important examples. During Spohr's lifetime and subsequent to it, the medium continued to flourish in the writings of eminent violinists like Jean-Baptiste-Charles Dancla (1817–1907). The duo repertoire ranged from easy pieces, like Guérin's *Duos faciles,* Op. 1, to showpieces like Spohr's Concertante for Two Violins, Op. 88, which he wrote in 1833 for performance at the Halberstadt Music Festival with Karl Friedrich Müller, the first violinist of the Müller Quartet.[10] Spohr's Op. 3 Duos were followed by three in Op. 9 (1806–7), three in Op. 39 (1816), Op. 48 (1808), the three of Op. 67 (1824), the above-mentioned Op. 88, Op. 148 (1853), Op. 150 (1854), and Op. 153 (1855). When we consider the fact that Spohr's last opus number was 154, the importance throughout his career of the duo for unaccompanied violins becomes clear.

SPOHR'S MATURITY

In 1805, Spohr left Brunswick, the town of his birth and childhood, to become concertmaster at Gotha. He held that post until 1812. There he met Dorothea (i.e., Dorette) Scheidler, a harpist possessing both an admirable technique and an elegant manner of expression. Spohr married her in February 1806. From the time of their first meeting until her death in 1834, he regularly wrote chamber pieces for their use on concert tours.

> The match was an ideal one; throughout the twenty-eight years of their marriage they remained devoted to one another. . . . The strength of their marriage lay partly in their shared musical lives. As a harpist Dorette became a distinguished virtuoso [*sic*]. . . . At the same time her well-developed critical instinct allowed her to take an informed interest in . . . her husband's creative work.[11]

The most significant works that Spohr composed for his wife were the various sonatas for harp and violin. The earliest of these, a Sonata in C minor, WoO 23, dates from 1805. In the next year, Spohr wrote the Sonata in B-flat major, Op. 16 as well as the Sonata in E-flat major, Op. 113. The Sonata in G major, Op. 115, followed in 1809. Another sonata, this one in D major, Op. 114, dates from 1811. With the exception of Op. 114, the sonatas are in the customary succession of three movements with the tempos fast-slow-fast. The D-major Sonata consists of only two movements. The second of these is a potpourri of themes taken from Mozart's *Die Zauberflöte* (1791). The last three sonatas, Opp. 113–15, use *scordatura* tunings. As Spohr explains in his autobiography:

> I conceived the idea of pitching the harp half a tone lower than the violin. . . . as the violin sounds most brilliantly in the cross or sharp notes, but the harp best in the B-tones or flat notes, when the fewest pedals possible are moved; I thereby obtained for both instruments the most favourable and most effective key-notes: for the violin namely, D and G; for the harp E[-flat] and A-flat. A second advantage was that from the

> lower tuning of the harp, a string would less frequently break. . . . From this time therefore, I wrote all my Compositions for harp and violin in that difference of keys.[12]

From 1813 to 1815, Spohr was active in Vienna. The Viennese years were particularly rich in chamber works, largely owing to a commission from Johann Tost "to compose as much chamber music as he liked, for which Tost would pay on a sliding scale . . . in proportion to the number of instruments involved."[13] Spohr's most populous chamber pieces, the Nonet in F major for violin, viola, cello, double bass, flute, oboe, clarinet, bassoon, and horn, Op. 31, and the Octet in E major for violin, two violas, cello, double bass, clarinet, and two horns, Op. 32, came into being under these circumstances; but not all of Spohr's Viennese chamber music was written for Tost. Spohr's final chamber work before leaving the city on 8 March was the String Quartet in C major, Op. 29, No. 2. The three quartets of Op. 29 are dedicated to Andreas Romberg (1767–1821), who had criticized some of Spohr's earlier quartets as being inferior to his orchestral music. Perhaps, therefore, Spohr's dedication of the quartets to Romberg was an invitation to the older composer to witness the advances he had made in the management of this exacting medium.

The several years following Spohr's departure from Vienna were devoted to touring in Germany, Switzerland, and Italy. From 1817 until 1819, he resided mainly in Frankfurt. In both Vienna and Frankfurt, Spohr functioned primarily as the conductor of operas; nevertheless, he continued to compose and perform chamber music. During the final segment of Spohr's career, the years from 1822 until his death, he was the *Hofkapellmeister* in Kassel.

During the 1820s, Dorette became increasingly interested in performance on the piano, apparently because her failing health made it difficult for her to play the harp. Spohr wrote a number of chamber works, such as the Quintet in C minor for piano, flute, clarinet, horn, and bassoon, Op. 52. In this particular work, the piano part is featured, and the remaining instruments are largely accompanimental. After Dorette's death in 1834, Spohr never again wrote for the harp.

In 1836, Spohr remarried; this time, to Marianne Pfeiffer, a talented pianist. In his subsequent chamber works, the piano assumes a more prominent role. "To a large extent, Spohr's burgeoning interest in piano composition sprang directly from the stimulus of Marianne's pianistic ability. . . . For a period of ten years, from 1836, he wrote no chamber music for strings alone, but a considerable amount with piano."[14]

Mostly late works, Spohr's chamber pieces with piano reflect both the consolidation of his compositional technique and the growing importance of the Romantic style; nevertheless, because Spohr did not play keyboard instruments of any sort, he seems not to have been fully aware of the piano's capabilities. Finding an idiomatic keyboard manner took time. His earliest attempts are often repetitious, and they suffer from a lack of variety in motivic and rhythmic elements. Similarly, he fails to exploit the full range of the instrument. In a different sense, however, Spohr's unfamiliarity with the piano was an advantage: the unbridled virtuosity of piano music by Kalkbrenner, Chopin, Liszt, and Mendelssohn defeats any attempts at creating a balanced ensemble.

Among Spohr's chamber music with keyboard, the Septet in A minor, Op. 147 is a particularly fine example. Written in 1852, it was intended for the court of Kassel, presumably with his wife at the piano. The second movement, Larghetto con moto, opens with a tranquil yet expansive melody for horn. The melody is echoed by the piano and then in turn by other instruments in the ensemble (flute, clarinet, bassoon, horn, violin, and cello). The movement contains elements that anticipate the style of Brahms. The tumultuous minuet, for instance, is filled with syncopations, shifted accents, and somber passages in minor mode. The clarinet melody of the trio is beautifully written, and it reveals the knowledge of the instrument that Spohr obtained through his association with Johann Simon Hermstedt (1778–1846) for whom he composed four clarinet concertos between 1808 and 1829. The final movement uses as one of its principal themes a descending, scalar motif that appeared earlier in the Larghetto. Throughout the piece, Spohr's use of imitative counterpoint is judicious, dramatic, and effective in creating genuine interplay among the seven instruments.

SPOHR'S STRING QUARTETS

The string quartet occupied a prominent place in Spohr's compositional activity. His thirty-four quartets span a period of fifty years, the earliest having been published in 1806, the last in 1856.[15] They are variable in style, and their particular characteristics depended upon the occasion for which each was written, the intended market for the publication, as well as the prevailing tastes and Spohr's own compositional interests at any given time. The firms that issued his quartets included Simrock, Steiner, Peters, Schlesinger, André, Breitkopf und Härtel, and others, all leading music publishers of the day. While their willingness to publish Spohr's chamber music may not offer proof of its quality, it nevertheless confirms the significance and influence of this repertoire during the nineteenth century.[16]

As a sample of Spohr's handling of the *quatuor concertante*, we may look at the second quartet of Op. 58, a set of three that, according to the composer, are "shorter, easier, and more effective" than his previous quartets of Op. 45.[17] Composition of the first two quartets, in E-flat major and A minor respectively, took place in Dresden during November and December 1821. The third quartet, in G major, was completed in March of the following year in Kassel.

The A-minor Quartet begins with a sonata-form movement in which the first violin carries the main theme, with its distinctive dotted rhythms, descending chromatic tones, and trills, as the lower strings accompany. The second strain, in the relative major, lies rather low in the first violin's range, but Spohr seems to have made the downward move in order to facilitate a more balanced dialogue with the cello, which takes up the new theme eight measures later. Attention shifts again to the first violin in the closing segment, and Spohr provides some brilliant writing with triplets, quintuplets, rapid chromatic figuration, and broken octaves as the exposition, which is to be repeated, draws to a close. Throughout the development section, Spohr recalls elements from the exposition—trills in the first violin, chromatic lines, and the dotted rhythm of the opening theme. The second theme, previously heard in C major, is recalled in A major; hence, the first violin is in a much higher range, and the music sounds much brighter and more vigorous than it had formerly. Apart from its transposition to A major, the closing theme appears with little change.

The second movement is a duple-meter set of variations in F major on a sixteen-measure theme in symmetrical binary form. Spohr gives two variations in which all four instruments are equally active before proceeding to the key of A major for what is at once a brief scherzo as well as a transformation of the theme. In the final variation, Spohr returns to F major and duple meter, but now the original theme, marked *dolce e cantabile*, sings out warmly in the cello part.

The concluding rondo is marked by Spohr "all' Espagnola," owing to the dactylic figure that appears in the inner voices in the first measure and as a motive throughout the movement. Tonalities familiar from the first movement, A minor, then E major and A major, return along with extensive chromaticism to give the whole piece a sense of cohesiveness. In its form as well as its florid writing for the first violin, the finale recalls the last movement of Haydn's String Quartet in E-flat, Op. 33, No. 2.

The String Quartet in A major, Op. 93, composed in 1835, was the last *quatuor brillant* to come from Spohr's pen. Its three movements, Allegro, Larghetto, and Rondo, are prefaced by a short introduction, an Andante, in which the cello has much of beauty and interest. Though formally comparable to the concerto, the virtuosic writing for the first violin in the three movements of this solo quartet produces an overall effect that is more lyrical than dramatic.

THE DOUBLE QUARTET

Spohr's most individual contribution to the genres of nineteenth-century chamber music is the "double quartet."

> The idea of combining two string quartets to form a Double-quartet, with the ensuing increase of voices, offers much scope for Spohr's predilection for contrapuntal writing, and also fullfils a desire to enrich the tone-colour in chamber music. Spohr gives this new form particular importance because he does not, like Mendelssohn in his well-known Op. 20, fuse the two quartets into an octet, but treats them as two separate, equally important groups, which can enter into the most varied relationships. As Spohr tells us in his memoirs, he set himself the task of using the two quartets in frequent contrast in the manner of double choirs, and saving the octet (that is, the combination of all the instruments) for the climaxes of the work. The alternating of the two quartets, i.e., the interplay either by repetition or in the form of a dialogue, had therefore to determine the general concept as well as the detail.[18]

The earliest of these works is Spohr's Double Quartet in D minor, Op. 65, of 1823. Op. 77 in E-flat major followed in 1827, Op. 87 in E minor in 1833, and Op. 136 in G minor in 1847. The first of the double quartets reveals a number of stylistic features in addition to those already mentioned. The homorhythmic opening statement by both quartets at a *forte* dynamic is striking, as is the enrichment of the first violin part by doubling by either the second violin or the viola at some interval below—often the octave, third, sixth, or tenth. Of particular importance is the liberation of the cello in quartet I from its role as harmonic bass. The instrument therefore enjoys unprecedented prominence as a melody instrument. Spohr makes good use of contrasting articulations. Extended passages for string "quintet," with the fifth string part chosen variously from quartet II, are frequently encountered. The first violin in quartet I generally functions as one of four virtuosi within a *quatuor brillant* texture. The early double-quartets are also useful as pedagogical pieces since the parts of quartet II are generally less difficult than those of quartet I. This feature, however, does not hold true in the later double-quartets.

In the spring of 1858, a little more than a year before Spohr's death, the British publishers Chappell and Cramer sponsored the construction of St. James's Hall in London. This hall had a seating capacity of 2,500—enormous for that time. Completion of the design by Owen Jones ran to £120,000. Cherubic figures of plaster were positioned in the lancet arches above the side windows. In their hands, these figures held scrolls inscribed with the names of the greatest composers of the western European tradition. There, beside the names of Mozart, Handel, Beethoven, Haydn, Weber, Gluck, Purcell, Rossini, and Cherubini, Spohr's name had its place of honor.[19]

EIGHT

Champions of Tradition: Mendelssohn, Schumann, and Brahms

THE ROLE OF CHAMBER MUSIC IN NINETEENTH-CENTURY CULTURE

The lifestyles of professional musicians changed radically in the early days of the historical style period that we generally call the Romantic era. Until about the middle of the eighteenth century, the typical musician might have expected to find employment in the home of a wealthy aristocrat, or in some ecclesiastical organization. The events of the later eighteenth century made both of these career opportunities obsolete. As a result of the Enlightenment, the power of the aristocracy and the Christian church were declining. Logic and reason replaced the dogma and divine right.

Music patronage was only one aspect of nineteenth-century life that was altered as a result of the great importance placed upon human intelligence. The development of a systematic method of inquiry led to technological advances that influenced all aspects of western European society. Farm machinery made it possible for a few individuals to do the work that had previously been accomplished only by the labor of many hands. Owing to the new relationship between personnel and productivity, many farmhands became superfluous. These displaced agrarians migrated en masse to growing urban centers. After their relocation, these people became the middle-class merchants and factory workers of Europe and America.

The physical layout of middle-class, urban homes differed from the homes of the landed aristocrats. The use of wrought iron in Europe and of steel in the United States, the numerous structural applications of reinforced concrete, Richard Trevithick's improvements in the design of steam engines, the development of generators and electric motors by Michael Faraday, the safe and practical implementation of elevators by Elisha G. Otis, and other technological advances made it possible for residential dwellings to be stacked one on top of another rather than being placed side by side on large plots of land. As a result of the Industrial Revolution, a single acre of land in an urban context could easily provide relatively comfortable residences for scores of people. This populace found their entertainment in the rapidly increasing number of music halls and opera houses that appeared in Europe and America. These venues for music, similar in many ways to a mass medium, depended upon contemporaneous advances in science and technology. Concert halls and opera houses were "of their time," but they were poorly suited to chamber ensembles.

In these concert halls, audiences lost their identities. Musicians could no longer write for known listeners in the way that Haydn composed his baryton trios for Prince Esterhazy, or that Beethoven wrote the *Archduke Trio* for his friend Rudolf. As a result, composers were forced to write according to their own inclinations rather than those of aristocratic or ecclesiastical patrons; hence, Romantic compositions tend to be highly personal. The cool logic and formal balance apparent in the music of the Age of the Enlightenment can already be seen fading into the distance in many of Beethoven's works. During the course of the nineteenth century, musical scores of a highly distinctive nature gradually came to replace the generic compositions of the late eighteenth century; consequently, the present-day music lover is more apt to know details about Beethoven's personal life—like the Heiligenstadt Testament, the phantom "Immortal Beloved," the composer's affliction with syphilis, his tragic loss of hearing, and so on—than about Haydn's or J. C. Bach's private affairs.

The persona of a particular Romantic composer is often manifested in chamber works with force equal to that in more stupendous works like Berlioz's *Symphonie fantastique*. It is for this reason that our discussions of Romantic chamber music will include more reflections upon the events of individual composer's lives than has been typical of our account up to this point. The great vanguards of romanticism—composers like Berlioz, Wagner, Verdi, and Liszt—were little concerned with the understated genres of chamber music. All four were progressives. Their activities were not limited to composition, but also embraced aesthetic theory, philosophy, and even politics. Their eyes were firmly fixed on the future.

At the same time that the avant-garde composers were proclaiming the music of the future, a growing number of scholars, performers, and composers began to examine historical and ethnological repertories with an academic rigor comparable to that already accepted as a convention within scientific disciplines. The investigations of diverse musics by Raphael Georg Kiesewetter (1773–1850), Friedrich Chrysander's foreword to his *Jahrbuch für musikalische Wissenschaft* (Yearbook for musical science, 1863), Guido Adler's organization with Philipp Spitta and Chrysander of the *Vierteljahrschrift für Musikwissenschaft* (Quarterly journal of musicology, 1884), and his mission statement in the opening essay in that journal, "Umfang, Methode und Ziel der Musikwissenschaft" (Scope, methodology, and objective of musicology, 1885), were harbingers of a growing desire to resurrect our musical heritage. At the same time, they were clear indications of the Romantic yearning for the distant, the exotic, and the mysterious.

During the nineteenth century, traditionally minded composers, such as Mendelssohn, Schumann, and Brahms, continued to write for small ensembles. Their handling of musical materials reflects their knowledge of historical forms and devices; nevertheless, their musical creations are of their time. For the Romantic composer, the key to writing successful chamber music was in discovering the diversity behind stereotypes, in building on rather than rejecting tradition, and in adapting compositional principles to suit their present artistic goals.

THE CHAMBER MUSIC OF FELIX MENDELSSOHN

Mendelssohn's activities ranged widely from his childhood until the time of his early death. As a wunderkind, he was not only a composer of extraordinary precocity, but also a gifted pianist and string player. His lifelong fascination with early music may justify his being ranked among the pioneers in the discipline of historical musicology. He enjoyed painting and sketching; moreover, Mendelssohn (1809–1847) was fortunate enough to have come from a family whose financial situation made it possible for the boy to travel widely, like the young Mozart, and to experience firsthand the important musical trends of the times. It has even been suggested that Mendelssohn's dedication to Germanic musical traditions stemmed, in fact, from his disappointment with the superficiality that he found in many of these trends.

> Mendelssohn's visit to Paris in company with his father in 1825 (actually his second visit—there had been an earlier one when Felix was only seven) proved a turning point in his career, stimulating both his critical

> and his creative faculties. Nowhere else in Europe could a young musician have met with such a range of talent and variety of outlook as was represented by Cherubini, Rossini, Meyerbeer, Auber, Liszt, Berlioz, Hummel, Onslow the prolific and popular dilettante composer of quartets and quintets, Baillot the violinist and teacher of violinists, and Reicha, flautist, composer and theorist, who had been a colleague of Beethoven's in the Elector's orchestra at Bonn and was to number both Berlioz and César Franck among his pupils. Felix thrived on the praise that came his way for his B minor Piano Quartet and other early compositions, but still more on the technical brilliance of many of the artists he met, and the string players especially: Viotti and Rodolphe Kreutzer, Habeneck and Baillot. But far from overwhelming him with their authority, these renowned personalities seemed to bring out the independence of his own character, so that he went out of his way to assert the claims of German music, especially J. S. Bach and Beethoven; like Spohr five years earlier, he reacted against the shallowness of much of the operatic, church, and salon music the French admired. He even found faults in the extemporisation of Liszt, the orchestration of Auber, and the operas of Rossini. When he returned from Paris it was with intellect and imagination stirred, but at the same time with a renewed faith in the solid virtues of the German classical tradition.[1]

German Baroque counterpoint and Austrian Classical formal clarity were, perhaps, the most important elements of Mendelssohn's musical inheritance. Counterpoint is an essential element even in very early compositions, such as the String Quartet in E-flat, which will be discussed a bit later. In his use of form, we can see the impact of Haydn, Mozart, and Beethoven. Mendelssohn ordinarily kept distinct breaks between movements, and in using introductions or interludes, he never allowed formal designs to become obscured. Mendelssohn was "neither an innovator, a creator of a special style, nor a composer who adhered to a specific school. He happened to be . . . a champion of old traditions rather than a sower of new seeds."[2] Mendelssohn's predictable use of genres and forms accounts for the accessibility of much of his music, and the model of the Viennese Classicists was largely responsible for the great importance that Mendelssohn attached to chamber music.

MENDELSSOHN'S EARLY CHAMBER WORKS

A series of three piano quartets were the first pieces that the composer deemed worthy of opus numbers. These Quartets, Op. 1 in C minor, Op.

2 in F minor, and Op. 3 in B minor, were composed between 1821 and 1825. In all three, the piano part is primary. The writing for the strings is often reminiscent of the old accompanied sonata. The Quartet, Op. 2, is dedicated to Felix's mentor, Karl Friedrich Zelter (1758–1832), who introduced the younger man to the music of Sebastian Bach.[3] The Quartet, Op. 3, is dedicated to another luminary, Johann Wolfgang von Goethe (1749–1832), who was personally acquainted with both Zelter and Mendelssohn. "For the average composer, and even for a prominent one, it was not easy to make Goethe's acquaintance beyond a purely initial stage of courtesy. . . . But by and by the grand old man became very fond of the youngster, and before long Felix kissed His Excellency after each performance."[4]

The piano quartets are of modest interest; nevertheless, they reveal hints of the genius that we expect to find in Mendelssohn's mature works. We can see him experimenting with the traditional minuet and trio, since already in Op. 2, that movement is replaced with one designated as an "Intermezzo." Also apparent is the use of thematic transformation and cyclic recollection of themes. These devices, common in Mendelssohn's early works, are rare—or, at least, extremely subtle—in the compositions of his maturity.

Cyclic composition is also employed in the Sextet in D major, Op. 110, which, despite the late opus number, was actually composed in 1824.[5] The most striking thematic recurrence takes place in the finale, which recalls the melody of the minuet. The instrumentation of this the piece is unusual: violin, two violas, cello, double bass, and piano.

Between 1823 and 1825, Mendelssohn also composed at least three sonatas for piano with an obbligato instrument: the Sonata in F minor, Op. 4, for violin and piano, the Sonata in C minor for viola and piano, and the Sonata in E-flat for Clarinet and Piano. The sonatas all employ a three-movement plan.

The Viola Sonata was composed between 23 November 1823 and 14 February 1824.[6] The first movement begins with a slow introduction, a structural element that appears consistently in Mendelssohn's sonatas with obbligato instruments. The Allegro movement that follows is in a conventional sonata form and includes a repetition of the exposition. The secondary tonality is E-flat major. Here is an early example of Mendelssohn's preference for third-related keys. (This tonal arrangement is clear in all six of his string quartets, which are ordered with movements in constellations of thirds.) The second movement is a minuet and trio in the tonic key; however, the trio is in common time. The finale consists of a theme and eight variations. The last variation, which begins Adagio, shows the viola to good advantage and places considerable demands upon the pianist, particularly in the scintillating *Allegro molto* section that concludes the work. As Mendelssohn's scores go, this piece has little counterpoint. It is, nevertheless, an appealing work that deserves to be heard more frequently.

The Sonata for Clarinet and Piano opens with an adagio introduction begun by the piano and later joined by the clarinet. A pedal point is sounded in the keyboard part as Mendelssohn stacks rich harmonies above it. The almost orchestral character of the piano part at this point is relieved by the unaccompanied clarinet, which plays a free, cadenza-like transitional passage leading into the movement proper and the principal tempo, allegro moderato. Throughout the movement—and the entire piece—Mendelssohn maintains a good balance between the two instruments. The second movement, Andante, begins with an extended passage for solo clarinet. The final cadence of the opening clarinet idea is elided with the entrance of the piano. The movement proceeds as an elegant duet with suave melodies much like those in the various "Songs without Words." The finale, which bears the tempo indication allegro moderato, is a cheery affair whose principal theme uses repeated notes in both the clarinet and piano parts. It includes much fine counterpoint in the fugato.

The Sonata in F minor, Op. 4, for violin and piano occupied a special place in Mendelssohn's heart and was the only one of these three sonatas that Mendelssohn published. He dedicated it to his close friend Eduard Rietz (1802–1832), with whom the composer studied the violin beginning in 1824.

The overall plan of the Violin Sonata is similar to that of the Clarinet Sonata insofar as both pieces have three movements and both contain first movements in sonata form prefaced by a slow introduction. In details too, such as the use of repeated notes within the context of a two-note appoggiatura motif, the two works exhibit similarities. The first movement of Op. 4, Adagio-Allegro moderato, reverses the scheme of the clarinet piece by beginning with an extended passage for the solo violin. The second movement, *Poco adagio*, is well written, but bespeaks a mood of melancholy that is almost theatrical. In the third movement, marked Allegro agitato, Mendelssohn tried to strike a balance by writing music of a serious character.

The Sonata in F major (1838) for violin and piano is a substantial composition; however, it was suppressed by the composer.[7] The work remained unknown until 1953, when Yehudi Menuhin made a practical edition.

The crown jewel of Mendelssohn's youthful chamber pieces—he was sixteen years old when he wrote this piece in 1825—is the String Octet in E-flat, Op. 20. The score, dedicated to Eduard Rietz, requires what amounts to two string quartets: four violins, two violas, and two celli. Mendelssohn intertwines all eight voices in a dense texture, yet each voice is thoroughly interdependent.

Formal designs in the Octet are the standard ones. Its four movements, Allegro moderato, ma con fuoco; Andante; Scherzo (Allegro leggierissimo); and Presto, follow the same arrangement typically found in Classical string quartets and symphonies. The only features of the piece that might appear as departures from eighteenth-century models are the use of duple meter for the Scherzo, the absence of a trio, and the highly contrapuntal texture of the finale. As for the duple meter of the Scherzo, we should recall that in the Scherzo of his Ninth Symphony, Beethoven had already used duple compound meter. Indeed, Mendelssohn's second movement (Andante) contains what appears to be a quotation of one of the principal themes of Beethoven's Scherzo.[8]

The Scherzo of the Octet is an early example of the brilliant yet airy manner that Mendelssohn cultivated in movements of this sort. Though the movement is light and amusing, it is not without compositional complexity; the principal theme is put into service as an accompanimental figure too, but it appears in this context in diminution. Mendelssohn was pleased with this movement, and he later scored it for orchestra as a substitute for the minuet of his Symphony in C minor, Op. 11.[9]

For his four-movement String Quintet in A major, Op. 18, Mendelssohn chose the more typical instrumentation of pairs of violins and violas with a single cello. The first movement, Allegro con moto, is a conventional sonata form whose secondary theme appears in various transformations in the final Allegro vivace. The second movement, Andante sostenuto, is in the key of F major and demonstrates Mendelssohn's fondness for arranging movements in third-related keys. As in the Octet, the Scherzo of the Quintet, marked Allegro di molto, is in duple meter and makes use of thematic imitation. The dynamics (predominantly *pianissimo*) and articulation (*sempre staccato*) recall the Scherzo of Op. 20. Though composed in 1826, the String Quintet did not appear in print until it was issued by Simrock of Berlin in 1832. This edition differs in several respects from the original version. For its publication, Mendelssohn inserted the second movement Intermezzo, moved the Scherzo from second to third place, and deleted the minuet and trio. The Intermezzo, which was composed in the year that the Quintet was published, is an elegy for Eduard Rietz who died on 22 January of that year.

Two works from Mendelssohn's youth remain to be discussed; the Piano Trio in C minor, whose four movements must have been written sometime around 1820, and the String Quartet in E-flat of 1823. The Piano Trio is an unusual one because it uses an ensemble of violin, viola, and piano instead of the more usual combination of violin, cello, and piano.[10] In Mendelssohn's later piano trios, the D-minor Trio, Op. 49 and the C-minor Trio, Op. 66, he used the conventional scoring.

MENDELSSOHN'S STRING QUARTETS

The popular conception of Mendelssohn's string quartet production reckons seven works for this medium: the A-minor Quartet, Op. 13 (1827), the E-flat major Quartet, Op. 12 (1829), the E-minor Quartet, Op. 44, No. 2 (1837), the E-flat major Quartet, Op. 44, No. 3 (1838), the D-major Quartet, Op. 44, No. 1 (1838), the F-minor Quartet, Op. 80 (1847), and the Quartet in E major, Op. 81 (1847). This list neglects the String Quartet in E-flat of 1823, but it includes the conglomeration of quartet movements that was pasted together by Breitkopf und Härtel and published after the composer's death as Op. 81. The opening Andante of this quartet, a set of variations in E major, and the second movement, a scherzo in A minor, were both composed in the last year of Mendelssohn's life as part of a projected but ultimately unfinished quartet. The two remaining movements, a Capriccio and a Fugue, were written in 1843 and 1827 respectively. From a formal and stylistic point of view, the combination of these diverse pieces is unconvincing. The tonality of the final movement is E-flat major. Mendelssohn invariably wrote the first and last movements of mulimovement cycles in the same key; hence, if the Op. 81 Quartet is to be performed at all, at the very least a transposition of the finale from E-flat to E major would be necessary. Even if someone were to make this transposition, Mendelssohn's style of 1827 differs from that of 1847.

The Quartet in E-flat, a youthful work without opus number, is an impressive piece.[11] The high quality of the writing throughout all movements lends support to Eric Werner's supposition that this quartet was performed for Louis Spohr when Mendelssohn visited him in Kassel in the company of his mentor, Zelter.[12] The composer's fondness for contrapuntal writing is apparent in the canonic passages of the second movement and the finale, which is a double fugue with *stretto*, augmentation, and other details. Mendelssohn's mastery of Classical pattern forms can be seen with equal clarity, particularly in the strict construction of the sonata-allegro design of the first movement. The writing for strings is idiomatic, but from time to time the first violin gets a disproportionate amount of attention.

Mendelssohn achieved mastery of the string quartet as a genre in his A-minor Quartet, Op. 13, which is traditional in its broad architectural design as well as in the forms of its individual movements. A more progressive feature, and one that came to be a hallmark of the Romantic style, is the use of thematic recurrence. The motivic core that dominates all four movements of the piece is the three-note figure that opens Mendelssohn's setting of Johann Gustav Droysen poem "Frage," the first in his set of Twelve Songs, Op. 9. Because of the prominence of this motif, the quartet may have some sort of programmatic significance.

The quartet opens with an adagio introduction in triple meter, in which the "Frage" motif is heard for the first time (meas. 13–15). The viola, which initiates many of the most important themes throughout, effects the transition to the allegro vivace tempo of the movement proper. The second movement, Adagio non lento, shows Mendelssohn's facility with counterpoint. The fugue subject of the second movement is taken up again, albeit in a thematic transformation, in the finale of the quartet. Mendelssohn replaces the conventional third movement with an Intermezzo at the tempo allegro di molto. The final movement, marked presto, begins in the subdominant key and eventually works its way back to the tonic. The fugue subject of the second movement returns in its original form (stated now by the first violin) in the transitional recitative leading to the restatement of the quartet's opening adagio.

The Quartet in E-flat, Op. 12—written *after* the Op. 13 quartet—also makes extensive use of cyclic recurrence. Similar too is the replacement of the minuet by a movement here designated as "Canzonetta." The finale uses progressive tonality, beginning in C minor and closing in the tonic major, E-flat.

These two quartets display most progressive conceptions. The use of thematic recurrence, particularly in the A-minor Quartet, actually anticipates developments of the mid-nineteenth century. Mendelssohn's early application of this device demonstrates his awareness of new directions in composition at the time. The prominence of cyclic composition in Mendelssohn's early works may also be indicative of a strong influence exerted upon him by Ludwig Berger (1777–1839), a pianist, pedagogue, and resident of Berlin, who was the piano instructor for young Felix and his sister, Fanny. The model of von Weber's *Der Freischütz* (1821) may also have been influential.

The published ordering of the three quartets in Op. 44 does not reflect

Con moto
Voice
Piano
f
dim.
dolce
Ist es wahr? Ist es wahr? dass du stets dort in dem Laub - gang, an der
Is it true? Is it true? that you wait there in the path be-neath the
mf
p
dolce
7
Pno.
Wein - wand mei - ner harrst und den Mond - schein und die
ar - bor just for me, and ask both moon and the
10
dim.
cresc.
Stern - lein auch nach mir be - fragst? Ist es wahr?
stars a - bout me? Is it true?

the chronology of their composition. Op. 44, No. 2 in E minor was completed in June 1837; Op. 44, No. 3 in E-flat followed in February 1838; Op. 44, No. 1, the D-major Quartet, was last in July 1838. Mendelssohn probably placed the D-major Quartet in first position when the set was published by Breitkopf und Härtel because it approximates the manner of the Viennese Classicists.

At the time Mendelssohn wrote the Op. 44 quartets, he was conductor of the Leipzig Gewandhaus Orchestra. The concertmaster was Ferdinand David (1810–1873), a close personal friend of Mendelssohn's and an experienced quartet player whom Mendelssohn appointed in 1843 as instructor of violin at the Leipzig Conservatory. Mendelssohn not only founded this institution, but also acted as its first director. He also engaged Robert Schumann as a member of that faculty for a brief time.

David was responsible for the first professional chamber music concerts in Leipzig.[13] His quartet premiered Op. 44, Nos. 2 and 3 at the Gewandhaus. Robert Schumann, in his glowing remarks about Mendelssohn's new quartets, informs us that the other players in the ensemble were [Karl Wilhelm] Ulrich on second violin, [Karl Traugott] Queisser on viola, and [Friedrich Wilhelm] Grenser on cello.[14]

Though less pervasive than in the A-minor Quartet, Op. 13, cyclic organization plays an important role in Op. 44, particularly in the third Quartet in E-flat, which is unified by a four-note motif that appears in the first, third, and fourth movements. In other respects, the quartets of Op. 44 are conservative. One scholar has called the set downright "anachronistic."[15]

Mendelssohn's last quartet, Op. 80 in F minor, is a unique work. Most of the piece was composed in the summer of 1847 during Mendelssohn's vacation at Interlaken, Switzerland. He continued to refine the score until September. The vacation was much needed: Felix's sister, Fanny Cäcilie Mendelssohn-Bartholdy Hensel (1805–1847), had died on 14 May. Felix had been closer to her than to any other human being, with the possible exception of his wife, Cécile Jeanrenaud. Fanny shared Felix's interest in music; had studied piano with Ludwig Berger; and had composed chamber pieces of her own including the Piano Quartet in A-flat (1822), the Adagio in E major for violin and piano (1823), a Fantasia in G minor (ca. 1830) and the Capriccio in A-flat major (1829), both for cello and piano, the String Quartet in E-flat (1834), and the Piano Trio in D minor (1846), which was published in 1850 as Op. 11.[16] Felix's letters to her often contain discussions of pieces that he was working on at the time. Her early death robbed Felix of a beloved sister, trusted friend, confidant, and colleague.

Mendelssohn's wild despair resulting from Fanny's death is apparent throughout the F-minor Quartet. The overriding affection throughout the piece is rage. Only in the third movement, an Adagio in A-flat major, do we find the tender melancholy that Mendelssohn expresses so often in his music. Traditional formal patterns are maintained—especially in the sonatas that constitute the first and last movements—but the smaller, harmonic components within the larger forms are articulated by figuration rather than melodies. Tremolando, syncopation, and harmonic audacities represent torrents of emotion. Double stops are used extensively, particularly in the Adagio and toward the close of the finale.

MENDELSSOHN'S LATE ENSEMBLE SONATAS

Mendelssohn's late works were written after 1833, the year in which he accepted a full-time position as conductor of the Düsseldorf Music and Theater Society and bid adieu to his childhood home in Berlin. In that same year, Mendelssohn composed his two Konzertstücke, Opp. 113 and 114, for clarinet, basset horn, and piano. These two works are fundamentally sonatas for piano with two obbligato instruments. Both have a three-movement plan of fast, moderate, fast. Though Op. 113 is somewhat diminutive in comparison with Mendelssohn's other ensemble sonatas, Op. 114 is proportioned in similar manner to the sonatas that we have already discussed. Both pieces were written specifically for Heinrich Joseph Baermann (1784–1847) and his son, Carl (1810–1885). The elder Baermann was perhaps the best-known clarinetist of the day. He was on intimate terms with Carl Maria von Weber, whose clarinet compositions he popularized throughout Europe. The vast majority of von Weber's clarinet pieces were written for and dedicated to Baermann. Meyerbeer was also acquainted with Baermann and composed the obbligato part in his cantata *Gli amori di Teolinda* for him.

Interesting, too, are the Sonatas, Opp. 45 and 58, for cello and piano, which Mendelssohn composed in 1838 and 1843 respectively. The first of these is in the key of B-flat major and exhibits the three-movement format that the composer preferred in pieces of this sort. The outer movements are bursting with energy, and both conclude with dazzling figuration for the bravura pianist. The movements are further related by their main themes: the opening theme of the third movement is a variant of the inversion of the main theme of the first movement. The preservation in the last movement's theme of the salient rhythms and intervals that characterized the first movement's theme make this relationship unmistakable. The polarized tonalities of the sonata-form first movement unfold as an arpeggiation of the tonic triad. The theme associated with the key of D is reminiscent of Schubert's Fantasy in F minor, Op. 103, in its juxtaposition of duplet and triplet subdivision of the beat. Within this sonata form, we find greater tonal variety than had been characteristic of eighteenth-century sonatas. Tonal plateaus are similarly less obvious because harmonic stability is immediately weakened by the coloristic and expressive use of chromatically altered tones. Felix composed the piece for his younger brother, Paul Hermann (1813–1874), who was an amateur cellist. Paul, incidentally, was entrusted by Felix's widow with the task of editing the various manuscript compositions that remained in the composer's estate.[17] He also edited and published a good deal of Felix's correspondence with members of the immediate family.

The Sonata in D major, Op. 58, was dedicated to Count Matwej Jurjewitsch Wielhorski (1794–1866). Wielhorski's musical activities were extensive, and as a young man he studied cello with Bernhard Heinrich Romberg (1767–1841). In a comparison with the Sonata in B-flat, Op. 45, the D-major Sonata has been described as "a bigger, more grandiose work in four movements."[18] Mendelssohn characteristically preferred the three-movement design in his ensemble sonatas. Although the B-flat Sonata contains four sets of double-bar lines, the tempo indications of the "four movements" are Allegro assai vivace; Allegretto scherzando; Adagio; and Molto Allegro e vivace. The Adagio, in the key of G major utilizes instrumental recitative. The piano part is generally homophonic, again suggesting the texture of recitative. The keyboard writing bears numerous instructions for coloristic effects, such as *arpeggiando col Pedale*, *una corda*, and *tutte le corde*, in addition to the standard sorts of dynamic instructions. The final, and perhaps most significant instruction, is the indication *attacca subito*. The movement that follows opens on a fully-diminished seventh-chord in the key of D major and concludes in the tonic key, B-flat major; thus, Op. 58 is better understood as a three-movement structure with a slow introduction to the last movement.

TWO LATE MASTERPIECES

In 1845, Mendelssohn composed two of his finest chamber works, the String Quintet in B-flat major, Op. 87, and the Piano Trio in C minor, Op. 66. In its rich textures, Op. 87 suggests orchestral writing. The second viola is used in places to double the cello part an octave higher, and double stops are plentiful in all four movements.

The first movement, Allegro vivace, features the first violin against tremolando chords in the lower four string parts. Though the movement is written in sonata form, Mendelssohn's approach to that form is more liberal than in his early works. The exposition, which continues up to measure 126, opens with a bold arpeggio figure in the first violin. The principal theme tumbles into triplet figuration that suggests a customary transition section by force of its harmonic mobility; nevertheless, all of this rhythmic and harmonic motion ultimately returns to the key of B-flat major and a repetition of the opening arpeggio figure in measure 41. A contrasting theme in F major is introduced in measure 53. The *forte* dynamic is replaced with *piano;* the subdivision of the beat into eighth notes is replaced with more deliberate quarter-note motion; and the diatonic arpeggios are abandoned in favor of chromatically colored imitations; nevertheless, the theme was suggested earlier in the quarter-note figure that appeared in the first violin part in measures 11 and 12. The exposition is not repeated, nor is it set off from the second half of the piece by the conventional double-bar line. The recapitulation (*fortissimo,* meas. 226), is rewritten with the principal theme now in the second violin, while the tonic chord supporting the theme is placed in first inversion in order to preserve the forward motion created by the descending bass line. The coda (meas. 350) combines the triplet figuration in the first violin with the final appearance of the arpeggio theme in the second violin. Double stops in all parts save the cello line produce a rich, eight-part texture in the last several bars, and bring the movement to a triumphant close.

The inner movements are two of Mendelssohn's finest. The Andante scherzando is a melodious affair in duple compound meter and set in the relative minor key. Its simplicity is interrupted from time to time with imitative passages—all easy to follow since Mendelssohn begins the figure with a trill and spaces the imitations at the distance of a single bar. The Adagio e lento movement begins in D minor, but gives way to the major mode of that key in the last seventeen measures. Though the first violin is the principal melodic voice, motifs from the main themes frequently migrate to the lower strings. The accompanimental figuration is pervaded by throbbing sixty-fourth and thirty-second notes, Lombardic rhythm, frequent double stops, and dramatic tremolandos that ultimately die away in a *tranquillo* closing.

The arpeggiated main theme and the first-inversion sonority of the first movement's exposition provided Mendelssohn with the opening theme of the finale, which outlines a descending B-flat major triad, but now decorated by neighboring tones within a brilliant cascade of sixteenth notes. Mendelssohn's use here of rondo form includes several statements of the refrain that are actually subtle variants of the original.

The C-minor Piano Trio, Op. 66, was completed in April 1845. When published a year later, it bore a dedication to Louis Spohr. In its formal structure, the piece is quite conservative. The four movements consist of a sonata, a tuneful slow movement reminiscent of his "songs without words," a delicate scherzo, and a rondo finale.

The thematic construction of the piece is fascinating. The opening piano theme appears in diminution as a countersubject to a second theme that Mendelssohn introduces in the strings while still in the tonic key. In his discussion of this piece, Basil Smallman notes several distinctive features: The second theme of the fourth movement later appears in augmentation as the third theme; this augmented version of the theme closely resembles the Lutheran chorale melody, *Gelobet seist du, Jesu Christ.* In addition, "The composer restricts the piano's role quite considerably in his search for a more homogeneous texture."[19]

Mendelssohn was one of the most influential musicians of the early nineteenth century. His reputation was an international one. As a composer, pianist, and conductor too, he was much in demand—particularly in England. It was for the Philharmonic Society of London that he composed his Fourth Symphony (1833). Shortly after his death, the "Mendelssohn Scholarship" funds were put in place, and the youthful Arthur Sullivan won that prize in 1856. Indeed, the pages of Sullivan's First Symphony are a tribute to the Mendelssohnian style from the first bar of the opening movement to the final fermata of the last. In his native land, Mendelssohn's work as a conductor and as founder and director of the Leipzig Conservatory was complemented by his unflagging support and encouragement for his friend and colleague Robert Schumann.

THE CHAMBER MUSIC OF ROBERT SCHUMANN

Schumann's first personal contact with Mendelssohn took place at the home of Carl and Henriette Voigt shortly after Mendelssohn's debut with the Gewandhaus Orchestra.[20] Mendelssohn frequently performed Schumann's compositions, and he "had a profound influence in advising him what kind of music to write and how." They became close friends in a short time. They regularly discussed "fairly private matters, including their dreams, their childhoods, and their feelings about mutual friends and acquaintances. Schumann (1810–1856) also spoke with Mendelssohn about marriage."[21] They shared an enthusiasm for the music of Johann Sebastian Bach, and Mendelssohn's performance of the *St. Matthew Passion* in Berlin in 1829 did much to enhance Bach's reputation in the nineteenth century. Later, in Leipzig, Mendelssohn conducted the work in 1841, again with great success. Subsequent concerts that Mendelssohn gave with the Gewandhaus Orchestra and as organ soloist at the Thomaskirche drew additional interest. Schumann pressed the *Neue Zeitschrift für Musik* into service for Bach scholarship, and, in 1850, he joined forces with Carl Friedrich Becker (1804–1877), Otto Jahn (1813–1869), Moritz Hauptmann (1792–1868), and the firm of Breitkopf und Härtel to form the Bach Gesellschaft (Bach society), which published the complete works of Bach in forty-six volumes. Schumann's fascination with Bach's music had far-reaching consequences. Not only did Schumann compose a set of six fugues using B, A, C, H (i.e., B-flat, A, C, B-natural) as a subject, but also, he developed great facility in using contrapuntal textures.[22]

Though Mendelssohn was only a year older than Schumann, the former man's career as a composer was already well under way in 1835, whereas the latter had composed rather little. Schumann's significant scores to that date included *Papillons*, finished in 1831, while 1835 saw the completion of the First Piano Sonata and *Carnaval*. He had founded the *Neue Zeitschrift für Musik* in 1834, and he was active as its editor and principal music critic until 1844.

Schumann was in the habit of using pseudonyms for the articles he wrote for the *Zeitschrift*. His quiet, thoughtful, and introspective writings were attributed to a figure named "Eusebius." The spontaneous outbursts of a youthful and energetic mind, on the other hand, were signed with the name "Florestan." These noms de plume appear not only in his prose writings, but also as cryptograms in his music.

Schumann was an eccentric individual. His maturity was an alternation between bursts of creative energy and fits of despair and depression; perhaps the duality of Schumann's own personality provided him with the imaginary figures Eusebius and Florestan. Schumann composed with ease during his periods of contentment, but when depressed, he produced little.

In January 1854, he suffered a mental breakdown and sought psychiatric aid. Ultimately, he died in a mental asylum in Endenich, near Bonn. In his last letter to his wife Clara Wieck Schumann (1819–1896), he sent "a drawing of Felix Mendelssohn . . . [to] put it into the Album. A priceless memento!"[23] That Schumann's final thoughts turned to his old friend and colleague demonstrates how highly he valued Mendelssohn's artistic insights and personal trust.

Schumann seems to have explored musical genres in a systematic way, as though perfecting one medium before progressing to the next. Chamber music was the focus of his attention during 1842. He had written a Piano Quartet in C minor as early as 1829, but he neither published it nor sought to have it performed. Apparently he composed no other chamber pieces until 1842.

Mendelssohn's string quartets, Op. 44, were partly responsible for Schumann's renewed interest in chamber music. Soon after their appearance, Schumann mentioned the idea of writing some quartets of his own to Clara. She asked him the simple but important question: "Do you know enough about the instruments."[24] Schumann decided that he did not, and so, the quartet project was held off until 1842. In the meantime, Schumann studied orchestration, and he actually began to learn how to play the violin.

The three quartets of Schumann's Op. 41 were dedicated to Mendelssohn. Given Mendelssohn's own devotion to the even-handed, sanguine formal designs of the Classical masters, it is hardly surprising that Schumann's quartets seem quite self-consciously to perpetuate the pattern forms of the later eighteenth century.

> Schumann's studies [of Haydn, Mozart, and Beethoven] . . . led him to extract general structural principles and apply them thoroughly within his own music, so that his sonata-form movements, in particular, unfold with a textbook clarity that is scarcely to be found in any "real" classical music.[25]

Schumann began his quartets of Op. 41 during the month of June "in a whirlwind of enthusiasm, sometimes beginning a new movement of one quartet before he had even finished the preceding quartet."[26] His birthday was on the eighth of that month, and by June 22, he had completed the A-major Quartet, which appeared in third place in the original publication. The first performance of the three quartets took place on 13 September 1842, the day on which Clara Schumann celebrated her twenty-third birthday.

The pieces were composed in rapid succession and exhibit certain melodic, rhythmic, and harmonic similarities, such as the singular pertinacity of the tonalities of F and A—both in the major and minor modes—throughout the three quartets. The First Quartet opens with an introduction in A minor (Andante espressivo) that leads to a sonata-form movement in F major (Allegro) beginning in measure 34. Paul Griffiths has noted that this tonal plan was used earlier but in reverse by Chopin in his Second Ballade.[27] Though usually placed in second position within sonata-allegro movements, the lyrical theme appears first in Chopin's piece (in the key of F major). Chopin relocates the transition to the secondary key (A minor) to the conclusion of the exposition, where it leads to a drastically abbreviated restatement of the exposition's polarization of F major and A minor. Following the development section, the recapitulation states the furious A-minor theme first. In the virtuosic coda, a ruined fragment of the opening lyrical melody, now transposed from the key of F to A and changed in mode from major to minor appears in the final measures of the piece. This Ballade is one of the most ingenious and original applications of sonata form in the pages of early Romantic music.

That Schumann knew Chopin's Ballade is clear: Chopin dedicated the piece to him. What is most remarkable is the fact that the Ballade is almost prophetic of Schumann's life, for it contains in its opening F-major theme the essence of the gentle poet and quiet thinker, Eusebius, while the A-minor figuration (marked *con fuoco*) embodies in its unsettled rhythms and aggressive character the person of Florestan. In the duel between these diametrically opposed personae, the delicacy of Eusebius is ultimately crushed by the reckless brutality of Florestan.

Whereas Chopin's Ballade is a single continuous movement beginning in F major and concluding in A minor, Schumann's Quartet is in four distinct movements, each separated by double-bar lines. Schumann's piece begins in A minor and ends in A major. This shift represents a change of mode, but not of tonality. At the same time, the principal tonality of the first movement is F major, not A minor. The second movement, a Scherzo with a contrasting Intermezzo, is in A minor. The third movement (Adagio) fluctuates between two tonal centers, D minor and F major; but the latter key ultimately wins out. The finale, which is a sonata-form movement, begins in A minor but concludes in the major mode.

The structural function of the first movement's introduction is curious. It is not uncommon for introductions to skirt around the main key of the movement to follow. In Classical compositions, the key of the dominant was regularly used for this purpose. Composers of the Romantic era often replaced the tonic-dominant axis with polarized tonalities arranged in thirds. What is so puzzling about this quartet, though, is the fact that in moving from the first to the fourth movement, we progress from F major to A major. On the basis of this information, we might conjecture that the introduction in A minor was actually added by Schumann after the four large movements were completed in order to bring the cycle into conformity with the tradition of beginning and ending an instrumental piece in the same key; however, this hypothesis seems unlikely since the nature of the first movement's principal theme is such that it would not be suitable as an opening. In short, though we may call it the "principal" theme of the sonata form, it does not possess the character of an opening theme.

Despite the unusual tonal design of Schumann's quartet, it is, in some respects, strikingly conservative. The first movement, in 6/8 meter, uses sonata form in the traditional manner. The exposition, which is to be repeated, contains two tonal levels with contrasting themes associated with each. The principal theme begins with a dotted quarter-note tied over the middle of the bar and then descends by step through the interval of a third. The secondary key (C major) and its concomitant theme are introduced in measure 99. This theme, though contrasting, is related to the opening motif, since the new theme begins with the same rhythmic motif, but it proceeds in the opposite direction from the first theme. An interesting countersubject consisting of iambic figures punctuated by eighth-note rests is also introduced at this point. The development and recapitulation sections proceed in a straightforward manner.

The regularity of formal detail within the individual movements of Schumann's quartets is perhaps best understood in light of the dedication to Mendelssohn, who was a champion of old traditions. Schumann's romanticism may have been tempered by the particularly Classical approach that Mendelssohn used in his own quartets of Op. 41. Schumann's emulation of Mendelssohn's quartets is also apparent in subtle details in the set of three quartets. For example, Mendelssohn's scherzos were not always in triple meter. Similarly, Schumann's scherzo in Op. 41, No. 1 substitutes 6/8 meter for simple triple meter. Likewise, the Intermezzo that takes the place of the conventional trio is in *alla breve*. Moreover, the very term *Intermezzo* may have been borrowed from Mendelssohn, since he replaced the minuet and trio with an intermezzo in his Piano Quartet in F minor, Op. 2. Finally, it was characteristic for Schumann to imbue his compositions with subtle allusions to persons, places, and events that were important to him. This proclivity can be seen in his Op. 1, the Theme and Variations on the Name "Abegg," the *Carnaval*, Op. 9, the Six Fugues on the Name of BACH, Op. 60, and many other pieces that employ cryptograms. It may be that Schumann hoped to make the dedication of his quartets to Mendelssohn the more meaningful by consciously imitating his friend's compositional manner.

An interesting musical allusion in the scherzo of Schumann's First Quartet is a borrowing from the music of Heinrich Marschner (1795–1861), a composer little known to present-day audiences, but who enjoyed an international reputation during his lifetime largely on account of his thirteen operas. Of these, *Der Vampyr* (1827) and *Hans Heiling* (1832) were the most popular. Though he made his livelihood as a stage composer and conductor in Dresden and Leipzig, he also wrote a substantial amount of chamber music, including piano quartets and trios, duets for violin and piano, music for piano four hands, and string quartets. In his study of the piano trio as a genre, Basil Smallman notes that "Schumann wrote a particularly favourable review of Marschner's G minor [piano] trio [Op. 111] in the *Neue Zeitschrift für Musik*" and further that Schumann "apparently took its scherzo as the model for the equivalent movement in his own A minor string quartet, Op. 41, No. 1."[28]

The Adagio of Schumann's First Quartet is one of his finest efforts in any medium. The recitative-like opening in D minor gives way to a movement in which slow-moving themes in half notes are played against syncopated figures in sixteenth notes, convoluted with ties. The first and second violins introduce the disjunct, angular, slow theme (doubled at the octave) while the cello plays an ascending, stepwise figure against more active viola figuration. In the course of the movement, the roles are reversed: the first violin line becomes the cello part (m. 20) and the viola plays the ascending, stepwise figure but now beneath the sixteenth-note movement in the first violin part. A transposed permutation of a similar type appears in measures 41 and following. The movement is rounded off by a reappearance of the opening recitative with a subtle extension of the passage in the viola part. The contrapuntal texture of this movement may have been intended as a simultaneous act of homage to Mendelssohn and Bach.

The finale, marked presto, is a terse sonata form in A minor with the secondary theme appearing in measure 63 (with the instruction *marcatissimo*) in the key of C major. The recapitulation (m. 218) enriches the material of the exposition with double and triple stops, doublings, and downward transpositions of an octave that create a rich, almost orchestral sonority. Noteworthy, too, are the thematic transformations of the secondary theme that appear in measure 238 and following. Again, contrapuntal devices are at work, and the cello part (m. 247) bears a paraphrase of the inversion of the secondary theme. It may well be the polyphonic ingenuity of this quartet that led Schumann to place it as the first in the set.

The Second Quartet in Op. 41, in F major, commences with a sonata-form movement (Allegro vivace) that is unusual in several respects: the opening theme appears in the first violin, but is subjected to developmental treatment (i.e., *stretto* between the second violin and the first) already in measures 33 and following of the exposition; further, Schumann hardly can be said to have provided the conventional secondary and closing themes. The exposition terminates with a canonic passage that leads to a closing motif in pairs of slurred eighth-notes. The development section is cleverly introduced by an Italian-sixth sonority that gives way to motivic manipulations of the opening theme. The recapitulation is literal at first. In this fashion, Schumann leads us into a false sense of security; however, the slurred eighth-notes of the closing motif appear, quite surprisingly, in the key of C. In another fascinating *léger de main*, Schumann employs the canonic imitations—now placed after rather than before the closing motif—in order to return to the tonic key of F major. At this point, the closing motif is stated in the "correct" key, and the movement proceeds to a satisfying close.

The lyric, second movement, in 12/8 time, is cast in the third-related key of A-flat major and bears the legend Andante, quasi Variazioni (slow, *as if* variations). The instruction is a puzzling one, because the movement clearly *is* a set of five variations with a coda. Schumann's trepidation in committing to the term *variation* stems from several unorthodox features of the movement. The theme is curious because of its length: thirty-two measures of this 112-measure movement. Bizarre, too, is the antiphonal construction of the theme. The melody is not a continuous one; instead, the tune regularly halts for half-measure intervals during which the inner voices either continue or echo important motifs; syncopations appear in one voice or another in every single measure. As the statement of the theme progresses, these syncopations become more prevalent, and beginning in measure 16, they are ubiquitous. Schumann calls attention to the pervasive nature of these syncopations with the performance instruction *un poco marcato* (which, incidentally, should probably appear in the first violin part in measure 20).

In conventional variations of the Classical era, each variation retained the harmonic design and phrase structure of the original, and a rhythmic crescendo was often employed in progressing from one variation to the next. In variations of this sort, the pulse remains the same, but the subdivision becomes ever smaller, moving, for example, from a theme in quarter notes, to a variation in eighth notes, to another in triplets, to a third in sixteenth notes, and so on. Schumann avoids this conventional rhythmic design; instead, the central variation in his set of five bears the tempo indication Molto più lento. This variation is a mere twelve measures long—shorter than the original theme. Here, the variation's fluid tempo and its concomitant reduction in length (by measures) show why Schumann was reluctant to head the movement with the designation *variations*. The design of this third variation shows that Schumann thought in terms of the duration perceived by the listener rather than in terms of symmetrical numbers of measures.

The above-cited eccentricities may account for Schumann's use of the term *quasi;* but he was not the first composer who included this alluring word in his performance instructions. As a pianist, Schumann could hardly have forgotten the most notorious "quasi" piece in the repertoire: Beethoven's Op. 27, No. 2, the famous *Moonlight Sonata*, which the composer called a *Sonata quasi una fantasia*.

Schumann derived his metrical plan for the Quartet movement from the Sonata's first movement. Beethoven's Adagio sostentuo is notated in cut time with triplet subdivisions of each beat and corresponds to Schumann's use of 12/8 time. The form of Schumann's Quartet movement likewise shows a debt to Beethoven's sonata, which is cast in an A-B-A form, with the A sections distinguished by a melody consisting of a dotted-rhythm pickup leading to a sustained note. The brief central portion takes place over a G-sharp pedal point, and the rhythmic movement of its melody consists of even quarter-notes drawn from a texture of triplet arpeggios. Schumann's movement parodies the A-B-A form of Beethoven's: The theme and the second variation are restated in altered form as the fifth variation and coda. The first variation, which acts as an interlude, is not accounted for in Schumann's varied restatement of the A section. The central portion, variations three and four, are set apart from the surrounding material by new tempo indications: Molto più lento and Un poco più vivace respectively.

As we have already remarked, syncopations appear in every measure of Schumann's variations, and, in many cases, these syncopations are in more than one voice. The source of this idea is close at hand: The second movement of Op. 27, No. 2, the minuet and trio (Allegretto) exhibits this same preoccupation with syncopated figures. Beethoven's Trio also contains a syncopation in every single measure. Perhaps Schumann's use of the word *quasi* in describing his variations was intended as an allusion to his model. If so, the hidden message would have been understood by Mendelssohn.

Schumann's Scherzo is an A-B-A form expanded by a coda of twenty-five measures. The arpeggio figures that serve as the principal subject of the C-minor Scherzo are of pianistic origin. One might again think of Beethoven's *Moonlight Sonata* as the inspiration, for its last movement is nothing more than an etude devoted to arpeggios played at lightning speed. Another curious feature of Schumann's Scherzo is the fact that its C-major Trio is actually in 2/4 meter. As we know, Mendelssohn was also fond of scherzos in meters other than simple triple time.

As we have pointed out in our discussion of Beethoven's chamber music, he was fond of employing expanded scherzo-and-trio form, with either an A: || BA: || form or a real five-section design that might be represented A-B-A-B-A. The coda of Schumann's Scherzo seems to take these formal plans as a point of departure for an interesting twist: the duple meter and characteristic thematic material of the Trio reappear; however, the 6/8 theme of the Scherzo section is intertwined with these musical gestures so that we have, in effect, a fully stated A-B-A plan with simultaneous, abbreviated restatements of B and A in the coda.

The finale of the F-major Quartet is a concise, sonata-allegro form (the recapitulation appears at the *a tempo* designation). It is, perhaps, an anachronistic feature that both halves of the binary form are repeated. Less conventional is the introduction of a descending scalar motif for the cello in the concluding measures of the development section (recalled later in the coda) which treats this motif imitatively—first in contrary motion between cello and first violin, and then in the two violins played off against the lower two strings. The prodigal use in the coda of double stops in all parts gives the conclusion of the piece a confident, assertive character.

The Third Quartet, in A major, is the most innovative. It commences with a seven-measure introduction (Andante espressivo) that contains several musical gestures that Schumann exploits during the course of this sonata-form movement. The interval of a falling fifth figures in the introduction as well as in the opening theme of the movement proper (Allegro molto moderato). The falling-fifth motif appears in the cello part in the concluding measure of the movement. Similarly, the rhythmic figure of a dotted eighth plus sixteenth (which appears at the end the first measure of the first violin part) forms an essential building block for the thematic material of all four movements. Schumann's introduction obscures the principal tonality of the piece by circling around the secondary dominant of A major, rather than elaborating the dominant chord of the home key. Indeed, as the Allegro portion begins, we hear a secondary-dominant-seventh cord in first inversion that wends its way to a firm cadence in A major three measures later. The cadence, incidentally, is delayed by a 4-3 suspension in the viola part.

The cello part is pitched unusually high throughout the movement. Curious, too, is the secondary theme in the key of C-sharp minor. The terse development section is followed by an unusual recapitulation (again, signaled by the indication *a tempo*) that reverses the order of themes as they had appeared in the exposition. This palindromic reprise dispenses with much of the music that had been heard in the first key area of the exposition, presumably owing to the fact that these ideas had already been treated in the development section.

The second movement (Assai agitato), in 3/8 time, is in the key of F-sharp minor. It is a hybrid one containing the characteristic triple meter and rhythmic drive of a scherzo; yet, formally, it is a set of four variations with a coda that offers an array of harmonic surprises. The theme—or, at least, the material that occupies the first forty-eight measures—is tuneful, but somewhat disconcerting owing to the fact that the melodic movement is riddled with syncopations. The first variation, which continues at the opening pace, is a polyphonic elaboration of a motif. This segment of forty-eight measures has the character of an old canzona. The second variation (L'istesso tempo) shifts to 2/4 meter and presents a more serious, ricercar-like series of imitations. The third variation, returning to 3/8 time, is marked Un poco Adagio. Here, for the first time, we can perceive the theme that has only been hinted at up to this point.

The final variation (Tempo risoluto), in 3/4 meter, is expansive and assertive, but shorter than any of the previous variations. The abbreviated variation leads to a coda of striking harmonic density. While the first violin toys with the intervals of fifths and fourths falling in a cascade from F^2, the inner voices move chromatically through a series of harmonic excursions that involve alternately the lowered and natural forms of the third of the tonic chord. Ultimately, the major form of the triad wins out. An interesting detail may be seen in the final measure of the first violin part, where the interval of an ascending fourth appears. This is not only a key motif in the main theme of the movement as it appears in the third variation, but also, the inversion of the descending fifth heard in the cello part at the conclusion of the first movement.

The third movement (Adagio molto) is in common time and the key of D major. It is one of Schumann's most complex inner movements. Two themes dominate the piece. The first, (Assai agitato), mostly in conjunct motion, is marked *sempre espressivo*, and exhibits the sort of plaintive melody familiar to us from Schumann's songs like "Seit ich ihn geseh'n," from *Frauenliebe und Leben*. The second theme is actually a six-note motif rather than a genuine melody, but the six notes are not all presented straightaway. Instead, Schumann prefigures the full statement of the motif with two- and three-note figures derived from it. These figures give unity to the quartet as a whole because they incorporate the intervals of rising fourths and falling fifths heard in earlier movements. Throughout the third movement, the two themes appear in various keys and with subtly modified figuration. The supple rhythmic figures in the inner voices—seldom repeated in exactly the same fashion—are particularly striking. The movement, though not a strict sonata form, includes a recapitulation when the principal theme returns (*espressivo*) harmonized with a first-inversion D-major triad. Here the bass line, originally played *arco* by the cello, is thoroughly rewritten with flowing, triplet filigree.

The finale, marked Allegro molto vivace and in cut time, is one of Schumann's most energetic creations. The opening theme is characterized by syncopated figures and lively, dotted rhythms. Because of its distinctive profile, this opening idea is easily recognized at each appearance—and it reappears six times. Though some commentators have associated this recurring material with rondo form, the movement lacks the symmetrical plan and tonal stability of a conventional rondo.[29] Instead, we might prefer to think in terms of Baroque *ritornello* structures, which allowed abbreviation, transposition, and fragmentation.

Schumann's formal plan might be designated with the letters A-B-A-C-A-D-A-B-A-C-A-D'-A-Coda. With the exception of transposition, the repetitions of the B and C sections preserve the original material. The D section, however, which was marked *Quasi Trio* at its first appearance, is significantly altered at its return. The triplet figuration and repeat signs are dropped, and the material is transposed from F major to E major. In the course of the varied restatement, E major assumes the role of dominant, and the last eight measures of the second Trio are cast in A major, thereby effecting a smooth transition to the final statement of the refrain. The coda derives from the vigorous dotted rhythms of the *ritornello* and the repeated-note triplets of episode C.

SCHUMANN'S CHAMBER MUSIC AFTER THE QUARTETS

In discussing the Quartets of Op. 41, we have noted a number of similarities to well-known pieces by Classical masters. Most of these models were to be found in works for solo piano. After completing Op. 41, Schumann never returned to the string quartet as a medium for his chamber music. Schumann's later chamber scores are remarkably diverse, but they invariably include piano. These later works include both large-scale pieces in three or four movements in traditional pattern forms as well as collections of miniatures arranged as instrumental cycles.

The large-scale works include the three piano trios: one in D minor,

Op. 63 (1847), another in F major, Op. 80 (1847), and the G-minor Trio, Op. 110 (1851).[30] In addition, there are the three sonatas for violin and piano: A minor, Op. 105; D minor, Op. 121 (both 1851); and the posthumous A-minor Sonata, which uses two movements Schumann wrote in 1853 for a collaborative work including movements by Johannes Brahms and Albert Dietrich and dedicated to Joseph Joachim.

The strengths of Schumann's piano trios are their rich and inventive use of contrapuntal textures, their ingenious and varied formal designs, and their integration of cyclic procedures and thematic transformation to achieve continuity. They sometimes suffer from overscoring of the piano part, unnecessary doublings, and excessive unison passages in which the violin part is duplicated by the piano.

Schumann's chamber music miniatures include the Adagio and Allegro in A-flat, Op. 70 (1849), for horn and piano; the Fantasy Pieces (*Fantasiestücke*), Op. 73 (1849), for clarinet and piano; the four Fantasy Pieces (*Fantasiestücke*), Op. 88 (1842), for piano, violin and cello; Three Romances, Op. 94 (1849), for piano and oboe; Five Pieces in Folk Style, Op. 102 (1849), for cello and piano, the four Fairy-tale Pictures (*Märchenbilder*), Op. 113 (1851), for piano and viola, and the four Fairy-tales (*Märchenerzählungen*), Op. 132 (1853) for piano, viola, and clarinet.

THE PIANO QUINTET IN E-FLAT, OP. 44

The most important work written after the string quartets is the Quintet in E-flat, Op. 44, for piano and strings. Schumann composed it concurrently with his Quartet, Op. 47, for piano and strings, which is also in E-flat. Both date from Schumann's "chamber music year," 1842. The Quintet was begun in September. While that score was still in progress, Schumann set to work on the Quartet and completed it in less than a week.[31]

The Quintet has become a staple of chamber music literature on account of its attractive melodic ideas, its rhythmic energy, and its unambiguous yet original formal designs. The piece is dedicated to Clara Schumann, and so the piano part is demanding; however, Schumann did not capitalize upon his wife's virtuosity at the expense of the collaborating instruments.

Robert had arranged for a private performance on 6 December at the home of Carl and Henriette Voigt. Owing to Clara's indisposition on that occasion, a substitute pianist was called in at the last moment: Felix Mendelssohn. He played the piece at sight and with great success. Later, he suggested to Schumann some revisions that were incorporated into the second trio of the scherzo.[32]

After Clara's recovery, she quickly took the Quintet into her repertoire and performed it at a private *matinée* on 8 January 1843. Subsequently, Clara played the piece whenever possible.[33] Her high estimation of the Quintet is also confirmed by the fact that Johannes Brahms, in anticipation of Clara's thirty-fifth birthday in 1854, arranged it as a four-hand piano piece.[34]

The first movement, marked Allegro brillante, demonstrates the musical genius of Schumann's alter egos, Florestan and Eusebius. The grandiose, energetic principal theme of this sonata-form movement is very similar that of Prince Louis Ferdinand's Piano Quintet, which must have served as a model for him both in instrumentation and specific musical details.

Schumann's indebtedness to the prince is apparent not only the intervallic and rhythmic structures of his themes, but also in the way Schumann distributes the themes over the course of the movement. Note in both pieces, for example, the several repetitions of the upward-leaping opening motif before it progresses to the transition. Equally conspicuous is the return of this motif immediately before the development section in both pieces. The fact that Schumann, like the prince, elects to repeat the exposition is quite remarkable in a composition of this vintage. (No such repetition appears in the first movement of the Piano Quartet, Op. 47.) Obviously, both Louis Ferdinand's Quintet and Schumann's have a key signature of three flats.

Schumann develops his principal theme immediately, and the opening eight-measure period concludes with an elided cadence introducing the first transformation of the subject. The motivic figures in the transition to the secondary theme, in the key of B-flat, stem from the opening theme. The development section begins with an unmistakable reiteration of the opening theme, but also, the eighth-note figuration in the keyboard part is a motif extracted from the theme and treated in diminution.

The soulful second theme first appears in the piano part with the dynamic instruction *piano* and the affective indication *dolce.* Here, we encounter both the tender heart of Eusebius and his wisdom as well; when the stringed instruments enter, they echo the secondary theme not only in its original guise, but also in a freely paraphrased inversion. Schumann's contrapuntal ingenuity is apparent throughout the Quintet, and even the most effusive Romantic melody has been crafted from the outset with an eye toward its potential for polyphonic manipulation.

The recapitulation, marked *a tempo* and *fortissimo,* contains some subtle modifications of the expository material—aside from the customary transpositions. Note, for example, how the accompanimental figuration in the

Piano Quintet, Op. 44

Robert Schumann

Allegro brillante 𝅗𝅥 = 108

first transformation of the theme (meas. 9–16) has been rewritten although the melodic structures have been retained intact (meas. 217–24). Similarly, the prefatory measures in the piano part (marked *dolce* and *piano*) just before the restatement of the secondary theme (m. 265) have been equipped with *arpeggiando* signs, thereby creating a completely different effect. (The arpeggios should be completed *before* the beat so that the principal melodic tone is reached at the downbeat of the measure.)

The second movement, which bears the indication *In modo d'una marcia* and the tempo indication *Un poco largamente*, drops to the relative minor. Whereas the contrasting moods of the opening movement had given the greater voice to Florestan, this funeral march is dominated by the melancholy of Eusebius. There is no historical information suggesting that this funeral march was precipitated by a particular event that befell Schumann or his intimates. Instead, the piece seems to be a concert funeral march of the sort written by Beethoven and Chopin.

The opening strain of Schumann's march presents a lugubrious theme in C minor with repeated notes punctuated by rhetorical pauses. A contrasting section in C major follows. Here, the first violin bears the main theme (*espressivo ma sempre piano*)—one of Schumann's most tearful confessions. This lyrical statement moves for the most part in half notes, the common denominator between the eighth-note subdivision of the beat in the lower strings and the quarter-note triplets in the piano part. This tranquil interlude concludes with a return to the opening funeral march figure in C minor. Rhythmic and melodic transformations are introduced for the central *Agitato* section, which alternates between A-flat major and F minor in its first half, and then moves to F major in the second. The F-minor section contains the theme of the opening strain of the funeral march in the left-hand piano part. A particularly touching effect is achieved in the F-major section by the return of the expressive, first violin theme in half notes, now stated a fourth higher. The movement concludes with a return to the key of C minor and a greatly abbreviated recapitulation of the opening theme.

The second movement is a short rondo with three statements of the funeral march in the tonic key with two different episodes rather than the three episodes that we would find in a full rondo with four statements of the refrain.[35] Again, we must remark Schumann's single-minded pursuit of particular thematic gestures. The second episode, for instance (*Agitato*), contains an unnerving rhythmic figure using *sforzandos* on the second beats of the measures and alternating constantly between triplet and duplet groupings within the beat. This figure, stated in the piano part, is a rhythmic diminution of the second-inversion F-minor chord that appears in the opening funeral march theme.

The third movement is a double scherzo and trio in the tonic and in 6/8 meter. The most striking feature of this movement is its exploration of scalar patterns in all forms, ascending and descending, in all instruments. Noteworthy, too, is the use of 2/4 meter for the second Trio—the one added at the request of Mendelssohn. Harmonically, this portion of the movement recalls the significance of the keys of A-flat major and F minor in the preceding movement. An energetic coda brings the movement to a close.

It is hard to imagine how any composer could follow three movements exhibiting such depth, vitality, and pathos with a satisfactory closing movement. Indeed, Schumann was compelled to create one of the most remarkable hybrid formal designs for this purpose. His solution was a movement that is a combination of sonata and rondo forms. The movement is remarkable, too, owing to its tonal design: The third movement ends in an ebullient surge of unequivocal E-flat major tonality, but the fourth movement commences in C minor, thus recalling the tonal relationship between the first and second movements. A transitional motif leads to a restatement of the opening figure in G minor. A third motif, consisting of a scalar figure through the interval of a fourth, finally states the E-flat major tonality, but E-flat is not secure at this point. An excursion into the key of G major (meas. 44) provides the polarized tonal level of the conventional sonata form, but the principal motif in the piano part is simply the filled-in-fourth figure in yet another rhythmic diminution. Indeed, the entire movement consists of one thematic transformation after another.

The most important thematic feature of the Quintet's finale is the coda, where Schumann combines the principal theme of the first movement in augmentation with a major-mode version of the finale theme within a double fugue; hence, the theme of the first movement is not merely restated in the last movement, but it is integrated and developed in an organic way. The thematic recurrence is not simply ornamental: it is essential.

Schumann's use of thematic transformation, his carefully calculated tonal plans—both within the individual movements and in regulating multimovement sets—and his cyclic reuse of themes yield highly integrated and convincing music. His deft handling of traditional pattern forms shows that Schumann possessed the diversity of a chameleon. For him, the choice between writing sprawling, programmatic cycles of wildly contrasting and loosely related fantasy pieces or composing highly integrated scores regulated by long-range architectonic plans was precisely that: a choice. It is

Piano Quintet, Op. 44, iv, coda

Robert Schumann

15
Vln. I
Vln. II
Vla.
Vc.
Pno.
sf
sf
sempre f
sf
sf
sf
sf
sf

21
Vln. I
Vln. II
Vla.
Vc.
Pno.
ff
sf
sempre f
sf
sf
sf
sf

ironic that his music has been criticized for both features at various times. In any case, the Piano Quintet alone must set to rest the oft-repeated accusation that Schumann was unable to exercise adequate control of form in his musical compositions.[36]

JOHANNES BRAHMS AND "THE NEW GERMAN SCHOOL"

In assessing the compositional style of Brahms (1833–1897), it is important to realize that he had no sympathy for the "New German School" headed by Wagner and Liszt. Musically and personally, he was more compatible with Robert and Clara Schumann, whom he met on 1 October 1853. After Brahms played his compositions for them, each expressed unbounded praise. In her diary, Clara described him as "one of those who comes as if sent straight from God." She went on to say that his works showed "exuberant imagination, depth of feeling, and mastery of form." She further remarked that "his things are very difficult."[37] Robert expressed his reaction in the famous article "Neue Bahnen," in which "he hailed the twenty-year-old Brahms as the new messiah of music."[38]

Because of his conservative aesthetics, Brahms rarely indulged in "program music." Nor did he rely upon brilliant orchestration or unusual instrumentation to any great extent. His approach to composition was more akin to that of the Renaissance composer; he wrote contrapuntal lines forming interesting and often unusual harmonies. These lines were regulated by equally interesting rhythmic designs. If a line were in danger of becoming obscured by dense counterpoint, he might employ in it a rhythmic pattern at variance with the surrounding voices in order to bring it out.

Similarly, Brahms expressed no interest in the more colossal genres of romanticism: He wrote neither operas, nor ballets, nor tone poems. In his symphonies, too, he avoided musical storytelling as well as the prodigious ensembles employed by many other late-Romantic composers. Instead, his interests gravitated naturally toward the genres and forms of the Classicists—especially chamber music.

BRAHMS AND BACH

Like Mendelssohn and Schumann before him, Brahms was keenly interested in the works of Johann Sebastian Bach. This repertoire was gradually making its way into the mainstream of European musical life as a result of the efforts of the Bach Gesellschaft and some enlightened performers, like Brahms, who regularly included selections from Bach's oeuvre on their concert programs. We know, for example, that Brahms was familiar with the preludes and fugues of the *The Well-Tempered Klavier* as early as 1848, when he gave his first piano recital, and on it, played a Bach fugue. Such programming would have been considered "very severe and unfamiliar concert-fare for the time."[39]

Later in his career, Brahms became close personal friends with the Handel scholar Friedrich Chrysander and the Bach scholar Philipp Spitta—himself a prolific composer of chamber music. Eusebius Mandyczewski, a noted musicologist who eventually became the director of the Gesellschaft der Musikfreunde in Vienna, was also an intimate of Brahms's. Mandyczewski saw to it that Brahms received the new editions of the Bach, Handel, and Schütz works as the individual volumes of their collected works were published.[40] Undoubtedly, Brahms's interest in early music was one of the factors that cemented his friendship with the Schumanns. "Clara Schumann herself copied half a dozen pieces by Palestrina and [Johann] Eccard" for Brahms.[41] We know, too, that Brahms was on the editorial board of the Bach Gesellschaft; that he included a cantata by Bach on the first program he presented as conductor of the Vienna Singakademie; and that he made realizations of continuo parts for Spitta's performances of Bach's works.[42]

Brahms's interest in the music of Bach left its unmistakable imprint on his own. In some instances, we can even discern "parodies" of Bach's compositions. In a few of his early works, Brahms was actually led astray by his awe for the master of the Thomaskirche, and so, cramped the pages of his scores with fugues of a rather stiff and pedantic nature. As he matured and came to grips with Bach's monumental polyphonic art, Brahms achieved a mastery of counterpoint seldom encountered in music of the Romantic era.

BRAHMS'S CHAMBER WORKS OF THE FIRST PERIOD: 1853–1865

Brahms's chamber music can be organized into three chronological periods. The first ranges from 1853, the year in which the twenty-year-old composer contributed the Scherzo for a four-movement Sonata for violin and piano written in collaboration with Robert Schumann and Albert Dietrich in honor of the violinist Joseph Joachim (1831–1907), to the completion of the Trio in E-flat major, Op. 40, for piano, violin, and horn of 1865. For the next eight years, Brahms wrote no chamber music. The second period commences with the two String Quartets in C minor and A minor,

Op. 51 of 1873, and continues until 1882, when he completed his String Quintet in F major, Op. 88. A four-year silence ended in 1886, when Brahms composed the Sonata in F major, Op. 99, for cello and piano. His final chamber pieces, completed in 1894, were the Sonatas in F minor and E-flat major, Op. 120, Nos. 1 and 2, for clarinet (or viola) and piano.

Important works from the first period include the Piano Trio in B major, Op. 8 (1854), the String Sextet in B-flat major, Op. 18 (1859–60), the Piano Quartet in G minor, Op. 25 (1857–61), and another piano quartet, this one in A major, Op. 26 (composition date uncertain). Though it is difficult to generalize about these pieces, Brahms seems to have been having difficulty managing thematic and formal structures. "In the early period . . . the methods of development do not seem to penetrate deeply into the themes; and theme and developments are somewhat separate."[43]

The Piano Trio, Op. 8, was Brahms's first multimovement chamber score to appear in print. In his monograph on the chamber music of Brahms, Daniel Gregory Mason gives details of the premiere.

> It is one of the ironies of music history that the first work in Brahms's great series of twenty-four masterpieces of chamber music—the Trio in B major, opus 8—should have come to its first performance . . . in America. The date was Tuesday, November 27, 1855. The place was Dodsworth's Hall, New York, on Broadway, opposite Eleventh Street and one door above Grace Church. The players were Theodore Thomas, violin, then only twenty years old, Carl Bergmann, cello, and William Mason, piano, a young man of twenty-six. The program, recorded in Dr. Mason's "Memories of a Musical Life," closed with the Brahms Trio, announced as "Grand Trio in B major, opus 8." . . . Dr. Mason's understatement that the piece was then played "for the first time in America" is misleading; it should read, "for the first time in the world."[44]

The Brahms Trio closed the first of the "Mason and Bergmann" chamber music programs of the 1855–56 season. On this occasion, the hall was well populated and included reviewers from both the *New York Times* and the *New York Dispatch*. Their respective comments follow:

> The trio in B [major] by Mr. Brahms is an early work written, we believe, at the age of eighteen. With many good points, and much sound musicianship, it possesses also the usual defects of a young writer, among which may be enumerated length and solidarity. The motivos [*sic*] seldom fall on the ear freshly; they suggest something that has been heard before, and induce a skeptical frame of mind, not altogether just,

> for the composer evidently has ideas of his own. In the elaboration of these ideas he is frequently original, always correct, and generally too lengthy.
>
> The Brahms Trio is a composition in the ultra new school of which we may say briefly that we do not yet understand it. Whether this be due to our dullness of perception, or lack of appreciation, or the intricate character of the music, we do not pretend to say. . . . Yet we feel obliged to Messrs. Mason and Bergmann for the opportunity they afforded us for hearing and becoming acquainted with this peculiar and *outré* style of music.[45]

Brahms revised Op. 8 thoroughly in 1889, deleting about one-third of the score. The excisions are far-reaching in all movements except the Scherzo.[46] Some have argued in favor of preserving the original version of the Trio "as a work in its own right."[47] To some extent, this has been done in recent years, and several good recordings of the early version are currently available; nevertheless, the temptation to compare the two versions is irresistible. Mason puts his finger on one of the most striking features of the 1854 Trio that Brahms altered in the 1889 piece, namely, "the adoption of a second and a third theme which do nothing to afford contrast to the thetic rhythm of the first, but turn its weightiness to downright heaviness by their pitiless insistence on beat One."[48] The introduction of a fugue subject toward the conclusion of the exposition (meas. 98–103) is even more problematic. The model for this subject was apparently Bach's B-minor fugue (number 24) in the first volume of *Well-Tempered Klavier.* Both subjects are constructed largely of chromatic dyads, and both terminate with a trill figure. The Bachian subject employs all twelve tones of the chromatic gamut, while Brahms's subject encompasses only ten as a result of the omission of the tones E-natural and F-sharp.

Brahms introduces the subject in measure 98, but is at a loss to do anything significant with it. After a few imitations, the idea is dropped, and the development begins. In measure 354 of the recapitulation, the unwieldy subject reappears in the cello. Again, Brahms is unable to achieve the musical interest that he admired in the fugue from *Well-Tempered Klavier.* In the revised version of the Trio, he removed these passages.

That Brahms, in 1889, was able to identify weaknesses in a piece that he had composed thirty-five years earlier is not surprising, but the extensive revision of this Trio may have been motivated by additional considerations. It is generally known that Schumann was fond of embedding hidden messages in his compositions. At other times, Schumann made allusions to lit-

Fugue in B minor, WTC, Vol 1, No. 24 Johann Sebastian Bach

Piano Trio, B major, Op. 8, meas. 94-103 Johannes Brahms

[Allegro con moto]

erature or other extramusical concepts. Brahms was familiar with the musical motifs and pet names that Schumann used to depict his wife, Clara. The themes of the 1854 version of the Piano Trio, Op. 8, included many such musical allusions.

> Its obvious allusions . . . [are] to Schubert ("Am Meer," No. 12 of *Schwanengesang* [D. 744]) and Beethoven (*An die ferne Geliebte*) in the Adagio and finale respectively. The latter speaks plainly enough; the recurrent melody of "Nimm sie hin denn, diese Lieder" is synonymous with its usage in Schumann's Fantasy op. 17. In both works, as in Beethoven's song-cycle, the music is offered as humble homage to an unattainable beauty. So presumably the other quotation will also mean its words.

> [Also] in 1854, Clara was practicing and performing the fourth Beethoven piano concerto, which resounds from the trio's finale. . . .Clara . . . is apparently the theme of the whole work—sometimes too apparently, as Brahms may later have realized.[49]

It has been suggested as well that even the choice of key for the trio was significant:

> [In] Schumann's opera *Genoveva* . . . Siegfried marches off to the wars, leaving his wife to the all too tender care of his steward Golo. . . . Brahms would have good reason to be thinking of that opera in 1854, . . . [for it] was due to appear on the autumn concert-programmes. It contains one of the last, and not the least apt or moving, of Schumann's own B minor Clara-themes—at Siegfried's words to Golo "take care of my wife."[50]

It is significant that all of these allusions "without exception, were omitted by Brahms from his second version, which is presented as absolute music—telling no tales, betraying no secrets. The first version is all but forgotten; and this too seems likely to have been a conscious aim."[51]

It remains unclear whether Brahms removed these personal allusions because he feared that what were once arcane messages for the intimate members of the Schumann circle would be readily comprehended by any intelligent musician of the late nineteenth century, or simply because he felt that these musical themes failed to come together to form a convincing musical score. The 1854 version of the Piano Trio is clearly laden with difficulties—both formal and aesthetic—that the composer removed in the later version of the piece.

Brahms revised another early work, the Piano Quartet in G minor, Op. 25 (1857–58), in order to make the piece more concise. Most of these cuts were confined to the third movement.[52]

The String Sextet in B-flat, Op. 18, was begun in 1859 and finished the following year. By writing for pairs of violins, violas, and cellos, Brahms avoided the difficulties of treating a single cello simultaneously as a functional bass line and an active participant in the presentation and development of the motivic substance of the piece. In short, the two cellos function in a capacity analogous to the host and hostess at a dinner party: each must, at times, look after the logistics of the event; on the other hand, their teamwork affords opportunities to each for more relaxed participation in the general conversation.

The melodic importance of the cello part is apparent even in the opening measures of the piece, where the first cello states the opening theme.

This theme is typically Brahmsian in its construction, consisting of two five-measure phrases leading up to the entrance of the violins.

With the exception of the Trio in E-flat major, Op. 40, for piano, violin, and horn, the first movements of Brahms's chamber compositions are in sonata form. The realization of this design in the Sextet in B-flat is especially clear, and includes a secondary theme—again stated by the first cello—beginning in measure 84 in the key of the dominant. The closing theme, stated by the first violin (meas. 115), uses the same rhythm (dotted quarter, eighth, quarter) that Brahms had employed in the exposition in the transition to the second theme. The exposition is delineated by a double bar line and includes a repeat. The end of the exposition is heralded by the expansion of the texture to eleven parts through the lavish use of double and triple stops.

The development section is essentially harmonic, though in its course, references are made to all three themes of the exposition. The climax of the development is reached in measures 230–58, where a crescendo passage is complemented by an enriched texture of double and triple stops, syncopation, and exploration of the extreme registers of both the cello and the first violin. This tremendous tension melts away almost imperceptibly to the recapitulation (m. 269), now with a modified form of the theme in the second cello part.

Whereas the principal theme had initially been stated at *poco forte*, Brahms instructs that the recapitulation should be *piano*. More than forty measures of the first-theme music are dropped from Brahms's initial recapitulation; however, the balance is restored when the first cello returns to the opening theme in its pristine form (meas. 363) toward the end of the movement.

The second movement, Andante, ma Moderato, is a set of six variations. Five of the variations are in D minor, but the fourth shifts to the parallel major. Both the choice of key and the string figuration suggest the influence of Bach's D-minor Chaconne, a piece that Brahms arranged—quite faithfully—as a piano etude for left hand. Brahms himself arranged these variations for piano solo.[53]

The third movement, a scherzo in F major, and the fourth, a rondo in B-flat major, are textbook examples of these forms. Regarding the finale, one critic has gone so far as to say that "the regularity of its design is almost painfully orthodox."[54] I would suggest, however, that Brahms's strict adherence to Classical pattern forms as well as such subtle deviations from it as we have observed in the recapitulation of the first movement enabled him to produce in this Sextet the finest chamber score of his first period.

Joseph Joachim, who led the premiere on 20 October 1860 in Hanover, frequently played the piece during his long and productive career. Similarly, Clara Schumann noted in her diary that the first performance in Leipzig, given at the Conservatory, was a great success. The Sextet was also well received at its premiere in Hamburg, and the publication of the piece by Simrock soon came into great demand.

The four-movement String Sextet in G major, Op. 36, was composed in the years 1864–65. This work reverses the scheme of internal movements found in Op. 18, and places the scherzo as the second movement with a set of variations as the third. The two string sextets stand apart from the other chamber works of Brahms's first period since they exclude the piano. As we listen to his works with piano, we must remember that the instruments that he used were different from those typically found in present-day performances. From 1856 until shortly after his move to Vienna in 1871, Brahms used a grand piano built by Conrad Graf (1782–1851) and presented to Clara Schumann for her wedding in 1840. This piano, which Robert Schumann had used, was donated by Brahms to the Gesellschaft der Musikfreunde in 1873.[55] Thereafter, he used a grand piano built in 1868 by the firm of J. B. Streicher (1796–1871).

> When we ponder the two pianos we know Brahms owned during his productive career, we find that one was a typical Viennese grand of the late 1830's, the other a conservative one of the late 1860's. Neither was a truly modern piano, if the cross-strung, iron-framed Steinway is the touchstone of the modern piano. To hear Brahms's music on an instrument like the Streicher is to realize that the thick textures we associate with his work, the sometimes muddy chords in the bass and the occasionally woolly sonorities, come cleaner and clearer on a lighter, straight-strung piano. Those textures, then, are not a fault of Brahms's piano composition. To be sure, any sensitive pianist can avoid making Brahms sound murky on a modern piano. The point is that the modern pianist must strive to avoid that effect, must work at lightening the dark colors, where Brahms himself, playing his Streicher, did not have to work at it.[56]

The chamber pieces with piano dating from Brahms's first chamber music period—specifically the two Piano Quartets, Opp. 25 and 26, the Piano Quintet, Op. 34, and the Trio in E-flat, Op. 40—were composed with the sound of the Graf instrument in mind. (This was lighter still than the sound of the Streicher.) The most frequently performed of these works is the expansive Piano Quintet in F minor, completed in the fall of 1864. The "thunderous" character associated with this piece is, to some extent, an anachronism.[57]

The history of this Quintet is complex: The piece began as a four-movement quintet for two violins, one viola, and two cellos. Joseph Joachim critiqued this version in a letter of 26 May 1863 to Clara Schumann:

> [Brahms] was here [in Hanover] for three days . . . and I was able to have his Quintette played for him. It is a great pity that the general effect of this piece, in spite of so much that is remarkable in it, should be unsatisfactory, and I was glad that Johannes, on hearing it himself, wished to alter it. A man of his strong character cannot accept anything on hearsay.[58]

In the winter of 1863–64, Brahms rescored the piece for two pianos. This version was known subsequently as Op. 34b.[59] The final version for piano with string quartet was completed during the late summer or early autumn of 1864.

The first movement is in sonata form. It commences with a unison subject for piano, first violin, and cello in F minor. The secondary key, C-sharp minor, is established in measure 34. The tonal scheme is simply a pair of third-related keys, F minor and D-flat minor, with the latter respelled as C-sharp minor. The closing theme (m. 74) is in the parallel major key, D-flat major. Brahms calls for a repetition of the exposition—a welcome feature given its complexity.

The development section of about eighty measures is in two almost equal portions treating the first and second themes respectively. A restatement of the opening theme in diminution appears in the first violin (meas. 96). This rhythmically altered statement is taken up briefly by the second violin and viola. The secondary theme, with its characteristic cross-rhythms (meas. 136), contributes the main substance of the development's second portion. The closing theme is omitted altogether from the development.

The beginning of the recapitulation is difficult to pinpoint. Brahms drops the unison statement of the principal theme and rewrites the opening bars so that the piano accompaniment is the first material we recognize from the exposition; however, this figuration is not preceded by a clear-cut dominant chord; thus, the return to F minor is weakly represented despite the familiar figuration. Only in the pickup beat to measure 173 do we have an unambiguous dominant-seventh chord cadencing directly to the tonic key and the principal theme. The secondary theme merits only a passing reference in the recapitulation. Brahms focuses instead on the closing theme. An extended coda (meas. 261) with the tempo indication *Poco sostenuto* brings the movement to a close.

The second movement, a straightforward song-form in the key of E major (Andante, un poco Adagio), affords a respite from the dense first movement. Whereas the outer sections consist largely of melodies doubled at the intervals of a third or tenth, the themes of the central portion appear in parallel sixths. An interesting but subtle modification of the principal theme is made at its return in measure 83, where the right-hand piano part is exchanged for the first-violin line and vice versa.

The third movement is a scherzo in C minor. Its three main themes are highly distinctive, the first being a syncopated figure in 6/8 time, the second, a sharply dotted motif in 2/4 time, and the third, a full-fisted, chordal passage of dotted quarter-notes in 6/8 meter. The Trio section is a more relaxed affair in C major, but it, too, contains touches for the connoisseur, such as the shift to 2/4 meter occurring in measure 226. This detail establishes a rhythmic and formal link with the preceding scherzo section. Another remarkable feature of this passage is the use of invertible counterpoint. Note how the cello line in measures 226 to 233 becomes the right-hand piano part in measures 234 to 241; similarly, the right-hand piano part in measures 226 to 233 moves to the first violin in measures 234 to 241. A conventional repetition of the scherzo follows the Trio.

The finale commences with a slow introduction (poco sostenuto) of forty measures. This ominous preface gives way to a tuneful theme (Allegro non troppo) stated by the cello, but soon taken up in the other voices. A contrasting theme and tonality appear beginning in measure 93 at the indication un pochettino più animato, and a densely scored idea characterized by triplet subdivision of the beat and syncopation serves in the capacity of a closing theme (meas. 125).

This opening segment of the finale suggests sonata form; however, it may be more accurate to speak of "sonata principle" rather than "form." Musical tension resulting from tonal and melodic contrast is important in creating direction and momentum in this movement. At the same time, points of thematic and tonal stability and instability are not quite so neatly sequestered from one another as they had been in earlier sonata forms. Brahms's "exposition" is already colored with passages that seem developmental in their use of thematic fragmentation, scalar alterations, and continuation and elaboration of rhythmic motifs. As a consequence, the traditional functions of the "development" and "recapitulation" sections have been usurped to a great extent. Accordingly, the reappearance of the main theme at measure 182, of the secondary theme at measure 251 (with the appropriate transposition), and of the closing idea at measure 283 constitutes a varied restatement rather than a recapitulation.

The varied restatement is followed by 150 measures of music in 6/8 time at the tempo Presto, non troppo. The themes here are derived from previous material, but the transformations are drastic. This portion of the movement serves as a coda, but its length and significance suggest that it also acts as another varied reprise.

The final chamber music essay of Brahms's first period is the four-movement Trio in E-flat, Op. 40, for piano, horn, and violin. Brahms began this unusual score in the spring of 1865 after the death of his mother. He gave the premiere himself on 5 December of that same year in Karlsruhe.[60]

The first movement, Andante, contains two distinct themes, the first in duple meter, the second in triple compound meter; however, these are merely played in alternation rather than being polarized as in a sonata. This structure was necessitated by Brahms's use of the *Waldhorn* rather than the valved horn—which, practically speaking, had already replaced the natural horn. Another consequence of the natural horn is that all movements are in the key of E-flat (the third movement, Adagio mesto, is in the parallel minor). The Trio of the second movement scherzo goes briefly into the key of A-flat minor.

Brahms approved the substitution of either cello or viola for the horn, but his preferred substitution was the viola. In any case, the thematic gestures—particularly in the scherzo (Allegro) and the finale (Allegro con brio)—are so idiomatic to the horn that neither of these substitutions is satisfactory.

The most compelling movement in the score is the third, which Brahms wrote as an elegy for his mother, Johanna Henrike Christiane (née Nissen). Her death was doubly traumatic to Brahms owing to its upsetting circumstances. Clara Schumann's letter of 19 July 1864 sets the scene:

> I was so shocked and saddened by your letter yesterday [informing me of the separation of your parents] that I feel I must write to you today. . . . I had not the faintest suspicion of any discord in your family; [thus], you will understand my alarm at your news. . . . I should not be surprised at your standing by your father, but in this case, knowing as I have for years your preference for your mother, it is incredible to me. I think it terribly sad that two people who have lived so long together, who are surrounded by grown-up children and who are almost standing on the edge of the grave, should separate. Naturally I cannot form any opinion as to who is right or wrong, and yet I cannot help thinking that

> if a misunderstanding arises as the result of a number of trifles, it is the woman's role to be conciliating. She ought to remember that it is her husband who bears the principal responsibility for the whole of the home, etc., etc. But if the husband is unfaithful or neglects his wife, or is a gambler or drunkard, then the wife cannot be blamed if she refuses to endure it all. I know, of course, that there can be no question of this in your father's case and am longing to hear the truth about the matter.[61]

During her stay in Hamburg between 30 November and 8 December of 1864, Clara had visited the Brahms family. She wrote the following to Johannes on 5 December:

> My heart is filled with anguish. . . . Oh what misery! Your mother and Elise were crying the whole time, and then there was your father who unburdened his heart to me; each of them in turn said they could answer before God for every word they had uttered. I assure you it has made me quite ill, for one's heart gets torn in two.[62]

On 6 February of 1865, Brahms wrote to Clara about his mother's final illness.

> Last Tuesday evening my mother returned in quite good spirits from a concert and even joked with Fritz as she got out of the carriage. Hardly had the latter driven away, however, when she complained that her tongue felt heavy, and my sister saw to her horror that her mouth was all drawn sideways and that her tongue was swollen and protruding. In spite of the fact that she was convinced that my mother had had a stroke, Elise had to comfort her and remain quietly at her side while my mother complained that the whole of her left side seemed paralyzed. After being brought home she believed herself to be quite well, and trusted Elise's comforting assurances that her chill would soon get better in bed. It was almost impossible to understand what she said, and the doctor told Elise at once how serious her condition was. In bed she was still able to address my sister in the tenderest way and to press her hand. Then she closed her eyes and fell gently to sleep. Heavy perspiration followed, then the death rattle, and at two o'clock on the following night she passed away.[63]

Under these heavy circumstances, Brahms penned the third movement of Op. 40. The movement, in 6/8 meter, commences with an *arpeggiando*, four-measure introduction by the piano. Then, largely in parallel thirds, the violin and horn play the first theme of the movement, an angular line riddled with chromatic tendency tones, and reminiscent of Bach's aria

"Seufzer, Tränen, Kummer, Not" from Cantata 21, *Ich hatte viel Bekümmernis.* A second theme is introduced (meas. 19) by the horn. This is imitated first by the violin, then by the piano. The second theme is immediately subjected to development. At measure 47, the first theme returns. At measure 69, this theme is transformed into a powerful, triumphant major-mode statement (*passionata*). As the movement draws to a close, the opening theme returns, and the brooding minor mode overtakes us once again.

The finale is the most ebullient element of the piece. This Allegro con brio movement in 6/8 meter is a miniature sonata form that has as its first theme a subject based on an arpeggiation of the E-flat-major chord with anacrusis, repeated tones, and passing tones. This melody is stated by the violin, then echoed by the horn (pickup to meas. 9). The second theme is another arpeggiated figure, this time based on the G-flat major triad. As the secondary idea draws to a close, we encounter the characteristic metrical permutations of this meter that we expect of Brahms: regrouping subdivisions to form three groups of two eighth-notes—hence simple 3/4 meter—syncopations of all sorts, use of the dotted quarter as the basic unit to create the impression of simple duple meter, and, of course, hemiola. The basic imagery of the movement is suffused with allusions to hunting. Perhaps Brahms was suggesting that life is a hunt in which every person eventually becomes the victim of the chase; death ultimately ensnares us all. Despite its grave content, the Trio has become one of Brahms's best-loved chamber works.[64] The Horn Trio was followed by an eight-year hiatus from chamber music composition.

THE SECOND CHAMBER-MUSIC PERIOD: 1873–1882

The two String Quartets, Op. 51, represent the culmination of years of work. We know that "Brahms destroyed more than twenty quartettes and in general probably published about half or less of what he composed."[65] Clara Schumann's diary mentions that Brahms showed her various quartet movements during the summer of 1869. Malcolm MacDonald supposes that these were actually "preliminary versions of his op. 51."[66] The composition of this pair of quartets occupied Brahms for at least four years. Several possible explanations for Brahms's glacial progress come to mind. As was the case with his well-known inertia in composing the First Symphony, Brahms must have been overawed by the contributions made by Beethoven to the genre. Indeed, it has been suggested that Beethoven's quartets of Op. 18 and Op. 59 were the direct models for those of Brahms's Op. 51.[67] By 1871, the year Brahms moved to Vienna, that city was self-conscious of its heritage as the home of the Classical style. The Viennese critic Eduard Hanslick was eager both to maintain that tradition and to ensure its continuation.

The two quartets that Brahms published in 1873 are conservative in their formal designs yet masterful in their ingenious counterpoint and manipulation of motivic resources. Both quartets follow the four-movement plan. The First Quartet, in C minor, begins with a sonata-from movement whose opening theme is transformed to become the principal theme of the finale, a truncated sonata movement. These outer movements include significantly proportioned codas. The internal movements are a triple-meter "Romanze" (Poco adagio) in A-flat major and a 4/8-meter Allegretto molto moderato e commodo in the key of F. The Allegretto contains a contrasting Trio. The Second Quartet, in A minor, also begins and ends with sonata movements. Again, thematic elements from the first movement infiltrate the finale. In this case, rhythmic motifs assume an importance equal to intervallic content in the cyclic structure. Probably the most unusual feature of the piece is the fact that both the second and third movements—marked Andante moderato and Quasi Menuetto, moderato respectively—remain in the tonic key of A. The Andante happens to be in the major mode, but the minuet returns to the minor form of the key.

The Piano Quartet in C minor, Op. 60, was completed in 1874 and published by Simrock in the following year, but its genesis can be traced to 1855. At that time, Brahms wrote the first movement (which was originally a half step higher) as well as an E-major Andante that may be the one that presently stands as the third movement. The 6/8-meter Scherzo in C minor and finale were added later.[68] The Quartet reveals problems already noted in conjunction with first-period works: a certain inconsistency in formal design, occasional awkwardness in managing the ensemble, and unnecessary density in texture, especially in the piano part.

The viola part often doubles the violin an octave below or the cello an octave above. This sort of doubling is particularly apparent in the finale. These passages almost invariably cause problems since even the slightest discrepancies in intonation or rhythm become noticeable. The piano part for much of this movement is a single line doubled at the octave.

Despite its spotty construction, the Quartet has moments of inspiration. The sonata design of the first movement is an ingenious one. The lyric second theme, which is announced in the piano part at (meas. 70), is one of Brahms's finest melodies. It becomes the basis of four variations that constitute the remainder of the exposition. This theme is in the key of E-flat major rather than the dominant key. The return of this theme in G major in the recapitulation (meas. 236 in the cello) is both novel and effective. On the one hand, we find the sort of third relations that were, by this point in the Romantic era, customary. At the same time, Brahms managed to save a special role for the key of the dominant. Finally, the stabilized tonal plateaus arpeggiate a C-minor triad, and thus grow organically from the tonic key of the piece. The third movement (Andante) contains fine contrapuntal passages. The finale, marked Allegro comodo, was revised shortly after its completion. Karl Geiringer remarks:

> Brahms, in his striving after compression, for once overshot the mark. As is shown by the manuscript (in the possession of the Gesellschaft der Musikfreunde), Brahms subsequently inserted b. 155–88 in order to mitigate the excessive conciseness of this movement. Moreover, he gave it, later on, a slower tempo.[69]

The Piano Quartet was followed in 1875 by the String Quartet, Op. 67 in B-flat major. The Hellmesberger Quartet played the premiere at the home of Theodor Billroth in 1876. Eduard Hanslick, who attended the event, gave a favorable verdict.[70] Brahms himself made the four-hand piano version.

The layout of the piece is conventional. The first movement, at a Vivace tempo, alternates sections of 6/8 and 2/4 and ultimately combines these contrasting meters in the F-major, second-key material in fascinating sesquialtera rhythms. Formally, the movement is a traditional sonata-allegro plan including the repetition of the exposition section and a conventional recapitulation (meas. 205).

The second movement, Allegro, is in the dominant key. The meter here, common time, is stable and presents a restful contrast to the rhythmic complexities of the opening movement. The design is an A-B-A' song form with extensive reworking of the opening material at its return. The codetta (meas. 81) contains interesting peripheral harmonies that set the listener up for the turbulent Agitato movement (Allegretto non troppo) that follows.

This movement in D minor, which strings play *con sordino*, is in triple meter and features the viola. Unusual is the use here of the old-fashioned *da capo* instruction (as opposed to a varied restatement). The movement is rounded off by an eighteen-measure codetta. Both Walter Frisch and Malcolm MacDonald suppose that this movement served Arnold Schönberg as the model for his String Quartet in D major of 1897.[71]

The finale is a set of eight variations on a folksy theme in 2/4 meter. They seem at once to summarize and to grow organically from the three preceding movements. In the first two variations, the sound of the viola is featured. The seventh variation (in 6/8 time, *doppio movimento*) retrieves the opening theme of the first movement. The thematic connection is made the more obvious by Brahms's reversion to the scoring used in the first movement: second violin and viola in parallel thirds. The final variation recalls the metrical complexities of the first movement and forms a sort of palindromic conclusion.

During the summers of 1878 and 1879, Brahms wrote his Sonata in G major, Op. 78, for violin and piano, which was his first score to use this instrumentation: This is odd, since Brahms's career as a professional musician began when the Hungarian violinist Eduard Reményi engaged him as his accompanist. From 1850 to 1852, the two concertized regularly. In 1878, Brahms completed Op. 77, the Concerto for Violin and Orchestra. Only after completing the concerto did Brahms undertake the composition of a sonata for violin and piano.

In 1880, Simrock published Brahms's sonata, which was constructed with a conventional three-movement plan: Vivace (6/4), Adagio in E-flat major (2/4), and Allegro molto moderato. Throughout the score, Brahms wrote lucid piano parts. The opening Vivace, in 6/4 meter, is a good example of the transparent, arpeggiated style that Brahms employs for the piano. Most of the time, the violin carries the principal melodies. The piano occasionally doubles the tune. The secondary key, D major, affords the piano the more conspicuous role, while the violin accompanies with pizzicato chords.

The ensuing Adagio drops down a major third to the more relaxed key of E-flat major. The piano leads off with the main theme in duple meter. Throughout this movement, Brahms explores the piano's lower register. The design of the movement is an A-B-A' song form with significant reworking of the A material at its reappearance. The piano part includes delicate triplet figuration, and the violin part is enhanced with double stops.

The finale, bearing the instruction Allegro molto moderato, commences with an idea that returns at regular intervals, but with the tonal flexibility of a Baroque *ritornello* rather than the restrictions of a Classical rondo refrain. Interesting, too, is the recollection in one of the episodes (meas. 83, violin) of the opening of the second movement. The movement includes curious paraphrases of two songs by Brahms, "Regenlied" and "Nachklang," Op. 59, Nos. 3 and 4 (1873) respectively. What Brahms may have intended by these allusions can only be guessed.

Brahms began the Piano Trio in C major, Op. 87, in March 1880 and finished the score in June 1882. Simrock issued the first edition in the following year. The first movement, an Allegro in 3/4 meter, commences with a theme stated in octaves by the strings. The theme is immediately followed by a varied restatement using imitation between the cello and violin and punctuated by rests. A more grandiose restatement appears at measure 33. The piano introduces both the secondary theme (meas. 57) and the closing theme (meas. 102). The development is a stormy one (meas. 129) based on a dotted rhythm from the exposition. The principal melodic interest of the development is its use of a variant of the opening theme. The recapitulation (meas. 209) is inflected by the minor mode. Beginning in measure 313, one of the transformations of the main theme assumes paramount importance and brings the movement to a dramatic close.

The second movement, a duple-meter set of variations marked Andante con moto in A minor, opens with the violin and cello presenting the main theme in octaves. The movement is given an unsettled feeling by the persistent use of syncopations in the piano accompaniment. The third variation is conspicuous for its dense texture created by double and triple stops in both the violin and cello parts. Noteworthy, too, is the antiphonal contrast that Brahms establishes between the strings and the piano. The fourth variation, in the parallel major mode, is a more relaxed piece of work in 6/8 time. The concluding variation spins out a lyrical melody in alternation between the two stringed instruments against an elegant, steadily arpeggiated piano accompaniment.

The ensuing Scherzo in the key of C minor in 6/8 meter is marked Presto. Its central section (poco meno presto) fluctuates between C major and E-flat major.[72] Formally, this portion is unusual because of its incomplete binary form. While the first portion of this subsection behaves as we might expect (i.e., presenting harmonic motion from tonic to dominant and utilizing a repeat bar), the second half of the form remains at the dominant level. The return to tonic coincides with the reappearance of the opening Presto material. Brahms wrote out the reprise, but only the six-measure closing deviates significantly from the original statement.

The finale, an Allegro giocoso movement in C major and common time, is a sonata-allegro form. The development features the opening theme. An extended pedal point leads to the recapitulation (meas. 117). In an expansive coda, Brahms uses the movement's main theme along with the theme of the first movement in augmentation.

While Brahms was at work on the Piano Trio in C major, he had the idea for the String Quintet in F major, Op. 88, and began composing it immediately in the spring of 1882. The piece was finished in short order—Brahms had already sent the completed score to Elisabet von Herzogenberg in July 1882.[73] Publication by Simrock followed in 1883. The original manuscript is in the collection of the Gesellschaft der Musikfreunde in Vienna.

For this Quintet, Brahms used two violins, two violas, and a single cello. Less traditional is the three-movement plan in which the second movement combines elements of the slow movement and scherzo under a single roof.

The first movement, an Allegro non troppo ma con brio in common time, utilizes two contrasting themes: the first, a lyrical tune, the second, distinctive for its use of triplets and cross rhythms. The second theme is in the key of A major, and so the tonal plan—moving from the relaxed flat key to the brighter sharp key—reflects the character of the themes. The development section picks up on the rhythmic intricacies of the second theme group. The recapitulation (m. 136) is enriched by double and triple stops in all instruments.

The second movement consists of five sections in the respective tempos Grave ed appassionato (3/4), Allegretto vivace (6/8), Grave, Presto (cut time), and Grave. The opening, C-sharp minor section and its repetitions are based on a sarabande Brahms wrote in 1855. The serious character of this Baroque dance pervades these three sections of the movement. The Allegretto in A major, too, has a certain high-minded purpose that fits it well between the surrounding sections. The presto portion, in A major, is less convincing and seems out of place. In the final measures of the movement, Brahms toys with varied repetitions of the cadential figure, flipping back and forth from minor to major in the manner of the Baroque cadence with a Picardy third. The movement as a whole breathes the spirit of the Baroque, and its contrasting sections are reminiscent of seventeenth-century *sonatas da chiesa.*

The last movement, too, shows influences of Baroque formal procedures, for it combines elements of fugue with structural aspects of the Classical sonata principle. Regarding this movement, Karl Geiringer has observed that "as the different themes . . . are nothing more than variations of the fugue-like main theme or in counterpoint to it, the inner unity . . . is perfectly preserved in spite of all its variety."[74] This organic relationship among the themes may have been inspired by similar structures that Brahms found in the variation canzonas of Frescobaldi and his contemporaries. We know that Brahms was particularly interested in the music of Frescobaldi, and that he had copied by hand various pieces for inclusion in his personal music library.[75] In many cases, Brahms copied from the extensive music collection of his close friend Gustav Nottebohm, at whose funeral Brahms gave the oration, and who bequeathed to Brahms various items within that collection.[76]

BRAHMS'S FINAL CHAMBER WORKS: 1886–1894

After the F-major Quintet, Brahms wrote no chamber music for four years. In the summer of 1886 when the composer was vacationing at Hofstetten, a Swiss resort near Thun, he wrote the Sonata in F major for cello and piano, Op. 99, the Sonata in A major for violin and piano, Op. 100, and the Piano Trio in C minor, Op. 101, and began the Sonata in D minor for violin and piano, Op. 108. This last work occupied him until 1888.[77]

The Sonata in F major for cello and piano exhibits a tendency toward compression and economy. The first movement calls for repetition of the exposition, which, at the first ending, comes to rest on an A-major chord; however, when the movement progresses to the development, A-major is transformed into F-sharp minor. This half-step relationship between F major and F-sharp minor is a critical structural element in each of the four movements of the Sonata. Though the development section commences with the stormy, opening theme, this idea soon gives way to some of the exposition's more subdued materials. Brahms highlights the change in affection with the instruction *molto piano e sempre legato.* The recapitulation (m. 128) is conventional.

The second movement (Adagio affettuoso, 2/4 meter) is in F-sharp major; thus, recalling the structural role of the half step. Its form essentially follows the three-section design of a song. The central portion, in F minor, reasserts the importance of the half step. The principal themes are introduced as subject and countersubject in the first two measures, and both instruments have ample opportunity to explore these themes in a series of voice exchanges. The piano part is written mainly in the treble clef. Dynamics are generally understated. The lowest range of the instrument is used sparingly, and such passages bear instructions like *dolce* or *piano.*

The third movement, Allegro passionato, does not follow the precise formal pattern of the scherzo-and-trio, yet its lively rhythm and 6/8 meter suggest the character of a scherzo, as does the movement's vivid contrast between the driving, F-minor material and the tranquil, F-major, central portion. Brahms rounds off the movement with the instruction *da capo sin al fine*—another archaic gesture.

The finale is one of the rare appearances of rondo form in the repertoire of the late Romantic era. In this rondo, Brahms departs from the customary procedure; the third reprise (m. 84) is in G-flat major. With this modification of the pattern form, Brahms at once made it more suitable for Romantic expression and, at the same time, reaffirmed the organic importance of the half step, albeit in its spelling as a Neapolitan here.

The Sonata in A major, Op. 100, for violin and piano, opens with a concise Allegro amabile in triple meter. The exposition is not repeated since the movement is one of exceptional formal clarity including the Classical tonic-dominant polarity, memorable themes, and traditional distribution of opening, secondary, and closing material. The closing theme uses a dotted rhythm that had already appeared in the secondary theme; hence, the structure is an integrated one. The recapitulation (m. 158) is condensed to make room for a fascinating coda (m. 227). This coda is a second recapitulation, presenting first the dotted rhythm of the closing theme (m. 243), then the main theme (m. 259). Viewed broadly, we see at once a palindromic recapitulation (with the order of themes reversed) and a "double recapitulation" sonata form.

The second movement combines traditional aspects of both a slow movement and scherzo: each of the three Andante tranquillo sections is followed by a contrasting Vivace. Whereas the former passages are in duple meter, the music of the Vivace segments is in triple meter.

In the finale, Brahms employs a rondo-variation design, so that at each recurrence (mm. 20, 63, 137), the rondo refrain is recognizable yet recognizably different. The movement, which bears the indications Allegretto grazioso (quasi andante), is also surprisingly restful—a characteristic not particularly associated with rondos or with finales in general.

The Piano Trio in C minor, Op. 101, is concise in expression and formal design. The first movement features a four-note motif, B (natural or flat), C, D, E-flat, heard in the opening measure, at the appearance of the second key area, at the beginning of the development, and in many permutations throughout the movement. Originally, the composer had called for a repetition of the exposition; however, upon further consideration he canceled the repeat sign.

The second movement is a scherzo of conventional formal design with the performance instruction Presto non assai. Clara Schumann admired this movement, noting in particular its poetic tenderness. The third movement, Andante grazioso, is a three-section song form employing changing meters. The finale continues the exploration of changing meters in a variable 6/8 meter. In the coda, however, of more than sixty measures, Brahms recalls his principal themes, and subjects them to transformation to produce an ebullient conclusion.

The D-minor Sonata, Op. 108, for violin and piano, begins with a sonata-form Allegro that polarizes the keys of D and F. The development is dominated by continuous eighth-note motion, which recalls the *Fortspinnung* of Baroque music, but which is exceptional for Brahms. The recapitulation, like the second recapitulation of the Sonata, Op. 100, is a palindromic one that presents theme two beginning at measure 185 and the opening theme beginning at measure 218.

The second movement, an Adagio in D major, is terse and uncomplicated. It consists of a lyrical strain that is then repeated with variation. The third movement, Un poco presto e con sentimento, is in F-sharp minor. This duple-meter movement is similarly terse and straightforward, save for the excursions into the keys of F major and D minor.

It took Brahms two years to complete Op. 108. MacDonald wonders whether the piece might have been "salvaged from some much earlier composition."[78] The finale (Presto agitato, 6/8 time) contains the heavy-handed writing noted in Brahms's early work. In length, it surpasses the first movement (which is a hefty 264 measures) by an additional 73; hence, the precision characteristic of Brahms's mature style is lacking. The lower extremities of the piano range are more extensively used than in any of the other late chamber scores. Though the dedicatee of this sonata, Hans von Bülow, was a pianist, the difficult part that Brahms wrote here seems primitive rather than virtuosic.

At the request of Joseph Joachim, who wanted a companion piece to perform with Op. 88, Brahms composed his String Quintet in G major, Op. 111 (1890) consisting of four exquisite movements in the sequence Allegro, non troppo ma con brio, Adagio, Un poco allegretto, and Vivace, ma non troppo presto.[79] The first movement is a sonata form with repeated exposition. The exposition presents two contrasted themes: the first, a vigorous, almost symphonic theme announced by the cello against tremolandi in the pairs of violins and violas; the second, a lyric idea that could easily have been a song. The dense scoring of the first theme apparently was considered problematic by a number of musicians close to the composer. Some thought was given to reworking the opening so as to allow the cello to be more easily heard.[80] In his monograph on Brahms, Geiringer gives the alternative opening that Brahms concocted, but notes that "in spite of the evident advantages of this arrangement . . . he retained the old version in print."[81] The development section is devoted primarily to sequences extracted from the main theme. The coda continues toying with the opening theme and contains many interesting transformations of it—some of them rather tender and quite unlike the original in character.

The internal movements, in D minor and G minor, employ more transparent textures and a more relaxed mood. There is no actual scherzo, though the third movement is skittish. The finale is a sonata-rondo form in which equal voice is allocated to complex imitative counterpoint and exuberantly cheerful melodies of Gypsy character.

Though the premiere of the G-major Quintet was actually given by the Rosé Quartet on 11 November 1890, Joachim's ensemble took the piece into their repertoire and played it regularly.[82] In his letter to Brahms of 22 March 1893, Joachim remarks that "the day before yesterday . . . we had an excellent performance of your G major Quintette in which [Alfredo] Piatti's playing was particularly happy. He is very much taken with the beginning, and I more especially with the deep and original Adagio, *one* of your most beautiful things."[83]

Brahms had thought seriously of retiring after the completion of Op. 111. Happily, this was not the case. His last opus was the set of organ Chorale Preludes, Op. 122; but before writing them, Brahms wrote four chamber pieces: the Clarinet Trio, Op. 114, the Clarinet Quintet, Op. 115, and the Two Clarinet Sonatas, Op. 120. The catalyst for these works was the uniquely expressive playing of Richard Bernhard Mühlfeld (1856–1907), the principal clarinetist of the Meiningen court orchestra. Brahms had performed his Piano Concerto No. 2, Op. 82, with the orchestra in 1881 and subsequently visited the court often for performances of his music. In his letter of 17 March 1891 written from Meiningen to Clara Schumann, Brahms tells her that the orchestra had played his symphonies and the *Variations on a Theme of Haydn*, Op. 56a. In addition, they had given Weber's F-minor Clarinet Concerto with Mühlfeld as the soloist. Brahms concludes, "It is impossible to play the clarinet better than Herr Mühlfeld does here."[84]

Brahms returned to Vienna inspired, content, and with an urge to write. He must have started the pieces shortly after his return, for already in a letter written from Ischl in July, Brahms remarked:

> Baroness [Helene von] Heldburg [of Meiningen] will have told you of a trio for pianoforte, violin and clarinet, and of a quintet for a string quartet and clarinet. If only for the pleasure of hearing these I am looking forward to Meiningen. You have never heard such a clarinet player as they have there in Mühlfeldt [*sic*]. He is absolutely the best I know. . . . The clarinet players in Vienna and many other places are quite fairly good in orchestra, but solo they give one no real pleasure.[85]

Brahms's A-minor Trio is an important contribution to the relatively seldom used ensemble of clarinet, cello, and piano. In musical substance, this score surpasses both Mozart's Trio in E-flat, K. 498, and Beethoven's Trio in B-flat, Op. 11.[86]

The first movement Allegro commences in A minor but concludes in the major mode. This sonata form dispenses with the repetition of the exposition. The second theme is a freely inverted paraphrase of the opening theme using certain elements of canonic imitation. Perhaps too conventional is the bland figuration—ascending and descending scale passages—that occupies so much of the development.

The Adagio second movement, in D major, is a song form with significant reworking of the return of the opening idea. The third movement, a triple-meter Andante grazioso, is an essentially lyrical piece. The work lacks a scherzo.

Of the four movements, the concluding Allegro—marked 2/4 (6/8)—is the most interesting. Brahms returns to A minor for this sonata-form finale. The second theme appears in E major (meas. 38), and the piano alone states the closing theme (meas. 58). In the recapitulation, the full ensemble plays the closing theme. The recapitulation omits the opening theme and begins with the second theme (meas. 136).

The "official" premiere of the Op. 114 Trio took place at the Singakademie in Berlin on 12 December 1891, but Brahms had played the piece at the Meiningen court on 24 November. The performers who assisted Brahms on that occasion were Richard Mühlfeld on the clarinet, and Robert Hausmann, who was the cellist of Joachim's Quartet from 1879 until 1907.

The Clarinet Quintet in B minor, Op. 115, was also written during the summer of 1891. Geiringer has pointed out that the four movements are thematically related, and that "the art of variation forms the basis of this Quintet."[87] Only in the final movement, a set of variations, does the structural premise of the piece become clear.

The head motif that informs the themes of all movements is heard at the outset of the piece, played by the two violins. The first movement, an Allegro in sonata form with a repetition of the exposition, is intensely lyrical, but within the movement, dramatic tremolando passages become increasingly prominent. These tremolandos provide a linking sonority with the second movement, where they reappear in the central section

The second movement, an Adagio in the parallel major, is an expanded A-B-A song form in which the central segment is multisectional. Brahms calls for muted strings (as in the slow movement of Mozart's Clarinet Quintet, K. 581). Tremolando passages in the strings recall the first movement. In the opening and closing sections, the harmonic foundation of the music is clear at all times, yet each voice moves as a different rate, some anticipating the target harmonies, others arriving at the meeting point tardily, by which time the other voices have already moved on. These points of missed harmonic coincidence result from linear movements in which melodic goals are constantly under- or overshot. For example, an anticipated tonic tone is delayed by a leading tone, or perhaps an appoggiatura; or, as the lines evolve, more complex combinations of double appoggiaturas delay the tonal objective of the melodic gestures still longer. The result is a sense of longing and Romantic anguish. The movement's unique effect also stems in part from those passages where the string quartet drops out from time to time, leaving the unaccompanied clarinet free to employ *rubato* in the quasi-improvisatory passages where the beat is subdivided irregularly into groups of five, six, nine, ten, or eleven notes. This movement is one of the most original, heartfelt, and poignant in all of Brahms's music.

The Andantino, which moves to the key of D major, extracts for its principal theme two three-note motifs from the first movement but stated here in augmented values. These motifs are subjected to various thematic transformations in the 2/4-meter section marked Presto non assai, ma con sentimento. The combination of rhythmic energy and delicacy that characterizes this movement recalls similar moments in Mendelssohn's scores.

The finale, in 2/4 meter and marked *con moto,* returns us to the key of B minor. Equally important as the tonal return to our point of origin, however, is the return of thematic ideas that originated in the first movement. In this closing movement, we have a theme in the design A-B-B with five variations and a twenty-nine-measure codetta. Each of the variations presents familiar motifs that have been derived from the main theme of the first movement. The strategy becomes clear in the codetta, where Brahms restates (in the first violin) the opening theme. Striking, too, is the parallel between the closing measures of the first movement and their only slightly modified restatement in the final measures of the entire piece.

The first performance of the Clarinet Quintet, which took place on that same concert of 12 December 1891 that introduced the Trio, was unique since Joachim's ensemble otherwise limited its repertoire to chamber music for strings. The sound of the group must also have been unique; Mühlfeld played on his beautifully fashioned clarinet built by the firm of Georg Ottensteiner (Munich), while the others played Stradivarius violins.

In May 1894, Mühlfeld visited Vienna to play in a music festival that had been arranged by some of Brahms's friends. Following the festival, Brahms set out for his perennial vacation at Ischl. During his vacation, he set to work on two sonatas, one in F minor and another in E-flat, for clarinet and piano. The pair, published as Op. 120, were his final chamber pieces.

Brahms allowed for the substitution of viola for the clarinet in both sonatas. He also made versions—with slightly rewritten piano parts—for violin. The two pieces were intended to be played as a pair. The F-minor Sonata consists of four movements in the sequence Allegro appassionato, Andante un poco Adagio, Allegretto grazioso, and Vivace. The first movement includes a false reprise in F-sharp minor during the development section and an extended coda marked *sostenuto ed espressivo.*[88] The two internal movements are in the relative major, A-flat. The third movement is a good-natured *Ländler.* The easygoing character of this movement is carried over into the rondo finale, which moves from the serious, minor mode to the parallel major.

The Sonata in E-flat major is in three movements: Allegro amabile, Allegro appassionato, and Andante con moto. All three movements are in E-flat, though the central movement is in the minor mode. This second movement, incidentally, is a tempestuous scherzo with a contrasting *sostenuto* section in B major as its core. Even this lyrical episode has a certain tension owing to its asymmetrical phrase shapes. The concluding movement, in 6/8 meter, is a set of five variations with a brief coda. The theme is a tranquil, chorale-like melody reminiscent of pieces in Schumann's *Scenes from Childhood.* Rhythmic variation seems to be Brahms's primary concern here; thus, we find syncopation in the first variation, triplet arpeggios in the second, thirty-second notes in duple meter in the third, a syncopated but much slower movement in the fourth, tumultuous cross-rhythms in the fifth—which veers into the minor mode—and a more relaxed pace in the coda, which returns to the major mode and bears the performance instruction *Più tranquillo.*

By the time of his death, Brahms had fulfilled the prophecies that Robert Schumann had made concerning him in his essay "Neue Bahnen." The young Brahms had begun awkwardly, with works too heavily burdened by his rich musical heritage: counterpoint and fugue, antique suites and dances, and allusions to classics of music literature; however, he eventually assimilated these eclectic musical materials, integrating them into his own distinctive voice in a way that was simultaneously traditional and progressive.

NINE

Nationalism in French Chamber Music of the Late Romantic Era: Franck, Debussy, Saint-Saëns, Fauré, and Ravel

MUSIC IN POST-NAPOLEONIC FRANCE

During the first half of the nineteenth century, the musical scene in Paris was dominated by three main operatic organizations: the Académie Royale de Musique, the Théâtre des Italiens, and the Opéra-Comique. Instrumental music had a limited appeal to the general public. Amateur players still performed chamber works in domestic settings. Professional concerts were sometimes given in the halls of instrument manufacturers like those of Erard and Pleyel.[1] Those given by Franz Liszt (1811–1886) at the Salle Erard in January and February 1837 included some of the piano trios of Beethoven. At the time, these were "totally unknown in Paris,"[2] and audiences there "were convinced that [his] late works were the product of a deranged mind."[3] At the 4 February concert, Liszt rearranged the items on the program, changing a Beethoven trio with one by Johann Peter Pixis. Apparently, neither the general public nor the critics were able to tell the difference.[4] Probably the most receptive audiences for chamber music programs in the early part of the century were those at the Paris Conservatory who heard the wind quintets of Anton Reicha. Outside of this limited populace, there was little appreciation for chamber music.

CONTINUOUS FORM IN THE WORKS OF CÉSAR FRANCK

Franck's music is highly organic. Generally beginning with a concise motif, he expands the motif immediately to create melodies as well as contrapuntal lines that produce harmonies. This insistence upon a motif, however, precludes the separation of stable and unstable harmonic areas that traditionally resulted in formal divisions into exposition and development. The pervasiveness of generative cells and their metamorphoses in Franck's scores results in highly cohesive yet unpredictable structures. Form evolves continuously in conjunction with motivic permutations.

Though generally considered a French composer, Franck (1822–1890) was born to German parents living in Belgium. He studied from 1830 until 1835 at the Conservatory of Liège, but in May 1835, the family relocated to Paris. There, Franck began lessons with Reicha, and studied counterpoint, fugue, and composition. Though these lessons lasted only a year—Reicha died in May 1836—they were influential. Reicha's enthusiasm for chamber music, and for the music of Beethoven particularly, seems to have been transmitted to the young scholar. That Franck chose to make his debut as a composer with a set of three piano trios, as Beethoven did, is strong evidence for this hypothesis, but more convincing still is the compositional method that Franck employed in these pieces, all written by the year 1840.

FRANCK'S PIANO TRIOS, OP. 1

Exactly when Franck began these early piano trios is unknown. The set of three trios, in F-sharp minor, B-flat major, and B minor respectively, actually led to a fourth, the Piano Trio in B minor, Op. 2. Franck completed the trios no later than 1842, the year in which he showed them to Liszt.

> The three Trios interested him enormously. He was exceedingly enthusiastic of the finale of the third, and told Franck that this movement seemed to him complete in itself and worthy of being published separately, and that, in this form, he would make a point of playing it and making it known in Germany.[5]

Even the opening page of the Trio in F-sharp minor contains elements that were to remain characteristic of Franck's style. The opening theme, stated in the piano, starts with a motivic cell consisting of the tone F-sharp ornamented with an upper neighbor. During the next several measures, the tone is ornamented with an upper third and then an upper sixth. In the fourth measure, the object of this intervallic expansion, the F-sharp an octave higher, is achieved. In the following four measures, the process is reversed, so that the eighth measure is identical to the first. This theme, in steady quarter notes at the tempo Andante con moto, becomes the generative cell that appears in each of the piece's three movements. This type of organic integration of gesture and form, inherited from Beethoven, becomes increasingly prominent in Franck's later works.

The form of the first movement of the F-sharp-minor Trio is also distinctive. Though its five sections are all rooted in the key of F-sharp, the mode regularly switches from minor to major and vice versa. For the minor mode segments of the movement (i.e., the first, third, and fifth), Franck uses the expanding subject already described; for the major-mode sections, he uses a contrasting idea that commences on the third of the key, ascends to the tonic, then descends through a full octave to the lower F-sharp. This descending gesture links the major-mode theme with the second half of the minor-mode theme where the same event occurs. Further unifying the two themes is the steady quarter-note rhythm of each against which Franck counterposes contrasting rhythmic figures: whole and half notes for the first theme, arpeggiated triplets for the second.

Within the five sections of the first movement, nondiatonic tones appear frequently. The longest and most harmonically diverse section is the third. Here Franck adds complexities of voice leading: a new melodic figure using dotted rhythms, triplets based on scalar configurations, and the whole- and half-note countersubject of the opening section. In short, we get the impression of a development within a sonata form. The F-sharp major theme as it appears in the fourth section is half the length it had been in the second section. The opening theme is preserved in its original dimensions (four measures of upward expansion followed by four measures of the inverse), but in this fifth and final section, pizzicato violin and cello join the piano. The movement combines aspects of a sonata, a set of double variations, and a rondo. Such hybridization of formal elements fascinated Franck throughout his career.

The second movement, a five-section scherzo and double trio in B minor, recalls Beethoven. As in the first movement, the tonal focus remains fixed in all five sections but simply switches from the minor mode to the parallel major. In the second trio, the B-major theme is a reworking of the F-sharp major theme from the first movement. Likewise, the final B-minor scherzo section has as its bass line a transformation of the opening figure from the first movement.

The scherzo leads without pause into the finale, the only movement of the piece that is a conventional sonata allegro design. The reappearance of the generative cell does not take place until the arrival of the secondary key (spelled as D-flat major rather than C-sharp major). Franck suggests the motif repeatedly before its actual statement. In the concluding pages of the movement, the ascending step of the generative cell is repeated in sequential fashion to achieve an expansive, ascending line in triplets. This line, in turn, suddenly shifts to half-note values for a luminous restatement of the major-mode subject from the first movement. As in many of Franck's works, the listener experiences a sense of triumph after adversity.

FRANCK'S LATER CHAMBER WORKS AND THE COMPOSERS OF THE SOCIÉTÉ NATIONALE DE MUSIQUE

Franck's late chamber works probably would not have been written had it not been for the Société Nationale de Musique. Many of them had their premieres on programs sponsored by the society. At the time, there was little encouragement for composers to write instrumental music. Camille Saint-Saëns complained that "a French composer who was daring enough to venture on to the terrain of instrumental music had no other means of getting his work performed than to give a concert himself and invite his friends and the critics. As for the general public, it was hopeless even to think about them."[6]

Changing this situation proved a difficult task; nevertheless, Romain Bussine, Alexis de Castillon, Gabriel Fauré, and Edouard Lalo, under the leadership of Franck and Saint-Saëns, joined together to found the Société in 1871. Their objective was to

> favour the production and diffusion of all serious musical works, published or unpublished, by French composers; and to encourage and bring to light . . . all musical experiments, whatever their form may be, provided they reveal high and artistic ambitions. . . . In a brotherly spirit, with complete self-abnegation and with the firm intention of helping each other to the best of their powers, members of the society will contribute, each in his own sphere of activity, to the study and hearing of the works they will be called upon to choose and perform.[7]

Many premieres took place under their auspices, but some were less than ideal. "Sometimes, performers sight-read their parts. . . . Lalo's cello and piano sonata, for example, was on the first program without any advance preparation; so too was one of Franck's early cyclical piano trios from 1841."[8]

Franck's three chamber music masterpieces, the Piano Quintet in F minor (1879), the Sonata in A Major (1886) for violin and piano, and the String Quartet in D major (1889), were all performed at Société programs.

By the time Franck wrote his Piano Quintet, the genre already had a considerable history: In addition to the Louis Ferdinand and Schumann quintets, noteworthy French examples that Franck would have known include the A-minor Quintet, Op. 14 of Saint-Saëns (1855), and the two of Louise Farrenc (1804–1875), A minor, Op. 30 (1842), and E major, Op. 31 (1845), both scored for piano, violin, viola, cello, and double bass.[9]

Franck's three-movement quintet had its premiere on 17 January 1880 with the Marsick–Rémy–van Waefelghem–Loys string quartet assisted by Saint-Saëns at the piano. The first movement begins in common time with strings alone. The first violin plays a passionate, dramatic figure (Molto moderato quasi lento) against sustained notes in the lower voices. By way of contrast, the piano enters with an expressive melody in 12/8 meter. A series of exchanges between assertive strings and the docile piano ensues. Gradually, the opening gestures are accelerated to a localized climax that quickly fades into a subdued lyricism from which the principal tempo of the movement, Allegro, emerges in the piano part. When the strings enter, their figuration focuses largely on the tone F ornamented first with a chromatic upper neighbor, then with a whole step neighbor, and finally with an upward leap of a fifth—the same sort of intervallic expansion that appeared years earlier in the Piano Trio in F-sharp. This gesture is modified at its appearance in the piano part (meas. 90), where it assumes its characteristic contour that Franck uses for the remainder of the first movement and at the conclusion of the third (meas. 428, Ritenuto un pochettino il tempo).

Since Franck uses the motifs as basic melodic unit, his harmonizations of them are quite variable; likewise, the process of development may begin during the course of exposition. Such metamorphoses of musical processes resulted in unprecedented formal structures, which, as the following anecdote suggests, are often difficult to understand.

> Franck was so delighted by the performance that immediately afterwards he went up to Saint-Saëns to thank him, saying that he would like to dedicate the work to him and handing over the original MS as a present. . . . Saint-Saëns made an ugly face, tossed the MS on to the piano, turned on his heel and strode away.
>
> . . . Saint-Saëns was utterly impossible in many ways but this behaviour was unforgivable and showed complete lack of breeding. Afterwards he expressed himself as hating the passionate warmth of the

> work. . . . The score, however, bore the inscription "To my friend Camille Saint-Saëns" and that inscription was not erased. . . . Vincent d'Indy tells the story and there is no reason to doubt its truth because several times Saint-Saëns expressed his hatred of Franck's music, speaking of it in terms of the greatest scorn.[10]

Eight years elapsed before Franck wrote another chamber-music score, the four-movement Sonata in A major for violin and piano. The germ cell of the sonata, the interval of a third, appears, relaxed and unhurried (Allegretto ben moderato), in the four-measure piano introduction to the opening statement of the solo violin, which begins with the same interval. The elaboration of the motif takes place within a loosely structured rounded binary movement without any separate development section. Momentum accumulates as Franck presses on to the second movement, Allegro. In this movement, which opens in D minor but concludes in the parallel major, the interval of the third is filled in, but the continuations of the theme recall the duarations of the theme in the first movement. The melodic contour of the piano's chords and its imitation in the violin in the Quasi lento section also stems from the first movement, where it appears first in the piano (meas. 11–13). These are but a few of the subtle links that connect the sonatas movements thematically.

The third movement, headed "Recitativo-Fantasia," returns to the relaxed atmosphere of the first movement. It bears the same designation, Ben moderato. Another fast movement follows. Though the finale has elements of rondo form, it might be more accurate to think of it as a ritornello structure since the returning theme appears in keys including C-sharp major and B-flat minor before its final restatement in A major. The refrain is a canon between the piano and the violin.

The use of *recitativo*, ritornello structure, and subjects designed for contrapuntal elaboration strongly suggests the influence of J. S. Bach and other Baroque composers. The fact that the sonata produces such an intensely Romantic impression, owing largely to its highly chromatic harmonies, may cause the listener to overlook the fact that the layout of movements in the tempo sequence slow-fast-slow-fast is reminiscent of the old Baroque sonata *da chiesa*.

Franck presented the score of the A-major Sonata to the Belgian violinist Eugène Ysaÿe (1858–1931), who was married in September 1886. On 16 December of that year, Ysaÿe gave the premiere on a program sponsored by the Cercle Artistique of Brussels. Ysaÿe repeated the work at the Société National program of 31 December 1887 with the pianist Léontine

Bordes-Pène (1858–1924). The sonata was an immediate success. Since Franck eschewed double stops and other technical features that might have restricted its performance to the violin, it was quickly taken up by flutists.

The first movement, Allegretto ben moderato, opens with a lilting melody in 9/8 meter. This tune, agreeable and inconspicuous, suggests the intervallic designs of many themes in the ensuing three movements. The second movement, Allegro, is the focal point of the work. It is a more intense treatment of the initial motivic cells. The third movement, Recitativo-Fantasia: Ben moderato–molto lento, is fragmented. It recalls the opening piano chords of the first movement and, after a tortuous, chromatic section, moves on to the movement's main theme. The finale is a canon between the piano and violin. Beginning in tranquility, the lines grow in intensity as they move through various major and minor keys. The movement comes full circle at the reprise of the opening material, but Franck, who generally preferred to conclude his works in a blaze of triumph, adds a coda in which the violin and piano join in a homophonic concluding statement.

The String Quartet is built upon a few motifs that reappear throughout the work, infusing it with a unity that can be sensed more than explained. Franck exerted great effort to achieve the organic design of the first movement. In his biography of the composer, Vincent d'Indy produces two versions of the opening segment that were ultimately discarded before the definitive, third version was accomplished.[11] The first movement is a compound form combining an A-B-A song form with a sonata design. The outer segments of the song form are in D major, while the contrasting central section moves from F minor to B-flat minor. The first half of the binary sonata form occurs between the A and B sections of the song, and the development and recapitulation portions of the second half appear following the B section of the song. Tonally, the sonata begins in D minor, moves to F major for the secondary tonality, through diverse keys in the development, and returns to D—with frequent use of the parallel major—for the recapitulation. These formal divisions can easily be perceived, since Franck maintains a slow tempo for all segments of the song form while he uses the allegro tempo for sonata elements. The insertion of slow segments in the first movement among the faster portions of the sonata plan may have been inspired by Beethoven's Piano Sonata in C Minor, Op. 13 (*Pathétique*). In Franck's manuscript, he took the unusual step of indicating the duration of the first movement as "17 minutes."[12]

The central movements, a scherzo and slow movement (Larghetto) in the keys of F-sharp and B major respectively, are more straightforward.

The scherzo, played for the most part with muted strings, is a tripartite form that moves from F-sharp minor to D and then back. In the closing portion of the movement, the modality shifts to F-sharp major, which becomes the dominant of the ensuing movement. The Larghetto is a song with a contrasting central portion (Appassionato).

The finale is one of Franck's greatest achievements. After some dramatic introductory gestures, he returns to the thematic material of the first movement. The opening strain of the song form is suggested in the first violin at the conclusion of the Poco lento section; it is then stated more extensively in the viola at the Allegro molto in the key of D major. As the second theme in this sonata-form movement, Franck uses a rhythmic variant (*pianississimo*) of the theme advanced by the cello in the exposition of the first movement. In the recapitulation, both themes appear in D, but they are reversed in a palindromic recapitulation. Between the restatements of these themes, Franck interjects reminiscences of the internal movements, first of the scherzo, then of the Larghetto.

The Société Nationale de Musique sponsored the Paris premiere on 19 April 1890. According to d'Indy, Franck was surprised by the resounding success of the quartet.[13]

THE TRANSFORMATION OF LATE NINETEENTH-CENTURY FRENCH ROMANTICISM: CLAUDE DEBUSSY

Debussy (1862–1918) stresses moods and atmospheres in his music. His works suggest rather than specify. Tone color, dynamics, and subtle fluctuations in tempo and texture are essential rather than ornamental; hence, even when using a small ensemble, Debussy creates extraordinarily colorful scores. His chamber works are few: the youthful Piano Trio (1880), String Quartet (1893), the Sonata (1915) for cello and piano, the Sonata (1915) for flute, viola, and harp, and the Sonata (1917) for violin and piano. Debussy's preference for mixed ensembles is an indication of the importance of sonority. The exceptional work, his string quartet, was probably written largely to demonstrate his technical mastery.

The piano trio was a strictly practical matter: Debussy, during the summer of 1880, was one of the house musicians of Countess Nadezhda von Meck. She was vacationing with family and friends at a villa in Fiesole, and she hired Debussy as pianist and pedagogue—for her children. Von Meck, best known as the benefactor of Tschaikovsky, wrote to him in October informing him that her "Frenchman" has written a fine piano trio. Several weeks later, her letter contained an ill-disguised prod that he, too, should write a trio. Debussy's trio, long considered lost, was reconstructed from manuscript materials and published in 1986. It is a four-movement work in a conventional, late Romantic manner.[14]

The string quartet was published as the First Quartet in G minor, Op. 10. It is the only one of Debussy's works that bears an opus number. Though the tonal focus of the piece is certainly G, that pitch is more often heard as the final of the Phrygian mode on G than diatonic G minor.

The four movements of the quartet, Animé et tres décidé; Assez vif et bien rythmé; Andantino, doucement expressif; and Très modéré—Très mouvementé et avec passion, are organized in the manner of Franck, with germinal motifs and thematic recurrences. In particular, the "recapitulative structure" of the finale seems to suggest Franck's architectonic approach.[15] Distinctive musical materials include whole-tone melodies, heterophonic textures, and a certain percussiveness in the second movement, a scherzo with two trios.[16] The last two features may have been inspired by the sounds of Javanese gamelan music that Debussy heard as early as 1887 at the Paris Conservatory and subsequently at the Paris World Exposition of 1889. Abram Loft has commented,

> The second movement is perhaps the musical chef's masterpiece in this quartet. At the beginning, as well as at several points later on, a wonderful mixture of sound flavors is layered together: a bowed line; a line of steady pizzicato triplets, constituting a drone; a third line of irregularly spaced triplet groupings, interspersed with occasional duplets; and a drone bass of drumlike, duplet rhythms enlivened with resonant chords.
>
> Reserved for one point in the movement is a splash of color produced by massed pizzicati in all four voices. The middle section is awash in the liquid tremolos of the middle voices. . . . Near the end (mm. 164–67), Debussy enjoys the side-by-side comparison of bowed and pizzicato settings of identical melodic figures.[17]

The premiere of the quartet was given by the Ysaÿe Quartet in Paris on 29 December 1893. Ernest Chausson (1855–1899), a friend of Debussy's and a composition pupil of Massenet's at the Paris Conservatory, had mixed reactions to the quartet. His criticisms provoked the designation "Premiere" in the title, since Debussy apparently intended to write a second, more refined quartet.

Having made a great impression with his *Prélude à l'après-midi d'un faune* in 1894, Debussy turned his attention toward larger, programmatic works. He did not revisit the medium of chamber music until shortly before his death.

In those years of World War I, all of European society was anxiously groping for some sort of stability. Neoclassicism met sociological and aesthetic needs rather neatly since its reduction of gargantuan Romantic ensembles was commensurate with economic conditions, and the revival of formal and textural clarity satisfied cravings for stability, tradition, and community. The war era was particularly difficult for Debussy, since he was dying with colon cancer; his first wife, Rosalie Texier, had attempted suicide; and his mistress, Emma Bardac, gave birth to their illegitimate daughter on 30 October 1905. The emotional states of Debussy and Europe generally rendered them receptive—perhaps even "vulnerable"—to the early music movement. In the summer of 1915, he began to compose a projected set of six sonatas for various instruments. The idea of "six" is itself neoclassical: During the Baroque, pieces were usually grouped in sets of six. In addition to the three sonatas cited, we know that Debussy had planned a fourth for oboe, horn, and harpsichord; a fifth for clarinet, bassoon, and piano, and one of undetermined instrumentation.

Formal designs, tempo indications, and movement labels in the three completed sonatas suggest Debussy's compositional models: François Couperin (1668–1733), Jean-Marie Leclair (1697–1764), and Jean-Philippe Rameau (1683–1764). Debussy's sonatas were his war effort for France: Beginning with the score for two pianos of *En blanc et noir* (in black and white; 1915), he began signing his name "Claude Debussy, musicien français." Each of the sonatas, as well as *En blanc et noir*, exhibits musical materials—especially in their use of modality and form—that are deliberately at odds with traditional Germanic constructive features.

The cello Sonata may originally have had some kind of programmatic motivation. The first movement is designated as a Prologue and focuses on two tonal areas, D minor and B-flat minor. The second movement is labeled Serenade. The finale, nominally in D minor, contains long stretches in Dorian mode on E (i.e., B-natural, F-sharp, and C-sharp), especially for the statement of the main theme five measures before [7] and its reprise eleven measures after [10]. The tempo of the movement commences with a quarter note equal to 92 beats per minute. The additional instructions Animé (lively) and Léger et nerveux (lightly and nervously) apply mainly to the glittering introductory passage that leads to the statement of the Dorian-mode theme. When the principal melody enters, however, it is considerably more relaxed. Lyrical sections (Rubato; Lento, molto rubato con morbidezza; and Largo) alternate with more animated passages (Con fuoco ed appassionato; Premier mouvement; Appassionato ed animando; and finally, Premier mouvement). The alternation of tempos clearly recalls Baroque sonata repertoire.

The instrumentation of the Sonata for Flute, Viola, and Harp (commonly called the "trio sonata") was initially to have been with oboe rather than viola; however, Debussy found it advantageous to use the viola, since it could act as a buffer between the cantabile lines of the flute and the plucked sonorities of the harp. Its three movements—Pastorale, Interlude, and Finale—derive from eighteenth-century models: The Pastorale is a free sonata form with a liberally transformed recapitulation; the performance instruction of the second movement is "tempo di minuetto"; the third movement uses a conventional harmonic idiom.

The Sonata for Violin and Piano, Debussy's last completed composition, shows another modification of sonata form. Whereas in the trio sonata Debussy exercised great liberty in the anticipated concluding restatement of themes of the first movement, he focuses in the Sonata for Violin and Piano on the structural role of tempos. Though the tempo indication is Allegro vivo, "because of the nature of its melodic material, it does not sound *allegro vivo* continuously throughout. In fact, one is not aware of a basic tempo until the music is well past the first principal theme of the movement."[18]

In their three-movement structures, the sonatas maintain a superficial connection with the Mozartian piano sonata, but the sectional design of the individual movements indicates a synthesis of Baroque elements, as does the toccata-like figuration in the Prologue of the Cello Sonata (at the instruction *Animando poco a poco*). An anachronistic element in all three sonatas is Debussy's use of cyclic unification: In the last movement of the Sonata for Cello and Piano, the cello arabesques of the final Largo passage recall the piano figuration at the outset of the first movement, and the repeated note patterns—bowed sometimes over the fingerboard (*sur la touche*), at other times at the bridge (*sur le chevalet*), and in still other instances in ordinary position (*position ordinaire*)—allude to the pitch reiterations in the Sérénade; in the third movement of the Sonata for Flute, Viola, and Harp, before the final acceleration to the cadence, Debussy, retrieves the opening intervals from the Pastorale (scored for the flute in both cases); in the finale of the Violin Sonata, the first theme of the first movement reappears.

In these sonatas, Debussy presents a neoclassical view of the genre and mixes musical elements from widely disparate historical periods: Renaissance modality, Baroque sectional contrast and toccata-like figuration, Classical three-movement layout, and Romantic recollection of themes. Remarkably, he was able to forge from this diversity a higher unity that seems natural, logical, and satisfying.

THE FRENCH CONSERVATIVES: CAMILLE SAINT-SAËNS AND GABRIEL FAURÉ

Saint-Saëns (1835–1921) entered the Paris Conservatory in 1848 at the age of thirteen and studied there until 1853. In 1861, he became professor of piano at the École Niedermeyer, where his outstanding student was Gabriel Fauré. Saint-Saëns was particularly fond of the sonatas of Mozart. The characteristics of this repertoire tempered his aesthetic principles for his entire career: He was attentive to color but avoided extravagant or shocking gestures; his works show sentiment, but not excessively; he preferred classical balance and formal order to experimentation; and—perhaps as a reaction against Wagner—he kept his music free of bombastic philosophical impediments.

His almost Classical outlook inclined him naturally to write much chamber music. His major contributions include two sonatas, Op. 75 in D (1885) and Op. 102 in E-flat (1896) for violin and piano; two for cello and piano, Op. 32 in C minor and Op. 123 in F (1872, 1905); the Quartet in B-flat, Op. 41 (1875) for piano, violin, viola, and cello; two string quartets, the First, Op. 112 in E minor (1899), and the Second, Op. 153 in G minor (1918); the A-minor Quintet, Op. 14 (1865), for piano, two violins, viola, and cello or double bass; the Piano Trio in F, Op. 18 (1867), and another in E minor, Op. 92 (1892); and—perhaps his finest pieces—the three sonatas of 1921, Op. 166 in D major for oboe and piano, Op. 167 in E-flat for clarinet and piano, and Op. 168 in G for bassoon and piano. Ironically, none of these conservative works achieved anything close to the popular fame of his most idiosyncratic chamber piece, *La carnaval des animaux* (Carnival of the animals; 1886, published 1922) for two pianos, two violins, viola, cello, double bass, flute, clarinet, harmonium, and xylophone.

The Oboe Sonata opens with an Andantino, a simple song form with a contrasting strain in E-flat. As the second movement opens, we hear, in the key of B-flat, the oboe's unmetered arabesques against slowly arpeggiated chords in the piano. This introductory music leads to an Allegretto in triple compound meter. The movement is rounded off by a return to the introductory arabesques. The cheerful finale in duple meter (Molto allegro) is admirable for the delicacy of the writing. Generous use of triplets prevents any feeling of squareness, and the oboe's phrases are amply spaced to permit optimal breath and embouchure control.

The Clarinet Sonata is written for the B-flat instrument. The opening Allegretto is interesting metrically, since it uses two-note figures within compound meter. As a result, the three-note groups within the bar begin alternately with the first and second notes of the accompanimental figure. The undulating accompaniment is at once stable and unstable—like a buoy that seems, despite its firm anchoring, to move about on the surface of the waters. Saint-Saëns expands the sonata to four movements by including a slow movement, Lento, in third position. The sonata concludes with a reprise of the opening of the first movement.

The Bassoon Sonata, according to the score layout, is a three-movement plan, but the finale opens with extended slow section, Molto adagio, that leads without pause into an Allegro moderato segment. The Molto adagio contains arabesques similar to those in the second movement of the Oboe Sonata.

MODAL AND TONAL SYNTHESIS IN THE WORKS OF GABRIEL FAURÉ

Of the French composers active in the early twentieth century, Gabriel Fauré (1845–1924) was the most important in the realm of chamber music. His ten major chamber works were composed during two chronological spans, the first (with four scores) from 1875 until 1905; the second (with six) from 1916 until 1921.

In these works, Fauré used almost every conventional chamber music scoring. One wonders whether, like Schumann, he had consciously set about a systematic exploration of media. The ensemble sonata is represented by four works: the sonatas in A, Op. 13 (1876) and E, Op. 108 (1917) for violin and piano; and the sonatas in D, Op. 109 (1917) and G, Op. 117 (1921) for cello and piano. Fauré wrote a single piano trio, Op. 120 in D (1923). He wrote two piano quartets, the First in C, Op. 15 (1879), the Second in G, Op. 45 (1886); and two piano quintets, the First in D, Op. 89 (1905), the Second, also in C, Op. 115 (1921). His final chamber score was the String Quartet in E, Op. 121 (1924), which he never lived to hear.

One cannot help but notice in this roster of scores the almost consistent presence of piano. This detail is not surprising since Fauré, who entered the École Niedermeyer de Musique Classique et Religieuse (Nidermeyer's school of classic and religious music) at the age of ten, studied piano there with Camille Saint-Saëns beginning in 1861. He also studied organ, an essential instrument in the Roman Catholic liturgies of nineteenth-century France.

During Fauré's formative years, he studied the plainchant repertoire extensively. The distinctive features of the various church modes led him to develop a melodic style rather different from the diatonic and chromatic manner of the Germans. A further important element of his studies was the improvisation at the organ of accompaniments for the chants. In the course of inventing harmonies to support these expansive, flowing chant lines, Fauré discovered many pleasing successions of chords that do not work in quite the same way as conventional functional harmonic progressions.[19]

Fauré, in fact, had a career as a church musician. Following his service in the Franco-Prussian War, he became organist at St. Sulpice, where he worked from 1871 until 1873. In 1874, he succeeded Saint-Saëns as organist at the Church of the Madeleine in Paris. It was there, in 1887, that he began work on his Requiem Mass. He held the post until 1905, when he was elected director of the Paris Conservatory. The roster of his students includes the names of Nadia Boulanger, Georges Enesco, Charles Koechlin, Maurcie Ravel, and Jean Roger-Ducasse. Enesco (1881–1955), like his mentor, went on to become a prolific composer of chamber music.

Fauré's flexible and often ingenious melodic and harmonic style was tempered by a careful preservation of Classical formal aspects. All of his chamber pieces are in three or four movements; sonata form is commonly used; and all ten pieces end in a functional harmonic major mode. Cyclic recollection of themes—though characteristic of much late-Romantic French music—is limited in Fauré's case to the Second Piano Quartet, and the Second Sonata for violin and piano.

In his First Sonata for violin and piano, Fauré demonstrated his ability to write in the conventional style of the late nineteenth century. Bravura string technique, glistening piano passages, memorable tunes, and Romantic expressivity are paramount. This four-movement work would have been consistent with the fare of the Parisian salons that Fauré frequented at the time. Of these, the most important were probably those of Saint-Saëns himself and that of the Princess Edmond de Polignac. In these environs, he socialized with the most important members of the French musical community: Henri Duparc, Emmanuel Chabrier, Vincent d'Indy, and Edouard Lalo.

The First Piano Quartet had its premiere at one of the 1879 concerts of the Société nationale. This four-movement work is Fauré's most popular chamber piece, and it is not hard to see why. The first movement is a sonata allegro form with a bold opening theme in C minor and a more sedate, secondary theme in E-flat major. Throughout the movement (but especially in the development), the opening theme emerges in many ingenious thematic transformations. Changing meters (6/8 and 2/4) in conjunction with lyrical piano tunes against pizzicato strings are the musical materials that produce this magical effect. The Adagio is a modified song form in which the opening strain appears in a greatly elaborated setting. One wonders whether Fauré did not have Cesar Franck's Prelude, Fugue, and Variation in mind when he constructed this lovely movement. The finale, in sonata form, does not use literal quotations from earlier movements; yet elements of the first movement (i.e., its distinctive rhythmic motifs) and the third (i.e., its generally ascending, conjunct melodies) suggest that Fauré had the cyclic constructive principle in mind, though his use of it is extraordinarily subtle.

Striking formal procedures emerge in the finale of the First Piano Quintet, where Fauré combines elements of the exposition's themes to suggest a restatement of the exposition. Similar adaptations of conventional formal designs are apparent in many of his other chamber pieces.

If anything distinguishes Fauré's melodic manner, it is his decided preference for long, *cantabile* lines. In many cases, these are accompanied in the piano part by virtuosic arpeggios based on rich but unusual harmonies.

Fauré's String Quartet is his only chamber score without piano. It exhibits a certain detached serenity that is not typical of his earlier chamber works. At the time of writing, Fauré was old; he was dying; and he was deaf. His circumstances paralleled those of Ludwig van Beethoven a century earlier. Fauré could easily identify with Beethoven's final musical manner, and the fact that that manner (most clearly manifested in the late quartets) was appropriated for his own final work seems an almost self-conscious and deliberate gesture.

As the quartet unfolds, one feature after another reinforces these valedictory associations. Like the late Beethoven quartets, Fauré's deviates from the four-movement pattern: It has three movements, Allegro moderato, Andante, and Allegro. In its textures, Fauré's quartet resembles those of late Beethoven in its preference for contrapuntal designs based on pervasive imitation. Most telling of all is the melodic style of Fauré's score: The "melodies" are not melodies at all; they are motifs—usually consisting of four notes—that are more abstract than tuneful. They bear a remarkable resemblance to the motifs of Beethoven's Galitzin quartets. Like Beethoven, the deaf Fauré seems to have withdrawn into an ascetic, transcendental state in which contemplation was more powerful than sensuous experience. The *cantabile* episodes of the central movement and the intriguing pizzicato passages of the finale fall upon the ear as recollections of vanished youth. At the same time, Fauré's technical mastery—and the genre in and of itself—is apropos for this final iteration.

MAURICE RAVEL

The crown jewel of Gabriel Fauré's composition class was Maurice Ravel (1875–1937), a student from an ethnically diverse household in which the father was French-Swiss, and the mother Basque. Shortly after his birth, the family relocated to Paris, where the boy began his studies at the Conservatoire in 1889 and continued there until 1895. He studied piano first, then, in 1897, composition with Fauré, and counterpoint with André Gédalge. In all areas, he was an exemplary student; however, his four attempts to win the renowned Prix de Rome (in 1901, 1902, 1903, and 1905 respectively) were unsuccessful. Ironically, it was during the years 1902–3 that he composed his String Quartet in F, a work now regarded as essential repertoire.

Of particular interest to Ravel was the music of Emmanuel Chabrier, Erik Satie, and Claude Debussy. As a mature composer, he met—through Serge Diaghilev and the Ballets Russes—Igor Stravinsky (1882–1971). Ravel acquired an international reputation early on, when his *Pavane pour une Infante défunte* was performed in its original piano solo version at a program given by the Société Nationale. By 1907, he had completed the magnificent score of *Rapsodie espagnole*, one of the most virtuosic examples of early twentieth-century orchestration.

Ravel's chamber scores are few, but the quantity is counterbalanced in this case by the remarkable quality of each work. His first chamber composition, the String Quartet in F, shows his mastery of traditional pattern forms: The first movement is a neatly executed sonata-allegro. The second, a scherzo, juxtaposes outer voices in 3/4 time with inner parts in 6/8 meter. The third, marked *Très lent*, is sparing of melodic materials. In the third movement, fragments of the first movement's main theme are manipulated against a slowly changing and serene harmonic backdrop. The tranquility of this movement stands in dramatic contrast to the verve of the finale (*Vif et agité*), a rhythmic labyrinth with constantly changing meters. It is fitting that Ravel chose to dedicate this distinctive score to his former composition teacher and lifelong friend Fauré. The premiere performance was given in Paris on 5 March 1904.

Ravel's Introduction and Allegro of 1906 uses the string quartet as the core ensemble but adds to it flute, clarinet, and harp. This unprecedented assembly of sonorities bespeaks the composer's interest in tone color as a compositional element of equal importance to harmony, melody, and rhythm. In this score, harp is the featured instrument—and for a very good reason?

In 1810, Sébastien Érard obtained a patent for the double action harp. Even today, his design remains the standard for harp construction. With his modifications, he enabled the harp to play in the major and minor keys of the entire chromatic scale. In 1905, just short of a century after Sébastien's pioneering work, the Érard firm commissioned Ravel to compose a piece for the double-action harp. The commission must have been a balm to Ravel, who, in 1905, had failed for the fourth and final time to win the Prix de Rome. He exerted the greatest care in working out the details of the score, which had its premiere performance in February 1907.

Ravel thought very highly of this piece, which was dedicated to M. A. Blondel, the director of the Érard firm at the time, and he chose it to be performed on 23 October 1928, when he was awarded an honorary degree from Oxford University.

The Allegro portion of the piece is basically a sonata, in which the harp is treated like a solo instrument in a concerto. Even though Ravel did not play the harp himself, he managed in the cadenza to use each of its seven pedals in all possible positions. The work is a compositional tour de force that had a lasting impact on all of Ravel's subsequent orchestral works that included harp.

Many years elapsed before Ravel composed his next chamber piece, the Trio in A minor of 1914. This four-movement score, dedicated to Ravel's former counterpoint instructor, André Gédalge, was published by Durand in 1915. For its premiere on 28 January 1915 for a concert benefiting the Red Cross, Ravel recruited the services of Alfredo Casella as pianist, George Enescu on violin, and Louis Feuillard as cellist.[20]

When Ravel began the Trio, he was near his Basque homeland; accordingly, he used a 3 + 2 + 3 rhythmic pattern of the *Zortzico* for the opening Modéré. The second movement is called *Pantoum* after a Malayan poetic form in which the second and fourth lines of a stanza become the first and third lines of the following one. Charles Baudelaire used the design in his *Harmonie du soir*; and, in all likelihood, these poems became Ravel's model. Exotic, too, is the third movement, a Passacaille, which uses a repeating bass line, but the movement is designed as an arch form in which the piano announces the theme, the other instruments join, harmonic plateaus escalate to a high point, and then the process is reversed to end with the piano solo as the movement had begun. The finale includes cyclic recollection of themes, but this fact is more sensed than perceived since the theme of the first movement appears here in inversion. Technical brilliance is required of all players in this scintillating conclusion.

Between 1920 and 1922, Ravel worked on his rarely heard Sonata for Violin and Cello. This four-movement work began as a single movement—the first, Allegro—that was dedicated to the memory of Claude Debussy in a 1920 issue of *Revue musicale.* He subsequently added the scherzo second movement (which he wrote twice before he was satisfied!), the Lento third movement, and the fast finale. This sonata differs from Ravel's previous scores, and it reflects his assimilation of eastern European techniques as manifested in works by composers like Bartók and Kódaly. Perhaps the influence of Alfredo Casella played a role in this eclectic approach as well.

Ravel's final score for chamber ensemble was his Sonata for violin and piano, which occupied him from 1923 until 1927. In this very late work, Ravel wrote in an abstract manner that makes no attempt to reconcile the sonorous differences of the percussive piano sounds and the bowed or plucked violin sounds. The second movement, "Blues," is inspired by American jazz, which was a novelty in France at the time. The third and final movement is a perpetual-motion piece based on a nervous rhythmic ostinato. Though he wrote the piece for Hélène Jourdan-Morhange, by the time he completed it her arthritis had ended her performing career. Georges Enesco gave the premiere with Ravel accompanying.

During the composition of the Sonata for Violin and Piano, Ravel completed the score of *Tzigane* in 1924. The title of the piece means "Gypsy," and it was composed specifically for Jelly d'Arányi, the Hungarian violinist for whom Béla Bartók had written his two sonatas for violin and piano in 1921 and 1922 respectively. It is not clear which version of *Tzigane* takes priority: Whether performed with solo violin and orchestra, or solo violin and piano, the fact is that both are authentic Ravel. Perhaps—as in the case of so many of Ravel's works—either version may be considered authentic. In any case, Ravel's score shows that he had studied carefully the works of Bartók and Kodály, and he could handle the demands of Gypsy fiddle playing along with the best of them.

The score of *Tzigane* is divided into two main sections, a slow, unaccompanied monologue for the violin that makes extraordinary technical demands on the player, and a contrasting, faster section with accompaniment. This pattern corresponds to the *lassù* (a slow, introductory passage to the traditional Hungarian *verbunkos* dance) followed by the exuberant Csárdás *friszka.* In either version, one can only marvel at Ravel's ability to write so idiomatically for the violin, while incorporating ethnically diverse musical materials that had only recently been introduced to the western European public.

TEN

National Schools from the Time of Smetana to the Mid-Twentieth Century

CENTRAL EUROPE: BEDŘICH SMETANA AND ANTONÍN DVOŘÁK

Throughout the nineteenth century, Italy, France, Germany, and Austria dominated the European musical scene. Politically, too, the last three of these countries exerted tremendous if not inordinate influence. The assertion of artistic autonomy thus became a venue for both patriotism and protest among artists working in marginalized countries, particularly those in the Bohemian regions of the Austrian Empire. The two most important composers who emerged from these surroundings were Bedřich Smetana (1824–1884) and Antonín Dvořák (1841–1904). Their efforts coincided with the founding of the Chamber Music Association of Prague, which was organized late in 1876 by leading aristocrats and intellectuals.[1]

Smetana's principal chamber works include his Piano Trio in G minor, Op. 15 (1855), the autobiographical String Quartet No. 1 in E minor (1876), which he called "From My Life," and his String Quartet No. 2 in D major (1883). The Trio is an attractive work in three movements (Moderato, Allegro, Presto) with many tempo variants in the second and third movements. The first movement contains strong influences of Liszt, whom Smetana knew personally and whose music he admired. Reminiscences of Robert Schumann can be heard throughout all three movements. The second movement consists of two contrasting strains that are varied in alternation, but the cello is relegated to a peripheral role. The finale is a reworking of an earlier piece. The main idea, a perpetuum mobile, is interrupted twice: first for a lyrical interlude featuring the cello, and a second time for a funeral march. When the original tempo returns, it is with the lyric theme thus combining two contrasting ideas. An abbreviated reprise of the perpetuum mobile serves as a codetta.

Smetana's piano trio is the first of many that were written as elegies. In this case, the death of the composer's four-year-old daughter provoked the composition. Later memorial trios were written by Dvořák, Tschaikovsky, Arensky, Rachmaninoff, and Shostakovich.

Events from Smetana's life provided the programmatic premise for the E-minor String Quartet. According to the composer's scenario, the first movement recollects his decision to devote his life to music; the second reflects his enthusiasm for dancing (shown here as a polka) and travel (represented by the call of the posthorn suggested by second violin and viola); the third recalls his romance with the woman who became his wife; the fourth begins as a celebration of Smetana's success, but toward the end of the movement, a shrill E^3 represents the sound he heard at the onset of his deafness. The first movement is a sonata form with contrasting themes. The first is explored in the development, the second dominates the recapitulation, and both are combined in the coda. The second movement, based on surprisingly elaborate polka tunes, is clearly nationalistic. The third movement is a recitative followed by a chorale-like theme and variations. Polka and other folk elements resurface in the finale. After the moment representing Smetana's deafness, musical reminiscences of the first movement fade away, suggesting the demise of the composer's life and career. The movement dies away as low strings play quiet pizzicato tones.

Smetana's Second Quartet is a compact but complex work. The composer himself anticipated that most would have difficulty understanding the formal ambiguity of the first movement.[2] Of the four movements, the first three are allegro, and the final one is presto. The second movement, based on a piece from 1849, is a tripartite form with polkas framing a relaxed passage in the manner of a trio. The third movement is dominated by furious tremolos amid which the cello introduces a subject that is treated in various contrapuntal textures and techniques though never achieving the status of a fugue. The finale is a ternary form with a codetta, but its harmonic design is bewildering. Chord streams flow variously from F major to D minor, but ultimately to D major.

Dvořák was a prolific composer of chamber music. His principal works include a sonata for violin and piano, eleven string quartets with opus numbers plus an additional three without, four piano trios, two piano quartets, three string quintets (one, Op. 77, B49 of 1875, with double bass), two piano quintets, and a string sextet.[3] Among his smaller chamber works are a terzetto for two violins and viola, and a sonatina for violin and piano. With these twenty-nine works, he outstrips even Brahms in terms of sheer quantity; moreover, we know that Dvořák destroyed many of his youthful chamber works.

A violist himself, Dvořák was enthusiastic about performing chamber music. His first opus was the String Quintet in A minor (1861), for two violins, two violas, and cello. The String Quartet in A, Op. 2 (1862) was written in celebration of the composer's rejection from military service. (As a Bohemian, he had no interest in supporting the Habsburg monarchy.) In short, the performance and composition of chamber music was an integral part of Dvořák's life.

Some of Dvořák's chamber scores merit attention because of their unique historical significance, while others simply have become staples in the repertoire. The string quartets in D minor, Op. 34, B75 (1877), E-flat, Op. 51, B92 (1879), and F, Op. 96, B179 (1893), and the String Quintet in E-flat, Op. 97, B180 (1893) are conspicuous among the former category. Op. 34 is in four movements: Allegro, Alla polka: Allegretto scherzando—Trio, Adagio, and Poco allegro. The most distinctive movement is the second, which elevates the polka to the status of high art in much the same fashion that Chopin treated the mazurka. The movement is not without irony, however, since it contains two conspicuous allusions to the finale of Beethoven's String Quartet Op. 18, No. 6 in B-flat, *La malinconia*. That Dvořák admired Beethoven's music above all other is well known, but the reason for the quotation probably has more to do with the fact that Dvořák dedicated this piece to Brahms. Dvořák had good reason to express his gratitude to Brahms since he had received stipends from the Austrian government for five years from 1874 to 1878. Eduard Hanslick and, beginning in 1875, Brahms sat on the selection committee.[4] In a letter of 23 January 1878, Dvořák made the initial request to dedicate the quartet to Brahms. The latter responded saying:

> You write somewhat hurriedly. When you add the many missing sharps, flats, and naturals . . . look also now and then rather closely at the notes themselves, the voice leading, etc. I hope you will forgive me; to express such wishes in these matters to a man like you is very presumptuous! For I accept them very thankfully as they are, and the dedication of the quartet I would regard as an honor done to me.[5]

Brahms made a point of advancing Dvořák and his music. He not only put him in touch with his own publisher, Fritz Simrock, but he recommended his compositions to Joseph Joachim and Josef Hellmesberger. Brahms and Dvořák thus began a relationship that soon developed into an enduring friendship. During Dvořák's historic visit to the United States from September 1892 until April 1895, Simrock was reluctant to send proofs across the Atlantic for correction; he therefore prevailed upon Brahms to do the proofing and editing of the String Quartet in F, Op. 96 (*American*), the String Quintet in E-flat, Op. 97, and the *Dumky Trio*, Op. 90 as well as several orchestral works. The final act of friendship took place in April 1897, when Dvořák was one of the pallbearers at Brahms's funeral.[6]

Jean Becker, the founder and first violinist of the Florentine Quartet, requested the E-flat Quartet, Op. 51. It was his wish that Dvořák write a piece using Slavonic musical elements. Dvořák worked on the piece from late 1878 until March 1879. It includes a variety of ethnic elements. Early in the first movement, the sonority of plucked strings plays a conspicuous and consistent role. This applies equally to the remaining three movements. Plucked strings, though plentiful in ensembles of Renaissance Europe, virtually vanished from the West in the Baroque era; however, the sound continued to be cultivated in folk ensembles of central and eastern Europe.

In the second movement, Dvořák writes some of his most inspired *dumky*. The *dumka* (singular) takes its inspiration from Slavonic ballads, usually of a brooding character; thus, *dumky* are something along the lines of American blues. The movement begins with pizzicato strings suggesting the folk instruments that would have been used to accompany the singing of a ballad. The ballad melody, in turn, is approximated in the highly coloristic and expressive melodies of the upper strings. In this particular set of *dumky*, Dvořák explores not only the baleful sort of *dumka*, but also more energetic sorts. At one point, he inserts something quite like a Viennese waltz segment. At other points contrast is provided by the rhythmic intricacies of the *furiant*.

The intensely lyrical Romanza provides maximal contrast with the energetic finale, which, as so often with Dvořák, is a sort of *perpetuum mobile* interspersed with fugatos and other interesting contrapuntal features. The prevailing rhythm of the finale stems from the *skocna*, a Bohemian and Moravian leaping dance in duple meter often performed by males who attempt to outdo each other in the height of their jumps.

The F-major Quartet, Op. 96, is known as the *American Quartet* because Dvořák composed the piece while vacationing with his family in Spillville, Iowa, a village of Czech immigrants who maintained their cultural traditions. Legend has it that Dvořák used various melodies and rhythmic patterns that he had encountered in African American and Native American musics; however, such claims have not been authenticated. At least, though, it is clear that national music was an issue that Dvořák was contemplating at the time. This is clearly the case with the String Quintet, Op. 97. The Larghetto (third movement) is a set of five variations on an original theme that Dvořák composed to fit Samuel Francis Smith's text of 1831, "My country 'tis of thee." The premieres of Opp. 96 and 97 were presented on New Year's Day, 1894, by the Kneisel Quartet in Boston.

Among Dvořák's chamber works for piano and strings, the Trio in F minor, Op. 65, B130 (1883), the A-major Piano Quintet, Op. 81, B155 (1887), and the *Dumky Trio*, Op. 90, B166, are the most frequently performed and recorded. The F-minor Trio reveals many distinctive traits of Dvořák's style. Performers at the premiere on 27 October 1883 included Ferdinand Lachner, violin, Alois Neruda, cello, and Dvořák at the piano. Its four movements are Allegro, Allegro grazioso, Poco adagio, and Allegro con brio. The third movement shows Dvořák's penchant for segmented melodies that do double duty in either linear or contrapuntal contexts. The tune is bifunctional in its modality, as well, and Dvořák uses it within A-flat major and G-sharp minor. The finale is a percussive *furiant* worked out in a sonata-rondo form. This is a distinctively Czech dance in which measures of triple and duple meter appear in alternation. Curiously, the episodes are Viennese waltzes. At the time, Dvořák was in a dilemma: As early as 1878, Brahms had hinted that Dvořák should move to Vienna.[7] According to the composer's son Otakar,

> Brahms tried to persuade Father to move to Vienna. . . . [He] offered as inducement . . . all of his capital, property and cash because Father had six children. Included in the offer were a couple of tenement houses located in Vienna. . . . Father thanked Brahms and declared that he was very impressed and moved by the surprising offer, but he was born a Czech and would stay a Czech for the rest of his life.[8]

Brahms did not give up easily, and apparently recruited the assistance of Eduard Hanslick to pressure Dvořák. In a letter of 11 July 1882, Hanslick pointed out the advantages that Dvořák would gain by moving to Vienna.[9] In the closing moments of the finale, Dvořák recalls the theme of the first movement, reminisces nostalgically on the waltz tune, then launches into a triumphant coda based on the furiant. Perhaps he thought that Brahms would better understand his refusal to move to Vienna if he did so in music.

The Piano Quintet, Op. 81 is actually Dvořák's second quintet. The first, a three-movement piece written in 1872, is also in A major. Despite a thorough revision of it in 1887, Dvořák was dissatisfied with the results. He started afresh and completed Op. 81 in that same year. The first movement, Allegro ma non tanto, is a vast sonata form with a repeated exposition. Dvořák moves from A major to C-sharp minor for the secondary tonality. The development section leads to an unusual recapitulation in which the music of the secondary key returns in F-sharp minor. The coda thus plays a vital role in reinstating the primary tonality of the piece. The second movement opens with a short introduction leading to a sonata-rondo in which the refrain is a *dumka*. Perhaps this movement suggested to Dvořák the idea of his Op. 90, the *Dumky Trio*. The third movement is a Czech furiant worked into the form of a scherzo and trio. The theme of the trio is a thematic transformation of the opening scherzo melody. The finale, in rondo form, includes the most elaborate counterpoint of the score.

Dvořák's Op. 90 is an atypical work. Much of the music is light and entertaining. The piece is a string of six *dumky* alternately in baleful but sometimes spritely moods (E-minor, C-sharp minor, A major, D minor, E-flat major, C minor); however, a *dumka* originally designated a Ukrainian folk ballad of somber character. Apparently Dvořák had a rather liberal interpretation of just what a *dumka* is.

Dvořák's last two string quartets, Opp. 105 and 106, were completed after his return to Czechoslovakia. Op. 106 in G major was actually finished before the A-flat Quartet, Op. 105, which he had started before leaving America. Both are in four movements, but the scherzo comes in second place in Op. 105 whereas it is in third place in Op. 106. The Adagio of the G-major Quartet roams through various tonalities in free variations on two contrasting themes. The concluding Allegro recalls the closing theme of the first movement.

NORWAY: EDVARD GRIEG

The musical talent of Edvard Grieg (1843–1907) was the discovery of the vivacious Norwegian violinist Ole Bull. Upon his recommendation, the young man was sent in 1858 to the Leipzig Conservatory, where he remained until 1862. He thus inherited the German Romantic legacy of Mendelssohn and Schumann. He became known as a nationalist mainly as a consequence of his founding of the Norwegian Academy of Music in 1867; nevertheless, his music is devoid of Norwegian folk tunes, indigenous dances, or other nationalistic elements, and he spoke scornfully of attempts to write nationalistic music. (Curiously, one of the rare instances of ethnic dance elements in his music is the Italian *saltarello* that appears in the finale of his G-minor String Quartet, Op. 27.)

His chamber works include the Sonata in F, Op. 8 (1865), the Sonata in G, Op. 13 (1867), and the Sonata in C minor, Op. 45 (1887), all for violin and piano, the String Quartet in G minor, Op. 27 (1878), and the Sonata in A minor, Op. 36 (1883) for cello and piano. A projected Piano Trio, String Quartet in F, and Piano Quintet in B-flat remain incomplete.[10]

The Third Violin Sonata is representative of Grieg at his best. Its three movements, Allegro, Allegretto, and Allegro animato, provide equal portions of virtuosity and lyricism. Formal designs are clear, and writing for both instruments is idiomatic.

RUSSIA: MIKHAIL IVANOVICH GLINKA, PYOTR ILYICH TSCHAIKOVSKY, AND NIKOLAI RIMSKY-KORSAKOV

Mikhail Ivanovich Glinka (1804–1857) is the earliest important figure in the Russian school. Most of his chamber works are youthful compositions that are heavily influenced by western European styles; however, some are scored for unusual combinations of winds and strings, and the double bass is often included. Glinka's most popular chamber score is his four-movement *Trio pathétique* (1832) for clarinet, bassoon, and piano.

Pyotr Ilyich Tschaikovsky (1840–1893) studied at the St. Petersburg Conservatory from 1862 until 1865, at which time he joined the faculty of the Moscow Conservatory. During the last three years of his studies, he composed ten individual movements for chamber ensembles including string trio and quartet, horn quartet, string quartet with harp, piano sextet (i.e., piano quintet with double bass), and *Harmoniemusik* for pairs of flutes, oboes, and clarinets with English horn and bass clarinet. By the time he wrote his "first" string quartet, he had already had extensive experience.

Tschaikovsky's three string quartets, in D, F, and E-flat minor respectively, all consist of four movements in conventional pattern forms; however, distinctive Russian elements are apparent in the use of folk songs, such as the tune from the Kaluga region that is the basis of the Andante cantabile of the First String Quartet, Op. 11 (1871), in the use of changing meters, as in the Scherzo of the Second String Quartet, Op. 22 (1874), and in the use of modal scales, as in the trio of the third movement of the Third String Quartet, Op. 30 (1876). Much of this music acquired nationalistic associations after the fact: The Andante cantabile of the First String Quartet, for instance, was performed at a concert in 1876 given in honor of Leo Tolstoy, who much admired the work and expressed his appreciation for it.

In the Third Quartet, the textures of the third movement, Andante funebre e doloroso, were suggested by the chanting of the Russian Orthodox funeral rite. Tschaikovsky arranged this movement only for violin and piano in 1877. The association was a purposeful one: The Quartet is dedicated to the memory of Ferdinand Laub, professor of violin at the Moscow Conservatory. At the premiere, given at the Conservatory on 18 March 1876, the first violin part was performed by Jan Hřimali, Laub's successor.

The death of another colleague inspired Tschaikovsky to write his Piano Trio in A minor, Op. 50. Nikolai Rubinstein, a virtuoso pianist, founder of the Moscow branch of the Russian Musical Society, the Moscow Conservatory, and the brother of Anton Rubinstein, died in Paris in March 1881. He had been an advocate of contemporary Russian music, and his support for Tschaikovsky was invaluable. The score of the Trio bears the inscription "To the memory of a great artist."

Writing to his benefactor Nadezhda von Meck on 25 January 1882 after completing the piece, Tschaikovsky remarked: "I can say with some conviction that my work is not all bad. But I am afraid, having written all my life for orchestra . . . [that] I may have arranged music of a symphonic character as a trio, instead of writing directly for the instruments. I have tried to avoid this, but I am not sure whether I have been successful." The piece is very grand, to be sure. Its unusual form consists of two large movements, the first, an extended sonata containing four main themes, is subtitled "Pezzo elegiaco." The second movement opens with a lyric theme in E major that Tschaikovsky heard sung by Russian peasants in May 1873 in the company of Rubinstein. It provides the basis for a dozen variations plus a coda. Apparently, each of these variations was associated with events of Rubinstein's life. Though we are in the dark about such details, the variations are highly distinctive: the sixth is an extended waltz; the eighth, a three-part fugue; and the tenth is a mazurka featuring the piano. The final variation and coda emphasize the obsequial character of the piece. The theme of the first movement returns in a dirge-like context, and the coda (Lugubre) invokes the rhythm of a funeral march.

Tschaikovsky's final chamber score was his string sextet called *Souvenir de Florence*, which he wrote after a vacation in that city. The first version of it was written in 1890, but he revised it extensively in late 1891 and in January 1892.

Rimsky-Korsakov (1844–1908) was a naval officer by profession, but after meeting Mily Balakiereff in 1861, he became increasingly interested in music. These two plus the composers Alexander Borodin, Cesar Cui, and Modest Mussorgsky constituted the nationalistic group known as the

"Mighty Five." Rimsky wrote a great deal of chamber music, including five string quartets (1875–97), the String Sextet in A major (1876), and the Quintet in B-flat (1876) for flute, clarinet, horn, bassoon, and piano. The most conspicuously nationalistc of these is his *String Quartet on Russian Themes* (1879). The Quintet for piano and winds is a skillfully written piece in three movements concluding with a rondo finale. In this movement, Rimsky provides each of the players with ample opportunity to demonstrate technical facility. In part, this singular facility at writing idiomatically for winds was acquired through his professional work as inspector of navy bands, a position he obtained in 1873, which required him to supervise the constitution of the ensembles, the purchase of instruments, and their maintenance.

NATIONAL SCHOOLS IN THE EARLY TWENTIETH CENTURY

Nationalistic sentiments provided the immediate cause for World War I when a Serb nationalist assassinated Archduke Francis Ferdinand and his wife in June 1914. When the map of Europe was redrawn at the conclusion of the war, one of the most significant changes was the creation of Czechoslovakia. The most important Moravian composer at the time was Leoš Janáček (1854–1928), who had won international fame with his opera *Jenůfa* (1904; prem. 1916). At the time Czechoslovakia became an independent nation, Janáček was already sixty-four years old; nevertheless, the event seems to have had a revitalizing effect on him. Though he had written various pieces for violin or cello and piano during the 1870s and 1880s, his three major chamber works, two string quartets (1924, 1928) and a wind sextet (1924), were written after the founding of the Czech nation.

The First String Quartet was inspired by Leo Tolstoy's short story "The Kreuzer Sonata." Tolstoy's story, which alludes to Beethoven's Sonata in A major, Op. 47, for violin and piano, is a story of a tragic marriage. Pózdnyshev introduces his wife, who plays the violin, to his friend Trukhachévski, who plays the piano. Together, they perform Beethoven's sonata for a gathering of friends. Several days later, Pózdnyshev arrives home unexpectedly and finds his wife with Trukhachévski. Presuming the worst, he draws a scimitar from his coat and murders her.

Within the context of the First String Quartet, the tense relationship between Pózdnyshev and his wife is apparent. Plaintive, baleful themes in long phrases are set in opposition with nervous, aggressive motifs whose articulation and phrasing are carefully indicated in the score—for the purpose of highlighting the warped outlook of Pózdnyshev. From a formal point of view, this juxtaposition of subjects and countersubjects is fascinating: Traditionally, opening themes, secondary themes, and closing themes had been manifestly different in character and had been designed to complement the polarity of tonalities in conventional pattern forms. In Janáček's quartet, however, the contrasting themes appear simultaneously. The programmatic element thus alters the musical form, even though Janáček preserves—in a token kind of way—the proper design of a four-movement string quartet.

Janáček's four movements are not ordered according to the standard plan. The first movement is an Adagio that opens with an ambiance of grief and sadness. Later, a contrasting theme, folklike in character, recalls the intervallic structure of the Lydian mode; but as it is stated in the quartet, the theme sounds more ironic and agitated than folksy. The second movement is simply marked Con moto (with movement), as are the third and fourth. In the last two movements, tempo alterations appear within the movements as follows: Vivace, Andante, Tempo primo; and Adagio, Maestoso, Tempo primo.

The third movement offers many opportunities to study Janáček's constructive methods. It contains ostinato patterns, superimposed ostinato patterns, additive rhythms, and many special effects that are highly idiomatic for solo strings when played by virtuoso performers. The third movement is the only one that contains a quotation from Beethoven's *Kreuzer Sonata*.

In all four movements, the configurations of half and whole steps do not conform to conventional scales or modes; thus, motivic contours are crucial. In the finale, Janáček takes pains to establish clear links with the first movement. These are marked with many performance instructions that, though they cannot be assigned to specific elements of Tolstoy's story, suggest a dramatic plan that Janáček had envisioned.

As this dramatic piece unfolds, Janáček capitalizes on the sonorous potential of the string quartet in ways unusual among western European composers. The sound of plucked strings was common among folk ensembles of eastern Europe. In all four movements, plucked, pizzicato tones are pervasive, as is the more aggressive pizzicato in which the string slaps against the fingerboard (often called "Bartók pizzicato," even though Monteverdi had used it in 1624).

The Wind Sextet, *Youth*, is so called because at the time of its composition, Janáček was assembling materials about his own childhood for his biographer Max Brod. Reminiscences were stimulated, as well, by a commemorative volume that was being issued by the Czech publisher Adolf Veselí in honor of the composer's seventieth birthday.

The four movements of this suite for winds are marked Allegro, Andante sostenuto, Vivace, Allegro animato: Presto. The second movement is a theme with variations, but its meters are upset by unexpected groupings. The third movement, in which the piccolo is featured, is a scherzo with two trios. The piccolo was intended to recall the sounds of fifes used in the Prussian recruitment bands that Janáček would have heard as a boy attending the Augustinian monastery in Brno. The finale recalls melodic and rhythmic motifs from the opening movement.

The first performance was given by six local virtuosi of Brno on 21 October 1924, but for a performance in the following month, on the 23 of November, Janáček recruited seven players from the Czech Philharmonic (with an additional player to render the piccolo part).[11]

Janáček called his Second String Quartet "Intimate Letters." The title alludes to the many letters—about six hundred!—he had written to Kamila Stösslová following their meeting in 1917.[12] Janáček spoke to Kamila openly in his letters about the romantic significance of their relationship and its impact on his quartet.[13] Significant, too, is the original instrumentation that Janáček had envisioned: with viola replaced by viola d'amore! As it is, the composer decided against the substitution; nevertheless, the viola is surely the dominant instrument in the ensemble. Perhaps the association of Kamila with this instrument was suggested by Liszt's *Faust Symphonie*, in which Faust is romantically involved with a much younger woman, who is represented in the second movement by the sound of viola.

When Janáček died, on 12 August 1928, it was in the arms of Kamila Stösslová rather than those of his wife, Zdenka. The sincerity of the Second String Quartet is confirmed further by the fact that shortly before his death, Janáček had changed his will to the advantage of Kamila, who died seven years later in 1935.

BARTÓK, KODÁLY, AND HUNGARY

Béla Bartók (1881–1945) and Zoltán Kodály (1882–1967) were avid nationalists. Nearly contemporary, they both decided to study at the Budapest Conservatory. Bartók began in 1899 and finished in 1903; Kodály began in 1900, completed his graduate work in 1906, and was appointed in that year to the faculty. In 1919, he became the director. Bartók was similarly successful, and in 1907, he became professor of piano, a post that he held until 1934, when he resigned to join the faculty of the Budapest Academy of Science.

Both had gone to Budapest to study with Hungarian nationalists rather than German pedants attempting to copy the style of Mendelssohn, or Viennese snobs who supposed that their geographical location made them the rightful heirs to the Classical tradition. The case of Ernö Dohnányi (1877–1960), whose training there from 1894 to 1897 quickly led to a successful career as a pianist and composer, was an encouraging precedent.[14]

Filled with enthusiasm, they were disappointed to encounter in Hans Kössler, their composition teacher, exactly what they had hoped to avoid. Kössler, a cousin of Max Reger, was a thoroughgoing German with little sympathy for Hungarian nationalism.

Nationalism led both Bartók and Kodály into ethnomusicology. Bartók first investigated folk songs in 1903, when he sent his mother two melodies and inquired whether she knew the words for them. By 1905, he and Kodály had joined forces on folk research.

Kodály's motivation seems to have been purely nationalistic, and he limited his purview of folk culture to Hungary. Bartók, however, quickly became interested in a wider variety of ethnic repertoires. Before long, he was traveling among Arabs, Bulgars, Romanians, Slovakians, Turks, and Walachians as well. One of his final research projects was the volume entitled *Serbo-Croatian Folk Songs*, which gives the texts and music for seventy-five women's songs that were preserved on phonodiscs in the Milman Parry Collection of Columbia University.[15] It was this broad perspective of diverse folk cultures—largely anthropological in nature—that led Bartók to his faculty position at the Budapest Academy of Science.

In his early, unpublished chamber pieces (several sonatas for violin and piano, a piano quartet, a string quartet, and a piano quintet, all composed between 1898 and 1904), folk elements are minimal. In later works, he synthesized western European and non-Western materials. These mature works include six string quartets composed between 1909 and 1939, two sonatas for violin and piano (1921, 1922), two rhapsodies for violin and piano (1928), a collection of forty-four duos for two violins (1931), the Sonata for Two Pianos and Percussion (1937), and *Contrasts* for violin, clarinet, and piano (1939).[16]

Ostinato patterns, pentatonic and modal melodies and harmonies, plucked string sonorities, percussion, declamatory rhythms inspired by the Hungarian language, heterophonic textures, rapidly reiterated tones, and melodic arabesques ornamenting structural tones figure prominently in Bartók's works. All of these elements take on a new life when applied to western European musical instruments and forms. He adds idiosyncratic features too, especially symmetrical structures, and a fascination with the sounds of nature mirrored in what the composer called "night music."

Among the Western classical composers that Bartók admired, Beethoven and Liszt figure prominently, probably because Bartók was a pianist and their works constituted the bulk of his repertoire. The motivic cell as the basic building block in Beethoven, and the thematic transformations in Liszt are combined in Bartók's music, especially in contrapuntal passages where imitation itself becomes a venue for transformations beyond "real" and "tonal" variants. Complex harmonies, polymodality, and polytonality are often by-products of music predicated on motives. If, for instance, a motif ascends from tonic through supertonic to mediant, then its literal inversion will fall from tonic through subtonic to flatted submediant. The ascending motif thus falls within the diatonic major mode, whereas the mirror image of the motif stems from the parallel minor key. In addition to this type of motivic chromaticism, Bartók also uses ornamental chromaticism, where a structural note is approached through or ornamented by a chromatic neighboring tone.

The Fourth String Quartet (1928; premiered by the Waldbauer-Kerpely Quartet, 1929) is a fine example of all these features. Its five-movement plan is symmetrical: The outer movements use the same motives, as do the second and fourth. The central movement is constructed in three segments, with the outer sections framing the central night music. The first movement is a sonata form, but, because of its five movements, Bartók used two scherzos, one as the second, and another as the fourth movement. The first scherzo, in a vigorous 6/8 meter with a contrasting trio in simple duple meter, is eerily evocative because of its use throughout of mutes on all instruments. This special sound effect provides a further link with the fourth movement, which is played pizzicato throughout on all instruments. In many instances, Bartók requires the string to be plucked with such force that it slaps against the fingerboard, thereby transforming the strings into genuine percussion instruments.[17] The finale, which begins with screaming dissonances and a wild, Magyar melody, has an ample store of distinctive sonorities, too, especially *col legno* chords (i.e., played with the wooden part of the bow rather than the strings). These special effects are paralleled in the first movement by microtonal glissandos; hence, virtually all aspects of this five-movement work are subsumed within a symmetrical design.

The two sonatas for violin and piano were both written for Jelly d'Aranyi, a Hungarian violinist who was living in England at the time. Despite their aggressively chromatic and dissonant harmonic style, Bartók performed them regularly during his concert tours—particularly the Second Sonata, which he preferred—and they were widely acclaimed.

The First Sonata includes three movements in the conventional sequence, Allegro, Adagio, Allegro, but observance of conventions ends there. Each instrument functions autonomously, and there is no attempt to find common ground for melodic materials. This is a characteristic that distinguishes the Second Sonata as well. The appeal of these pieces arises from the binary relationship of instruments, and from the highly idiomatic and virtuosic writing that Bartók provides for each player. The opening Allegro of the First Sonata follows the outline of sonata form in only the most general way. The second movement has a clearer design, which includes three large sections, each with two subsections: the first for unaccompanied violin, the second for the instrumental duo. The first and third sections are related by their more transparent textures, especially in the solo violin segments. The middle section, by contrast, is more thickly scored. Except for the central, lyric episode, the finale is a rondo written in *perpetuum mobile* rhythms that evoke Hungarian peasant music. Primitive fiddling, with its insistence on open strings, is here converted to virtuosic writing that clings to the G-string for many measures at a time. Pizzicato and glissando passages provide contrast within the episodes.

The Second Sonata, much more compact than the First, is in two movements, Molto moderato and Allegretto. This succession of movements may have been inspired by the slow *lassú* and the fast *friss* pairings of *verbunkos* music.

The Sonata for Two Pianos and Percussion is actually a quartet for two pianists and two percussionists. At the time, this scoring was absolutely unprecedented. Subsequently, it became the model for at least two important compositions. Bartók's sonata and its descendants are discussed in chapter 15.

The clarinetist Benny Goodman commissioned *Contrasts*. Joseph Szigeti was the violinist, and Bartók the pianist. Bartók began the piece with the premise of the pairing of the *lassú* (Verbunkos) and the *friss* (Sebes). He expanded that pattern by the insertion of a slow, intermediary movement labeled *Pihenö* (rest). Bartók requires an A clarinet for the first and second movements and the trio of the third, with the rest of the last movement played on B-flat clarinet. In the last movement only—and there, for only part of the movement—Bartók uses *scordatura* for the violin, retuning the G and E strings to G-sharp and E-flat. He advises in the score that the player have two fiddles at hand, one with the adjusted tuning, the other with the conventional tuning, so that at the appropriate moment, the change may be made expeditiously.

The chamber music of Kodály consists exclusively of early works written before he achieved fame in 1923 with the premiere of *Psalmus Hungaricus.* Thereafter, he composed only for large ensembles. His principal chamber pieces include two string quartets, Opp. 2 and 10 (1909, 1918), the Sonata, Op. 4 (1910), for cello and piano, the Sonatina (1909) for cello and piano, the Duo, Op. 7 (1914), for violin and cello, and the Serenade, Op. 12 (1920), for two violins and viola. In addition, there are several youthful works for string trio, string quartet, and violin and piano.

The Sonata for cello and piano was a two-movement work originally, but Kodály later decided to add the conventional, third movement. Having completed the movement, he determined that it did not quite match the style of the earlier piece; thus, the Sonatina came into being. It was published separately in 1965.

The First String Quartet, monothematic and cyclic in structure, includes a tune very much like the Hungarian folk song "Lement a nap a maga járásán" (The sun descended along its path), but Kodály stated that the similarity to the tune was coincidental and not planned precompositionally; nevertheless, he spotted the parallels himself and placed the tune as an introduction to the first movement that he had already written. The coda of the movement is—quite disturbingly—a funeral march. The second movement makes extensive use of counterpoint, first as simple fugato, then as a more complex combination of subjects in a double fugue. The third movement is a scherzo and trio, and the finale consisting of an introduction followed by six variations and a coda. Snippets of themes from the first and third movements are heard in this introduction. The quartet is dedicated to Kodály's wife, Emma, perhaps because its premiere on 17 March 1910 at Budapest's Royal Hall coincided with her birthday; or, perhaps because *she* wrote the fourth variation. Emma's hand in the composition may account for the unusually accessible and traditional character of the finale.

The premiere of the First Quartet was an important event because it occasioned the formation of the Waldbauer-Kerpely Quartet, an ensemble that consisted initially of Imre Waldbauer, János Temesváry, Antal Molnár (who, in 1936, published the first monograph devoted to Kodály), and Jeno Kerpely. Just two days after premiering Kodály's quartet, the gave the premiere of Bartók's First String Quartet. The ensemble continued to promote new music until 1945, when Waldbauer and Kerpely immigrated to the United States.

Kodály's Duo for violin and cello is a highly contrapuntal work in three movements. In the second movement (Adagio), Kodály transforms the theme into the subject of a double fugue. Throughout the piece, the composer's own performance skills as a violinist are apparent.

The Serenade for two violins and viola was an especially important work for Kodály's career: It was featured in 1920 at a preliminary conference of what would become in 1922 the International Society for Contemporary Music. At subsequent ISCM festivals, Kodály's works were frequently heard.

Kodály's Second String Quartet is more adventurous and tautly constructed than the First. It consists of two movements, an Allegro followed by a multisectional Andante, quasi recitativo—Allegro giocoso. The former is roughly in sonata form, but its themes are transformations of two main motifs: The core of the first, stated by the first violin after four introductory measures, is a pentatonic melody; the second, which appears in the second violin part at measure 13, uses three pitches (D, E, G-sharp) in rotating metrical contexts. Both motifs pass among all the instruments, and their interactions These same motifs provide the basis of the recitativo that opens the second movement, but their subsequent expansions result in a wide variety of distinctly tuneful melodies. Within this compact quartet, Kodály synthesizes pentatonic and chromatic elements, motifs and melodies, as well as linear and harmonic materials to produce a highly organic yet hybridized work.

CHARLES IVES AND THE UNITED STATES

Ives (1874–1954) began his career in music at age fourteen when he became the organist of the First Baptist Church of Danbury, Connecticut, in 1889. Following his studies at Yale from 1894 to 1898 with the composers Horatio Parker and Dudley Buck, Ives returned to the organ bench and remained active in that capacity until resigning his post at Central Presbyterian Church in New York City in 1902. His experiences were thus practical and academic. His practical nature as well as his admiration for the New England transcendentalist thinkers inclined him toward the music of his environment, such as hymn tunes, patriotic songs, dance melodies, and band music.[18]

Ives cherished the interaction of composer and performer, and he thought of his music as a living organism rather than as an absolute commodity. As a consequence, he frequently revised pieces for new contexts, transforming what was originally a chamber work into a symphonic work—such as the first movement of the First String Quartet, which became the third movement of the Fourth Symphony. Apparently, however, the First String Quartet is already a transformation of four organ solos that Ives used in church services. The titles of the movements—Chorale, Prelude, Offertory, and Postlude—certainly suggest this origin. In other instances, such as his Second Piano Sonata, the *Concord Sonata,* Ives invites performance by piano solo throughout, or, at various points, with stringed instruments and flute. In such a performance, the *Concord Sonata* would be chamber music. The point is: To the tally of Ives's chamber works, pieces with variable scoring might be added.

The core of Ives's chamber output includes two string quartets (1909, 1915), four sonatas for violin and piano (1913–16), and one Piano Trio (1915). In addition, he wrote smaller pieces for various instrumentations including "Practice for String Quartet in Holding Your Own" and "An Old Song Deranged" (both 1903) for clarinet/English horn, harp/guitar, violin/viola, viola, and two celli; Scherzo for String Quartet (1904), "From the Steeples and the Mountains" (1906) for trumpet, trombone, and four sets of bells; Prelude on "Eventide" for baritone/trombone, two violins, and organ; "Scherzo: All the Way around and back," for clarinet/flute, bugle/trumpet, bells/horn, violin, two pianos/piano four hands (both 1908); "Take-Off No. 3" (1909), for clarinet, bassoon, trumpet, and piano; "Largo risoluto" Nos. 1 and 2 (1909, 1910) for piano quintet; "Scherzo: Over the Pavements" (1910; rev. 1927) for piccolo, clarinet, bassoon/baritone saxophone, trumpet, three trombones, cymbals, bass drum, and piano; "The Gong on the Hook and Ladder" (1912) for string quartet or quintet with piano; "Halloween" (1914) for piano quintet with optional percussion; "In Re con moto et al" (1916; rev. 1924) for piano quintet; "Decoration Day" (1919) for violin and piano; and the Largo (1934) for violin, clarinet, and piano.

The earliest of the sonatas for violin and piano is the so-called Pre-first Sonata, which was begun around 1899 and subsequently ransacked for various movements of the later four sonatas and the Largo of 1934. The sonatas are all three-movement pieces, but formal aspects of individual movements are not classical pattern forms, save for the occasional ternary song-form.[19] In all of the sonatas, hymn tunes—as opposed to parlor songs, marches, and so on—are more prominent than in any of his other works.[20] Technically, they are less demanding than most of Ives's compositions, and in the Fourth Sonata, he wrote the violin part with the intention of having his nephew Moss White Ives play it.[21] The spirituality and accessibility of the sonatas are indicative of Ives's sensitivity to distinctions among musical genres. These scores represent his most homely and traditional style despite localized musical audacities. The traditional aspect has more to do with Ives's preservation of the character of domestic chamber music than with details of particular musical events.

Ives composed his First String Quartet in 1896 during his studies at Yale with Horatio Parker. It quotes hymn tunes, and probably originated as organ music for services. The first movement is a double fugue based on "Missionary Hymn" and "Coronation." The music is conservative yet elegant; Ives later scored it for orchestra and incorporated it as the third movement of his Fourth Symphony. Those who question Ives's competence in writing tonal music need to look carefully at the skill with which Ives has woven these two classic, America tunes into a contrapuntal edifice that is impressive yet deeply touching.

The remaining three movements are more adventurous, but the finale most closely resembles classic Ives: In it, the march rhythms of the main theme,"Webb" ("Stand up! Stand up for Jesus!"), dominate the score, but quotations in triple meter from the second movement soon drift into the ongoing music to create intricate polyrhythms in the work's jubilant conclusion. By the time the piece was performed publicly, Ives had been dead for three years.

Ives was provoked into writing his Second Quartet by attending performances by the Kneisel Quartet. He found their repertoire traditional to the point of triteness, and their audiences, consisting of polite old ladies and gentlemen, offended him equally. He began the Second Quartet, as he says, partly in anger, partly in jest, and in the hopes of hearing something new from a medium that appeared to him threadbare.

Eventually, he got serious about the piece and worked on it from 1907 until 1913. Ultimately, it came to have three movements: "Discussions," "Arguments," and "The Call of the Mountains." The first is a dense web in which all four instruments play all the time. The rhythmic profiles of the lines are largely independent, and harmonies are highly dissonant. The second movement has more diverse textures and includes strange juxtapositions of bitingly modern passages with others that sound like traditional Romantic quartet literature. This curious stylistic mixture can only be understood by looking at the score, where Ives penned mocking comments above these later passages—much in the manner of his "Unanswered Question." Most of these passages are assigned to the second violin, which Ives associates with a fictitious violinist named Rollo Finck. The allusion is probably to Henry Theophilus Finck (1854–1926), who studied at Harvard with John Knowles Paine, visited Berlin and Vienna, and was the music critic for the *New York Evening Post* and the *Nation* from 1881 to 1924. He wrote monographs on Richard Wagner, Edvard Grieg, Richard

Missionary Hymn

Lowell Mason

Coronation

Oliver Holden

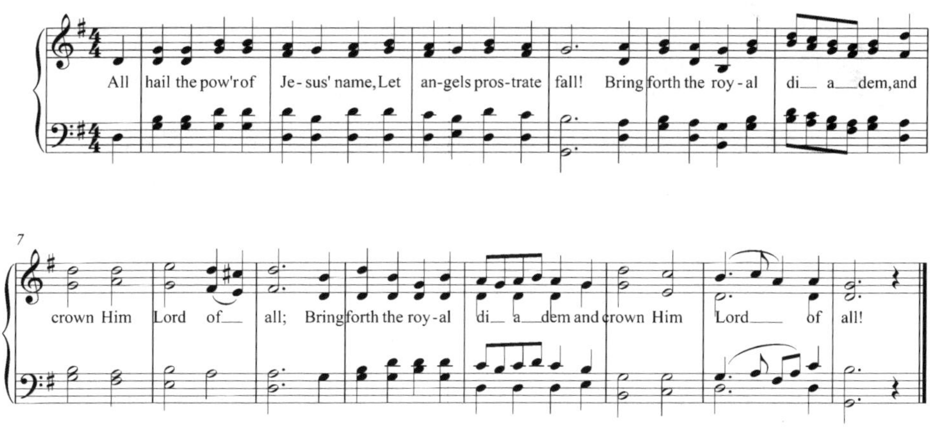

Strauss, and Jules Massenet. Apparently, Ives saw him as one of the reasons why New York City's musical life at the time was rooted in the past.

In the finale of the quartet, Ives returns to the difficult idiom and dense textures of the first movement. All three movements contain quotations of familiar tunes. Those in the first and second are secular and patriotic tunes, but those in the third are hymn tunes. Ives's use of "Nettleton" ("Come, Thou fount of every blessing") is so veiled as easily to escape notice, but toward the end of the movement, an ostinato line in the cello is played against a very clear statement of Lowell Mason's tune "Bethany." The movement has been called "transcendentalist";[22] however, Ives may have been aiming not so much for sublimity as ironic humor: He indicated on the score that the piece was "for four men who converse, discuss, argue (politics), fight, shake hands, shut up, then walk up the mountainside to view the firmament." Here, Ives may have intended a pun since—at least according to traditional metaphysical cosmology—these four men on the mountaintop might have been "Nearer, My God, to Thee."

Ives's chamber works, like all of his music, are scrapbooks in which the collage of musical materials reflects the diversity of his life and culture. Quotation, paraphrase, and parody all play roles in these collages. Quotation seems generally to pose a neutral view, whereas paraphrase frequently is nostalgic, dreamy, or idealistic, and parody is humorous, ironic, or mocking. These are not coincidental traits of Ives's music. They are part of the aesthetic philosophy—influenced especially by Ralph Waldo Emerson—that he formulated early in his career and maintained for the remainder of his life. Emerson's essay on art articulates this viewpoint clearly:

> The artist must employ the symbols in use in his day and nation to convey his enlarged sense to his fellow-men. Thus the new in art is always formed out of the old. The Genius of the Hour always sets his ineffaceable seal on the work and gives it an inexpressible charm for the imagination. . . . No man can quite emancipate himself from his age and country, or produce a model in which the education, the religion, the politics, usages and arts of his times shall have no share.[23]

It was this ideology that enabled Ives to create a distinctively American style of art music from vernacular musical materials of the time.

ELEVEN

Nationalism and Tradition: Schoenberg and the Austro-German Avant-Garde

Histories of music rarely speak of Arnold Schoenberg (1874–1951) as a nationalist or as a traditionalist; however, he was definitive in asserting both his status as a German composer and as a continuation of the German musical heritage. Josef Rufer, who studied composition with Schoenberg and was his assistant at the Prussian Academy of Arts from 1925 until 1933, quotes an article by Schoenberg that begins with the statement: "Whenever I think about music, I never visualize . . . any other than German music."[1] When he formulated the precepts of serialism, Schoenberg told Rufer: "Today I succeeded in something by which I have assured the dominance of German music for the next century."[2] On another occasion, when seeking an appointment to teach composition, Schoenberg described himself as "an educated Brahmsian, Beethovenian, and Mozartian."[3] In his essay of 1931 entitled "National Music," Schoenberg lists Bach and Mozart as primary influences and Beethoven, Brahms, and Wagner as secondary models.[4]

Schoenberg was deeply hurt when the president of the Prussian Academy, Max von Schillings, in accordance with National Socialist anti-Semitic policies, denounced Jewish faculty members. Schoenberg recoiled in pain, declaring to Anton Webern in a letter of 4 August 1933 that he had separated himself from whatever connections he had had with the Occident; however, his protestations were more rhetorical than realistic. Webern sent the letter to Alban Berg with the observation that "[Schoenberg] has shaken me deeply. Even if I regard his departure from the Occident *humanly* as possible (I don't believe it . . .) there remains for me the unshakeable fact of his musical works, for which there is only one description: German."[5]

Nationalism in Schoenberg's music is demonstrated through his alliance with German musical traditions. At the precise moment when he ostensibly broke with that tradition, he took pains to demonstrate that on the contrary, he was maintaining and continuing that tradition; thus, in his first serial work, the Suite, Op. 25 (1923), he replaced the perfunctory designation *Stück* (piece), which he had often used to label earlier pieces, with highly indicative designations: Prelude, Gavotte, Musette, Menuett, and Gigue.

Because he was a composer who valued his musical heritage, Schoenberg attached great significance to chamber music, as his output demonstrates. His principal chamber scores include an early String Quartet in D (1897); four additional works for that medium—Op. 7 (1905), Op. 10 (1908), Op. 30 (1927), Op. 37 (1936)—the string sextet *Verklärte Nacht*, Op. 4 (Transfigured night; 1899); *Pierrot Lunaire*, Op. 21, for flute/piccolo, clarinet/bass clarinet, violin/viola, cello, piano, and speaking voice reciting surrealist poems by Albert Giraud in German translation by Otto Erich Hartleben; the Serenade, Op. 24 (1923) for clarinet, bass clarinet, mandolin, guitar, violin, viola, cello, and bass voice; the Wind Quintet, Op. 26 (1924); the Suite, Op. 29 (1926) for two clarinets, bass clarinet, violin, viola, cello, and piano; *Ode to Napoleon*, Op. 41 (1945) for string quartet and reciter; the String Trio, Op. 45 (1946), and the Phantasy, Op. 47 (1949) for violin and piano.[6]

Verklärte Nacht has established an enduring place in the repertoire, and rightly so. The piece uses Wagnerian techniques of sequence and leitmotif to construct a tone poem in the manner of Strauss, albeit for chamber ensemble in this case. Schoenberg indicated on the title page of the manuscript that the piece is based on Richard Dehmel's poem by the same title; however, the manuscript does not include the text of the poem. Similarly, when Schoenberg gave the score to Dreililien Verlag for publication, it was without the poem. Max Marschalk, the director of the firm, had to write to the composer requesting the poem in order to include it with the published score. In early performances of the piece, programs did not include the poem either.[7]

The poem is in five stanzas of irregular length. Individual lines have variable numbers of syllables, and rhyme schemes are erratic. The third and fifth stanzas are the shortest, with four and three lines respectively. The first stanza amounts to a set design; the second lays bare the crux of the drama: a woman has become pregnant out of wedlock; she is uncertain how her present companion will respond; the third stanza is an interlude leading to the man's response; in the fourth stanza, he magnanimously reassures her that he accepts her and her child; the brief final stanza lowers the curtain on the happy trio immersed in tranquil ecstasy.[8] In notes provided by the composer for the Hollywood String Quartet's recording of the piece, he related particular musical events to certain lines of the poem; however, his aim was to capture the ambience of the poetic images rather than to write onomatopoeic music. Instrumentation is sometimes anthropomorphic—with rather obvious instances equating the man and woman walking through the woods with the sounds of viola and cello respectively, yet here too Schoenberg does not maintain this assignment of instruments slavishly.

Arnold Rosé and the Rosé Quartet gave the premiere of *Verklärte Nacht* on 18 March 1902. They repeated the work in 1903 on a program that had been rehearsed in the presence of Gustav Mahler. It was in this context that the two composers met for the first time.[9] In a performance of 1912, Dehmel heard Schoenberg's piece for the first time. He wrote the composer a note of thanks in which he calls the piece "wonderful" and states that he was "enthralled" by the music. Similarly enthusiastic responses led Schoenberg to arrange the work for string orchestra in 1917.

The First String Quartet shows the influence of Richard Strauss insofar as Schoenberg adopts his procedure, familiar from the tone poems *Also sprach Zarathustra* (1896) and *Ein Heldenleben* (1898) of combining multiple movements as a continuum. In the Quartet, the sections are clear from the headings: Nicht zu rasch (not too fast), Kräftig (powerfully), Mäßig: Langsame Viertel (evenly: slow quarter-note), Mäßig: Heiter (evenly: jovial). Harmonies are highly chromatic, but imitative counterpoint and highly melodic passages appear throughout the piece. Schoenberg draws from the Classical tradition as well, particularly in the second section, which uses for its first motif a figure borrowed from the minuet of Haydn's String Quartet in D major, Op. 20, No. 4, Hob. III/34. Later, he draws from the "Theme russe" section of the third movement of Beethoven's Quartet in E minor, Op. 59, No. 2. The allusion is confirmed by the contour of Schoenberg's melody, its countersubject, and the characteristic imitations of both.

The String Quartet, Op. 10 broke new ground for Schoenberg. In it, he wrote two essentially traditional quartet movements. The second of these is a scherzo whose trio quotes the familiar tune "Ach, du lieber Augustin, alles ist hin" (Alas, my dear Augustin, all is lost). This is apparently an allusion to the fact that his first wife, Mathilde Zemlinsky, had left him for the painter Richard Gerstl.[10] Schoenberg adds soprano soloist in the third and fourth movements, which use two poems, "Litenai" (Litany) and "Entrückung" (Transcendance), from Stefan George's collection *Der siebente Ring* (The seventh ring; 1907). The former poem is a prayer for comfort amid earthly turmoil, the later, a sublimation of human misery that leads Schoenberg to transcend not only his personal circumstances but the restrictions of tonality as well. Here, he lines out a tone row of the pitches G-sharp, B, G, F-sharp, A-sharp, D, F, E, D-sharp, C-sharp, A, C. While the movement is not constructed in strict serial fashion, it nevertheless anticipates aspects of the compositional style that Schoenberg developed in 1923.

The nature of dodecaphony was elucidated in Schoenberg's essay of 1923 entitled simply "Twelve-Tone Composition."[11] In the first sentence, he states: "In twelve-tone composition consonances (major and minor triads) and also the simpler dissonances (diminished triads and seventh chords)—in fact almost everything that used to make up the ebb and flow of harmony—are, as far as possible, avoided." He explains that this approach in no way diminishes the significance of harmonies (i.e., simultaneous sonorities) or motives and phrases (i.e., successive sonorities), but that the application of these will be different in homophonic and polyphonic music. In his closing remarks, Schoenberg stresses that comprehensibility of the musical idea is presumed regardless of whether the sonorities are presented simultaneously or successively. He makes the further interesting observation that the ease or difficulty of comprehensibility of the original idea will affect both the tempo and the development of the musical premise.

In transforming these theories into music, Schoenberg worked initially with pieces for piano solo and chamber ensembles—specifically, the Serenade, Op. 24, the Wind Quintet, Op. 26, and the Suite, Op. 29.[12] The Serenade is an appealing work, largely owing to its fascinating constellation of timbres and interesting rhythmic motifs. In this and other twelve-tone pieces, Schoenberg generally uses metrical and formal patterns more akin to traditional repertoire than he had in his free pan-tonal works. Each of the seven movements is highly profiled from a constructive point of view. Schoenberg's labels—Marsch, Menuett, Variationen, Sonett nr. 217 von Petrarca, Tanzscene, Lied ohne Worte, and Finale—help to orient the listener to particular aspects of each movement, but these are often subverted by the intrusion of disparate musical topics.[13] In the opening march, for example, the opening duple meter is almost immediately contradicted by allusions to the triple meter and melodic contours of Viennese waltzes. This montage of materials is brought under control by clearly articulated formal designs, which frequently include literal repeats. In the case of the minuet, Schoenberg follows the Classical model exactly and provides a contrasting trio that is followed by the repetition of the minuet, then the coda. The theme of the third movement is clearly labeled, as are each of its five variations and coda. The only strictly serial movement is the fourth, which is based on the row E, D, E-flat, C-flat, C, D-flat, A-flat, G-flat, A, F, G, B-flat, which is heard first in segments played by the violin, bass clarinet, cello, and viola. These are clearly identified in the score by the designation *Hauptstimme* (main line), an instruction that Schoenberg began using in 1909 in his Five Pieces for Orchestra, Op. 16. The tone row appears as the vocal line thirteen times, each time with different rhythmic designs.[14] The ensuing dance scene consists of a waltz and an Austrian Länder stated in alternation. The sixth movement is a tranquil Adagio played *pianissimo* and with muted strings throughout. The line for the violin, which is the soloist, moves quickly throughout its register in a free pan-tonal style, yet its effect is intensely lyrical. The finale recalls the opening march and then cites salient passages from earlier movement, although special emphasis is given to the *Ländler* theme.

Schoenberg's Wind Quintet, Op. 26 is his first score to realize the full potential of serialism. The prime form of the row, which consists of the tones E-flat, G, A, B, C-sharp, C, B-flat, D, E, F-sharp, A-flat, F, is identified as the main line in the flute part. Within the four movements of the piece, Schoenberg focuses at various times on particular pitch sets extracted from the row and its transformations. In so doing, he hoped to achieve a formal effect comparable to the components of traditional tonal forms. This formal partitioning is aided by consistency of dynamics, tempo, melodic contours, and other parameters as well; thus, the first movement is a sonata form with a coda, the second, a scherzo and trio with coda, the third, a ternary song form, and the last, a rondo. It is in the rondo that Schoenberg comes closest to accomplishing his goal of a clearly comprehensible form.

In his initial plans for the Suite, Op. 29, Schoenberg had envisioned a seven-movement work. The finished product, dedicated to his new wife, Gertrud née Kolisch, consists of four movements—Overture, Dance Steps, Theme and Variations, and Gigue—that retain some elements of those originally projected. The first, which was to have been in 6/8 meter, "light, elegant, snazzy, and bluffing," became the Overture and retained those very characteristics. Of the Foxtrot, only the duple meter and shifting tempos remained in the Dance Steps movement. The next two items of the first plan, a waltz and a slow movement self-portrait of the composer, were dropped. Friedrich Silcher's setting of "Änchen von Tharau" (long notes in the clarinet) is the theme of the third movement, which consists of four variations and a coda. The sentiments of the first stanza continue throughout the remaining five of the complete poem.

Ännchen von Tharau ist's, die mir gefällt,
Sie ist mein Leben, mein Gut und mein Geld.
Ännchen von Tharau hat wieder ihr Herz
Auf mich gerichtet in Lieb' und in Schmerz.
Ännchen von Tharau, mein Reichthum, mein Gut,
Du meine Seele, mein Fleisch und mein Blut!

(Annie from Tharau! May she live in good health!
She is my life, my goodness, my wealth.
Annie from Tharau devotes her whole heart
To me, both in joy and when pain doth smart.
Annie from Tharau, you make my life whole:
You are my flesh, and my blood, and my soul.)

Schoenberg replaced the last two movements of the original plan with a Gigue in 12/8 meter at a lively tempo and in a typically Baroque, contrapuntal texture. These features are interrupted from time to time, particularly for recollections of the Dance Steps movement and an extended reminiscence of the "Änchen" theme.

"Änchen von Tharau" Friedrich Silcher

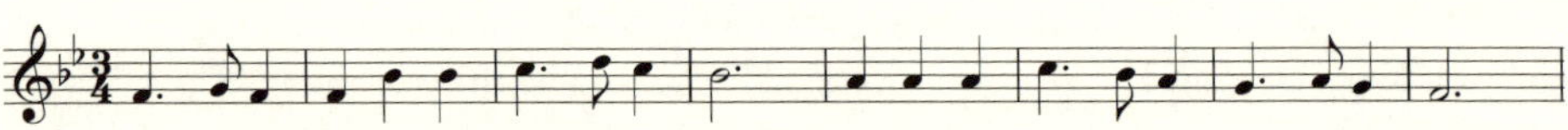

Schoenberg's Third and Fourth String Quartets (1927, 1936) were both commissioned by Elizabeth Sprague Coolidge, and both were premiered by the Kolisch Quartet (the former in Vienna, the latter in Los Angeles).[15] Both are in four movements and retain close ties with traditional formal designs. They also preserve the typically serious character of the genre insofar as they contain no compositional games—such as the syllabic distribution of eleven-syllable lines over the twelve tones of the row in the Petrarch Sonnet of the Serenade, or the incorporation of an unambiguously tonal melody within the serial fabric of the third movement of the Suite. The two quartets are nevertheless quite different because the Third makes little use of special string effects, whereas the Fourth relies on *sul ponticello*, harmonics, pizzicato, and other distinctive sonorities.

In his String Trio, Schoenberg reacted to his near-fatal heart attack on 2 August 1946. At the time, he had already accepted a commission from A. Tillman Meritt for a piece to be performed on a chamber-music program with other new works by Walter Piston and Bohuslav Martinů. He had determined before the attack that the piece would be a continuous movement with three principal subjects separated by two episodes.[16] The details of Schoenberg's brush with death are recounted in his own essay "Mein Todesfall" (My fatality) as well as in recollections of his friends and colleagues to whom he explained the significance of particular musical events.[17] Sudden, loud outbursts are generally associated with the many injections Schoenberg was given; wildly juxtaposed musical segments recall the composer's unconscious and delirious states; and variously remembered and abandoned musical languages reflect both his state of mind at the time and his general relationship with his German musical heritage.[18]

The creative conceptions behind Schoenberg's Trio greatly impressed one of his literary friends, Thomas Mann, who was then writing his novel *Doctor Faustus: The Life of the German Composer Adrian Leverkühn as Narrated by Friends.* Mann was intrigued by the dichotomy between the almost impossible technical demands of Schoenberg's Trio and the rewards of its fascinating tonal effects. This dialectic was incorporated by Mann into a chapter on the imaginary composer's chamber music. (In the novel, Leverkühn is syphillitic, a detail that Schoenberg greatly resented.)

Schoenberg's *Ode to Napoleon* exists in two versions. The first, for reciter, string quartet, and piano, fulfilled the requirements of the commission that he received from the League of Composers in 1942 for a chamber work. In fact, the premiere of the piece on 23 November 1944 was hardly a chamber work at all, having been given by Artur Rodzinsky conducting the string section of the New York Philharmonic with Mack Harrell, speaker, and Eduard Steuermann, pianist. For this version, "Schoenberg made the necessary additions to the original score."[19] Even in its original instrumentation, the *Ode* differs sharply from Schoenberg's authentic chamber scores in several ways. Most conspicuous is the absence of traditional pattern forms within this through-composed piece. While vocal resources had been used previously in the Second String Quartet, their pervasiveness in the *Ode* precludes the kind of interaction among elements of the ensemble that is characteristic of chamber music. This circumstance arose from two grounds: The first was Schoenberg's intention of making a political statement in condemnation of Hitler, the second was his selection of a gargantuan text—nineteen strophes of nine lines each! The *Ode to Napoleon*, in its original version, is thus chamber music only insofar as it uses an ensemble of six players.

ANTON WEBERN

Similar small ensembles with solo voices appear commonly in the works of Schoenberg's pupil Anton Webern. Among these are Six Songs with four instruments, Op. 14; Five Songs with Five instruments, Op. 15; Five Canons for soprano, clarinet, and bass clarinet, Op. 16; Three Folk Songs with three instruments, Op. 17, and Three Songs with E-flat Clarinet and Guitar, Op. 18. In these works, too, the demands of setting texts often inhibit the characteristic interactions among instruments of chamber ensembles; however, Webern's predilection for canonic writing helped to minimize this impediment.

Webern composed an impressive number of purely instrumental chamber works, and his first known compositions (discovered in 1965) are two pieces for cello and piano. Before his official "Opus 1," the Passacaglia for orchestra, Webern had completed almost two dozen instrumental chamber scores, mainly for string quartet and piano quintet.[20] His Five Movements, Op. 5 (1909) for string quartet thus represents a very advanced stage of his compositional development rather than an initial essay in this medium. Each of them is highly contrasted in affection, duration, and sonority. The third and shortest is not quite a minute; the fifth and longest is slightly over four minutes. In all five, Webern, who was himself a cellist, makes extensive use of distinctive string sonorites including pizzicato, *sul ponticello*, harmonics, *con sordino*. The third movement, which has the character of a scherzo, was inspired by Schoenberg's Second String Quartet, Op. 10. Webern had heard the premiere of Op. 10 given by the Rosé Quartet in Vienna on 21 December 1908. In fact, Webern's movement uses thematic materials taken from the Scherzo of Schoenberg's Quartet. More recent study of Op. 5 indicates that the influence of Schoenberg's Op. 10 is far more pervasive in Webern's Op. 5, and that the motivic figure that becomes the head motif of "Ich fühle luft von anderen planeten" was converted by Webern into a structural plan at least for the fourth of his movements.[21]

Arnold Rosé first heard Webern's Op. 5 when the composer played the pieces for him on the piano. At the time, Rosé expressed interest in performing them with his quartet; this they did on 29 June 1912, although the premiere had taken place in Vienna on 8 February 1910. Schoenberg was equally enthusiastic about the pieces, and he wrote to the publisher Fritz Simrock recommending them as well as the Passacaglia, Op. 1, and the Four Pieces, Op. 7 (1910) for violin and piano. Although they were not accepted for publication, the Five Movements attracted attention, and they were featured on a program of 8 August 1922 that was sponsored by what became the International Society for Contemporary Music (ISCM) three days later on 11 August. The performance was given by the Amar Quartet, whose members were Licco Amar, Walter Casper, Paul Hindemith, and Maurits Frank.[22]

Webern rewrote the Five Movements in 1928–29 for string orchestra, and this version of the pieces was given under Fabien Sevitzky—Serge Koussevitzky's nephew—in Philadelphia on 26 March 1930. In revamping the pieces, he envisioned an ensemble of about eighty players and often expanded the score at times to fourteen staves; thus, it was not simply an "arrangement" of the chamber music. Webern submitted this version (along with Opp. 19–21) on 3 February 1931 in his successful bid for the Music Prize of the City of Vienna. This award gave Webern considerable notoriety in musical circles in addition to a sizable cash stipend. On 13 April of that year, the quartet version was the opening number of the first all-Webern concert. According to Webern, a performance of the string-orchestra version requires about seventeen minutes.[23] Even allowing a minute or two extra for performance by the larger forces, one must conclude that most string quartet performances are excessively fast.

During the years from 1911 to 1913, Webern had considered expanding Op. 5. Eventually rejecting this idea, he assembled four movements as a string quartet in 1911. In 1913, he composed two additional movements that were placed as outer movements to the existing four. The set of six became the Bagatelles, Op. 9, for string quartet. Webern may have felt the need to expand the four-movement string quartet of 1911 on account of the extreme brevity of the pieces, a feature to which the title (i.e., "trifles") alludes.[24] The Amar Quartet, with Paul Hindemith on viola, gave the premiere of Op. 9 on 19 July 1924 at the prestigious Donaueschingen Festival. In a lecture that he gave on 12 February 1932, Webern explained the significance of Op. 9 as follows:

> The Bagatelles for string quartet [are] all very short, lasting about two minutes. . . . Here I had the feeling that when the twelve notes [of the chromatic scale] had all been played, the piece was over. . . . In my sketchbook, I wrote out the chromatic scale and crossed off individual

> notes. . . . In short, a law came into being: Until all twelve notes have appeared none of them may occur again. The most important thing is that each successive "run" of the twelve notes marked a division with the piece, idea, or theme.[25]

Webern's aphoristic manner is still more prominent in the Three Little Pieces, Op. 11 (1914), which were the indirect result of a request from his father. An enthusiastic music lover, the elder Webern suggested that his son might try to write a longish piece for cello and piano. Webern began work on it immediately, finished a single movement of a sonata, but became distracted by the idea of writing several small pieces. The Three Little Pieces (nine, thirteen, and ten measures respectively) thus came into being. Webern presented them to his father as a birthday present, apparently indicating that he planned to continue work on the sonata. Within two weeks, World War I had begun, and so the sonata remains an impressive torso of the projected two-movement work. The first performance of Op. 11 was given on 2 December 1924 by Maurits Frank, cello, and Eduard Zuckmayer, piano. The cello sonata was premiered by Gregor Piatigorsky accompanied by Victor Babin on 3 June 1970.

The String Trio, Op. 20 (1927) was originally planned as a three-movement work, but Webern ultimately rejected the third movement. The two movements were published by Universal Edition in 1927, and the premiere was given by Rudolf Kolisch, violin, Eugen Lehner, viola, and Benar Heifetz, cello, in Vienna on 16 January 1928. By the time he began the Trio, Webern had embraced Schoenberg's method of composing with twelve tones; however, the sequence of movements in many of Webern's works does not always reflect the order of their composition. In the case of the Trio, the second movement, Sehr getragen und ausdrucksvoll (very lightly and expressively), was originally intended as the first movement; thus, it has the depth, character, and sonata form typically associated with first movements of Classical scores. It also contains the primary form of the tone row that pervades both movements. When Webern changed the design of the piece, he placed what would have been an internal movement, Sehr langsam (very slowly) in first position; however, by this point, the row transformations are well advanced.[26]

The details of row variations were of little concern to most audiences during Webern's time, and most critics decried the Trio along with its advanced serial techniques. When Licco Amar, Paul Hindemith, and Maurits Frank played it on 21 May 1928, the response was quite uniformly negative. On 13 September, when members of the Kolisch Quartet played the piece at the Siena conference of the ISCM, disturbances in the hall during the second movement forced the performers to begin the movement anew. At its conclusion, the concert hall became pandemonium.[27] Ironically, this austere, difficult work was the first music by Webern to be recorded on a commercial record label. This release in 1939, which featured the Kathleen Washbourne Trio on Decca Records, was sent to the composer in October of that year.

Webern's Quartet, Op. 22 (1930) was written and dedicated to the architect Adolf Loos on the occasion of his sixtieth birthday. The piece was planned in 1928 as a three-movement work, but Webern ultimately produced two movements. These were originally to have been the third (rondo) and second (slow), but they became second and first. Other aspects of the score changed during its creation: At first, Webern had envisioned a concerto for violin, clarinet, horn, piano, and string orchestra, but by mid-1929 he settled on an ensemble of violin, clarinet, tenor saxophone, and piano. By then, he had softened his position regarding literal repetitions within scores, admitting that comprehensibility required at least some reiteration. This occurs most conspicuously in the first movement, which is essentially a binary form with repeats of both segments, all of which are framed by a prelude and epilogue. Throughout the work, small motivic cells are put forth then inverted, much like opening measures of Brahms's Symphony No. 4.[28] The premiere performance was given in Vienna on 13 April 1931 by Rudolf Kolisch, violin; Johann Löw, clarinet; Leopold Wlach, saxophone; and Eduard Steuermann, piano.

On 23 November 1937, Elizabeth Sprague Coolidge wrote to Webern requesting a wind quintet; however, Rudolf Kolisch managed to persuade her to ask for a string quartet instead. There was a good reason for this: Webern was already at work on what became his Op. 28 (1938), a piece that he had conceived and entered into his sketchbook over a year previously, on 17 November 1936. There, the three movements are given as Langsam (slow), Rondo, and Fugue. By the time Webern received the commission, he had already completed two movements of the string quartet and was working on a third. The change in specifications of the commission was most welcome since the agreement stipulated that the piece should be ready for its first performance in July 1938. The Kolisch Quartet gave the premiere at the Tenth Berkshire Festival of Chamber Music, Pittsfield, Massachusetts, on 22 September 1938. In that performance, the movements were in the order Gemächlich (unhurried), Mäßig (evenly),

Sehr fließend (very flowing); however, Webern—against the advice of Kolisch—changed the ordering of the printed edition so that these became the second, first, and third movements.

Op. 28 is a highly contrapuntal work whose three movements make extensive use of canon, fugue, and stretto. Formal details likewise stem from the Classical heritage, and antecedent-consequent pairings, variation procedure, ternary song form, scherzo and trio, and fugue contribute the designs of the movements.[29] The row consists of a series of three tetrachords each spanning a minor third: D-flat, C, E-flat, D / F-sharp, G, E, F / A, G-sharp, B, B-flat. The outer two tetrachords are transpositions of the B-flat, A, C, H motif. The central one gives the motif in retrograde transposition. If the central tetrachord is bisected and combined with the outer tetrachords, the resulting hexachords are related in that the second is the retrograde inversion of the first. Webern uses the row both as three tetrachords and two hexachords.

ALBAN BERG

In general, Berg preferred to compose for large ensembles, but his three chamber works, the First String Quartet, Op. 3 (1910), Four Pieces, Op. 5 (1913) for clarinet and piano, and the *Lyric Suite* (1926) for string quartet, are flawlessly written and have become standard repertoire.

The completion of Op. 3 marked the end of Berg's apprenticeship with Schoenberg, but the piece is rife with the expressive characteristics and sonic effects of Schoenberg's own early works for string ensembles. It was for this very reason that Berg decided not to dedicate the piece to Schoenberg.[30] The Quartet consists of two movements, the first being a sonata and coda, the second, a rondo with varied reprises interspersed with four episodes. The first movement commences with a quick descending figure that settles on the tone B. Both the theme and its accompaniment focus on chromatic expansions to form melodic and harmonic wedges. In its linear expansion, the first theme moves upward until it reaches a minor third, but the continuation of the main theme, with its downward expansions from the minor third, to a major third, and then to a fourth, provides a contrasting motif despite its derivation from the organic process of expansion. The second theme opens with a conspicuous ascending fifth, followed immediately by the descending version of this same interval. The brief development section is followed by a recapitulation in which motifs of the opening theme are thoroughly reworked, often in an intensely lyrical way.

The four pieces of Berg's Op. 5, for clarinet and piano, were modeled on the Six Little Pieces, Op. 19 (1911) for piano by Schoenberg.[31] In addition, several contain allusions or quotations from *Till Eulenspiegel* and *Death and Transfiguration* of Richard Strauss.[32] Berg apparently chose the four-movement plan in order to follow the Classical tradition in which the first movement is an Allegro, the second an Adagio, the third a Scherzo and Trio, and the fourth a Rondo finale.[33] The pieces, which are dedicated to Schoenberg, are highly coloristic and suggest the influence of Debussy. The challenges of the pieces are musical rather than technical—assuming the ability for flutter-tonguing. They were first performed at a program of the Society for Private Musical Performances on 17 October 1919.

Berg's magnum opus of chamber music is his Second String Quartet, known as the *Lyric Suite.* The piece is an astonishing cross-referencing of musical, personal, and artistic developments in Berg's life, and as one unravels the strands of allusions, the depth of Berg's melancholy genius becomes increasingly clear.

The sequence of six movements begins with a medial tempo and affection, Allegretto gioviale. The ensuing movements alternate bipolar intensifications of tempos and affections: Andante amoroso, Allegro misterioso, Adagio appassionato, Presto delirando, Largo desolato. The number twenty-three, which Berg considered his fateful number, provides the common denominator for the number of measures in five of the movements.[34] Quotations from the *Lyric Symphony* of Alexander Zemlinsky, Schoenberg's only composition teacher, and from Wagner's *Tristan und Isolde* indicated from the outset that the work had extramusical associations. The secret story behind the piece remained a mystery until 1977, when Berg's heavily annotated gift score to Hanna Fuchs-Robettin was discovered among the possessions of her daughter, Dorothea Robetin, in Mifflinburg, Pennsylvania, by George Perle.[35] That score contained a previously unknown vocal setting of Stefan George's German translation of "De profundis" from Baudelaire's *Les fleurs du mal;* moreover, the motivic cell A, B-flat, F, H (= C) was recognized as a permutation of the initials in *A*lban *B*erg and *H*anna *F*uchs.

Berg went to great pains to incorporate these cryptograms in his music. The row as it appears in the first movement consists of F, E, C, A, G, D, A-flat, D-flat, E-flat, G-flat, B-flat, B. In the second movement, the fourth and tenth tones are exchanged. At the opening of the third movement, the latter form of the row is transposed to begin on B-flat, thus yielding the tetrachord derived from their initials, B-flat, A, F, B (= C-flat), as the head motif of the Allegro misterioso—Trio estatico movement.[36] The Trio, which reaches the *fortissimo* dynamic, is played throughout with mutes.

This would appear ironic; however, the annotated score shows that Berg knew that his and Hanna's mutual passions, intense though they may be, would have to remain suppressed and secret.

This embedded subject of the row is not its only remarkable feature, since it is an all-interval row; moreover, Berg designed it to accommodate within the context of strict serial procedure an exact quotation in the middle (meas. 26, 27) of the last movement, Largo desolato, of the Tristan Chord. "Through serial operations, Wagner's motives (the Tristan Chord set-types [0, 2, 5, 8], the cello melody [0, 1, 2, 6], and the canonic subject [0, 1, 2, 3, 7] saturate Berg's composition. . . . particularly the last movement."[37] Astonishingly, this masterfully crafted and highly expressive work was Berg's first strict twelve-tone composition.

PAUL HINDEMITH

Though he is often cited as the primary exponent of expressionism in music, Paul Hindemith (1895–1963) wrote a substantial number of scores that are not radically modern. As a string player himself, Hindemith was a violinist in Adolf Rebner's quartet before World War I, and after his tour of duty, he was the violist in Licco Amar's quartet from 1921 until 1929. It was during the 1920s that he became increasingly concerned about the widening gap between composer and audience. He addressed this situation by participating in the Donaueschingen Festival for contermporary music from its inception in 1921 until 1930 as well as by composing *Gebrauchsmusik* (utility music)—pieces directed to the intelligent music lover who may not be a professional musician. His *Gebrauchsmusik* includes pieces for children, movies, radio, and sonatas for nearly every instrument.

Hindemith's six sonatas of Op. 11 (1919) include four accompanied sonatas: two, Nos. 1 and 2, for violin and piano, one, No. 3, for cello and piano, and one, No. 4, for viola and piano; the remaining two, Nos. 5 and 6, are for solo viola and violin respectively. The sonatas of Op. 25 (1923) again mix solo and accompanied sonatas, those with piano being Op. 25 No. 2 for viola *d'amore*, and No. 4 for viola. (The viola *d'amore* fell out of use at the close of the Baroque era, but experienced a revival in the early twentieth century when early-music groups became increasingly interested in original instrumentation.) Subsequent sonatas with one obbligato instrument and piano include one each for flute (1936), bassoon (1938), oboe (1938), clarinet (1939), trumpet (1939), English horn (1941), trombone (1941), cello (1942), double bass (1949), and bass tuba (1955), and two each for violin (E, 1935; C, 1939) and horn (F, 1939; alto horn, E-flat, 1943), which can also be played on alto saxophone.

In addition to these, Hindemith wrote seven string quartets (1915, 1918, 1920, 1921, 1923, 1943, 1945); two string trios (1924, 1933); a Trio (1928) for viola, heckelphone/saxophone, and piano; a wind quintet (1923); a Quintet (1923; rev. 1954) for clarinet and strings; a Quartet (1938) for clarinet, violin, piano, and cello; a Septet (1948) for flute, oboe, clarinet, trumpet, horn, bass clarinet, and bassoon; a Sonata (1952) for four horns; and an Octet (1958) for clarinet, bassoon, horn, violin, two violas, cello, and double bass.

TWELVE

The Continuation of Tonality in the Twentieth Century

Many composers at the close of the nineteenth century were attempting to find new ways to use sonorities inherited from the tonal tradition. Some devised ingenious new applications of sounds that, though familiar, are contextualized in ways that depart from functional harmonic paradigms. These composers might be considered conservative, at least superficially; nevertheless, their objectives were no less inventive than those of Schoenberg and his followers although their means were more readily acceptable to the typical musician and devotee of the time. Many—but not all—composers who took this moderate approach were trained in conservatories. The conservatory system evolved primarily during the Romantic era, with the Paris Conservatory leading the way in 1795. Other cultural centers followed and set up schools of music. With few exceptions (such as the conservatories at Dessau and the Berlin Meisterschule, established in 1829 and 1833 respectively), conservatory instruction was intended to train capable performers. "Composition" in those contexts consisted mainly of instruction in music theory and basso continuo. Schools of this sort sprang up in Prague (1811), Breslau (1815), Vienna (1817), Berlin (1822), Geneva (1835), Leipzig (1843), St. Petersburg (1862), and Moscow (1866). In the United States, Baltimore's Peabody Conservatory opened in 1857. Oberlin College Conservatory (1865), the Cincinnati Conservatory (1867), and the New England Conservatory (1867), the largest of the three, were intended primarily for training teachers.

A concurrent development that fostered conservative attitudes was the rise of historical musicology as a discipline. Repertoires were increasingly treated as museum pieces, and historical musical styles became models that young composers were encouraged to imitate. Nations boasting rich musical traditions—especially Germany, Austria, France, and Italy—became destinations for many musicians making pilgrimages from culturally remote areas, and the composers considered paragons of those traditions led to epigones among the aspiring populations.

The impact of conservatory training and historical musicology can be discerned in the works of so many composers that it would be impossible to survey them all; nevertheless, in some exceptional cases aspiring composers progressed beyond imitation in order to make distinctive contributions to the chamber music repertoire. Among these are the Scandinavians Carl Nielsen (1865–1931) and Jean Sibelius (1865–1957); the British Ralph Vaughan Williams (1872–1958) and Benjamin Britten (1913–1976); and the Americans George Whitefield Chadwick (1845–1931), Amy Beach (1867–1944), Arthur Foote (1853–1937), Walter Piston (1874–1976), Vincent Persichetti (1915–1987), Aaron Copland (1900–1990), and Ronald Caltabiano (b. 1959).

SCANDINAVIANS: CARL NIELSEN AND JEAN SIBELIUS

In his youth, Nielsen played piano, violin, bugle, cornet, and trombone. He often performed with his father at weddings, civic ceremonies, and occasions that prompted the creation of ad hoc bands. Nielsen attributed his contrapuntal skills to his habit of improvising countersubjects to popular tunes at such events. That he was an intensely poetic individual is clear from his autobiographical account of his childhood.[1] In it, he relates musical experiences that inspired him: listening to dance music, folk songs, overtures, the symphonies of Haydn and Mozart, Beethoven, the *Well Tempered Clavier* of Bach, and the string quartets of Ignaz Pleyel and George Onslow.[2] The account ends with the composer's departure on 1 January 1884 to study at the Copenhagen Conservatory with Niels Gade.

Gade (1817–1890) was an internationally known figure, largely owing to the advocacy of Robert Schumann and Felix Mendelssohn. Gade's First Symphony (1842) was premiered by Mendelssohn and the Leipzig Gewandhaus Orchestra. Gade became *Kapellmeister* of the Gewandhaus upon Mendelssohn's death in 1847. He returned to Denmark the next year and became a prominent figure in musical circles. In 1866, he was among the founders of the Copenhagen Conservatory and served for a time as its director. A prolific composer of chamber music, Gade wrote three sonatas for violin and piano, two quartets, two quintets, one sextet, and one octet, all for strings, as well as elegant and substantial Fantasy Pieces for clarinet and piano.

When Nielsen applied for admission to Gade's composition studio, he did so—successfully—with the Andante of his String Quartet in D minor. In 1915, Nielsen became a professor at the Conservatory, and in 1930, he was named honorary director. He embraced both Gade's conservative approach to composition and his fondness for chamber music. Fittingly, it was with a chamber work that Nielsen first achieved international fame.[3] In the course of his career, Nielsen wrote three sonatas for violin and piano, *Fantasistykker* (fantasy pieces; one in G minor ca. 1881 for clarinet and piano, two in Op. 2 of 1889 for oboe and piano), a piano trio, six string quartets—the first two of which he chose not to publish, a string quintet, the lament *Ved en ung kunstners Baare* (At the bier of a young artist; 1910) for string quartet and bass, the *Canto serioso* (Serious song; 1913) for horn and piano, the "Serenata in vano" (Futile serenade; 1914), for clarinet, bassoon, horn, cello, and bass (1914), and his most popular chamber piece, the Wind Quintet, Op. 43 (1922).[4]

Nielsen's G-minor Sonata of 1882 for violin and piano as well as the D-minor String Quartet and the Piano Trio in G major (both 1883) were written for use by himself and his friends. He never sought to publish them. Even after studies at the Conservatory, he withheld his scores from publication; thus, the four-movement String Quintet in G (1888; 2.2.1), despite its clarity of form, idiomatic writing, expressive melodies and harmonies (especially in the second movement Adagio), and its energetic rhythms (Allegretto scherzando and finale) was unavailable until six years after his death. Nielsen played the second violin at the premiere of the Quintet on 28 April 1889, but we have no account of his reaction to it.

In the case of the string quartets, Nielsen clearly fussed about details prior to publication. His first published quartet was Op. 5 in F minor, which he wrote in 1890, but he had already written the String Quartet in G minor, Op. 13, in 1888. That score remained unpublished until Nielsen revised it in 1898. A similar process took place with the String Quartet in E-flat, Op. 14, which originated in 1898 but was revised in 1900. His Fourth Quartet in F, Op. 44, first appeared in 1906 with the title *Piacevolezza* (Pleasantry), but it did not acquire its generic title and higher opus number until its revision in 1919. All six quartets, at least in their original versions, are early works completed by 1906. They tend, consequently, to be more conservative than later works.

In his quartets, Nielsen uses traditional forms and movement layouts:

All have four movements with outer movements in sonata-allegro or sonata-rondo from; second movements are ternary song-forms; and third movements use scherzo-and-trio design.[5] Some passages, such as the opening of the second movement (Andante sostenuto) of the String Quartet in E-flat, Op. 14, reveal fluid harmonic designs. This passage bears striking similarities to the opening of the Quartet in C, K. 465, of Mozart, a composer whose works Nielsen prized above all others. Schubertian fluctuation between parallel major and minor is common, as are third-related keys (often enharmonically spelled). Chromaticism for Nielsen was not so much a localized phenomenon as a process of continuous movement among keys. He is concerned with overall unity, and to this end, he regularly employs cyclic recollection of themes, such as the "Résumé" of themes in the recapitulation of the finale of Op. 13. Combination of themes also occurs, but not in the traditional, Schumannesque way. When Nielsen combines themes—as, for example, in the coda to the finale of Op. 5—he draws the most distinctive motifs from his themes and synthesizes them within a new context.

The reconstruction of thematic and harmonic events occurs in Nielsen's sonatas for violin and piano as well. In the First Sonata, again in the coda, music segments previously heard are reordered so as to impart new significance to them, both affectively and structurally. "There is hardly a new bar here in terms of pitch or rhythmic motifs; but virtually every connection is new."[6] The organic relationships among musical gestures provided Nielsen with a means to unify his works without reliance upon a conventional tonal center. This is apparent in the fact that his Sonata, Op. 35 (1912) for violin and piano bears no designation of key whatsoever. The main theme of the second movement finale appears quite conventional at first, but at subsequent hearings, its metrical shapes are altered as are the tonal regions in which it is stated. When the movement ends this process of drifting tonality and changing metrical shape, it does so without the invocation of a traditional tonic key. "Though Nielsen's music is generally in a recognizable key, . . . his use of these keys is unlike common-practice tonality. Even though Nielsen incorporates some standard functional progressions, . . . his scope of chromatic inflexions within reach of any given tonic is just as wide as Schoenberg's. . . . The continual tonal flux complements the other continually evolving aspects of his music."[7]

Nielsen's occasional works, *Ved en ung kunstners baare*, the *Canto serioso*, and the "Serenata in vano" are substantial pieces worthy of performance. The first was written for the funeral of Oluf Hartmann, a painter and acquaintance of Nielsen's via the Neergaard family, whom Nielsen visited at their country home with regularity. The texture of this lament is generally homophonic and without rhythmic complexities, but the harmonic successions are often surprising and always intensely expressive. The score was heard again in 1931 at Nielsen's own funeral. The *Canto serioso* was a test piece written by Nielsen in his capacity as conductor of the Copenhagen Royal Court Orchestra from 1908 to 1914. He was particularly interested in hearing how applicants might manage "arpeggios, difficult intervals, the tone in the bottom register, musical understanding, etc."[8] Nielsen made the transcription of the Canto for cello and piano that was published by Skandinavisk Musikforlag in 1944. The "Serenata" was composed for a tour of musicians from the Copenhagen Royal Court Orchestra in 1914 as a companion piece to Beethoven's Septet, Op. 20. Its simple program outlines successive romantic overtures by musicians beneath the balcony of a young woman. The musicians strike up an exit march, undaunted by their serenade's failure to elicit any response whatsoever from the young lady.

Nielsen's most frequently performed chamber score is his three-movement Wind Quintet, Op. 43. According to popular Nielsen legend, the composer phoned the pianist Christian Christiansen one evening in the fall of 1921, heard music by Mozart in the background, and went straightaway to Christiansen's home to hear this rehearsal. The instrumentalists there, in addition to Christiansen, were Paul Hagemann, flute, Svend Christian Felumb, oboe, Aage Oxenvad, clarinet, Hans Sørensen, horn, and Knud Lassen, bassoon, all members of the Copenhagen Wind Quintet. One detail, however, raises doubts about what they were performing: Mozart never wrote a wind quintet or a sinfonia concertante with winds including flute. The best scoring match among Mozart's works is his Quintet, K. 452 for piano, oboe, clarinet, horn, and bassoon.

Nielsen played winds himself, so he knew well what to do with those instruments. In the Quintet, he demonstrated not only the technical capacities of the instruments, but also something of the personalities of each of the players. The first movement is a sonata form; the second a minuet and trio in which melody does not always correspond to the anticipated triple meter; and the third, which is prefaced by a prelude in which the oboist plays *cor anglais*, is a set of eleven variations including solo variations for bassoon and horn, and concluding with an Andantino festivo. Nielsen chose the theme for his variations from his collection of [49] *Hymns and Sacred Songs* (1914) for solo voice. The tune used in the Quintet is "Min Jesus, lad mit Hjerte få" (My Jesus, make me love you with all my heart). The last movement was performed at the composer's funeral in 1931.

Jean Sibelius

Sibelius was a violinist and he played in a domestic trio with his brother, Christian, on cello, and his sister, Linda, at the piano. He also played in a string quartet in Hämeenlinna, the town to which he moved with his mother (pregnant at the time with Christian) and sister following the premature death of his father in 1868. It was for such homely ensembles that Sibelius wrote his earliest works, largely pieces for string quartet, string duos and trios, and movements for violin and/or cello and piano.

Sibelius moved to Helsinki in the fall of 1885 to study law at the university, but he soon gave this up in preference for studies at the Helsinki Music Institute, which Martin Wegelius (1846–1906) founded in 1882. Having been trained at the conservatories in Vienna, Leipzig, and Munich, Wegelius was well versed in Austro-German music and pedagogy. Sibelius was his star pupil and taught at the Helsinki Music Institute from 1892 until 1900; in 1939, it was renamed the Sibelius Academy in anticipation of his seventy-fifth birthday.

Sibelius wrote his first substantial chamber score, the Quartet in A minor (1889), in the spring semester of his senior year at Wegelius's Institute.[9] Ferruccio Busoni, professor of piano at the nstitute, sight-read the piece in the composer's presence—a feat that impressed Sibelius as much as the Quartet impressed Busoni. In May 1889, the music critic Karl Flodin commended the piece following its performance there by the Institute's quartet. The double scherzo and trio form of the third movement, whose two episodes are in B-flat and F minor respectively, seems to have been modeled after Beethoven, whereas the Dorian mode motifs in the first movement may have been inspired by the music of Grieg.

The success of this piece along with the recommendation of Wegelius won Sibelius a grant for a year of study in Germany. His composition lessons there with Albert Becker were frustrating, as Sibelius found him pedantic. One of the larger works that Sibelius composed in Germany was his five-movement Piano Quintet in G minor (1890), but Wegelius was not enthusiastic about the piece. Upon returning to Helsinki in late summer, Sibelius composed the Quartet in B-flat, Op. 4 (1890). From October of 1890 until June 1891, Sibelius studied privately and at the conservatory in Vienna with Karl Goldmark and Robert Fuchs.

In many ways, these trips to Berlin and Vienna were turning points for Sibelius. His experiences with orchestral music in Helsinki had been limited. Although Robert Kajanus founded the Helsinki Orchestral Association in 1882 (renamed the Philharmonic Society in 1895), the ensemble had fewer than fifty players during that entire period; thus, the contemporary orchestral scores of Gustav Mahler (1860–1911) and Richard Strauss (1864–1949) were inaccessible to the young Sibelius, except in score. Once he heard this music, he turned away from chamber music almost entirely. Among the late works are only two substantial chamber pieces: the three-movement Sonatina in E major, Op. 80 (1915) for violin and piano, and the five-movement String Quartet in D minor, Op. 56 (1909).

The D-minor Quartet is most often known by its nickname, *Voces intimæ* (inner voices). In a score for a friend, Sibelius penciled these words over the three *ppp* chords that appear in measure 21 of the third movement, Adagio. At the time he composed this quartet, Sibelius had severe throat problems, which he presumed were symptoms of cancer. He actually did have a tumor, but it was benign and was successfully removed; nonetheless, *Voces intimæ* is marked throughout by either somber resignation or fierce energy. In its form, too, the piece is ambivalent, sometimes invoking pattern forms but almost invariably pushing them beyond the breaking point. The dialectics within the score's expressive content and constructive features result in a powerfully disconcerting work. Had Sibelius composed only this piece, his status as a great composer would remain without question.

The first movement, in D minor, opens with an Andante dialogue between first violin and cello, but the passage is more than "introductory" since the opening themes grow out of its rhythms and contours. Sonata principle underpins the structure of the movement, but movement from one tonal plane to another is the result of voice leading rather than conventional modulation. The secondary key/theme area (**1** in the exposition, **6** in the recapitulation) is so riddled with chromatic alterations and sudden harmonic shifts that it has little of the stability typical of the subsidiary domain. The development is appropriately brief—because the piece has already included tremendous harmonic movement, as it will in the recapitulation; hence the typical role of the development is no longer applicable. The recapitulation arrives as the key of D minor before the actual restatement of the opening theme (**4**-3). The secondary theme is transposed to D, as might be expected, but Sibelius takes it on a detour ending on A; thus, the second movement, a Vivace in A major, seems to be a continuation of the first rather than a fresh start. This impression is enforced by the quotation of a passage from the recapitulation of the first movement shortly before the end of the second. Note too that the final cadences in both movements consist of half-step motion from G-sharp to an unharmonized A.

Given the principal tonality of D minor, neither of these movements provides harmonic closure; thus, the third movement, Adagio, is an inevitable continuation of the previous movement(s). Sibelius has enticed his listeners down this path for a good reason. This movement opens in D minor, thus offering the potential of being the harmonic goal of what has passed; however, Sibelius straightaway begins to undermine D minor, and by measure 3, the implied tonic is F major. Soon, the mode changes to F minor. An extended argument ensues, in which E minor (i.e., the key of the *voces intimæ* chords) vies with the two forms of F—major and minor—for hegemony. This harmonic instability is paralleled in the rhythmic instability of the lines, which are almost all syncopated; however, the beat is so consistently obscured, that without the score in hand, it is difficult to perceive any syncopations as such. At points where Sibelius intends to establish a tonic, he does so by introducing imitations of a motif derived from the opening violin melody. At its first appearance, it contains seven notes (four rising + three falling), but in subsequent imitative passages, it is altered. As the movement draws toward its close, F seems to be the harmonic goal, but the harmonic progress of the movement is diverted in a coda in which the motif previously used for imitation becomes the principal melodic strand with a new, homophonic accompaniment. The motif is tortured by invading keys, is interrupted by the *voces intimæ* chords, now in C-sharp minor, but is ultimately transformed into an ascending, diatonic scale *mi, fa, sol, la, ti, do.*

The arrival at F major offers expressive repose following the harmonic tensions contained within the third movement; nevertheless, it does not satisfactorily conclude the motion from D to A of the previous movements; thus, another movement becomes necessary: the fourth, Allegretto (ma pesante). This triple-meter movement consists of five sections arranged in the manner of a rondo. The A section is a rustic, almost Haydnesque minuet that falls into head and tail motifs. The first violin dominates the other three instruments in the head motif, but it is the more evenly distributed material of the tail motif that becomes the primary concern in the restatements of A. The contrasting music of B is a gigue in homophonic texture that appears first in G minor, later in B minor. Although the movement provides a harmonically satisfactory ending in D, its formal clarity and metrical regularity ally it so strongly to penultimate movements in Classical string quartets that a more weighty finale is virtually expected.

The fifth and final movement, an Allegro in D minor, is formidable indeed! The writing for the first violin is reminiscent of the *quatuor brillant,* but the brilliance is required of the other three players too. In its short, rapidly reiterated motifs and suddenly shifting harmonies, the piece anticipates the music of Bartók. This movement is a torrent of energy that culminates in unison cascades of D-minor scales. Its duple-meter pulse is constant throughout, but in the closing sixteen measures, Sibelius shifts to triplet division of the beat for a thrice reiterated cadential progression that becomes a perfect authentic cadence only in its final statement.

Ironically, the *Andante festivo* (1922) for string quartet, which was commissioned to celebrate the twenty-fifth anniversary of the opening of a factory in Säynätsalo, is better known than *Voces intimæ*. Sibelius is partially responsible for this cruel twist of fate since he subsequently arranged the piece for string orchestra. At the request of Olin Downes, the *New York Times* critic charged with supervision of the musical festivities of the 1939 World's Fair in New York, Sibelius conducted this version of the piece on New Year's Day of 1939 in studio performance that was broadcast worldwide as part of Finland's participation in the exposition. It is also performed at the opening of the annual Sibelius Festival in Loviisa, Finland, and has become associated with the composer in much the same way as his hymn "Finlandia," which is quite similar in style.

BRITISH: RALPH VAUGHAN WILLIAMS AND BENJAMIN BRITTEN

Coming from a well-to-do family as he did, Vaughan Williams (1872–1958) was exposed to high culture from his childhood. Traditional instruction in strings and keyboard was complemented by study of John Stainer's *Theory of Harmony*, which was published in 1872, the year of Vaughan Williams's birth. His formal training was at the Royal College of Music, London, where his composition teacher as Sir Charles Hubert Hastings Parry. From 1892 until 1895, he pursued a double major in history and music at Trinity College, Cambridge, where he studied composition with Charles Wood. Vaughan Williams was well informed regarding his British musical heritage, and his study of English Renaissance polyphony revealed to him sonorities and textures, especially streams for first-inversion triads called *faburden*, which he later used in his own works. After completion of his degrees, he returned to the Royal College of Music to study composition with Charles Villiers Stanford. Two Continental sojourns, the first in 1897 to study with Max Bruch, the second in 1908 to work with Maurice Ravel, rounded out his training. During these formative years, he wrote his first chamber pieces: a string quartet (1897), a quintet (1898) for clarinet, horn, and piano trio, and a piano quintet (1903) scored, like Schubert's, with double bass, and the Ballad and Scherzo (1904) for string quintet (2.2.1). These were never published, nor did Vaughan Williams count them among his works.

The principal chamber works from his maturity include the String Quartet in G minor (1908, rev. 1921), the Phantasy Quintet (2.2.1; 1912), Six Studies in English Folksong (1926) for cello (or violin, viola, clarinet) and piano, *Household Music* (1941), String Quartet No. 2 in A minor (1942), and the Sonata in A minor (1954) for violin and piano.

Vaughan Williams wrote the G-minor Quartet shortly after returning from his three months of study with Ravel. It had its premiere in London in November 1909, but Vaughan Williams revised it in 1921 for impending performances by André Mangeot and his associates. Themes of the four-movement Quartet frequently suggest prose rhythms, reveal modal influences, are treated in imitation, and are subject to thematic transformation. All of these features are already apparent in the opening theme of the first movement, its transformation into the second theme, and in the appropriation of the ascending fourth with which it begins in each of the subsequent movements' themes. Formal designs are conservative, especially in the lovely Minuet and Trio. The playful use of pizzicato in the Trio section is one of many string effects that Vaughan Williams uses effectively throughout the piece. The Romance, in a variable 5/4 meter, is the most freely structured and subdued movement. It contrasts with the energetic finale whose pizzicato sonorities relate it to the second movement as does its use of classical form, in this case, a rondo. In the final episode, the opening theme of the first movement returns in imitative counterpoint. Having established the texture, Vaughan Williams proceeds in the final refrain to treat the rondo theme in a series of imitations leading to a powerful stretto that concludes the work. In this and other chamber works, Vaughan Williams uses the designation "solo" to show where one instrument assumes the primary melodic role and others accompany. A sign follows such passages to indicate where the solo function ceases.

The philanthropy of the wealthy entrepreneur Walter Wilson Cobbett played a crucial role in the genesis of Vaughan Williams's Phantasy Quintet. Himself an amateur violinist and collector of fine violins, Cobbett, in 1905, instituted the Cobbett Competitions and Commissions for chamber music.[10] The requirement for the first Cobbett Competition was the composition of a "phantasy" scored for string quartet. Submitted pieces were to resemble seventeenth-century British fancys—or phantasies, in Cobbett's preferred spelling—insofar as they would be (1) one continuous movement, (2) of moderate length, and (3) comprised of different sections of contrasting character. These broad guidelines afforded composers great latitude. The 1905 competition yielded seventy-six manuscripts, but in the years that followed, phantasy quartets and quintets enjoyed a resurgence in popularity.[11] Vaughan Williams wrote the Phantasy Quartet at Cobbett's request. It is dedicated to him and the players of the London String Quartet, who, assisted by violist James Lockyer, played the premiere in Aeolian Hall, London, on 23 March 1914. For that program, the composer supplied a note about the piece:

> It is in four very short movements, which succeed each other without a break. There is one principal theme (given out by the viola at the start) which runs through every movement—
>
> Prelude (in slow 3/2 time)
>
> Scherzo (this is a quick movement—the longest of the four).
>
> "Alla sarabanda." (Here the cello is silent and the other instruments are muted.)
>
> Burlesca. (This movement is, for the most part, in the form of a "basso ostinato.")

The main theme is largely a pentatonic scale on F, but Vaughan Williams freely embellishes the structural tones with ornamental tones beyond the theoretical scope of the pentatonic scale.

The String Quartet No. 2 in A minor bears the subtitle "For Jean on her Birthday." The woman named here is Jean Stewart, the violist of the Menges String Quartet.[12] It is for this reason that the principal themes of each movement are stated first by the viola. For her birthday in February 1943, Vaughan Williams sent via Ursula Wood (who became Mrs. Ursula Vaughan Williams on 7 February 1953), the first two movements of the Quartet with a note indicating that "the scherzo refuses to materialize."[13] The first movement is a sonata form with a greatly abbreviated recapitulation. The second movement, "Romance," is a fantasy in G minor in which passages in imitative counterpoint are punctuated with episodes in homophonic texture; however, the episodes use cross-relations that recall voice leading of Elizabethan repertoire. When the Scherzo and Epilogue did materialize, both drew upon earlier works. For the Scherzo, Vaughan Williams used a theme from a film score for *The 49th Parallel.* The subject of the Epilogue was taken from music for a film entitled "Joan of Arc" that never came to fruition. The Epilogue is much like the Romance in its use of neo-Renaissance imitative counterpoint, but the tonal plot of the movement is unorthodox, beginning in F major and moving midway through to D major. The composer included a little pun in the subtitle of the Epilogue: "Greetings from Joan to Jean."

Another instance of Vaughan Williams's resurrecting older scores occurs in the Sonata in A minor for violin and piano, which was composed for the violinist Frederick Grinke. Ginke joined with pianist Michael Mulliner on 12 October 1954 to give the first performance of the piece on a BBC broadcast in honor of the composer's eighty-second birthday. The three movements of the Sonata are a contrapuntal Fantasia, an energetic Scherzo, and the finale, a set of six variations on a theme lifted from his piano quintet of 1903. The contrapuntal ingenuity of the finale is impressive, with the first variation using the theme in inversion, the second treating it in canon, the fourth again in inversion, and the fifth using both canon and inversion. The movement concludes with a recollection of the opening motif of the first movement.

Both the *Six Studies in English Folksong* and the *Household Music* are modest yet touching and effective works. The former were written for May Muhlke, who gave the premiere with Anne Muhlke at the piano on 4 June 1926 at an English Folk Dance Society Festival in Scala Theatre, London. The first five pieces are lyrical and expressive, and the last energetic. None presents technical difficulties for either player; thus, they are useful pieces for beginning chamber players. This is equally true of the *Household Music*, which Vaughan Williams wrote as his contribution to the war effort. In a lecture of 1940 entitled "The Composer in Wartime," he asserted that it was the artist's obligation to "use his skill, his knowledge, his sense of beauty in the service of his fellow men."[14] Heeding his own advice, he composed three settings of Welsh hymn tunes for string quartet with horn *ad libitum*, or for any other instrumentation at hand. The first movement is a fantasia on "Crug-y-bar," the second a scherzo on "St. Denio," and the last a set of eight variations on "Aberystwyth." The Blech Quartet premiered the set on 4 October 1941 in Wigmore Hall, London.

In his youth, Benjamin Britten (1913–1976) enjoyed musical advantages similar to those described in the case of Vaughan Williams. He began the study of composition with Frank Bridge (1879–1941) at the age of eight; consequently, he composed prolifically while still a boy. He entered the Royal College of Music, London, in 1930, studied composition with John Ireland (1879–1962), and by nineteen, had already written significant chamber works, such as the Movement (1930) for wind sextet and the two phantasies of 1932.[15]

Britten scored his Sextet for standard wind quintet with bass clarinet (i.e., the same instrumentation used by Janáček in *Mládí*). It is a substantial, interesting, and attractive work that should be heard more frequently.[16]

The phantasies—a String Quintet in F minor (2.2.1), and a Quartet for oboe and strings—were both inspired by the Cobbett Compeition. Cobbett himself was present on 22 July 1932 when the prize-winning Quintet had its premiere at the Royal College. The Quartet won no prize, but Britten designated it as Op. 2, and it brought him international attention. Following its premiere on 21 November 1933 at St. John's Institute, Westminster, by Leon Goosens (oboe), André Mangeot (violin), Eric Bray (viola), and Jack Shinebourne (cello), it was featured on 5 April 1934 at the ISCM Festival in Florence. At their 1936 conference in Barcelona, the ISCM hosted the premiere of Britten's Suite, Op. 6 (1935) for violin and piano.

The two phantasies are vastly different pieces. The Quintet might be described as polythematic since each of its sections focuses on a different motif drawn from the somber cello melody that opens the piece (Andante). This material serves as both a transition from the Allegro scherzando and a link to the Andante lento. Finally, it appears as a varied reprise of the opening. One wonders whether Britten may have composed the motive-based sections first and then drawn from them the material for the opening theme. In the Quartet, which is a monothematic phantasy, Britten derives almost everything from a reiterated tone and its expansion to a third. One particular strength of the Quartet is the way in which Britten summarizes its various motifs, bringing them to a climax and resolving their accumulated tension in the final section.

The *Temporal Variations* (1936) for oboe and piano were an experiment in educing a wide variety of moods from severely restricted musical materials. The contrasting movements, designated respectively as Oration, March, Exercises, Commination, Chorale, Waltz, Polka, and Resolution, contain some intriguing moments, but Britten ultimately decided to withhold the score.

Britten's music for string quartet includes the early Rhapsody (1929), Quartettino (1930), String Quartet in D (1931), Alla marcia (1933), and Three Divertimenti (1936); his mature works are the String Quartet No. 1 in D (1941), No. 2 in C (1945), and No. 3 in E (1975). The youthful works reflect Britten's study of the music of Schoenberg and Berg, composers whom Bridge admired. Other influences can be heard, too, as in the third and final movement of the Quartet in D of 1931, for example, which shows his fascination with the music of Bartók. Britten rejected the *Alla Marcia;*

however, he appropriated portions of it, expanded them, and rescored them for string orchestra to accompany the song "Parade" in his song cycle *Les illuminations* (1939). The Three Divertimenti (March, Waltz, and Burlesque; 1936) are movements salvaged from a five-movement suite of 1933 that materialized only in part. Each of them explores string effects in a masterful way, but the tremendously energetic Burlesque uses these techniques within a movement reminiscent of Bartók.

Quartet No. 1 in D (1941) was written for Elizabeth Sprague Coolidge. Britten had a ready contact with her through his teacher Frank Bridge and his wife, Ethel, who were personal friends of Mrs. Coolidge. Frank played viola, and Ethel, violin. They were enthusiastic about chamber music, and Mrs. Coolidge responded with equal enthusiasm.[17] When Britten left England in 1939 because of World War II, he came to the United States equipped with a letter of introduction from Bridge. In 1941, Mrs. Coolidge commissioned Britten to write a string quartet, the score was completed during June and July of that year. The premiere by the Coolidge String Quartet took place on 21 September in Los Angeles.[18] They played the piece again at the Library of Congress Founder's Day Program on 30 October 1941. During the ceremony, Mrs. Coolidge awarded Britten the Coolidge Medal for outstanding achievement in the field of chamber music.

The First String Quartet is exquisitely beautiful and filled with appealing sonorities, but it is also suffused by a tension that is perceptible from the outset. The key signature and broad outlines of first movement's intervallic content—both harmonic and melodic—suggest orthodoxy, as does the work's traditional four-movement layout including sonata, scherzo (F major), lyric Andante (B-flat major), and sonata-rondo finale (D major). Closer scrutiny shows conflicting strands, such as the largely E-Phrygian melody of the second violin within the prevailing D-major harmony, or the cello's persistent C-natural in the second theme (Allegro vivo). The piece presents formal curiosities as well: The opening theme is relaxed, and the second is animated; thus, the classic sonata allegro design is reversed. Unusual, too, is the fact the two sections are juxtaposed without a transition section, and the second theme's unsettling C-natural links it to the development's harmonic processes. During the development, a transformation of the opening theme returns in F. The ensuing reprise of the Allegro wends its way back to D major in measure 119, but the Lydian motifs (now on D) undermine the sense of recapitulation, while the conflicting E of the opening is worked into a triplet figure using the tones F-sharp, D, and E in rotation over the course of almost two dozen measures. The restatement of the music from the opening and secondary tempos is greatly compressed, but it retains the alien C-natural and subverts the dissipation of tension characteristic of classical sonata forms.

The Scherzo is an asymmetrical arch form in which roughly the first third increases in intensity—specifically dynamics, rhythmic activity, and register—while the remainder of the piece reduces these tensions one layer at a time in the stated order. The materials for the third movement are drawn from the first, but as with that movement, harmonic security is elusive. The contradiction of B-flat major by C major begins in the third measure. Midway through the movement, C-major triads flung across all parts act as a gateway to the central portion, but there too, conflicting tonalities arise: D and F. These conflicts persist in the final section of the movement and are resolved in favor of B-flat major only in the final measures; however, that sonority is sounded as though a phantom—*pianissisimo*, in second inversion, and with the first violin on B-flat^2.

Lydian inflections, emphasis on thirds, and tonal conflicts among B-flat, F, and D unify the finale with the previous three movements. Even in the bold, closing flourish, the scalar rush upward from E moves through F-sharp and G-sharp in approaching a unison D, which is followed by a full D-major triad.

The String Quartet No. 2 in C (1945) was written for the 250th anniversary of the death of Henry Purcell, a composer whose works Britten admired, performed, and, to some extent, imitated. The premiere was given in Wigmore Hall, London, on 21 November 1945 by the Zorian Quartet. Of the three movements in this score, there is little to suggest the influence of Purcell in the first, which is pervaded by shadows of sonata form. Most of the movement's motifs are derived from the opening leap of an upward major tenth from tonic to mediant and then eventually from the third to the fifth scale degree. This leaping tenth and its continuation soon appears in G, then D. The movement from mediant to dominant scale degrees never happens in quite the same way; however, the turn figure used in its third statement plays a crucial role in the remainder of the movement. Britten reinstates C in a varied statement of the tenth in the cello against more animated counterpoint. Structurally, the reappearance of C is reminiscent of the classical repetition of the exposition; however, Britten's scheme is more varied, and he moves from C to F-Lydian, G, and B-flat-Lydian. The B-natural of F-Lydian and the E-natural of B-flat-Lydian effectively cancel the sense of movement to subdominant tonalities while simultaneously implying the enduring primacy of C. The implication is soon realized, and the return of C effectively thwarts all efforts to establish a secondary tonal region. Glissandos fill in the leaping tenths at the commencement of the development section. Britten places these glissandos as a background for the turn figure, which now appears in inversion, augmentation, and polytonal contexts. The return to C (letter M) is unmistakable yet frustratingly brief. The coda (nine measures after letter O) is an ethereal prolongation of the opening tenth from C to E, heard now in all voices, during which the turn motif is sounded in augmentation as the top note in the strummed cello chords (*quasi arpa*). The movement is one of Britten's most ingenious and satisfying creations. While acknowledging the tradition of first-movement form, he draws from it unprecedented results as a consequence of a harmonic idiom originating in the combination of various scales and modes that are primarily linear constructions.

The formal design of the C-minor Scherzo movement is more straightforward. Its Trio is a freely executed basso ostinato on a six-measure theme (letter D). The ground bass assumes greater importance in the finale, which Britten calls "Chacony"—a clear reference to Purcell, who wrote many such pieces. The nine-measure pattern in sarabande rhythm is stated *unisono* at the opening.

Eighteen of the twenty variations follow the nine-measure pattern of the main theme. Variations are grouped into sets of six by cadenzas for cello, viola, and first violin respectively. In the final variation and coda, Britten takes pains to contradict, evade, or otherwise escape the underlying tonal authority of C major. Britten's tonal language arises from the conflicts between modality and tonality, and between linear and harmonic construction. This tonal idiom is his most significant allusion to Purcell, who wrote at a time when nascent functional harmony was emerging from traditional modal counterpoint. The movement, about twenty minutes' length, is longer than Beethoven's *Grosse Fuge* by about 25 percent. As we know, Beethoven's publishers rejected the movement as the finale for Op. 130 because of its magnitude and musical intensity. Britten's Chacony is similarly overpowering, but what colossal music!

Britten's String Quartet No. 3 (1975) was his last instrumental work. He died on 4 December 1976, just a few weeks before the premiere on 19 December by the Amadeus Quartet at Snape Maltings Concert Hall. The five movements of the piece are arranged in complementary pairs (i.e., 1 and 5, 2 and 4) with the central movement, a lyrical piece for violin, acting as a fulcrum. Some materials in the Quartet are derived from his last opera, *Death in Venice* (1973). This connection is clarified in the last movement, an epilogic Recitative and Passacaglia that Britten called "La Serenissima," the traditional nickname for the city of Venice.

String Quartet No. 2, iii, Chacony Benjamin Britten

Two additional Britten works merit attention. These are his *Lachrymae: Reflections on a Song of John Dowland*, Op. 48 (1950) for viola and piano, and his Sonata in C, Op. 65 (1960) for cello and piano. The former was written for William Primrose, who gave the premiere with Britten at the piano on 20 June 1950 at the Aldegurgh Festival. The latter work was composed for Mstislav Rostropovich, who gave the first performance with Britten at Aldeburgh on 7 July 1961.

The title of the viola piece is misleading: The song used as the premise for most of its ten movements is "If my complaints could passions move." The famous *lachrymæ* (i.e., tears) tune, "Flow, my tears," is mentioned only in the sixth variation. Britten arranged the piece for viola and string orchestra in 1976.

The Cello Sonata consists of five movements: Dialogo, Scherzo-pizzicato, Elegia, Marcia, and Moto perpetuo. This succession of movements is similar to that in late eighteenth-century divertimentos—especially in the conspicuous use of a march. The first movement, in sonata form, balances well with the energetic finale. The Scherzo and Marcia are also structural counterparts. The elegy, in keeping with the divertimento tradition, is the most lyrical and expressive of the five. Throughout the piece, Britten employs bitonality (in the march) and octatonic configurations (especially in the last movement), features that he would have associated with Russian composers generally.[19]

AMERICANS

George Whitefield Chadwick. Though he lived into the third decade of the twentieth century, Chadwick wrote all of his chamber music by 1898, the year he completed his String Quartet No. 5 in D minor. Having gone from his native Massachusetts to Leipzig to study with Salomon Jadassohn (1831–1902) and then to Munich for further work with Joseph Rheinberger (1839–1901), Chadwick became intimate with the Austro-German musical tradition.[20] He made his mark as a composer first in Germany with performances of two movements from his String Quartet in G minor (1878) and, on another program, of his String Quartet No. 2 in C major (1879) and an orchestral overture entitled *Rip van Winkle.* All of these had been written under the watchful eye of Jadassohn, who was "almost a father" to Chadwick.[21] Rheinberger was an intimidating but effective teacher who trained his students "beyond the elements of music as taught at home by Lowell Mason and exposed them to expressive possibilities wider than the church choir or brass band."[22]

When he left Munich for Boston in March 1880, Chadwick already had some reputation as a composer and had received favorable reviews in formidable journals including *Dwight's Journal of Music,* the *Musikalisches Wochenblatt,* and the *Neue Zeitschrift für Musik.*[23] In 1882, he was appointed to teach composition and instrumentation at the New England Conservatory. He became the director in 1897 and worked there until his retirement in 1930.[24]

Chadwick's mature chamber works begin with his String Quartet No. 3 in D (1885), which is dedicated to the composer Arthur Foote. Its premiere was on 9 March 1887. The following year, the Kneisel Quartet played it on a program devoted exclusively to Chadwick's music. The piece survived only in performing parts until 1986 when Chadwick's full score was discovered quite by accident in a used bookshop in New York City. That score is important since it provides alternate readings for some passages that were incorrectly written by the copyist who made the parts.[25] The second movement, a theme with variations in D minor, shows strong influences of the variations of Schubert's *Death and the Maiden* quartet. Impressive, too, is the finale (Allegro vivace, D major), which includes extensive and complex counterpoint.

Chadwick's String Quartet No. 4 in E minor was composed in the wake of Antonín Dvořák's tenure at the National Conservatory of Music in New York City. Chadwick knew him, his music, and his concern with nationalism. He also knew the players of the Kneisel Quartet, who had given the premiere of Dvořák's *American Quartet,* Op. 96 on 1 January 1894. Chadwick dedicated his Quartet to Franz Kneisel, and he and his Quartet played Chadwick's Fourth for the first time on 21 December 1896 in Association Hall, Boston. These factors may account for the prominence of folk elements, such as the prominent pentatonic (G, A, B, D, E) melody in the first movement, the tune of the duple meter scherzo, which sounds very much like the hymn tunes in *Southern Harmony*, as well as the metrical irregularity and Phrygian inflection of the descending supertonic of the eight-measure theme of the finale. This theme becomes the basis of something roughly like a passacaglia; thus, these features permeate the entire fabric of the movement.

Chadwick's String Quartet No. 5 in D minor was written for a quartet in which Timothée Adamowski played first violin and his brother Josef played cello. Josef was on the NEC faculty and was, therefore, a colleague of Chadwick's. As with the Third and Fourth Quartets, this one exhibits a lyricism that is reminiscent of folk melodies. Their organization within clearly articulated forms again suggests the influence of Dvořák; however, Chadwick tends to changes tonalities more rapidly, even within the context of relaxed, inner movements. The finale is rich in imitative counterpoint, but the polyphony is predicated on lyric subjects, thus preserving the general character of the movement.

Considering that Chadwick played keyboard instruments, it is surprising that he scored with piano only in his Piano Quintet in E-flat of 1887. The tonality of the piece and its musical gestures owe much to Schumann, both his Piano Quintet and his Piano Concerto in A minor. Chadwick played the premiere of the piece with the Kneisel Quartet on 23 January 1888 in Chickering Hall, Boston, both to his own and critics' satisfaction. In 1890, it was issued in Leipzig and Boston by Arthur P. Schmidt, and was thus one of Chadwick's earliest published works.

Chadwick was a generous and supportive man who was eager to help fellow musicians both at NEC and in the larger community of Boston. He expressed this camaraderie elegantly to Amy Beach in a letter written immediately after the premiere of her *Gaelic Symphony* in 1896: "I always feel a thrill of pride myself whenever I hear a fine new work by any one of us, and as such, you will have to be counted as, whether you will or not, one of the boys."[26]

Amy Marcy Cheny. At the age of eighteen, Cheny married Dr. Henry Harris Aubrey Beach, a prominent Bostonian surgeon who was forty-three at the time. From that moment until Dr. Beach's death in 1910, Amy's professional name was Mrs. H. H. A. Beach (1867–1944). Her principal chamber scores are the Sonata in A minor, Op. 34 (1896) for violin and piano (also arranged for flute and piano); Piano Quintet in F-sharp minor, Op. 67 (1907); Theme and [6] Variations, Op. 80 (1916) for flute and string quartet; String Quartet in A minor, Op. 89 (1929); and Piano Trio in A minor, Op. 150 (1938).

The Sonata and the Quintet are expansive and demanding works that Beach performed regularly. The premiere of the Sonata in January 1897 with Franz Kneisel marked the beginning of Beach's association with him and the Kneisel Quartet, who took her Quintet into their repertoire. During her European tour following the deaths of her husband and then of her mother, Clara Cheny on 18 February 1911, she played both works frequently.[27] The Sonata was already known in Germany since it had been played there on 28 October 1899 by pianist Teresa Carreño and violinist Carl Halir. Both pieces were warmly received in the German cities where Beach performed. Had it not been for the mobilization of troops for World War I, she might well have remained in that favorable environment.

Even before her return to the United States, Beach had been booked for "at least thirty concerts."[28] Her concert of 16 December 1914 at Steinert Hall, Boston, was particularly important. The audience included George Whitefield Chadwick, Arthur Foote, and Horatio Parker in addition to the leading music critics of Boston. Five major Boston papers subsequently echoed Chadwick's praise of Beach's musicianship, both as performer and composer.

In both the Sonata and the Quintet, musical materials are handled skillfully, but traditionally. One contemporary critic remarked concerning the Sonata that "The weakness of the work lies . . . in its total lack of original ideas."[29] This criticism does not apply to Beach's later works, however, and some of her chamber music, such as the single movement String Quartet, shows impressive originality and independent thinking. For her musical materials, she used three Eskimo or Inuit tunes, treating them sometimes within imaginative harmonic contexts, at other times in imitative counterpoint, and in still other cases more rhapsodically throughout the various sections within the Quartet.[30] The tunes are austere in their simplicity, and Beach assumes the same general attitude in her treatment of them. Most of the textures are a result of the linear progress of voices, chromaticism is pervasive but not conventionally Romantic, and extensive dissonant passages sometimes obscure tonal focus. This Quartet is at once intense in its harmonic idiom, yet reserved and understated in its lyrical expression.

The Quartet must have held a special place in Beach's own opinion since she originally designated it as Op. 79—thus suggesting that it originated around 1918—but when she put the piece in final form in January 1929, she changed the opus number to 89. This decade-long gestation contrasts with the compositional histories of other pieces, such as her Sonata for Violin and Piano, which, though much longer than the twenty-minute Quartet, she completed in six weeks.[31] Ironically, the Quartet was heard only in a handful of private performances—mostly bad—during the composer's lifetime. A public performance was given in November 1942, when it was heard as part of the celebration in Washington, D.C., of Beach's seventy-fifth birthday.[32] It was among the few of her chamber works not published during her lifetime despite the fact that Arthur P. Schmidt Company had accepted it for publication.[33] First the Great Depression, then World War II prevented Schmidt from issuing the piece.

Beach started her Piano Trio at the MacDowell Colony, Peterborough, New Hampshire, on 2 June 1938 and finished it on the eighteenth. In it, she used some of her older pieces. Her song "Allein," Op. 35, No. 2, figures prominently in the second movement, Lento espressivo, which uses two lyrical segments based on the song and its novel yet sumptuous harmonies to frame a fast central section in duple meter that acts as a scherzo—exactly as Franck had done in his *Grand pièce symphonique* (1862). This scherzo section, incidentally, is based on a setting of the Inuit song "The Returning Hunter" from Beach's suite for piano, *Eskimos* (1907). Owing to the dual function of the second movement, the third movement is the finale.

Arthur Foote. The numerous chamber works of Foote (1853–1937) include String Quartet No. 1 in G minor (1883), Piano Trio No. 1 in C minor (1882), Sonata in G minor (1889) for violin and piano, Piano Quartet in C, (1890), String Quartet No. 2 in E (1893), Piano Quintet in A minor (1897), Piano Trio No. 2 in B (1907), String Quartet No. 3 in D (1907), and Nocturne and Scherzo (1918) for flute and string quartet. The nocturne is better known in its orchestral version, "Night Piece" for flute and orchestra.

Foote studied at the New England Conservatory of Music, then with John Knowles Paine at Harvard University, where he received the first master's degree in music awarded by any American university. His primary instrument was piano (though he played organ too), and from 1921 until his death, he taught piano at NEC. His chamber works including piano are especially attractive, though all are written in a later Romantic harmonic style with clear, memorable melodies and classically inspired formal designs.

THIRTEEN

Strictly Confidential: The Chamber Music of Dmitri Shostakovich

SOCIAL REALIST OR VICTIM?

The principal chamber works of Shostakovich consist of two piano trios (Op. 8, 1923; Op. 67, 1944), sonatas for cello and piano, violin and piano, and viola and piano (Op. 40, 1934; Op. 134, 1968; Op. 147, 1975), the Piano Quintet in G minor (Op. 57, 1940), and fifteen string quartets written between 1938 and 1974. String Quartet No. 1 in C major, Op. 49 is an easygoing work that he wrote for the Glazunoff Quartet, which consisted of his colleagues on the string faculty of the St. Petersburg Conservatory.[1] Shostakovich's remaining chamber works reveal ethnic elements that sound, at times, distinctively Russian, and at other times, distinctively Jewish.[2]

Unraveling the informational knots inherent both in Shostakovich's music and in commentaries about it is a complex task. Some see him as a social realist who advanced the agenda of the Communist Party, while others view him as the helpless victim of a ruthless, totalitarian regime. The publication of the composer's memoirs in 1979 has led to a rejection of both images, and has given us the portrait of a composer who conformed to Soviet guidelines in a superficial way while embedding encoded messages of rebellion, criticism, and ironic commentary in at least some of his scores.[3]

As a young composer, Shostakovich focused on public genres, such as symphony, opera, and ballet. These were the media that formed the tastes of the general public; thus, composers who were sincere about advancing

Soviet ideology devoted their efforts to these genres. Chamber music, on the other hand, was considered elitist music.[4] In the early years of his career, Shostakovich produced only a handful of chamber works. His youthful Piano Trio in C minor, Op. 8 was written following the death of his father, Dmitri Boleslavovich, in February 1922. To help support the family during the hard times that ensued, Shostakovich improvised on the piano to accompany silent films. It was there, in the cinema, that he and his musical companions learned the score for this elegiac trio, his first chamber work. The Trio is a single movement in a richly Romantic style. Little of the characteristic Shostakovich can be heard in the piece, save for his uncanny ability to switch effortlessly from lush lyricism to impish, scherzo-like gestures. Shostakovich did not regard this production of his youth as a significant work, and it only became known after Boris Tishchenko (b. 1939) made an edition of the piece and restored the final twenty-two measures that had been lost from the piano part.

The Sonata in D minor for cello and piano was written before he first ran afoul of Soviet authorities in 1936.[5] Its four movements include an expansive but conventional sonata-allegro first movement, a brief Allegro that seems almost like a transition to the third movement, a Largo of real emotional depth, and a virtuosic Allegro finale. The piece is dedicated to Victor Kubatsky, a cellist whom Shostakovich met in 1925 and who remained one of the composer's closest friends. Kubatsky and Shostakovich gave the first performance in St. Petersburg on 25 December 1934. Interpreters of the sonata should be aware of the comments of Arnold Ferkelman, a cellist who played the sonata with Shostakovich:

> Dmitri Dmitriyevich was a brilliant pianist and had an incredible technique. . . . He knew all the music from memory, not just his own sonata. . . . He liked playing quickly and loudly, and he took incredibly fast tempi. I never succeeded in getting any other pianist to take such tempi. His playing was on the dry side, but on the other hand he played very loudly.[6]

The Piano Quintet in G minor was apparently to have been the composer's second string quartet; however, he had an urge to travel at the time. He realized that if he wrote a piano quintet, he would be invited to tour with whatever ensemble was performing the piece.[7] The first performance of the Quintet, given by the Beethoven Quartet with the composer in Moscow on 23 November 1940, was greeted with enthusiasm. The Leningrad premiere with the Glazunoff Quartet was equally successful.

It was in the score of the Piano Trio No. 2 in E minor that Shostakovich found his characteristic voice as a composer of chamber music. As with many piano trios by central European and Russian composers previously surveyed, this one is an elegy: It was begun late in 1943 probably in memory of his student Veniamin Fleyshman, who had been killed defending Leningrad on 14 September 1941. In 1943, Shostakovich undertook a completion of Fleyshman's opera, *Rothschild's Violin*, an opera on a Jewish theme. On 11 February 1944, the musicologist Ivan Sollertinsky died. Shostakovich wrote to the widow that "Ivan Ivanovich was my very closest and dearest friend. . . . To live without him will be unbearably difficult."[8] Apparently, Shostakovich changed the dedicatee of his memorial piece, and fired with devotion, he resumed work on 15 February, completing all four movements by 13 August.

It was during these months that Shostakovich read news reports about the Nazi death camps where Jews awaiting their own deaths were forced to dance beside the graves into which their bodies would soon be thrown. The composer embodies these frantic dances in the finale of his Trio; thus, Shostakovich's expression of personal grief as a result of Sollertinsky's death was complemented in the Trio by another and equally powerful sentiment: outrage at the deaths of thousands at the hands of totalitarian regimes that targeted specific citizens among their populations as the objects of their hatred.[9]

Although Ivan Ivanovich Sollertinsky became the offical dedicatee of the Trio, the work's genesis in connection with Fleyshman's death left its traces. "Shostakovich recognized the uniqueness of both the Holocaust and the Jewish experience. Furthermore, against official Soviet policy, he identified the Holocaust as a particularly Jewish catastrophe: the Jews were the primary victims and it was they who would . . . bear the scars of this experience in their collective psyche";[10] however, in the Trio and in other works, Shostakovich uses Jewish musical topics as a broader signal indicative of the victimization of humanity.[11]

The shadow of death pervades the entire Trio. The very choice of this medium is portentous; the ghostly harmonics of the canonic opening arouse further suspicions; the apparent joviality of the brief second movement is undercut by the harmonic shifts that disrupt the diatonic goals of its music; the passacaglia design of the third movement "is a twentieth-century variation on the baroque topic of the lament bass with the descending chromatic tetrachord. [However], the chromatic descent takes place not in the bass, but in the upper voice of the right hand, which chromatically connects F4 down to B3 (omitting only C#4)."[12] The concluding Allegretto is an unusual rondo that recalls both the canonic E-minor theme of the first movement and the B-flat minor passacaglia theme as the piece draws toward its close; thus, even without knowledge of the compositional circumstances of this piece, the finale can in no way be read as a positive conclusion.

Anguish is embedded into the movement's structural materials; so, too, is the dilemma of Jews at the hands of anti-Semitic governments. "Shostakovich deliberately adopts in much of the movement a Jewish folk idiom: jaunty, highly accented, metrically regular dance rhythms; the pizzicati, strummed multiple-stop chords and soloistic effects of the Jewish fiddler; and the ubiquitous flattened-second scale degree and melodic augmented seconds."[13]

That Jews were the victims of Nazi executioners in this specific instance does not preclude a broader interpretation of Shostakovich's grief and outrage. The composer's quotation from the Trio in his String Quartet No. 8 in C minor, Op. 110 (1960) shows that his musical outcry was addressed as much to Stalin in the U.S.S.R. as to Hitler. Ironically, the Trio won the Stalin Prize (class II) in 1946.

String Quartet No. 2 in A major, Op. 68, was the first of fourteen quartets Shostakovich wrote for the Beethoven Quartet: Dmitri Tsyganov, Vasily Shirinsky, Vadim Borisovsky, and Sergei Shirinsky.[14] Shostakovich dedicated his Second Quartet to Vissarion Shebalin (1902–1963), a composer on the faculty of the Moscow Conservatory from 1928, its director from 1942 until 1948, the teacher of Tikhon Khrennikov (1913–2007), Edison Denisov (1929–1996), and Sophia Gubaidulina (b. 1931), and a chamber-music enthusiast. Shebalin wrote nine string quartets, the Piano Trio in A, Op. 39 (1947), the sonatas, Op. 51, No. 1 for violin and piano (1958), Op. 51, No. 2 for viola and piano (1954), and Op. 54, No. 3 for cello and piano.[15]

Shostakovich grew cordial with the players of the Beethoven Quartet and dedicated string quartets No. 3 in F major, Op. 73 (1946) and No. 5 in B-flat major, Op. 92 (1952) to them. Years later, as the inevitable end of their years together approached, he penned individual quartets dedicated to each player: Nos. 11 in F minor, Op. 122 (1966) to the memory of Vasily Shirinsky, 12 in D-flat major, Op. 133 (1968) to Tsyganov, 13 in B-flat minor, Op. 138 (1970) to Borisovsky, and 14 in F-sharp major, Op. 142 (1973) to Sergei Shirinsky. He rounded out the set of memorial quartets with No. 15 in E-flat minor, Op. 144 (1974)—for himself! Owing to the sudden death of the cellist, Sergei Shirinsky, on 18 October 1974, the premiere was entrusted to the Taneyev Quartet. This final quartet consists of six adagios designated respectively as Elegy, Serenade, Intermezzo, Nocturne, Funeral March, and Epilogue.

Piano Trio, Op. 67, iv

Dmitri Shostakovich

As these brief historical comments on the quartets show, Shostakovich viewed the string quartet as a highly personal medium. His Eighth Quartet, Op. 110 (1960), is so intimate that it may be considered his musical autobiography. He revealed his intentions in writing the piece in the following letter of 19 July 1960 to his lifelong friend Isaak Glickman:

> I wrote an ideologically deficient quartet nobody needs. I reflected that if I die some day then it's hardly likely anyone will write a work dedicated to my memory. So I decided to write one myself. You could even write on the cover: "Dedicated to the memory of the composer of this quartet."[16]

Shostakovich penned the Eighth Quartet during a trip to Dresden, where *Five Days and Five Nights*, directed by Leo Arnshtam, was being filmed. Shostakovich was to create the score for the movie, which recounts the bombing of that city during World War II. In his public remarks and the formal dedication of the piece, he indicated that it is was written "in memory of the victims of fascism and war"; however, the musical materials of the Quartet suggest a more specific victim. Embedded within the Quartet are quotations from Shostakovich's Symphonies Nos. 1 and 5, the Jewish theme from the finale of the Trio, Op. 67, cello Concerto No. 1, the Russian song "Languishing in Prison," and "Sergei, my love," an aria from his opera *Lady Macbeth of the Mzensk District.* The work's five movements proceed without break and are unified by a recurring motif, the motto D, S, C, H (i.e., D, E-flat, C, B-natural) which appears in all of them.[17]

Of the three largo movements (1, 4, and 5), the first and last are the most densely contrapuntal elaborations of the motto. The second movement, a frantic Allegro molto juxtaposing the Jewish theme of Op. 67 with statements of the motto in augmentation, leads without break into the third, an Allegretto, which is a surrealistic waltz. In the fourth movement, the first violin plays the prison song in C-sharp minor within the texture of a recitative; however, the threefold repetitions of *fortissimo* chords in the lower strings are not "supportive," as they would be in a typical *recitativo.* They seem instead to be foreboding, almost menacing. The tone of the concluding Largo becomes gloomy at the reappearance of the motto, where Shostakovich calls for muted strings. The movement ends in utter desolation with a theme recalled from the first movement.

The premiere of Op. 110 took place in St. Petersburg on 2 October 1960. The Moscow premiere, also given by the Beethoven Quartet, followed on 9 October. Despite its somber message, the Eighth Quartet was immediately recognized as masterpiece.

Many of the concealed meanings of the piece are now common knowledge, but the verifiable existence in the music of encrypted messages gives rise to further questions relating to it specifically and Shostakovich's works in general: Do we hear the quotation of the First Symphony differently if we understand that the person to whom that symphony was dedicated, Misha Kvardi, a close friend of Shostakovich's from their student days at the St. Petersburg Conservatory, was arrested and executed in 1929? What is the significance of the Jewish elements in the finale of Quartet No. 4 in D major, Op. 83 (1949), which, though completed early in 1950, was withheld from performance until after the death of Stalin in 1953? What is the meaning of the quotation in No. 5 in B-flat major, Op. 92 (1952) of a theme from the Trio (1949) for clarinet, violin, and piano of Galina Ustvolskaya, who had been among Shostakovich's students at the Conservatory? Why, in No. 12 in D-flat major, Op. 133 (1968), presented to Dmitri Tsiganov for his sixty-fifth birthday on 12 March 1968, does Shostakovich use a twelve-tone row—the epitome of formalism—in the opening cello theme? These and other curious features can hardly have happened by accident.

TWO LATE SONATAS

Leonid Kogan and David Oistrakh were the leading Soviet violinists of the mid-twentieth century. Shostakovich first encountered Oistrakh in 1935 when he won the first prize in the second All-Union Competition. Soon afterward, Shostakovich and Oistrakh were members of a Soviet delegation of performers visiting Turkey. The two joined with the cellist Milos Sádlo in performances of Shostakovich's Trio, Op. 67, which they eventually recorded.[18] In 1947 and 1948, while working on the First Violin Concerto, Shostakovich consulted with Oistrakh about the feasibility of certain passages. Oistrakh gave the premiere of the Concerto with the Leningrad Philharmonic Orchestra on 29 October 1955, and Shostakovich dedicated both this and the Second Violin Concerto to him. In anticipation of Oistrakh's sixtieth birthday in September 1968, Shostakovich had begun writing his Sonata, Op. 134 (1968) for violin and piano; however, the score was not completed until 23 October of that year.

The pianist Svyatoslav Richter was recruited to present the official premieres of the Sonata with Oistrakh.[19] These were on 3 May 1969 in Moscow and on 23 September of that year in St. Petersburg. A preview of the piece had been given on 8 January 1969 at a conference of the Russian Union of Composers with the pianist Moisey Vainberg.

The Violin Sonata was written shortly after String Quartet No. 12, which, as we have noted, uses twelve-tone elements within a clearly tonal context. The same is true of the Sonata. The opening Andante movement presents the twelve-note series followed by its inversion in the piano. In subsequent permutations of the theme, the violin enters with a counter-subject. These two ideas, alternatively manipulated by piano and violin, become the main material of the movement. Frequently the texture is astonishingly sparse with the violin and piano playing in two-part counterpoint. The second movement (Allegretto) is an energetic scherzo, and the finale (Largo-Andante) is a passacaglia prefaced by an eight-measure introduction based on twelve-tone elements. The passacaglia theme is stated pizzicato by the violin. The entrance of the piano initiates a series of lean, austere contrapuntal variations, but Shostakovich includes variations that function essentially as cadenzas, first for the piano, then for the violin. A motif from the first movement—easily identifiable owing to its ornamental trills—appears in the final moments of the movement.

Shostakovich's ultimate composition, the Sonata, Op. 147 (1975) for viola and piano, was composed between 25 June and 6 July while the composer was on his deathbed. The piece is dedicated to Fyodor Druzhinin, violist of the Beethoven Quartet at the time, and he gave the first public performance of the piece in St. Petersburg on 1 October 1975. Of its three movements—Moderato, Allegretto, and Adagio—the second and third contain explicit quotations: The former quotation, providing the most cheerful and energetic music of the piece, comes from his early opera after Gogol entitled *The Gamblers;* the later, heavy with pathos, appropriates the opening motif from the first movement of Beethoven's *Moonlight Sonata;* a less obvious quotation, also from Beethoven, is the fugue subject of the Piano Sonata in A-flat major, Op. 110. This pair of Beethoven quotations, one familiar and transparent, the other unfamiliar and opaque, may well have been chosen to reflect Shostakovich's feelings about his own output, specifically, that Soviet apparatchiks may interpret his works to advance party agendas, but that their deep, inner meanings would forever elude them.

LATER SOVIET COMPOSERS: SOFIA GUBAIDULINA, EDISON DENISOV, ALFRED SCHNITTKE

Shostakovich was a role model for the generation of Soviet composers born during the second quarter of the twentieth century. Not only his musicianship, but also, his personal sincerity were a source of inspiration. He was generous with his encouragement of young composers, and many, including Edison Denisov (1929–1996), Boris Tishchenko, and Sofia Gubaidulina (b. 1931) benefited from his support and guidance.[20]

The very prolific Denisov studied at the Moscow Conservatory with Shebalin. In 1959, he was appointed to teach instrumentation. His works include pieces for conventional chamber ensembles, such as his sonatas for flute and piano (1960), violin and piano (1963), alto saxophone and piano (1970), and clarinet and piano (1993), Suite (1961) for cello and piano, String Quartet No. 2 (1961), Wind Quintet (1969), Piano Quintet (1987), Clarinet Quintet (1987), and Quartet (1989) for flute, violin, viola, and cello.

Denisov generally writes in an expanded tonal idiom, but sudden shifts in register, discontinuity of phrases, and other features that disrupt traditional musical progress give his music a novel sound. Sometimes, as in the finale of the two-movement Wind Quintet, these antics are amusing, if not downright comical. He also use makes effective use of extended instrumental techniques, such as flutter-tonguing, multiphonics, and microtones. He draws freely from various styles including jazz and be-bop, as can be seen in the third movement (Allegro moderato) of the fantastically difficult Sonata for Alto Saxophone and Piano. Formal designs take their point of departure from Classical models, but are freely altered. In the Sonata for Flute and Piano, for instance, he writes a continuous piece in three sections, with the tempo scheme slow, fast, slow. The first, slow section comprises about half of the entire piece and functions as an exposition. The second, fast section is about one-quarter of the piece and serves as a development section. The final section of the piece—about one quarter of its total length—is another slow section that is clearly a recapitulation of the opening section. The three sections taken together thus suggest a multimovement design in which each section corresponds to exposition, development, and recapitulation. This format is often called a "supersonata" or a "sonata in one."

His chamber works are often scored for unconventional ensembles. The *Romantische Musik* (Romantic music; 1968), for example, is for oboe, violin, viola, cello, and harp. In some instances, such as the Trio (1981) for oboe, cello, and harpsichord, he writes modern music for early-music ensembles.[21] Among his most exotic instrumentations are those of "Diane dans le vent d'automne" (Diana in the autumn wind; 1984) for viola, piano, vibraphone, and double bass, which became the first of the *Three Pictures after Paul Klee* (1985) for oboe, horn, piano, vibraphone, viola, and double bass. The pieces are dedicated to Igor Boguslavsky, whose playing is featured in the second movement, "Senecio," which is a viola solo. The third movement, "Child on the Platform," is pointillistic and borders on atonality. The Trio for oboe, cello, and harpsichord reflects Denisov's fascination with the sonorities of collegium instruments, but he was equally interested in their repertoire; thus, he wrote several compositions inspired by the music of Bach, the most important of which is *Es ist genug* (It is enough; 1984) for viola and piano. This piece is a dual homage alluding both to Bach's version of the chorale and Berg's use of it in his Violin Concerto (1935).[22]

Sofia Gubaidulina (b. 1931) was born during the decade that "saw the most savage persecution of religion in the entire Soviet period."[23] The Law on Religious Associations of 8 April 1929 remained in force until October 1990. This law "limited the rights of religious believers to the performance of religious services in registered buildings, and made almost every other kind of religious witness or activity illegal."[24] These policies caused difficulties for Gubaidulina, who is a deeply spiritual and religious individual. Her own statements about her expression of religious convictions in art are unequivocal:

> All my works are religious. . . . I've never written non-religious pieces. . . . I feel a great desire to realize my religious needs within art. . . . For us, the artists, it is absolutely necessary to experience this religious reunion with the highest essence of our souls. Without it, we would be unable to work with such an inspiration. I understand the word "religion" in its direct meaning: as *re-ligio* (*re-legato*), that is, a restoration of legato between me (my soul) and God. By means of my religious activity I restore this interrupted connexion. Life interrupts this connextion: it leads me away, into different troubles, and God leaves me at these times. This is unbearable pain: by creating, through our art, we strive to restore this legato.[25]

The conflict between Gubaidulina's inspiration and Soviet policy sometimes left her no choice but to conceal the religious basis of some of her pieces. At the Moscow premiere of her *Seven Words* (1982) for cello, bayan, and strings, for example, the relationship between the instrumental movements and New Testament scriptures went unmentioned, even though the music contains metaphors alluding to the events of the Passion; moreover, Gubaidulina quotes the melody for "I thirst" as it appeared in the *Seven Words* of Heinrich Schütz.[26]

The title of Gubaidulina's *In croce* (In the cross) tells us something about its religious inspiration as well as its musical materials. Originally scored in 1979 for cello and organ, the piece was arranged for cello and bayan in

1992 for the accordionist Elsbeth Moser. The themes of *In croce* reflect the perpendicular beams of the cross in their antithetical construction and disparate registers: The organ begins with diatonic arpeggios in a high register, while the cello begins in a low register with consistently chromatic lines. As the piece progresses, the organ part moves into a progressively lower tessitura while the cello moves into a higher one. About two-thirds through the piece (i.e., at the horizontal beam of the cross) Gubaidulina introduces an extended monologue for the cello, the single episode in the piece in which the polyphonic capacities of the instrument are explored. When the organ part resumes, its writing is chromatic. Following a varied reprise of the opening material, the cello brings the piece to its close with a slow glissando back to its original, low register.

In croce draws from Christian heritage, which is not surprising since Gubaidulina is a member of the Russian Orthodox Church. In other works, she takes a more ecumenical approach. Her personal history predisposed her toward religious eclecticism: Her father was Tatar, and her paternal grandfather was a mullah; her mother was Russian, but of both Jewish and Christian ancestry.[27] A blend of spiritual perspectives illuminates Gubaidulina's score for flute, viola, and harp entitled *Garden of Joys and Sorrows.* This colorful ensemble—used previously by Debussy—explores thoughts inspired by two literary sources, "Sayat-Nova," a poem by Iv Oganov, and *Stimmen* by Francisco Tanzer (1921–2003).[28] The "garden" of the title is the locale of Oganov's poem as well as an Islamic symbol for paradise. Tanzer's Western verses consider the concept of borders such as those between nations, religions, life and death, creativity and imagination, joys and sorrows. The roughly twenty-five-minute piece abounds in distinctive sonorities including diatonic arpeggios, chromatic motifs, long glissandos, spirals of short, microtonal glissandos, pizzicatos, sul ponticello, and harmonics. These sonorities are woven into an intricate web of recurrences that lead to the recitation *ad libitum* of Tanzer's verses:

When is it really over?
What is the true end?
All boundaries are driven into the earth
With a piece of wood
Or the imprint of a shoe.
Until then . . .
Here is the boundary.
All that is artificial.
Tomorrow we will play
Another game.

In addition to these works whose distinctive titles are indicative of their spiritual orientation, Gubaidulina has written many other chamber works including some with generic titles. Among these are *Der Seiltänzer* (The tightrope dancer; 1993) for violin and piano; Meditation on the Bach Chorale "Vor deinem Thron tret ich hiermit" (1993) for harpsichord and string quintet; Pantomime (1966) for double bass and piano; a Piano Quintet (1957); *Quasi hoquetus* (In the manner of a hocket; 1984) for viola, bassoon (or cello), and piano; a Sonata (1975) for double bass and piano; a Sonata (*Rejoice!* 1981) for violin and cello; four string quartets (1971, 1987, 1987, 1993); a String Trio (1989) for violin, viola, and cello; a Sonata (*Detto I;* 1978) for organ and percussion (1 player); Five Etudes (1965) for harp, double bass, and percussion (1 player); a wealth of pieces for ensembles with percussion; and the *Hommage à T. S. Eliot* (1991) for soprano, clarinet, bassoon, horn, violins 1 and 2, viola, cello, and double bass. This last work was requested by the violinist Gidon Kremer, whose advocacy of Gubaidulina's Violin Concerto (*Offertorium;* 1980) has done much to spread her reputation. The premiere of *Hommage à T. S. Eliot* shared the program with Schubert's Octet in F major, Op. 166, D. 803, and the commission from Philharmonie of Cologne specified that the piece should have the same instrumentation. In her Fourth Quartet, Gubaidulina capitalized on the adventurous performances that have typified the repertoire of the Kronos Quartet over the years. In this single-movement piece, she actually combines *three* quartets, two recorded in advance, and one performing live. Kronos gave the first performance of this highly original work in 1994.

Gubaidulina has articulated the religious intentions behind some of her pieces. In other cases, the titles are suggestive. With her numerous works that simply bear generic titles, the mysteries have yet to be unraveled; but, if we take her at her word, the mysteries are there. "I can't think of any way to explain the existence of art other than as a means to express something greater than ourselves. I can't reach a single musical decision except with the goal of making a connection to God."[29]

Alfred Schnittke (1934–1998) was one of the most talented and prolific Soviet composers. Through his contacts with Filip Gershkovich, a native of Vienna and an admirer of its musical heritage, both ancient and modern, Schnittke became familiar with the music of Schoenberg, Webern, and Berg.[30] Gershkovich shared his insights about modern music with Denisov and Gubaidulina, too; thus, this group of modernists provided mutual support in their exploration of contemporary techniques while being scorned by the apparatchiks of the Soviet establishment.

Schnittke's String Quartet No. 1 (1966) was written during the height of his enthusiasm for contemporary techniques and is serial throughout its three movements. Like Schoenberg, Schnittke chose movement titles that suggested a connection with musical tradition: Sonata, Canon, and Cadenza. The titles were of no avail, and after the Quartet's premiere by the Borodin Quartet on 7 May 1967, it was filed in the "anti-Soviet" drawer.

In his next major chamber score, the Serenade (1968) for clarinet, violin, double bass, percussion, and piano, he explored another contemporary style: mobile form. In Senza tempo, the first of its three movements, the clarinet begins with an inverted smear that sounds like the opening of Gershwin's *Rhapsody in Blue* turned upside down. After this smear, the five instrumentalists, like a committee gone haywire, make simultaneous statements of their musical contentions. In each of their statements, we hear the unmistakable influence of American jazz, which was generally held in reproach by the Union of Soviet Composers. The percussionist acts as moderator, and at five junctures in the Introduction, he brings the cacophonous group to order with bangs of the gavel—in this case, motifs of three, five, seven, nine, and eleven notes respectively on the bells. The second movement, devoid of jazzy elements, is a subdued Lento primarily for clarinet and piano. Here, the pianist is asked to play trills directly on the strings, scratch the windings of the strings with the fingernails, and play clusters. Schnittke returns to the idioms of mobile form and jazz in the Allegretto finale. As the movement draws to its close, reminiscences of the first movement are heard, and the bells too return, but here they are given an elaborate cadenza. The mélange of five returns briefly before the clarinet brings the piece to its conclusion.

The year 1968 also saw the creation of Schnittke's Sonata No. 2 for violin and piano, one of his boldest experiments in polystylism, the collage-like juxtaposition of musical styles and techniques that eventually became Schnittke's trademark.[31] The music originated as a film score for Andrei Khrzhanovsky's cartoon-film *Glass Accordion*, which uses images ranging from the Italian Renaissance to paintings of Salvador Dalí but has no verbal content whatsoever. The Sonata, subtitled "Quasi una sonata," contains conspicuous links with Western musical traditions, such as the motif B, A, C, H (i.e., B-flat, A, C, B-natural) and the principle of opposing musical elements that has characterized the sonata as a genre since the time of Haydn and Mozart. In Schnittke's piece, polarized tonalities are replaced by tonal and atonal materials. Although it is written as a single, continuous movement, its three subsections give the impression of a multimovement composition.

Among Schnittke's many film scores is one for *The Adventures of a Dentist* (1965). In 1972, Schnittke transformed this music into the *Suite in Olden Style,* a straightforward foray into neoclassicism for violin and harpsichord or piano. There is hardly anything by way of stylistic parody in the piece. Not only is the ensemble a typical Baroque one, but also the harmonic style, rhythmic details, formal designs, and ornamentations within the movements are generally authentic. Schnittke must have felt that the piece was too tame, so he rescored it in 1986 for an anachronistic ensemble of viola d'amore, harpsichord, vibraphone, marimba, glockenspiel, and bells. The Suite consists of a Pastorale (in the manner of a Siciliano), Ballet, Minuet, Fugue, and Pantomime.

The death of Maria Vogel, Schnittke's mother, prompted him to compose the Piano Quintet (1976), a five-movement work that opens with a piano solo reminiscent of the music of Shostakovich. The body of the first movement suggests sonata principles: The first musical topic is largely triadic. The polarity of musical materials, therefore, is between the linear and the vertical, the chromatic and the triadic, the atonal and the tonal. Within this context, tone clusters play a conspicuous role. The second movement is a waltz, but it is—like Ravel's *La valse*—deranged and disoriented, a parody of a paradigm representing elegance, stability, and grandeur, but now attired in tattered ball gowns and torn tuxedos. In the waltz, Schnittke uses thematic transformations of a theme from the first movement. A concluding tone cluster (like a cinematographic fade-out) leads to the third movement, which uses previous musical images in altered states. At this point, Schnittke modified the classical four-movement plan by placing after the Andante third movement a still slower Lento as the fourth. The association with fade-out techniques in film seems especially appropriate here, and Schnittke uses clusters like painkillers for a dying victim. At the end of the ordeal, we reach the Moderato pastorale. This fifth movement is not a "finale." It has nothing to do with traditional concluding movements; instead, it is like the ending (happy) to a film. Schnittke has given a couple of hints to verify his intention of a happy ending: The tempo indication reminds us of another five-movement work, Beethoven's *Pastoral Symphony,* Op. 68; to confirm the allusion, Schnittke quotes Beethoven's theme from the concluding Allegretto of that piece, which, according to Beethoven's scenario, represents "glad and grateful feelings after the storm." Perhaps we are to conclude that Maria Vogel died a holy, peaceful death. Schnittke's Piano Quintet is one of his most powerful yet reassuring statements. Apparently, he felt as much since he later made an orchestral version of the work entitled *In memoriam.*

An unmetered, angular, and brooding monologue for unaccompanied cello opens Schnittke's Sonata (1978) for cello and piano. When the latter instrument enters, it is with material conspicuously similar to the opening of the first movement of Beethoven's Sonata in E-flat major, *Les adieux*, Op. 81a. The cello and piano alternate intense monologues in the brief first movement. The second is a moto perpetuo in which the instruments seem to assume an adversarial role, much like the disposition of instruments in Bartók's two Violin Sonatas. The concluding Largo commences with a baleful cello theme devoid of meter, periodic structure, or tempo. The tune develops into a cantilena recalling Beethoven's "Farewell" motif in the piano part, but now, with new material in the cello. Articulation serves a structural function in this piece, and closing statements—cadence patterns in the first movement, closing phrases in the second, and final periods in the third—use pizzicato in the cello part; moreover, a durational crescendo takes place as the piece unfolds: Each movement lasts approximately twice as long as the previous one (i.e., three minutes, six minutes, twelve minutes). This architectural design is, if not unprecedented, then, at least, rare.

Schnittke's *Stille Musik* (Tranquil music; 1979) for violin and cello was his next chamber work. A substantial movement of six or seven minutes' duration, the piece is, as the title suggests, tranquil. In addition to its inherent musical charm, its unusual instrumentation is enticing.

String Quartet No. 2 (1980) is dedicated to the memory of Larissa Shepitko, the film director with whom Schnittke had collaborated on several films and who died in an automobile accident at the age of forty-one. It was commissioned by Universal Edition and was the compulsory piece for that year's International String Quartet Competition at Evian. The four-movement quartet begins with string harmonics that evolve in imitative contrapuntal texture. If not an allusion to the opening of the Piano Trio, Op. 67 of Shostakovich, then, at least, that work served as the model for Schnittke's short opening movement. The second movement, Agitato, the longest of the four, generally exhibits frantic superficial rhythmic activity, but the underlying harmonies are simple and change slowly, and the formal design of the movement is a fairly straightforward rondo with varied reprises plus a coda. Some of the themes—probably those in the tranquil sections of the coda—were apparently drawn from sixteenth- and seventeenth-century Russian-Orthodox chant. The melodic style, rhythmic contours, and texture of Russian church music are increasingly apparent in the third movement, Mesto, and the last, Moderato, both of which are constructed in the manner of a litany with modifications of each iteration.

Some statements venture into polytonality, others employ harmonics that recall the opening movement (again à la Shostakovich, Op. 67). The last movement begins and ends inaudibly—*quasi niente*, according to Schnittke's direction. The effect is mesmerizing.

In 1982 Schnittke became a Roman Catholic. For practical purposes, he generally made his confession in the Russian Orthodox Church.

In the three movements of String Quartet No. 3 (1983), polystylism involves the use of cadence patterns from the Stabat Mater of Orlando di Lassus, the subject of Beethoven's *Grosse Fuge*, and Shostakovich's D, S, C, H motto. Additional allusions appear in subsequent movements: The Agitato (second movement) borrows its theme from the second subject of Beethoven's *Pathétique Sonata*, Op. 13, a piece that Schnittke, as a pianist, would have known well. The Pesante (third movement) references the last song of Mahler's *Lieder eines fahrenden Gesellen* (Songs of a wayfarer). The text reeks with feelings of alienation, feelings that Schnittke is known to have shared: "Die zwei blauen Augen von meinem Schatz, die haben mich in die weite Welt geschickt. . . . O Augen blau, warum habt ihr mich angeblickt? Nun hab' ich ewig Leid und Grämen" (The two blue eyes of my beloved, they have exiled me into the wide world. . . . O blue eyes, why did you look upon me? Now I have perpetual sorrow and grief).[32] The introduction, juxtaposition, transformation, and recombination of these musical referents in the course of the piece results in a troubling score heavy with implications but offering neither solutions nor even the slightest sense of closure.

The String Trio (1985) for violin, viola, and cello was commissioned by the Alban Berg Gesellschaft to celebrate the centennial of Berg's birth. Oleg Krysa, Fyodor Druzhinin, and Valentin Feigin gave the premiere at the Moscow Conservatory on 2 June 1985. Several weeks later, on 19 July, Schnittke had a stroke—the first of half a dozen that he suffered before his death in 1998. After this first stroke, he was declared clinically dead three times. To the amazement of all, he rallied and went on to compose a great deal more music including two alternate versions of the Trio: One in 1987 that he called Trio Sonata was scored for chamber orchestra; the other, dating from 1992, is the Piano Trio. This last version was premiered by Mark Lubotsky, Mstislav Rostropovich, and the composer's wife, Irina Schnittke, on 25 May 1993 at Evian.

In all three versions, the piece is essentially the same: two movements, Moderato and Adagio, using the same themes are played without pause. The prominence of the tones A, B, E, G (i.e., A, B-flat, E, G) suggests that Schnittke used letters from Alban Berg's name to generate one of the main motifs of the piece.[33]

Schnittke's final chamber works include a variety of smaller occasional pieces written as birthday greetings or memorials. The noteworthy exceptions are his austere String Quartet No. 4 (1989), the longest of his quartets, with three Lento movements separated by an Allegro and Vivace respectively, and the Sonata No. 3 (1994) for violin and piano, which was premiered by Mark Lubotsky and Irina Schnittke on 10 October 1994 in Moscow. These pieces are not much concerned with polystylism. The textures in both are generally sparse—a characteristic feature of his late works in all genres—perhaps as a consequence of impaired motor control following multiple strokes.

CHAMBER MUSIC OF THE SATELLITE NATIONS: WITOLD LUTOSLAWSKI, KRZYSZTOF PENDERECKI, ALEXANDER ARUTIUNIAN

Russian social-realist policies affected composers in Socialist Republics. The Pole Witold Lutoslawski (1913–1994) was among them. His major chamber works include his String Quartet (1964), an essay in mobile form consisting of an introductory first movement followed by the principal, second movement, and his Partita (1984) for violin and piano. Modest yet interesting pieces that merit attention include *Epitaph* (1979) for oboe and piano, and Grave (1981) for cello and piano.[34]

Krzysztof Penderecki (b. 1933), also in Poland, is best known for his large-ensemble works that explore myriad possibilities of texture, register, dynamics, articulation, and so forth. These sound-mass compositions include pieces such as his *Threnody for the Victims of Hiroshima*. This style tends to be less useful in chamber scores, though his two string quartets (1960, 1968) are essentially in this manner. More typical of his chamber style are the String Trio (1990) for violin, viola, and cello, and the exquisitely beautiful Quartet (1993) for clarinet, violin, viola, and cello, consisting of four movements (Adagio, Vivacissimo, Tempo di valse, Larghetto) that are titled Notturno, Scherzo, Serenade, and Abschied (departure). These recent works are closer stylistically to the music of Shostakovich. Intense lyricism pervades the outer, slow movements, both of which call for clarinet in A. The Scherzo, which seems in its extensive unison writing to recall the "Intermede" of Messiaen's *Quatuor pour la fin du temps*, is in a traditional formal design and employs the characteristic fast, triple meter. All movements have clear functional harmonic implications, and the final movement closes with an F-major triad. This engaging work will doubtless become a classic in the relatively sparse repertoire for this ensemble. Pendercki's most recent chamber score is his two-movement Sextet (2000) for clarinet, horn, string trio, and piano.[35]

The Armenian composer Alexander Arutiunian (b. 1920) joined the Union of Composers in 1939, studied at the Moscow Conservatory with Genrik Litinsky (1901–1985) and Nikolai Peiko (1916–1995), and won the state prize of the U.S.S.R. in 1949. Arutiunian's chamber works are few, but skillfully written, challenging yet not unreasonably difficult, and appealing both to listeners and performers. His most important works are the *Retro-Sonata* (1983) for viola and piano, the Suite (1983) for wind quintet, the *Poem-Sonata* (1985) for violin and piano, and the Suite (1992) for clarinet, violin, and piano. This last piece consists of four movements, Introduction, Scherzo, Dialog, and Final. It is one of over 200 pieces commissioned by the Verdehr Trio, whose players include Walter Verdehr, violin, Elsa Ludewig-Verdehr, clarinet, and Gary Kirkpatrick, piano. As in much of his music, elements of Armenian folk music pervade this colorful score.

FOURTEEN

Two Fugitives from the Soviet Bloc: György Ligeti and Karel Husa

The Ligeti family settled in Transylvania at the end of the nineteenth century and became residents of Hungary. (Since then, the town of his birth has become part of Romania.) Following the trends among Hungarian nationalists at the time, they changed their German family name, Auer, to an approximation of it in Hungarian: Ligeti.[1] From 1941 until 1943, György Ligeti (1923–2006) attended Cluj Conservatory, where he studied composition with Ferenc Farkas. In 1944, Ligeti was conscripted and—since he was a Jew—assigned to perilous labor, transporting explosives. During the Holocaust, he lost both his father and his brother to the death camp at Auschwitz. In 1945, Ligeti resumed music studies at the Budapest Academy of Music, first with with Sándor Veress and then with Farkas. Ligeti completed the program in 1949 and joined the faculty as a teacher of harmony and counterpoint in the following year.

Government censors monitored closely the musical output of innovative young composers like Ligeti. Works in a quasi-Bartókian style were permitted, but adventures like *Musica ricercata* for solo piano were prohibited. During the 1950s, Liget experimented with serialism and other modern techniques.

These experiments coincided with the Hungarian revolution of October 1956. Imre Nagy appealed to the United Nations for aid against Soviet domination. With popular support, he became premier of Hungary and organized a neutral government. The Soviet response was decisive: Nagy was abducted and executed. Fearing for their own lives, approximately 190,000 refugees fled the country in the following months. Ligeti explained that his escape was possible in December 1956 because the frontiers remained open, though Soviet forces had surrounded Budapest.

> The railway people organized trains for people who wanted to go [to] . . . the Austrian frontier; of course, they never arrived at the frontier. The train stopped at every station, and they telephoned ahead to the next station to find out if there were Russian soldiers there.
>
> I and my wife took the train one day. . . . There had been some mistake and the warning had failed: the train was surrounded by Russian military. But they didn't have enough people to cover the whole train. . . . We in our end very quickly got out and into the town. Somebody told us to go to the post office. . . . The next day, the postman took us . . . with ten or twelve people hidden under mailbags.
>
> Then we were dropped quite close to the frontier . . . within the prohibited zone, with Russians patrolling. . . . We knew we had reached the border when we fell into the mud where the mines had been: the mines had been cleared during the revolution, because Austria refused to have trade with Hungary while the border was mined.[2]

After he arrived in western Europe, Ligeti worked during 1957 and 1958 at West German Radio in Cologne, where he became acquainted with Karlheinz Stockhausen (1928–2007) and the music of the avant-garde, especially that of Pierre Boulez (b. 1925). Ligeti soon became involved with the Darmstadt Festivals, participating as an attendant in 1957 and 1958, and then as a lecturer annually from 1959 until 1972. He taught there again in 1976, and his works were featured in 1980 and 1984.

Ligeti wrote rather little chamber music, but several of his chamber works are quite extraordinary. Some of his pieces, such as his early String Quartet No. 1, *Metamorphoses nocturnes* (Nocturnal metamorphoses; 1954) and the Six Bagatelles (1956) for wind quintet, show the influence of Bartók. Both scores are tremendously variegated with occasional strands of imitation, modal tunes in a largely homophonic texture, sometimes including considerable dissonance, and allusions to functional harmony. The Bagatelles were actually extracted from his collection of piano pieces called *Musica ricercata* (1953). From these, he selected the third, fifth, and seventh through tenth movements; four exhibit unbounded energy and biting rhythms, while the remaining two—placed second and fifth in the set of six—are slow and melancholic.

In his later works, Ligeti often built sonic complexes from minuscule elements that could be altered gradually by a predetermined process. Early Renaissance polyphony provided one of the models for this structural approach. In particular, Ligeti was fascinated by the way in which Ockeghem used "stagnating structures [in which] the individual voices are constantly overlapping, just like waves washing one over another."[3]

The Ten Pieces (1968) for wind quintet, commissioned by the Stockholm Philharmonic, is a good example of such overlapping, individual voices—what he once called "supersaturated polyphony." The pieces are terse, ranging from half a minute to about three minutes in length. At times, the entire ensemble is pervaded by terse motifs—as in the eighth piece, Allegro con delicatezza; nevertheless, Ligeti occasionally draws solo voices from these amorphous clouds of sound. Ligeti has the flute change, at times, to alto flute and piccolo, and the oboe to *cor anglais* and oboe *d'amore*. The harmonic idiom is highly dissonant and marked by dramatic contrasts. Tone clusters, tone color, register, texture, and density also play crucial roles in these scores.

The five-movement String Quartet No. 2 (1968) employs many of the same compositional principles; the first, second, and fifth movements exhibit Ligeti's penchant for heavily imbricated polyphony. Likewise, the importance of compact musical particles subject to subtle modification is particularly apparent in the central movement, "Come un meccanismo di precisione" (in the manner of a mechanism of precision). All five movements are actually transformations of one basic musical idea; thus, despite all of its modernity, the piece exhibits the organic construction that has been characteristic of the string quartet as a genre since the time of Beethoven.

The Trio (1982) for violin, horn, and piano shares the same instrumentation as Brahms's Op. 40—a composition Ligeti admired. The rhythmic complexities of the first movement show the influence of American minimalism. The Bulgarian rhythms of the second movement are again reminiscent of Bartók. The third movement recalls a traditional scherzo and trio, while the finale, a Lamento, reverts to Ligeti's manner of the 1950s. The footprint of Brahms's piece is apparent in Ligeti's pervasive use of horn fifths, a motif prominent in the final movement of Brahms's Op. 40. Ligeti's writing for the horn recalls Brahms's use of the natural horn in Op. 40. In the Ligeti Trio, though a valved horn is essential, he tends to write sections in which he changes the fundamental of the horn by depressing a single valve. Within these sections, he limits the notes to those of the corresponding harmonic series or readily available through modification of the embouchure. Ligeti's writing for the horn exploits the "out-of-tune" notes; rather than avoiding them, he integrated them as a part of the timbre of the instrument specifically noting that the natural mistunings should not be corrected. He creates a variegated microtonal system by always changing the fundamental of the horn. Some phrases begin on the same pitch and are essentially the same, but they are notated in different keys (i.e., with a different valve depressed), so the tunings of the notes are completely different, thereby changing the sound of the phrase.[4]

Karel Husa (b. 1921) had hoped to become an engineer, but when the Nazis took control of Czechoslovakia in March 1939, one of their first actions was to close the technical school in Prague on 18 November of that year.[5] Husa, who had played violin since the age of eight, ultimately found himself at the Prague Conservatory in the composition class of Jaroslav Řidky. Husa studied there from 1941 until 1945. He continued with Ridky for graduate work at the Academy of Musical Arts in Prague, but much of this degree program was completed abroad owing to the fact that Husa had won a French Government Fellowship to study at the École Normale de Musique in Paris. There, from 1946 to 1948, he studied with Arthur Honegger (1892–1955). In addition, he took private composition lessons with Nadia Boulanger (1887–1979) from 1946 to 1949. During a short visit to Prague in the summer of 1947, Husa enjoyed twofold triumph: the completion of his diploma at the Academy of Musical Arts, and the premiere of his Sinfonietta (1945) by the Czech Radio Symphony Orchestra. The piece was such a success that it was selected by the Czech Academy of Arts and Sciences in 1948 as the winner of its annual prize.

The year 1948 was an ironic one for Husa: It was a year of accolades and the year in which the marriage of his sister brought him back to Czechoslovakia, but it was also the year when he was exiled from his native land. He and his music were banned from that moment until the dissolution of the Soviet Union in 1989. When his mother, Božena Husová *née* Dongresová, died in 1955, Husa's family refrained from informing him of the news for fear that he would come to her funeral and be arrested by the Communist authorities. Husa and his music were not welcome in the Czech Republic until 1989, when the Communist regime fell from power. Husa, for the first time since 1948, returned to his native land in 1990. On 13 February of that year, in Smetana Hall in Prague, he led the Czech premiere of his monumental *Music for Prague 1968.* That performance was nationally televised.

Husa has written in virtually all genres; however, the tally of his chamber works—twenty-two pieces to date—clearly indicates the emphasis he has consistently placed on small ensembles. Early chamber pieces include his String Quartet, Op. 2 (1943), the Suite, Op. 5 (1945) for viola and piano, and the Sonatina, Op. 6 (1945) for violin and piano. The Quartet, Op.

2, was played privately at the time, but Husa never reckoned it as his "first" quartet. Presently, it is generally designated as the quartet "Nulty," the Czech word for zero.

The work that Husa reckoned as his String Quartet No. 1 (1948),[6] was dedicated to and premiered by the Smetana Quartet at the Prague Music Festival on 23 May 1948. During the Darmstadt Festvial of 1950, a student quartet from the Darmstadt Institute performed the work. In that same year, the Quatuor Haydn presented the piece at Brussels conference of the International Society for Contemporary Music. In 1951, the piece was heard both at the Frankfurt Festival and at the renowned Donaueschingen Festival. Written during his student days in Paris while working with Arthur Honegger and Nadia Boulanger, String Quartet No. 1 established Husa's reputation in contemporary music. With it, he captured his first two prizes in composition: the Lili Boulanger Prize (1950) and the Bilthoven Contemporary Music Festival Prize (1952).

Husa's growing reputation did not spare him from sentiments of remorse over the virtual loss of his homeland. Perhaps this was the stimulus for his composition of *Evocations de Slovaquie* (1951), a trio for clarinet, viola, and cello in three movements titled "Mountain," "Night," and "Dance." This music makes it clear that most of Husa's recollections of his native land were pleasant ones. The colorful, virtuosic clarinet solo and the dancelike rhythms in the string parts of the opening movement are sheer energy and *joie de vivre*. The subdued second movement, which features the strings, is contemplative. The final movement returns the spotlight to the clarinet part, which was realized first by Maurice Cliquenois. Here, Husa places emphasis on short motifs, manipulating them with additive rhythms and changing meters. At times, they are reiterated to the point that they become ostinato patterns. According to Husa, this curious chamber ensemble was his approximation of Slovakian folk groups that he had heard in that country.

The Parrenin Quartet commissioned Husa's String Quartet No. 2 (1953) and gave its premiere on 23 October 1954 at the Centre de Documentation sur la Musique in Paris. On 28 April 1958, the Walden Quartet gave the U.S. premiere of the piece at Cornell University's Festival of Contemporary Arts. Quartet No. 2 is divided into three movements of almost equal length. The outer movements open with Adagio passages, in both cases commencing with high strings rhetorically introducing sparse, angular lines that evade tonal centers but also eschew twelve-note constructive features. Noteworthy, too, are the varied and interestingly juxtaposed timbres involving variously conventional *arco* bowing, pizzicato, *sul ponticello*, and other striking sonorities. The intervallic content of the Adagios plays a larger role in movement construction; thus, the angular intervals heard at the opening of the first movement appear in imitative contrapuntal texture about two-thirds through the movement. The central Lento assai shares the character of these Adagios, but now in a greatly prolonged context. The writing for the strings is idiomatic and tremendously diverse. Rhythmic motifs and recurring pitch-class sets give the piece a sense of unity and musical logic. The balanced design of the three movements gives the whole composition an appealing architectonic shape. Finally, Husa assessed accurately the capacity of mid-twentieth-century audiences to listen to music such as this: It is long enough to provide musical depth, but the piece concludes before it overwhelms—about eighteen minutes.

One of Husa's most popular chamber pieces is the *Élégie et rondeau* for saxophone and piano. The German saxophonist Sigurd M. Rascher commissioned a solo saxophone work from Husa in 1958. The composer decided to use *Élégie* (1957), originally a piano solo written in memory of his mother, and arrange it for saxophone and piano. According to Husa, the mood of *Élégie* is similar both to the books of elegiac poetry by the existentialist poet Rainer Maria von Rilke (1875–1926) as well as much of the elegiac poetry of ancient Greece.[7] Rascher presented the premiere of this version at the Eastman School of Music, Rochester, New York, on 12 June 1960. The distinctive feature of Rascher's playing was his facility in the *altissimo* register (i.e., any note above F^2); Husa exploited this facility in the climax of the *Élégie*, which occurs roughly two-thirds through the piece (or, approximately at the Golden Ratio).

The *rondeau* was composed later, as Husa wished to add a contrasting movement that was light and nimble. This movement commences with both instruments quietly playing isolated rhythmic and melodic cells. As the movement progresses, these cells gradually coalesce to form intricate, virtuosic passages. Similarly, the harmonies "expand from simple sounds such as single notes and diads to chords that become more complicated."[8] Rascher gave the premiere of the combined pieces *Élégie et rondeau* in London at Wigmore Hall on 12 December 1960.[9] Husa's only other score for saxophone and piano is "Postcard from Home" (1994), a free treatment of two melodies, "Echo in the Mountains" and "Homeland, Goodbye," in Husa's *Twelve Moravian Songs* (1956). "Postcard" was written for John Sampen, who gave the premiere.

When the Parrenin Quartet toured the United States in 1959, they included Husa's Second String Quartet among their repertoire. It was at one of their concerts at the University of Chicago that George Sopkin, cellist of the Fine Arts Quartet, heard the piece. He prevailed upon his colleagues to take Husa's quartet into their repertoire. In 1967, the Fine Arts Foundation of Chicago provided funds for the Fine Arts Quartet to commission a new work. They chose Karel Husa. The work he wrote is his String Quartet No. 3. The piece is dodecaphonic, but the application of the procedure is liberal. Octave doublings, microtonal writing, and passages written in a free, pan-tonal style pervade the score.

The choreographer Dennis Nahat conceived of a ballet set to String Quartet No. 3 during a performance of the piece in New York City. Titled *Ontogeny*, the balletic interpretation depicts the conception of a human being. The Royal Swedish Ballet's premiere of Nahat's version on 29 November 1970 was a success, as was a subsequent production in Cleveland, where it has been performed on a regular basis. Nahat eventually won an award in 1986 for *Ontogeny*.

String Quartet No. 3 received many accolades. Among the admirers were the composers William Schuman, Samuel Adler, and Otto Luening. Without Husa's knowledge, the Fine Arts Quartet nominated the piece for a Pulitzer Prize. When the selection committee called the Husa household with the decision, the composer's wife, Simone, thought the call was solicitation. She indicated that they were "not interested in winning any prizes." The committee then called Husa at his Ithaca College office, and, after an explanation, Husa gladly accepted the award.

In 1968, Husa composed his Divertimento for brass quintet. This medium, for two trumpets, horn, trombone, and tuba or bass trombone, is a relative newcomer to the standard chamber ensembles thus far discussed in this book. The decisive first step toward the modern brass quintet was the formation of the New York Brass Ensemble in 1954. Two of its members, Robert Nagel (trumpet) and Harvey Phillips (tuba) organized the New York Brass Quintet. Arnold Fromme, also a member of the New York Brass Ensemble at one time, organized the American Brass Quintet in 1960; he chose to use bass trombone instead of tuba. As a consequence of their pioneering work, major contributions to the repertoire for this ensemble have been made by composers including Gunther Schuller (1961, 1993), Vincent Persichetti (1968), Elliott Carter (1974; bass trombone), Jacob Druckman (*Other Voices*, 1976), Peter Maxwell Davies (1981; Two Motets, 1982; *Pole Star*, 1982), Leslie Bassett (1988; tuba), Ned Rorem (*Diversions*, 1989; tuba), Leonard Bernstein (*Dance Suite*, 1990; optional percussion) and, of course, Karel Husa.

Husa's Divertimento, for two B-flat trumpets, horn in F, trombone, and tuba, consists of four movements: Overture, Scherzo, Song, and Slovak

Dance. These pieces are actually twice reworked selections from his *Eight Czech Duets* (1955) for piano four hands; they had first been arranged as the Divertimento (1958) for brass ensemble and percussion. Their style is reminiscent of Bartók. Highly rhythmic passages dominate in the first, second, and fourth movements. The plaintive and melancholy Song (titled "Evening" in the original, piano version) makes extensive use of various types of mutes. Polytonal passages add a degree of dissonance; however, these tend to be amusing and almost humorous. The Slovak Dance, a continuous accelerando with changing meters, is the longest and most interesting movement of the four.

The far more ambitious *Landscapes* for brass quintet (trumpets in C—with first also playing piccolo trumpet—horn, trombone, tuba) is a three-movement blockbuster that was commissioned by and dedicated to the Western Brass Quintet for an American Bicentennial celebration. They played the premiere in Kalamazoo, Michigan, on 17 October 1977. Although the movement titles, "Northern Woods," "Northern Lakes," and "Voyageurs," were added after the completion of the piece, they illuminate Husa's visions of America as it might have been viewed for the first time by explorers. The use of French for the title of the final movement reminds us that the first explorers of the Great Lakes region and Canada were French. This movement, according to Husa, is "one continuous and progressive crescendo." The second movement, like the Song of the Divertimento, makes extensive use of mutes, now coupled with microtonal inflections of pitches, slides, and glissandos.

It is remarkable that this relatively new medium had reached such levels of sophistication within approximately a quarter of a century. *Landscapes* is a staggering accomplishment not only because of the novelty of the ensemble, but also because it is hard to imagine how a composer who is not himself a brass player could possibly have managed to acquire such an intimate and intricate understanding of how these instruments work. Commenting on the piece, one reviewer noted:

> Because of all of the special effects . . . one cannot resist the temptation to compare the work with Bartók string quartets, which stretched the coloristic possibilities of that ensemble years ago. Indeed this work first strikes the player as a veritable compendium of the special effects possible on brasses. Many of these effects may at first seem gimmicky, but, as with Bartók string quartets, when the whole effect is heard, the result is unique and convincing. . . . It is unfailingly well-received by audiences of all ages.[10]

As part of its thirtieth-anniversary celebration, the Koussevitzky Foundation commissioned Husa's Sonata for Violin and Piano. On 31 March 1974, Ani Kavafian (violin) and Richard Goode (piano) gave the first performance at New York's Alice Tully Hall. In response to the premiere, John Rockwell wrote in the *New York Times:*

> What Mr. Husa has done is combine many of the most fascinating techniques of string and piano writing of recent years into the context of a highly virtuosic display piece of the old school. The work hardly sounds like a 19th-century sonata, but its coloristic ingenuity and expressivity suggest one all the same. Occasionally one felt that Mr. Husa might have cut the piece here and there. But the overflowing abundance of his ideas made most of it seem more than worthwhile.[11]

In the prefatory notes, Husa discusses how the events he has witnessed, "continuous wars, senseless destruction of nature, killing of animals . . . man's incredible accomplishments in space," all contributed to the piece. Interesting sonorities in the piece include quarter tones on the violin and plucking of the piano strings.

Recollections (1982) and Five Poems (1994) are substantial contributions to the repertoire for woodwind quintet, the former also including piano. Both are about twenty minutes' duration. *Recollections* marked the 200th anniversary of Dutch-American diplomatic relations. The combination of woodwind quintet and piano has seldom been used—Francis Poulenc's Sextet (1939), is one example. The premiere of this six-movement composition on 28 October at Coolidge Auditorium of the Library of Congress took place with three other premieres of pieces commissioned for the occasion: the Concerto *da camera* for violin, piano, and winds, Op. 60 (1982) by the American James Cohn (b. 1928); "And They Shall Reign Forever," for mezzo-soprano, clarinet, French horn, piano, and percussion (1982) by the Dutch composer Ton de Leeuv (1926–1996); and the Divertimento for violin, piano, winds, and double bass (1982) by de Leeuv's student Tristan Keuris (1946–1996).

The Koussevitzky Foundation commissioned the Five Poems. Each of the movements was inspired in some way by birds. Husa has always been inspired by nature, particularly while he lived at his vacation home on Cayuga Lake. He also had easy access to the Ornithology Lab of Cornell University—unlike Messiaen, who twice came to Ithaca for the sole purpose of visiting that facility. The movements are "Walking Birds," "Happy Bird," "Lamenting Bird with a Dead Bird," "Fighting Birds," "Birds Flying High." The Quintet of the Americas presented the premiere on 10 February 1995 at Weill Recital Hall at Carnegie Hall.

Husa's *Sonata a tre* was written specifically for the Verdehr Trio: Walter Verdehr (violin), Elsa Ludwig-Verdehr (clarinet), and Gary Kirkpatrick (piano). For them, Husa composed the *Sonata a tre* as a "program ender" displaying virtuosic potentials of each of the instruments. The first movement features the violin ("With Intensity"), the second, piano ("With Sensitivity"), and the third, clarinet ("With Velocity"). *Sonata a tre* was premiered in Hong Kong on 23 March 1982.

Husa's Variations (1984) for piano quartet are a major contribution to contemporary chamber music. They were commissioned by the National Endowment for the Arts on behalf of a consortium of three chamber ensembles: the Atlanta Virtuosi, the Rowe Quartet, and the New England Piano Quartette. The Atlanta Virtuosi gave the first performance on 20 May 1984 with premieres by the other two ensembles on 15 July 1984 and 23 January 1985, respectively.

Husa worked on the piece from the summer of 1983 until spring of the following year. The twenty-seven pages of sketches show many interesting features, including the working out of various compositional cells, some of which combine to form twelve-tone sets. These sets are not used pervasively, as in classic dodecaphonic composition; nevertheless, the configurations of the cells show a fascination with pitches bounded within intervals not exceeding a major third and arranged as successive whole tones, half steps plus whole steps, and successive semitones. These sonorities provide the "theme" of Husa's variations, which are not at all variations on a fixed melodic idea in the traditional sense. As the composer notes in his prefatory remarks, "The work explores . . . the alternations of sounds, intevals, chords, and forms in permutations, mirroring, and other techniques. Combinations of bell-like sounds are applied throughout the different sections and always slightly modified"; thus, a cell in what we might call "closed position" may subsequently appear in a pointillistic spacing with its tones dispersed across several octaves. These cells are varied in rhythm, dynamics, articulation, and sonority.

The sketches show other interesting compositional premises too: One page is labeled "Study in Unison," another, "Elegiac Litany." Although Husa did not employ either of these titles in the final piece, their thumbprints remain. The "Study in Unison"—possibly inspired by the "Intermède" of Messiaen's *Quatuor pour la fin du temps*—turned out to be a somewhat different piece. In Husa's realisation of this compositional premise, a single, expansive, and rhythmically energetic line is broken up (*hocket* style) into trichordal segments flung among the four participating instruments (at the point marked Prestissimo at rehearsal "C"). The litany corresponds to the Moderato molto section at rehearsal "M," where the composer plays with chromatic expansions of the trichordal cells. The variations contain a further unifying factor, specifically, a four-note *groupetto* with which the piece opens. These tones—sounded in the manner of grace notes in most cases—pop up here and there in slightly modified form throughout the work. In this respect, the piece invokes the cyclic compositional manner of nineteenth-century Romantic music as cultivated by Wagner, Liszt, and others. The concluding measures of the work remind us of Bartók, on the one hand, with the trichordal cells moving in contrary motion, and Wagner, on the other, with the concluding recollection of the *grupetto* leading to a final, abysmal statement of the trichord C-sharp, B, A (using the A that is the lowest available pitch on the conventional piano keyboard).

Husa's Variations for piano quartet are one of his most intricate and fascinating conceptions. They are not what would be called "easy listening"; however, they are characteristic of chamber music since the late nineteenth-century in their nuance, complexity, and delicacy. Those willing to go beyond the initial hearing will be well rewarded for their efforts.

Husa's String Quartet No. 4, *Poems* (1989) features six movements titled "Bells," "Sunlight," "Darkness," "Hope," "Wild Birds," and "Freedom," all of which combine to produce what the composer Earl George (1924–1994) called a "tour de force of colorful sound production."[12] Even though there is no direct correlation with any known poem, the Quartet does reflect on themes that have interested Husa throught his career. For example, "Bells" can be understood as relating to *Music for Prague 1968*, where on of the musical motifs was inspired by the tolling of Prague's many bell towers. "Wild Birds," a cheerful movement, speaks to Husa's fascination with nature. Composed in Ithaca, New York, the piece was premiered at the International Janáček Music Festival in Brno, Czechoslovakia, on 12 October 1991.

FIFTEEN

Benchmarks: Chamber Music Masterpieces since circa 1920

The expense and logistical challenges involved with rehearsing large ensembles as well as the diversity and novelty of many musical styles cultivated since 1900 have been powerful stimuli for the composition of chamber music. Because tone color has assumed greater importance in music since the time of Debussy, many of these chamber works have unique or distinctively modified instrumentations. Other factors, such as polycultural synthesis, advances in electronic and other technological devices, philosophies, and religious beliefs, have played a role in shaping chamber music composed during approximately the last seventy-five years. This chapter will present a sampling of some of the most important of these works.

IGOR STRAVINSKY'S OCTET (1923)

In the course of his career, Igor Stravinsky (1882–1971) first cultivated a late-Romantic, Russian nationalist style, then, beginning in 1919, a neoclassical style, and finally, from 1951 onward, a style based on serial permutations of sets. The Octet (1923) for flute, clarinet, and pairs of bassoons, trumpets (C and A), and trombones (tenor and bass) came into being at the juncture of Stravinsky's Russian and neoclassical style periods.

All three movements of the Octet are predicated on Classical pattern forms: The opening Sinfonia is designed as a sonata form in E-flat with a secondary tonal center of D. Like many late eighteenth-century sonatas, it begins with a slow introduction (Lento). The arrival of the main theme (Allegro moderato) is highlighted by drastic changes in meter (from triple to duple), texture (from independent lines to unison tutti), and dynamics (from *piano* to *forte*). The development section and ultimate return of the main theme in E-flat are distinctively profiled as well.[1] The second movement (Andantino) is an octatonic waltz theme with five variations centered on D. This movement was Stravinsky's first use of variation technique. His preference here is for strict variations that preserve the original melody intact; however, there is one novel feature: The first variation (labeled A) returns twice, always at the same tonal level and in essentially identical form. The result is a movement combining variation technique and rondo form. For the finale, Stravinsky writes a five-section design in which the odd-numbered components are centered on C and the even-numbered ones are of ambivalent tonality. Whereas the majority of the previous music was self-consciously neo-Baroque in its textures and motor rhythms, the final, brief return to C is colored by the syncopations and harmonies of pop music, especially jazz.

Stravinsky's neoclassicism has been criticized by many, including Serge Prokofiev, but his combination in the Octet of Classical forms, Baroque textures, and Russian octatonicism—which even dictates the succession of the movements' tonal centers: E-flat, D, and C—is extraordinarily subtle and effective.[2] The composer conducted the first performance at the Paris Opera on 18 October 1923. It was his first appearance of many on the podium.

Stravinsky's other important chamber works are his five-movement suite for violin and piano called *Duo concertante* (1932) and the Septet (1953) for clarinet, horn, bassoon, piano, violin, viola, and cello. Both exhibit the same deft synthesis of elements drawn from various historical styles with aggressively modern techniques. Though it was originally a ballet with orchestra, *Pulcinella* exists in three chamber versions—all by Stravinsky. The earliest of these (1925) is the five-movement Suite for Violin and Piano. For Gregor Piatagorsky, Stravinsky arranged five movements for cello and piano to make the *Suite Italienne* (1932), and in the following year, he arranged six movements—also called *Suite Italienne*—for the violinist Samuel Dushkin.

EDGARD VARÈSE'S *Octandre* (1923)

According to Milton Babbitt, *Octandre* (1923) is "probably Varèse's best known and most widely performed ensemble work."[3] This is surprising in view of its uncommon instrumentation: "Octandrous" flowers are those having eight stamens; correspondingly, Varèse's composition is scored for eight instruments: flute (piccolo), clarinet (E-flat clarinet), oboe, bassoon, horn, trumpet, trombone, and double bass. Perhaps the success of the piece rests in its remarkably concise melodic premise—successive chromatic tones of a tetrachord—and the inventive deployment of these limited resources. In stating the successive half steps of the tetrachord, Varèse displaces the second, thereby establishing a secondary motif consisting of a whole step followed by a half step. The first motif is an all-combinatorial tetrachord; the second spans the interval of a minor third, which, when projected to form a diminished seventh chord, forms the basis of another all-combinatorial tetrachord. Although Varèse does not pursue the possibilities of these tetrachords in a systematic way, he does use them to give form and cohesion to the individual movements and, by thematic recall, to the cycle of three.

Throughout the piece, the single tone displaced to create the trichordal motif virtually becomes a third motif. Varèse uses reiterated single tones not only in each of the three movements, but in every single tempo segment within the movements. Note, too, the isolated tone is dispersed to every possible register and instrument (including piccolo and E-flat clarinet) in the course of the piece. This compositional feature clarifies one important principle in the music of Varèse: The traditional presumption of "octave equivalence must be ruled out, . . . for events in one octave occur in a place fundamentally different from events in any other octave. Thus the property of pitch class disappears."[4] Whenever these reiterated tones appear, Varèse varies not only their register, but also their durations. This technique reaches its climax in the penultimate section of the third movement (Subitement très vif et nerveux).

This intricate process of motivic derivation and thematic cross referencing is supported by Varèse's highly colorful instrumentation. For example, the first movement's opening motto appears transposed by a tritone at the conclusion of that movement; in both instances, it is played by the oboe. These motivic webs leave virtually no room for doubling of pitches; the single instance of doubling appears in measure 29. Intricate, too, are Varèse's metrical designs, which include $1\frac{1}{2}/4$, $2\frac{1}{2}/4$, $3\frac{1}{2}/4$, and $4\frac{1}{2}/4$. These meters could easily be converted to conventional meters (i.e., 3/8, 5/8, 7/8, 9/8); however, such a conversion would change the number and position of stresses within each measure.

The first performance of *Octandre* was conducted by Robert Schmitz on 13 January 1924 at the Vanderbilt Theatre, New York. It was published in that same year by J. Curwen & Sons.[5] That performance was sponsored by the International Composers' Guild, an organization founded in 1921 by Varèse and Carlos Salzedo for the purpose of providing performance venues for contemporary music.

BARTÓK'S SONATA FOR TWO PIANOS AND PERCUSSION (1937)

A commission in May 1937 from the Basel chapter of the International Society for Contemporary Music led Bartók to compose this three-movement sonata for two pianos and two percussionists.[6] It begins with a substantial introduction (Assai lento) that anticipates the second of the two themes (theme 1A and 1B) in the opening statement of the ensuing sonata movement (Allegro). A contrasting subject makes its appearance before the restatement of theme 1B at the conclusion of the exposition. The central development section makes extensive use of ostinatos and thematic inversion. In the recapitulation, imitative counterpoint creates what seems more like a second development section, which, in turn, ends with the recollection of the first subject. The second movement (Lento ma non troppo) is a simple A-B-A song form, and the finale combines elements of sonata and rondo.

The first performance of the Sonata was given in Basel on 16 January 1938 with Bartók and his wife Ditta Pásztory as pianists, Fritz Schiesser and Philipp Rühling as percussionists, and Paul Sacher, conductor.[7] Of the seven percussion instruments—three tympani, bass drum, cymbals, tam-tam, side drum with snares, side drum without snares, and xylophone—all save the xylophone and tympani are played by each percussionist at some point. The Sonata is tonal throughout, with the three movements focused on C, F, and C respectively; however, symmetrical structures, reiteration of identical motifs, and modal inflections lead to a greatly expanded tonal palate. Bartók's characteristic rhythmic energy is apparent even in slow passages.

The ensemble of Bartók's Sonata became the starting point of many derivative works including *Linea* (1973), for two pianists, vibraphone, and marimba, by Luciano Berio (1925–2003); *Music for a Summer Evening* (Makrokosmos III; 1974) for two amplified pianos and percussion, by George Crumb (b. 1929); and *Sur incises* (1996/98), by Pierre Boulez (b. 1925), a forty-minute roller-coaster ride for three pianos, three harps, and three percussionists, who play vibraphones, marimba, steel drums, crotales, glockenspiel, timpani, and tubular bells.

Berio's *Linea* shows influences of minimalism in its strictly limited pitch collections. Adjacent chromatic tones are separated into disjunct groups heard variously in approximates closed or open positions. As the work unfolds, is a continuous piece comprised of twelve short segments: The first, fourth, and sixth are labeled Manège I, II, III; the second and eighth are designated Entrée I, II; the third, fifth, seventh, and eleventh are Ensemble I, II, III, IV; the ninth and tenth are Coda I and II; Berio calls the twelfth and last segment Notturno. The sections called "manège" (*Fr.* trick, little game) lack meter signatures and bar lines; the two "entrée" segments are relaxed and fluid. In addition, they exhibit more transparent and spacious textures than the other movements. The four "ensembles" exhibit the greatest rhythmic activity and textural density. The two "codas" extract distinctive aspects of the contrasting types of segments heard during the course of the work. The Notturno provides a tranquil epilogue to the whole set.

Berio is most particular about the use of sustaining pedal by vibraphone and both pianos, and he typically changes the resonance of repeated motifs as a form of variation. The piano parts sometimes include chords, but surprisingly long stretches of the piece use the instrument as a monophonic voice. Berio's use of understated dynamics softens the impact of the feverish rhythmic activity and textural density of the piece. This approach was probably inspired by the Prestissimo con sordino movement of the Fourth String Quartet of Bartók, a composer Berio very much admired.[8]

Crumb's *Music for a Summer Evening* is in five movements: "Nocturnal Sounds," "Wanderer-Fantasy," "The Advent," "Myth," and "Music of the Starry Night." Its percussion battery is an extensive one including vibraphone, glockenspiel, glass wind chimes, bamboo wind chimes, tubular bells, Japanese temple bells, crotales, bell tree, claves, maracas, sleighbells, wood blocks, temple blocks, large and small triangles, log drum, bass drum, bongo drums, and large tympano, large and small tamtams, large and small suspended cymbals, sizzle cymbals, detached flat cymbal, thunder sheet, sistrum, and Tibetan prayer stones. Both the percussionists and pianists play additional instruments, including slide whistles, jug, alto recorder, guiro (scraper), thumb piano, and *quijada* (rattle).

According to the composer, the first, third, and fifth movements are the weightiest, while the second and fourth act as interludes. The first is headed with a quotation from the twentieth-century poet Salvatore Quasimodo, the third with one from the seventeenth-century mathematician and philosopher Blaise Pascal, and the fifth with one from the turn-of-the-century poet Rainer Maria von Rilke. Pattern forms are not used, but the elaboration of motivic cells provides coherence. The finale includes conspicuous quotations (clearly labeled in the score) from Bach's Fugue in D-sharp minor from book 2 of the *Well-Tempered Clavier.* The music as well as the poetic references suggest a soundscape for a dream. The first performance was given by pianists Gilbert Kalisch and James Freeman and percussionists Raymond des Roches and Richard Fitz at Swarthmore College on 30 March 1974.

Sur incises is a vast elaboration of a nine-page piece for piano solo entitled "Incises" (1994), which was composed for the 1994 Umberto Micheli Piano Competition in Milan. At that competition, a group of judges chaired by Luciano Berio selected Gianluca Cascioli's performance as the winning interpretation of "Incises." The piece, of course, is virtuosic and exploits the characteristic sonorities and capabilities of the piano. Cascades of notes tumble over the entire range of the instrument (A_4, the lowest note on the instrument, is heard in the opening gesture); reiterated tones, frequently combined with expanding and contracting dynamic levels; wedges formed by expanding or contracting intervals and registers are another essential element.

In *Sur incises,* Boulez uses the three harps and percussion battery to accentuate the characteristic yet tremendously diverse sounds produced by a modern, acoustic piano. In this respect, Boulez's intentions were clearly aligned with those of Bartók in his score of the Sonata for two pianos and percussion. The connection between the two works is confirmed by the fact that Boulez dedicated the score of *Sur incises* to Paul Sacher on the occasion of his ninetieth birthday. The score won the University of Louisville's Grawemeyer Award for Music Composition in 2001. The Paul Sacher Stiftung, in Basel, Switzerland, is the repository for the archives of many leading contemporary composers including Boulez.

MESSIAEN AND THE *Quatuor pour la fin du temps* (1941)

No greater practical constraints can be imagined than those that a composer would have faced in a Nazi concentration camp during the 1940s. It was precisely in such circumstances that Olivier Messiaen (1908–1992) composed his chamber-music classic, the *Quatuor pour la fin du temps* (Quartet for the end of time; 1941).

Messiaen had been conscripted to service, but owing to his poor eyesight, he was assigned to a post at Verdun as a paramedic. In May 1940, the Germans invaded. After a futile flight to Nancy, he was captured and interned at Görlitz, in Silesia, in a Nazi camp known as compound VIIIA.

There his fellow prisoners included the violinist Jean Lee Boulaire, the clarinetist Henri Akoka, and the cellist Etienne Pasquier.[9] The only cello available was missing one string. Boulaire and Akoka had been allowed to keep their instruments when they entered the camp. For these two and the handicapped cellist, Messiaen first wrote what is now the fourth movement, "Intermède." The remainder of the quartet (save for the third movement, "Abîme des oiseaux") includes piano—the one that became available to the prisoner-musicians was an upright piano in disrepair. The first performance was given on 15 January 1941 with the composer at the piano assisted by his three friends. For Messiaen, it was the musical experience of his life. Approximately five thousand inmates listened with a concentration and perception that the composer experienced neither before nor afterward.

At the head of the score, Messiaen wrote verses 1 through 7 of chapter 10 of the Revelation of St. John the Divine:

> I saw an angel full of strength descending from the sky, clad with a cloud and having a rainbow over his head. His face was like the sun, his feet like columns of fire. He set his right foot on the sea, his left foot on the earth and, standing on the sea and on the earth, he raised his hand to the sky and swore by Him who lives in the centuries of centuries, saying: "There shall be no more Time, but on the day of the seventh Angel's trumpet the mystery of God shall be accomplished."[10]

The relationship between Messiaen's personal religious views and his music is a complex one. He once stated:

> The first idea that I wished to express—and the most important—is the existence of the truths of the Catholic faith. I've the good fortune to be a Catholic; I was born a believer, and it happens that the Scriptures struck me even as a child. So a number of my works are intended to bring out the theological truths of the Catholic faith. That is the first aspect of my work, the noblest and, doubtless, the most useful and valuable; perhaps the only one which I won't regret at the hour of my death.[11]

Messiaen's theological views pervade the complex musical idiom of the quartet. He reminds us that "most of the arts are unsuited to the expression of religious truth: only music, the most immaterial of all, comes closest to it."[12] Here, irony confronts us since Messiaen effaces this "immateriality" by the programmatic titles for each of the quartet's eight movements; furthermore, each title is accompanied by a detailed prose explanation.

That a concentration camp could not negate the presence of God in all things and in all places, found a natural parallel in the music of birds and the sounds of drops of water that could be heard even within the barbed-wire enclosures of the camp. In order to appreciate these sounds in the quartet and other works, it is helpful to note Messiaen's observation that:

> The phenomenon of nature is . . . beautiful and calming, and, for me, ornithological work is not only an element of consolation in my researches into musical aesthetics, but also a factor of health. It's perhaps thanks to this work that I've been able to resist the misfortunes and complications of life.[13]

The irony here is twofold: Messiaen not only attaches material meanings to immaterial music by invoking nature's sounds, but in so doing, he acknowledges the power of time. The composer noted that "all of God's creations are enclosed in Time, and Time is one of God's strangest creatures because it is totally opposed to Him who is Eternal by nature, to Him who is without beginning, end, or succession."[14]

Messiaen suggests the ending of time through musical materials. Sometimes he constructs themes based upon non-retrogradable rhythms (i.e., palindromic patterns in which time past and time future are identical). Repetitious figures and rhythmic cycles are employed—especially in the first movement—to provide coherence. Though the thirteenth-century Indian theorist Sârngadeva presented such cycles in his treatise *Sangîta-ratnakâra* (Ocean of music), they are not unique to his theory; similar rhythmic patterns appear in western Europe's rhythmic modes as well as in isorhythmic motets of the Ars nova. In the first movement, Messiaen uses panisorhythmic structures combining dissimilar cycles of durations and sonorities. The various instrumental parts thus unfold in a manner analogous to planets moving through their unique orbits. Paul Griffiths has estimated that the cycles as they appear at the beginning of the piece would not come into alignment again for approximately two hours.[15] The seventeen-duration plan of the opening piano part may serve as an example.

Litanies, which have played an important part in Christian liturgies since the fifth century, also influenced Messiaen's score. Their repetitious structure induces a sort of spiritual intoxication in which one becomes oblivious to the world and to time. Messiaen's use of recurrence—particularly the links between the second and seventh movements, and the fifth and eighth—enhances this sense of timelessness. Finally, the eight-movement plan is significant. "This 'Quartet' consists of eight movements.

Why? Seven is the perfect number, the creation of 6 days sanctified by the holy Sabbath; the 7th day of repose extends into eternity and becomes the 8th day of indefectible light, of unalterable peace."

In *Quatuor*, Messiaen used previously composed music for the fifth movement, "Louange à l'éternité de Jésus" (Paean to the eternity of Jesus), and the last movement, "Louange à l'immortalité de Jésus" (Paean to the immortality of Jesus). The former is drawn from the *Fête des belles eaux* (Celebration of beautiful water; 1937), scored for six *ondes martenot*, the latter from the *Diptyque* (1930) for organ solo. In addition to *Quatuor*, Messiaen wrote only two chamber works: *Merle noir* (Blackbird; 1951 for flute and piano), and the *Pièce* (1991) for piano quintet.

LUCIANO BERIO, CHAMBER MUSIC (1953) AND PIERRE BOULEZ, LE MARTEAU SANS MAÎTRE (1954)

When traditional poetry is set to music, the intelligibility of the text almost always assumes a primary role, thereby impeding—if not virtually precluding—the equality of elements that is the life's blood of chamber music ensembles. Late nineteenth-century French symbolist poets began using words for their sonorous qualities as well as for their "meanings." The liberation of words from syntax and connotation was accomplished by the Italian Futurist poets of the early twentieth century, who advanced the concept of *parole in liberta* (liberated words). The works of James Joyce (1882–1941) exhibit similar tendencies, which led in his later works to a host of technical innovations including interior monologue (i.e., stream of consciousness), invented words, puns, double meanings, symbolic parallels drawn from a wide variety of sources, and other methods of presentation that range from the obscure to the unintelligible. These trends have changed the way musicians interested in vocal chamber music look at texts.

Pierre Boulez (b. 1925) has addressed these issues in his essay "Sound and Word," where he remarks: "When one envisages the 'putting to music' of the poem . . . a series of questions relating to declamation, to prosody is posed. Is one going to sing the poem, 'recite' it, speak it? All the vocal means enter into play, and upon these diverse particularities of emission depend the transmission and . . . intelligibility of the text."[16] A poem is an autonomous work of art with inherent sonorities, rhythms, and intervals; thus, as Boulez candidly states, singing a poem results in the "destruction of the poem."[17] Operating on the premise that a poem's inherent sonorities are irreconcilable with those that the poem inspires in the mind of the composer, Boulez brushes aside the issue of intelligibility: "If you wish to 'understand' the text, then read it."[18]

Berio's *Chamber Music* takes its title from an early set of Joyce's poems published in London by Charles Elkin Mathews in 1907. Berio selected three poems, "Strings in the earth and air," "All day I hear the noise of waters," and "Winds of May," and set them for mezzo-soprano, clarinet, cello, and harp. His approach to the voice at that time was influenced by two factors: the singing of Cathy Berberian, whom he had married in 1950, and the music of Luigi Dallapiccola, with whom Berio studied during the Berkshire Music Festival at Tanglewood in 1952.

Dallapiccola, best known for his one-act opera *Il prigioniero* (1949), was the leading serialist in Italy after World War II. In *Chamber Music*, Berio uses serial techniques as well; however, his tone row is designed "to furnish lyrical opportunities rather than to expunge tonal and triadic echoes."[19]

For the outer two poems, Berio used the opening lines of the poems as titles. For the central song, he has gone farther into the poetic text to find his title as well as the defining feature of the song's vocal line:

All day I hear the noise of water
Making moan,
Sad as the sea-bird is, when going

Forth alone,
He hears the winds cry to the waters'
Monotone.

The drab recitation of the text is masterfully counterbalanced by the brilliant instrumental writing, which amounts to a tone poem in miniature.

For *Le marteau sans maître*, Boulez chose three short poems by the French surrealist poet René Char (1907–1988), which appeared in his 1934 publication by the same title. The texts are as follows:[20]

L'ARTISANAT FURIEUX
la roulette rouge au bord du clou
et cadavre dans le panier
et chevaux de labours dans le fer à cheval
je rêve la tête sur la pointe de mon
couteau le Pérou

BEL ÉDIFICE ET LES PRESSENTIMENTS
j' écoute marcher dans mes jambes
la mer morte vagues par-dessus tête
enfant la jetée-promenade sauvage
homme l'ilussion imitée
des yeus purs dans le bois
cherchent et pleurant la tête habitable

BOURREAUX DE SOLITUDE
le pas s'et eloigné, le marcheur s'est tu
sur le cadran de l'limitation
le balancier lance sa charge de granit
réflexe

The score exists in two editions, the first, published in 1954 and used for the premiere at the 1955 Baden-Baden Festival on 18 June 1955, and a revised version of 1957, which bears a dedication to Hans Rosbaud, who conducted the premiere. The earlier version has seven movements rather than nine, and their sequence is different from that in the final version. Both are scored for alto and six instrumentalists playing alto flute (i.e., in G), guitar, vibraphone, xylorimba, percussion, and viola. "All these instruments have a medium pitch register, [which is] an important consideration since they are to accompany a contralto voice. . . . The nature of the instrumentation supports the nature of the voice in both tessitura and colour." The composer notes further that the instrumentation represents a "chain linking each instrument to the next by a feature common to both

. . . : voice-flute, breath; flute-viola, monody; viola-guitar, plucked strings; guitar-vibraphone, long resonance; vibraphone-xylophone, struck bars of metal or wood."[21] In using these instruments, Boulez has taken care to vary the ensemble from one piece to another. This, he says is a "deliberate, direct reference to [Schoenberg's] *Pierrot lunaire.*"[22] Each of the vocal movements became the kernel for a cycle of movements: "l'artisanat furieux" inspired a prelude and a postlude; "bourreaux de solitude" provoked three commentaries; and "bel édifice et les pressentiments" suggested to Boulez the idea of a variation. In arranging the sequence of these purely instrumental movements that followed in the aftermath of the vocal movements, Boulez made no attempt to keep the cycles together; instead, he interspersed items from the various cycles in one larger cycle of increasing complexity. According to the composer, "It's only the last piece ["bel édifice et les pressentiments"—double] that, to some extent, offers the solution, the key to this labyrinth."[23] The most important process that takes place in this final movement is the equalization of vocal and instrumental elements. During the preceding movements, the voice periodically emerged to declaim the words of the poems, but in the final movement, the voice is used to hum rather than to utter words. The constantly changing timbres, textures, and dynamics result in a piece that can be appreciated for its sonorous beauty if not for its cognitive intricacies.

LEON KIRCHNER, STRING QUARTET NO. 3 (1966)

The highly evocative scores of Leon Kirchner (1919–2009) have been recognized repeatedly as major accomplishments in contemporary idioms. His First and Second string quartets (1949, 1958) both won awards, but his Third Quartet (1966) earned him the prestigious Pulitzer Prize in 1967.

In addition to the three previously mentioned string quartets, Kirchner's principal chamber works include the Duo (1947) for violin and piano, the Sonata concertante (1952) for violin and piano, the First Piano Trio (1954), and the Second Piano Trio (1993). Additional chamber pieces include Two Duos (1988) and Triptych (1988) for violin and cello. The latter consists of the Two Duos with a central movement for cello solo dating from 1986.

Arnold Schoenberg, Ernst Bloch, and Roger Sessions were among Kirchner's mentors. Given this highly diversified background, Kirchner has eschewed reliance upon any single contemporary ideology; instead, he has drawn resources from each of these composers' idioms as well as from his personal experiences as a pianist and conductor. His music is totally chromatic, but that chromaticism may sound at one moment lush and Romantic, in the manner of Richard Strauss or Gustav Mahler, or more akin to the free pan-tonal works of Schoenberg or Berg in the next. He tends to write single, continuous movements; nevertheless, lyrical adagios, energetic scherzos, and other familiar types of movements can be found embedded within the larger designs. Kirchner has no interest in being a radical. His preference for traditional chamber music genres is evidence of that; however, like Schoenberg, he has freely broadened traditional approaches to these genres and their concomitant ensembles when it suited his expressive goals to do so.

A case in point is his Third String Quartet, which combines this most traditional of chamber-music ensembles with electronically synthesized sounds that Kirchner created on the Buchla synthesizer.[24] From 1954 until 1961, Kirchner was on the faculty of Mills College in Oakland, California. It was there that he became interested in electronic music. At the same time in San Francisco, Donald Buchla was developing technological support for composers. Buchla had refined his synthesizers to enable electronic strands to be integrated with live performance. While Kirchner admits that electronics have given musicians new insights into the creation and application of musical materials, he nevertheless finds claims of the potential of electronic media greatly exaggerated. He is more interested in "the combinations of instruments with electronic sounds and filters. Instrumental qualities are then somehow reflected, extended, and adumbrated in interesting ways. Human involvement is, of course, essential; for the problems of composition remain the primary factors. I set out to produce a meaningful and musical confrontation between new electronic sounds and those of the traditional string quartet."[25]

The Third String Quartet is a continuous piece that lasts a bit under twenty minutes; nevertheless, it consists of eleven contrasting sections (so numbered by the composer), much like an ancient canzona. These seem variously to be introductory, expository, transitional, or developmental. At some points, Kirchner writes exclusively for the acoustical ensemble; in other passages, it dominates; in others, it functions in dialogue with the electronic sounds, or with the electronic sounds as accompaniment. Though prominent in many segments of the piece, especially the opening of the "Scenario: Tape Cadenza," the synthesized sounds never become the primary sonic events.

The notation of the score is ingenious. Traditional notation is used for the quartet, and freely created graphics, including lines, ovals, circles, sawtooth shapes, and so on, represent the electronic sounds. Arrows and lines drawn through the image of a loudspeaker indicate where the electronic tape should be activated and deactivated; consequently, no two performances will ever be identical.

Other composers have written pieces that combine acoustical instruments with electronic elements. Noteworthy among these are *Musica su due dimensioni* (1952) for flute, cymbals, and electronically altered sounds, by Bruno Maderna (1920–1973), which is probably the earliest such work; *Delizie contente che l'alme beate* (1973), a marvelous fantasia for wind quintet and electronic sounds by Jacob Druckman (1928–1996) based on a Baroque aria by Francesco Cavalli; the series of *Synchronisms*—all with electronics—by Mario Davidovsky (b. 1934), including No. 1 (1963) for flute, No. 2 (1964) for flute, clarinet, violin, cello, No. 3 (1965) for cello, No. 5 (1969) for percussion ensemble, No. 6 (1970) for piano, No. 8 (1974) for woodwind quintet, No. 9 (1988) for violin, and No. 10 (1992) for guitar. *As If* (1982), for violin, viola, cello, and electronics, by Paul Lansky (b. 1944), consists of four movements titled respectively "In Preparation," "At a Distance," "In Practice," and "In Distinction." Impressive, too, is his score *Values of Time* (1987) for wind quintet, string quartet, and electronic sounds. Lansky has also written purely acoustical chamber works including two string quartets (1967, 1971) and *Crossworks* (1975) for flute, clarinet, violin, cello, and piano.

STEVE REICH, *Violin Phase* (1967)

In exactly the same year that Kirchner won the Pulitzer for his electronic quartet, Steve Reich (b. 1937) set out on a closely related but essentially different path: By using first one, then two, and finally three prerecorded tracks of the musical patterns that constitute *Violin Phase* (1967), Reich creates a constantly changing superimposition of motifs, rhythms, and textures. Though highly repetitious, the music is never the same. A further irony of the piece has to do with its status as chamber music. While its texture consists largely of four totally independent parts, all four of the parts are performed by a single violinist.

Violin Phase is a landmark in the history of the largely American style known as minimalism. In his later works, Reich created the same effects without the use of prerecorded material. His Octet (1979) for flute/piccolo, clarinet / bass clarinet, two pianos, two violins, viola, and cello is a more colorful realization of the same concept.

Minimalism has been significantly transformed in the works of John Adams (b. 1947), whose principal chamber works to date include *Shaker Loops* (1978; rev. 1982), *John's Book of Alleged Dances* (1994)—eleven fancifully titled movements for string quartet, six of which include electronically altered sounds of a prepared piano, and *Road Movies* (1995) for violin and piano. While retaining repetitious patterns within the context of ever changing relationships, Adams tends to color his musical modules with chromatic elements. In some instances, the resulting harmonies are strikingly Romantic. The rhythms of the *Alleged Dances* are drawn from a wide variety of musics: In addition to classical items, such as the pavane, the habanera, and *scherzando* polymeters in 12/8 time, Adams gets toes tapping with energetic hoedowns, the perpetual motion of Western-swing fiddle music, and the syncopations of turn-of-the-century ragtime. Some of the movements are less concerned with appealing to a large audience, and they contain very imaginative and refined writing. "Alligator Escalator," which includes no electronics or prerecorded sounds, is an excellent example.

GEORGE CRUMB, *Black Angels* (1970)

In the formation of his style, George Crumb (b. 1924) has embraced diverse historical influences as well as elements of folk music from the hills of his native West Virginia. Bartók, Webern, Ives, Messiaen, and Berio are important, but he attributes the most profound influence to Debussy. Crumb's fascination with folk instruments has led him to discover fantastic uses of color and timbre. He does not shun pop, rock, or jazz, each of which contributes something to his style. He is equally delighted to hear unfamiliar sounds in Asian, African, South American, and other non-Western repertoires. Electronic music fascinates him, and he considers Mario Davidovsky "the most elegant of all the electronic composers whose music I know."[26] Crumb's forays into the electronic world, however, are limited to amplification.

His invented techniques for playing traditional acoustical instruments often produce what sounds like electronic music, but without the technological and logistical impediments of electronics. He routinely expects instrumentalists to use their voices too, and he asks variously for hissing, howling, shouting, screaming, whispering, and so on. In the opening of *Vox balænæ* (Voice of the whale; 1971), the flutist must sing into the instrument and play it simultaneously to approximate the actual humpback whale songs of which Crumb had heard tape recordings. In *Black Angels* (1970) for electric string quartet with maracas, tam-tam, and water-tuned goblets, his players are required to count in a quasi-ritualistic way in German, French, Russian, Hungarian, Japanese, and Swahili. In both of these pieces, music is complemented by drama. In *Vox balænæ*, the three players (flute, cello, piano) perform bathed in aquamarine lighting and in masks.

Symbolism pervades all of Crumb's music, but is especially apparent in *Black Angels*, which is subtitled "Thirteen Images from the Dark Land." The score is dated "Friday 13 March 1970 (in tempore belli)." This was the height of the Vietnam War. The quartet may therefore be viewed as a parable exploring the fall from grace in the first movement, "Departure," spiritual emptiness in the second, "Absence," and redemption in the third, "Return." Numerology (often imperceptible without the score) informs the structure of the piece, and the numbers seven and thirteen affect the choice of intervals, durations, motivic patterns, and other details.

The sonic resources of *Black Angels* include a conventional string quartet but with amplification. Extended techniques, such as stopping the strings with thimble-covered fingers, bowing on the wrong side of the strings, and so on. frequently result in quasi-electronic sounds. References to tonal music include paraphrases of the *Dies irae*, Schubert's *Death and the Maiden*, and an original sarabande in a neotonal style. The trill is used as a motif to represent the fallen angel—this via Tartini's famous "Devil's Trill Sonata."

CHOU WEN-CHUNG, *Echoes from the Gorge* (1989)

Echoes from the Gorge is not the first Western music for ensembles consisting only of percussion. The fifth and sixth *Rítmicas* (1930) of the Afro-Cuban composer Amadeo Roldan (1900–1939) and *Ionisation* (1931) of Edgard Varèse (1883–1965) were the earliest such pieces.[27] John Cage (1912–1992) began experimenting with ensembles of this sort in his percussion Quartet (1935), which does not specify instrumentation. Cage welcomed serendipitous scorings including pots, pans, and other kitchen ware, garbage cans, pieces of furniture, and so on. In his later pieces entitled *First Construction in Metal* (1939), *Second Construction* (1940), and *Third Construction* (1941), unconventional percussion items are specified. Lou Harrison (b. 1917) also combined classical and "junk" instruments, such as brake drums and iron tubs. His three-movement Suite (1942) for percussion is representative not only of this trend, but also of a technique generally known as metric modulation. In the seven-movement suite *Los Dioses Aztecas*, Op. 107 (Aztec gods; 1959), Gardner Read (1913–2005) specifies both pitched and unpitched percussion with exactitude. This massive work of about a half-hour's duration requires six percussionists and no fewer than sixty percussion instruments. An extraordinary number of percussion pieces have been written by William Kraft (b. 1923), whose academic training was complemented by practical experience he gained as percussionist for the Los Angeles Philharmonic from 1955 to 1981. In 1958, he completed *Momentum*, requiring eight players, and his Suite, which requires four. Kraft's series of pieces called *Encounters* (eleven composed between 1975 and 1998) are for various instruments, invariably with percussion. *Encounters I*, "Soliloquy," (1975) is for a single percussionist with tape; others are for trumpet, trombone, saxophone, English horn, violin, cello, and so forth. Some Encounters—Nos. VI and VII—are for percussion ensembles: roto-toms and percussion quartet in the former, two percussionists playing various instruments in the latter. Kraft writes for four percussionists in Theme and Variations (1956) and the Quartet (1988). The former piece, composed exactly ten years after Benjamin Britten's score of *Young Person's Guide to the Orchestra*, employs an organizational scheme no doubt derived from that piece: Kraft's "Theme" is followed by four variations, the first is scored for cymbals, snare drum, bass drum, and tympani; the second for idiophones of metal and wood; the third for membraphones; and the fourth draws freely from all departments in a fascinating mix and match of timbres and pitches.

Multiculturalism provides the foundation for the music of the remarkable Chinese-American composer Chou Wen-chung (b. 1923). Chou heard percussion ensembles of Chinese instruments as a young man before immigrating to the United States in the fall of 1946, but by the time he began *Echoes from the Gorge* in 1970, he was already intimately familiar with Varèse's *Ionisation;* hence, his fantastically colorful scoring of represents an amalgamation of Chinese and Western timbres and techniques.[28] The instrumentation calls for a vast array of percussion including concert castanets, clave, cowbells, bongos, congas, low snare drum, metal chimes, sizzle cymbal, finger bell, gong (small, high, and low), Chinese cymbal (small and large cup), crash cymbal (high and low), tamtam (high and low), Chinese tom-tom (high and low), timbales, bass drum (high and low), parade drum (high and low), ride cymbal (high and low), gong (high and low), wood blocks, tom-tom, high snare drum, bamboo chimes, small cymbal, metal sheet, and temple blocks.[29]

Traditional Chinese *qin* music is rich in variations of sonorities accomplished by specific finger movements. In *Echoes from the Gorge*, Chou achieves similar effects by using a wide variety of contact locations and sticks—for example, he may instruct that the instrument be struck on the cup, at the rim, near the back edge, or even rolling gradually from one location to another.[30] Some of the instruments listed here appear in more than one of the four groups; hence, the composer has been able to highlight either similar or different timbres within the groups. In fact, the role of transethnicity in *Echoes* goes far beyond its instrumentation. Chinese philosophy, aesthetics, and arts also played a role in Chou's conception.

Echoes occupied Chou for almost twenty years. He commenced work in the summer of 1970 when he was Guest Composition Teacher and Composer-in-Residence at the Berkshire Music Center at Tanglewood. He resumed composition there in the following summer. Owing to the demands made upon him as chairman of the Music Division at Columbia University, a position that he held from 1969 to 1989, he put the score aside. Further time constraints came with Chou's founding of the Center for U.S.-China Arts Exchange in 1978. Finally, in 1988, he returned to the score and completed it in 1989. The New Music Consort gave the first performance at the Lila Acheson Wallace Auditorium in New York City on 27 April, 1989.[31]

At the heart of the piece are its six rhythmic modes, which are based on permutations of the durational ratios 3:2:1 and their aggregates. These ratios were suggested to Chou by the writings of Lao-tzu, the semimythical founder of Taoism.[32] Stanza 42 of the *Tao-te ching* reads as follows:

> The number one of the Way was born.
> A diad from this monad formed.
> The diad next a triad made;
> The triad bred the myriad,
> Each holding *yang*
> And held by *yin*,
> Whose powers' balanced interaction
> Brings all ten thousand to fruition.[33]

In his poems, Lao-tzu imbues the number one with cosmological significance. "The term *yi*, 'One,' a single horizontal stroke, represents the dividing line between the unmanifest and the manifest, between Dao and the ten thousand. On one side of the line life emerges in spontaneous profusion (*min-min*, helter-skelter). At life's end all things cross back to the unmanifest state, to negation."[34] This single horizontal stroke can also form the central line of a trigram, the figures used in the classic Confucian text known as the *I ching* (book of changes). Contrary to popular Western beliefs, this volume is not merely a book of divination; rather, it is predicated upon three philosophical premises: the dynamic balance of opposites, the evolution of events as a process, and the inevitability of change. These concepts—along with the trigrams and hexagrams formed by the combination of trigrams—became the cornerstones of Chou's "variable modes." The first of Chou's scores to employ the variable modes is *Metaphors* (1961) for wind orchestra. By the time he composed *Echoes*, Chou had discovered that these variable modes could be applied to parameters other than organizing pitch; they could also serve to regulate elements such as duration, timbre, register, and so on. In this respect, Chou's expansion of the function of his variable modes is analogous to the expansion of dodecaphonic principles within the context of "total" or "integral" serialism implied in some works by Anton Webern and subsequently elucidated in detail in compositions by Milton Babbitt (1916–2011), Pierre Boulez, Luigi Nono (1924–1990), Karlheinz Stockhausen (1928–2007), and others.

The roles of *yin* and *yang* also play an important part in Chou's *Echoes*. Initially, *yin* and *yang* were understood as "natural, equal forces interacting in a balanced manner."[35] Subsequently [the concept of] *yin* and *yang* polarity was applied more broadly. Yang might represent "heaven, large kingdoms, sovereigns, males, and so on, while *yin* is associated with earth, small kingdoms, vassals, females, and so on."[36] In the trigrams of the *I ching*, *yang* are represented by an unbroken line, and *yin* by the line broken into halves. From bottom to top, the three lines in a trigram correspond to earth, humanity, and heaven. The maximum number of different trigrams is eight. If we represent *yin* (a broken line) by 0 and *yang* (a solid line) by 1, the possibilities become the following: 000/001/010/011/100/101/110/111. When trigrams are paired to create hexagrams, the total number possible is sixty-four. Combining the cosmological Taoist numerology associated with one, then two, then three (or, the durational ratios 3:2:1 or rhythmic motifs consisting of one, two, or three elements) with the *yin-yang* lines of the trigrams, Chou represents *yin* and *yang* by various groupings of six elements. Since the note value used in the 3:2:1 series may be a quarter (i.e., dotted half, half, quarter), and eight (dotted quarter, quarter, eighth), or any other, arbitrarily selected note value, the traditional compositional procedures of augmentation and diminution are inherent in Chou's theoretical plan.[37]

The "Prelude: Exploring the Modes" presents six rhythmic motifs that, in permutations and transformations, provide the durational foundations of the score. The Prelude is followed by twelve continuous sections, each with a citation of some evocative image familiar from classical Chinese landscape paintings: "Raindrops on Bamboo Leaves," "Echoes from the Gorge," "Autumn Pond," "Clear Moon," "Shadows in the Ravine," "Old Tree by the Cold Spring," "Sonorous Stones," "Droplets down the Rocks,"

"Drifting Clouds," "Rolling Pearls," "Peaks and Cascades," and "Falling Rocks and Flying Spray."[38]

Yin is reflected in the series 3 + 2 + 1 and 3 + 1 + 2, whereas 5 + 1 and 4 + 2 represent *yang*. "A rhythmic mode is thus formed by combining a 3- and a 2-group unit in either order."[39] A trigram of 001 type might therefore become the following:

3 + 2 + 1	3 + 1 + 2	5 + 1
0	0	1

This trigram might then be paired with its reciprocal trigram, 100 (*yin-yang* polarity), within a hexagram. In the design of *Echoes*, Chou favors nine hexagrams that—in the *I ching*—are numbered as follows: 11, 12, 17, 18, 42, 53, 54, 63, 64. The adjacent hexagrams (i.e., 11, 12; 17, 18; 53, 54; 63, 64) happen also to be retrogrades of each other: 111000, 000111; 100110, 011001; 001011, 110100; 101010, 010101.[40] The traditional compositional principles of retrograde and inversion are thus inherent in the constitution of the various hexagrams.

Although the score includes precise metronomic indications and time signatures, the temporal progress of the piece is not based on meter; moreover, the structural elements briefly surveyed here provide coherence not only within individual sections of the piece, but throughout the superstructure of the entire piece.

The role of transethnicism in *Echoes*—and in all of Chou's other works—goes far beyond the simple combination of Asian and Western instruments, or using a Chinese folk tune with a pentatonic harmonization. His synthesis of Asian and Western elements is both pervasive and organic. Soon after leaving New England Conservatory in 1948, he relocated to New York City, where he composed Three Folk Songs (1950) for harp and flute. Chou subsequently composed his Suite (1951) for harp and wind quintet, and the very adventurous score *Cursive* (1963) for flute and piano. Because the flute is capable of minute fluctuations in pitch, varying speeds of vibrato, microtonal trills, and so forth, Chou felt it necessary to endow the piano with some comparable timbral variety. In certain passages, the strings must be prepared with wooden slabs, metal slabs, and metal chains. He suggests bookshelf brackets, rulers, triangular scales, ball-chains, and the like. At other times, the pianist plays inside the instrument, variously stopping, tapping, or plucking the strings, or playing glissandos. *Cursive* contains important structural elements that relate directly to Chou's system of variable modes used in his mature works, particularly the use of augmented triads whose thirds are motivically elaborated variously as successive whole tones or as a minor third plus a semitone. Despite the origin of these motifs within compact intervallic boundaries, the motifs are often stated in widely separated registers; thus, abstract concepts of pitch (i.e., without reference to that pitch's location within a precise octave) do not apply in this piece. Accordingly, Chou devised what he calls a "Continuous Intensity Scale," which associates specific dynamics with particular pitches and registers of each of the two instruments.

Ancient Chinese *qin* music inspired *Yü Ko* (1965) for violin, alto flute, English horn, bass clarinet, trombone, bass trombone, piano, and two percussionists. This zither-type instrument (usually with seven silk strings) has a subtle sound that may be likened to that of the Western clavichord: A person speaking at a normal dynamic level will essentially drown the instrument out. Like the clavichord, the *qin* is capable of great nuance in inflection and dynamics. Because its strings are plucked with the fingers (rather than struck, as are the strings of a clavichord), the method of plucking (e.g., with the fleshy part of the fingertip, with the fingernail, with a bit of each, at some particular point close or far from the bridge, etc.) shapes the resulting sound. Chou uses an actual *qin* melody, the "Fisherman's Song," in *Yü Ko*. Because of the musical structure of the tune, Chou's harmonic and melodic style are heavily pentatonic.

Additional chamber works of interest include *Ceremonial* (1968) for three trumpets and three trombones; and *Yün* (1969) for flute, clarinet in B-flat, bassoon, horn, trumpet in B-flat, trombone, two percussionists, and piano. *Yün*, largely because of Chou's commitments at Columbia University and with the music of his mentor, Edgard Varèse, was followed by a long silence that was finally broken with his completion of *Echoes from the Gorge*. Since then, Chou has been consistently prolific.

The fascinating score of *Windswept Peaks* (1990) is a double duo for violin and cello in dialogue with the paired clarinet and piano. Although it is performed as a continuum, it has clearly discernable sections with verbal clues indicating the affection of the music. At the time Chou was working on the piece, he was powerfully influenced by the Tiananmen Square episode and its aftermath in June 1989. To an extent, the dialectic between the two duos of Windswept Peaks is an allegory relating to the traditional role of literati (文人, "wenren") in dialogue with society in general. As he notes in the preface to the score, "The image of windswept peaks suggest the unadorned beauty of inner strength." In this and subsequent scores, Chou's system of variable modes is fully realized and pervasively implemented. Rhythmic structures are similarly the outgrowth of his scheme of rhythmic modes. The relationships of rhythmic designs, pitch patterns, dynamics, and timbres are regulated by *yin/yang* correspondences traditionally associated in Chinese astronomy and philosophy with woman/moon in complementation with man/sun respectively. In designing the piece, Chou has used Asian premises in a manner that clearly parallels the integral serial pieces of Milton Babbitt, Pierre Boulez, and others.

Chou's two string quartets, *Clouds* (1996) and *Streams* (2002), were written for and premiered by the Brentano Quartet. String Quartet No. 1, dedicated to the composer's wife, the pianists Yi-an *née* Chang, is structured in five distinct movements. It was Chou's intention to pay homage to two musical traditions, that of the Western string quartet, the traditional movements of which can easily be perceived, and *qin* music. Although *qin* repertoire is soloistic, it is relevant to chamber music because, as Chou points out, *qin* music was typically composed by the *qin* player specifically for particular guests invited for a particular musical occasion; thus, there was an intimacy, a meeting of minds, that is characteristic of chamber music. The first movement of *Clouds*—the longest and most varied in tempo, texture, and mood of all—seems almost as though Chou had composed it to be a quartet complete unto itself.[41] In fact, it is an expansive metamorphosis in which the processes of exposition and development are merged.[42] The second movement, Leggierezza, has very much the character of a traditional scherzo. The Larghetto nostalgico, the third movement, is one of the highlights of string-quartet repertoire. Strings are with mutes throughout. Dynamics are subdued. Melodic movement is generally limited to a single voice, but that melodic material is distributed quite evenly among the four instruments. That Chou's earliest linguistic experience was with a toned language is clearly reflected in the careful shaping of each tone in the melodic line. The fourth movement, Presto con fuoco, keeps the same pulse for every measure even though the measures cycle constantly through combinations of three to eight beats. Each statement of the cycle is a continuous *accelerando*. Chou cycles through the series six times. This unique isometric ostinato recalls something of the character of the isorhythmic motets of the Ars nova and the basso ostinato structures of Baroque music; however, this particular application of those concepts is novel. The finale is unique in Chou's works since it is a condensed recapitulation, often verbatim or with slight modifications such as octave transpositions, of the first movement. Chou could easily have continued the process of transformation that he initiated in the first movement. His choice to harken back to a distant memory, recalling it essentially but not exactly, intensifies the nostalgic and essentially Romantic aesthetic of this music.

Chou's Second String Quartet, *Streams*, began as a commission from the Brentano Quartet for a work responding to Bach's *Art of the Fugue*. The resulting composition was his *Contrapunctus Variabilis* (2002), which the Brentano players premiered at Middlebury College on 8 November 2002. This movement begins with an astonishing Introduction in which rich, tutti chords quite like those in his String Quartet No. 1 form the aggressive, *ying* character of the opening. This is immediately countered by a *yin* passage played *sotto voce* and at a much slower tempo. The ensuing movement is a quadruple fugue using all of the permutations of subject and answer that one would expect in a traditional fugue. Chou—like Beethoven with the four-note motif of the Galitzin quartets—became fascinated with the possibilities of his subject and expanded it with three additional movements. The second movement, an elegy written in memory of the composer's brother, Wen-tsing, recalls the Larghetto nostalgico of the First Quartet both in its precise shaping of individual tones within the melodic lines and in the use of muted strings. The third movement, Allegretto grazioso, takes its point of departure from the Presto con fuoco of String Quartet No. 1. It is a double canon that constantly accelerates during its sixty-two-measure duration. Chou likens the movement to his experiences during the compositional process in which "severe recurrent pain . . . would intensify mercilessly to an unbearable climax when it would suddenly subside, very much in the manner of the arpeggio that abruptly concludes the movement."[43] The last movement, "Episodes and Coda," makes extensive use of double stops in recapitulating three expositions of the fugue. The Coda is a varied and condensed restatement of the Introduction to the first movement.

Twilight Colors (2007) is ingeniously conceived to get three trios of contrasting timbres out of six players and scored for flute / alto flute, oboe / English horn, clarinet / bass clarinet, and violin, viola, and cello. The timbres are an essential element of this piece, which owes a debt not only to seventeenth-century Chinese brush painting but also to the Luminist painters of the Hudson River School. The four movements and coda are headed with suggestive titles: "A Thread of Light," "Colors of Dawn," "In the Mist," Mountain Peaks Rising," and "Their Silhouettes Neither Parallel nor Contrary."

His most recent composition, *Eternal Pine* (2009), was originally conceived for an ensemble of traditional Korean instruments. Soon after its premiere, Chou made extensive revisions to the piece, shortened it, and rescored it for a Western instrumentation consisting of flute, clarinet, violin, cello, percussion (one player: bass drum, four tom-toms, two dome cymbals, two crash cymbals, cncerro, and bell), and piano.

Table of Chamber Pieces According to Ensemble Size

Note: Basso continuo is counted as a single performer. In repertoire using electronics, the person operating the electronic equipment is counted as a performer.

TWO PERFORMERS

Adams, John
- *Road Movies*, violin, piano

Arutiunian, Alexander
- *Poem-Sonata*, violin, piano
- *Retro-Sonata*, viola, piano
- Suite: clarinet, violin, piano

Bach, Johann Sebastian
- Sonata: viola *da Gamba*, basso continuo, G major, S. 1027

Bartók, Béla
- Duos: forty-four, two violins
- Rhapsodies: violin, piano, No. 1 (1928); No. 2 (1928)
- Sonatas: violin, piano, No. 1 (1921); No. 2 (1922)

Beethoven, Ludwig van
- Sonatas: cello, piano, Op. 5
- Sonata: violin, piano, Op. 96

Berg, Alban
- Four pieces: clarinet, piano, Op. 5

Brahms, Johannes
- Sonata: cello, piano, F major, Op. 99
- Sonatas: clarinet, piano, F minor, Op. 120, No. 1; E-flat major, Op. 120, No. 2
- Sonatas: violin, piano, FAE Scherzo; G major, Op. 78; A major, Op. 100; D minor, Op. 108
- *Variations on a Theme of Haydn*, Op. 56b

Britten, Benjamin
Lachrymae: Reflections on a Song of John Dowland, Op. 48, viola. Piano
Sonata: cello, piano, C, Op. 65
Temporal Variations, oboe, piano

Chou Wen-chung
Cursive, flute, piano
Three Folk Songs, harp, flute

Davidovsky, Mario
Synchronisms: flute, electronics, No. 1; cello, electronics, No. 3; percussion, electronics, No. 5; piano, electronics, No. 6; violin, electronics, No. 9; guitar, electronics, No. 10

Debussy, Claude
En blanc et noir, 2 pianos
Sonata: cello, piano
Sonata: violin, piano

Denisov, Edison
Es ist genug, viola, piano
Sonata: alto saxophone, piano (1970)
Sonata: clarinet, piano (1993)
Sonata: flute, piano (1960)
Sonata: violin, piano (1963)
Suite: cello, piano (1961)

Fauré, Gabriel
Sonata: cello, piano, D major, Op. 109; G major, Op. 117
Sonata: violin, piano, A major, Op. 13; E major, Op. 108

Foote, Arthur
Sonata: violin, piano, G minor

Franck, César
Sonata: violin (flute), piano, A major

Grieg, Edvard
Sonata: cello, piano, A minor, Op. 36
Sonatas: violin, piano, F major, Op. 8; G major, Op. 13; C minor, Op. 45

Gubaidulina, Sophia
In croce, cello, organ *or* cello, bayan
Pantomime, double bass, piano
Der Seiltänzer, violin, piano
Sonata: double bass, piano
Sonata: *Detto I*, organ, percussion
Sonata: *Rejoice!*, violin, cello

Guérin, Emmanuel
Duos faciles, Op. 1 (violins)

Hindemith, Paul
Sonata: alto saxophone, piano (E-flat, 1943)
Sonata: bassoon, piano (1938)
Sonata: cello, piano, Op. 11, No. 3; Kleine Sonata (1942)
Sonata: clarinet, piano (1939)
Sonata: double bass, piano (1949)
Sonata: English horn, piano (1941)

Sonata: four horns (1952)
Sonata: oboe, piano (1938)
Sonata: trombone, piano (1941)
Sonata: trumpet, piano (1939)
Sonata: tuba, piano (1955)
Sonata: viola *d'amore*, piano, Op. 25, No. 2 (1922)
Sonatas: horn, piano (F, 1939; E-flat, 1943)
Sonatas: viola, piano, Op. 11, No. 4; Op. 25, No. 4
Sonatas: violin, piano, Op. 11, Nos. 1, 2; in E (1935); in C (1939)

Husa, Karel
Eight Czech Duets, piano, four hands
Élégie et rondeau, saxophone, piano
"Postcard from Home," saxophone, piano
Sonata: violin, piano (1973)
Twelve Moravian Songs, voice, piano

Ives, Charles
"Decoration Day," violin, piano
Sonatas: violin, piano, No. 1; No. 2; No. 3; No. 4

Kirchner, Leon
Duo: violin, piano
Duos: violin, cello

Kódaly, Zoltán
Duo: violin, cello, Op. 12
Sonata: cello, piano, Op. 4
Sonatina: cello, piano (1909)

Lutoslawski, Witold
Epitaph, oboe, piano
Grave, cello, piano
Partita: violin, piano

Mendelssohn, Felix
Sonatas: cello, piano, B-flat, Op. 45; D, Op. 58
Sonatas: violin, piano: F minor, Op. 4; C minor, viola, piano; E-flat clarinet, piano

Mendelssohn-Bartholdy Hensel, Fanny Cäcilie
Adagio: violin, piano, E major
Capriccio: cello, piano, A-flat major
Fantasia: cello, piano, G minor

Messiaen, Olivier
Merle noir, flute, piano

Mozart, Wolfgang Amadeus
Fugue, K. 426, piano 4 hands; *see also* K. 546, string quartet, double bass
Sonatas: violin, piano, K. 10, 59, 60, 296, 304, 305, 454, 526, 547

Nielsen, Carl
Canto serioso, horn, piano
Fantasistykker: clarinet, piano, G minor; oboe, piano, Op. 2
Sonata: violin, piano, G-minor (unpublished); No. 2, Op. 35

Prokofiev, Serge
Sonata: flute, piano, Op. 94
Sonata: violin, piano, Op. 80
Sonata: cello, piano, Op. 119
Ravel, Maurice
Sonata: violin, cello
Sonata: violin, piano
Tzigane, violin, piano
Rheinberger, Joseph
Sonata: violin, piano, Op. 77, Op. 105
Sonata: cello, piano, Op. 92
Saint-Saëns, Camille
Sonata: bassoon, piano, G major, Op. 168
Sonatas: cello, piano, C minor, Op. 32; F major, Op. 123
Sonata: clarinet, piano, E-flat major, Op. 167
Sonata: oboe, piano D major, Op. 166
Sonatas: violin, piano, D major, Op. 75; E-flat major, Op. 102
Schnittke, Alfred
Sonata: cello, piano (1978)
Sonatas: violin, piano, No. 2 (1968); No. 3 (1994)
Stille Musik, violin, cello
Suite in Olden Style, violin, harpsichord or piano; rev. 1986, viola *d'amore*, harpsichord, vibraphone, marimba, Glockenspiel, bells
Schoenberg (Schönberg), Arnold
Phantasy: violin, piano, Op. 47 (1949)
Schubert, Franz Peter
Fantasie: piano, 4 hands, F minor, Op. 103, D. 940
Grande marche funebrè, piano 4 hands Op. 55, D. 859
Grande marche heroïque, piano 4 hands Op. 66, D. 885
Grandes marches, piano 4 hands Op. 40, D. 819
Marches characteristiques, piano 4 hands Op. 121, D. 886
Marches heroïques, piano 4 hands, Op. 27, D. 602
Marches militaires, piano 4 hands, Op. 51, D. 733
Polonaises: piano, 4 hands, Op. 61; D. 824; Op. 75, D. 599
Rondo: piano, 4 hands, A major, Op. 107, D 951
Sonatas: piano, 4 hands, B-flat major, Op. 30, D. 617; C major, Op. 140, D. 812
Variationen über ein Franzosisches Lied, Op. 10, D 624
Schumann, Robert
Adagio and Allegro in A-flat, horn, piano, Op. 70
Fantasiestücke: clarinet, piano, Op. 73
Five Pieces in Folk Style, cello, piano, Op. 102
Märchenbilder, piano, viola, Op. 113
Sonatas: violin, piano: A minor, Op. 105; D minor, Op. 121; A minor, Op. posth.
Three Romances, piano, oboe, Op. 94
Shebalin, Vissarion
Sonata: cello, piano, Op. 54, No. 3

Sonata: viola, piano, Op. 51, No. 2
Sonata: violin, piano, Op. 51, No. 1
Shostakovich, Dmitri Dmitriyevich
Sonata: cello, piano, D minor, Op. 40
Sonata: viola, piano, Op. 147
Sonata: violin, piano, Op. 134
Sibelius, Jean
Sonatina: E major, violin, piano, Op. 80
Spohr, Louis
Concertante: two violins, Op. 88
Duos: violins, Op. 3; Op. 9; Op. 39; Op. 48; Op. 67; Op. 148; Op. 150; Op. 153
Stravinsky, Igor
Duo concertante, violin, piano
Suite Italienne, cello, piano; violin, piano
Tartini, Giuseppe
"Devil's Trill Sonata"
Vaughan Williams, Ralph
Six Studies in English Folksong, cello (or violin, viola, clarinet), piano
Sonata: violin, piano, A minor (1954)
Webern, Anton
Four Pieces: violin, piano, Op. 7
Three Little Pieces: cello, piano, Op. 11

THREE PERFORMERS

Bach, Johann Sebastian
Sonata: two flutes, basso continuo, G major, S. 1039
Bartók, Béla
Contrasts, violin, clarinet, piano
Beach, Amy
Trio: piano, strings, A minor, Op. 150
Beethoven, Ludwig van
Trio: B-flat, clarinet, cello, piano, Op. 11
Trios: piano, Op. 1, Nos. 1–3; Op. 70, Nos. 1, 2; Op. 97 *Archduke Trio*
Trios: strings, Op. 3; Op. 9
Berio, Luciano
Linea, two pianists, vibraphone, marimba
Brahms, Johannes
Trio: piano, clarinet, cello, Op. 114
Trio: piano, violin, horn, E-flat major, Op. 40
Trios: piano, strings, B major, Op. 8; C major, Op. 87; C minor, Op. 101
Buxtehude, Dieterich
Singet dem Herrn ein neues Lied, BuxWV 98, violin, soprano, basso continuo
Crumb, George
Vox balænæ, flute, cello, piano, lighting, costumes

Debussy, Claude
Sonata: flute, viola, harp
Trio: piano, strings (1880)
Denisov, Edison
Trio: oboe, cello, harpsichord
Dvořák, Antonín
Trios: strings, F minor, Op. 65, B130; E minor, Op. 90, B166
Fauré, Gabriel
Trio: piano, strings, D major, Op. 120
Foote, Arthur
Trios: piano, strings, No. 1, C minor; No. 2, B
Franck, Cesar
Trios: piano, strings, Op. 1, Nos. 1–3; Op. 2
Friedrich Christian Ludwig, Prince of Prussia
Trios: A-flat major, piano, strings, Op. 2; E-flat major, Op. 3; E-flat major, Op. 10
Glinka, Mikhail Ivanovich
Trio: clarinet, bassoon, piano/violin, cello, piano, *Trio pathetique* (1832)
Gubaidulina, Sophia
Garden of Joys and Sorrows, flute, viola, harp
Five Etudes: harp, double bass, percussion
Quasi hoquetus, viola, bassoon (or cello), piano
Trio: violin, viola, cello (1989)
Haydn, Franz Joseph
Trios: piano, strings, Hob. XV/6, XV/7, XV/8, XV/39, XV/41
Trios: strings, Hob. V/8, V/D6, V/E-flat 1, V/G 7, Op. 53
Hindemith, Paul
Trios: strings, 1924; 1933
Trio: string, wind (heckelphone/saxophone), piano, 1928
Husa, Karel
Evocations de Slovaquie, clarinet, viola, cello
Sonata a tre, clarinet, violin, piano
Ives, Charles
Largo, violin, clarinet, piano
Trio: piano, strings (1911; rev. 1915)
Kódaly, Zoltán
Serenade: two violins, viola, Op. 12
Ligeti, György
Trio: violin, horn, piano (1982)
Maderna, Bruno
Musica su due dimensioni, flute, cymbals, electronically altered sounds
Marschner, Heinrich
Trio: piano, strings, G minor, Op. 111
Mendelssohn, Felix
Konzertstücke: clarinet, basset horn, piano, Opp. 113, 114
Trios: piano, violin, viola, C minor; piano, strings, D minor, Op. 49; C minor, Op. 66

Mendelssohn-Bartholdy Hensel, Fanny Cäcilie
Trio: piano, strings, D minor, Op. 11
Mozart, Wolfgang Amadeus
Trio: clarinet, viola, piano, E-flat, K. 498, *Kegelstatt*
Trios: piano, strings, K. 254, 496, 502, 542, 548, 564
Trio: strings, E-flat major, K. 563
Nielsen, Carl
Trio: piano, strings, G major (unpublished)
Penderecki, Krzysztof
Trio: violin, viola, cello (1991)
Rameau, Jean Philippe
Pieces de clavecin en concert: violin/flute, viol/cello, harpsichord (1741)
Ravel, Maurice
Trio: piano, strings, A minor
Rheinberger, Joseph
Trios: piano, strings, D minor, Op. 34 (1862/67); G major, Op. 112 (1878); B-flat major, Op. 121 (1880); F major, Op. 191a (1898)
Saint-Saëns, Camille
Trios: piano, strings, F major, Op. 18; E minor, Op. 92
Schnittke, Alfred
Trio: violin, viola, cello (1985)
Suite in Olden Style, violin, harpsichord or piano; rev. 1986, viola *d'amore*, harpsichord, vibraphone, marimba, Glockenspiel, bells
Schoenberg (Schönberg), Arnold
Trio: strings, Op. 45
Schubert, Franz Peter
Auf dem Strom, soprano, horn, piano, Op. 119, D. 943
Der Hirt auf dem Felsen, soprano, clarinet, piano, Op. 129, D. 965
Trios: piano, strings, B-flat, Op. 99, D. 898; E major, Op. 100, D. 929
Schumann, Robert
Fantasiestücke: piano, violin, cello, Op. 88
Märchenerzählungen, piano, viola, clarinet, Op. 132
Trios: piano, strings, D minor, Op. 63; F major, Op. 80; G minor, Op. 110
Shebalin, Vissarion
Trio: piano, strings, A, Op. 39
Shostakovich, Dmitri Dmitriyevich
Trios: piano, strings, C minor, Op. 8; E minor, Op. 67
Smetana, Bedřich
Trio: piano, strings, G minor, Op. 15
Tschaikovsky, Pyotr Ilyich
Trio: piano, strings, A minor, Op. 50
Ustvolskaya, Galina
Trio: clarinet, violin, piano (1949)
Vaughan Williams, Ralph
Six Studies in English Folksong, cello (or violin, viola, clarinet), piano

Webern, Anton
- Five canons: soprano, clarinet, bass clarinet, Op. 16 (1924)
- Trio: violin, viola, cello, Op. 20 (1927)
- Songs: soprano, clarinet, guitar, Op. 18 (1925)

Zemlinsky, Alexander
- Trio: clarinet/violin, cello, piano, D minor, Op. 3 (1896)

FOUR PERFORMERS

Adams, John
- *John's Book of Alleged Dances*, string quartet, electronically altered sounds

Bach, Johann Sebastian
- *Musikalisches Opfer*, S. 1079, flute, violin, cello, basso continuo

Bartók, Béla
- Quartets: strings, No. 1 (1909); No. 2 (1917); No. 3 (1927); No. 4 (1929); No. 5 (1934); No. 6 (1939)
- Sonata: two pianos, percussion (2 players)

Beach, Amy
- Quartet: strings, A minor, Op. 89

Beethoven, Ludwig van
- Quartets, strings: Op. 18 Nos. 1–6; Op. 59, Nos. 1–3, *Razumovsky Quartets;* Op. 74, *Harp Quartet;* Op. 95, *Quartetto serioso;* Op. 127; Op. 131; Op. 132; Op. 130; Op. 135

Berg, Alban
- Quartets: strings, No. 1, Op. 3; No. 2, *Lyric Suite*

Berio, Luciano
- *Chamber Music*, mezzo-soprano, clarinet, cello, harp

Brahms, Johannes
- Quartet: piano, strings, G minor, Op. 25; A major, Op. 26; C minor, Op. 60
- Quartets: strings, C minor, Op. 51, No. 1; A minor, Op. 51, No. 2; B-flat, Op. 67

Britten, Benjamin
- Quartet: oboe, strings, Op. 2
- Quartets: strings, Rhapsody (1929); Quartettino (1930); String Quartet in D (1931); Alla marcia (1933); Three Divertimenti (1936); No. 1 D; No. 2 C; No. 3 E

Cage, John
- *Third Construction*, 4 percussionists
- *Second Construction*, 4 percussionists

Chadwick, George Whitefield
- Quartets: stings, No. 1, G minor (1878); No. 2, C major (1879); No. 3, D (1885); No. 4, E minor; No. 5, D minor

Chou Wen-chung
- *Contrapunctus Variabilis*, string quartet
- *Echoes from the Gorge*, percussion, 4 players
- Quartets: strings, No. 1, *Clouds* (1966); No. 2, *Streams* (2002)
- *Windswept Peaks*, violin, cello, clarinet, piano

Crumb, George
Black Angels, string quartet, maracas, tam-tam, water-tuned goblets, amplification
Music for a Summer Evening (Makrokosmos III; 1974), two amplified pianos, percussion, 2 players
Debussy, Claude
Quartet: strings, G minor, Op. 10
Denisov, Edison
"Diane dans le vent d'automne," viola, piano, vibraphone, double bass
Quartet: flute, violin, viola, cello
Quartet: strings, No. 2
Dvořák, Antonín
Quartets: strings, D minor, Op. 34, B75; E-flat, Op. 51, B92; F, Op. 96, B179, *American Quartet;* G major, Op. 106, B192; A-flat Quartet, Op. 105, B193
Fauré, Gabriel
Quartets: piano, strings, C major, Op. 15; G major, Op. 45
Quartet: strings, E major, Op. 121
Foote, Arthur
Quartet: piano, strings, C
Quartet: strings, No. 1. G minor; No. 2, E; No. 3, D
Franck, César
Quartet: strings, D major
Friedrich Christian Ludwig, Prince of Prussia
Andante with Variations, piano quartet, Op. 4
Quartets: piano, strings, E-flat major, Op. 5; F minor, Op. 6; E-flat major, Op. 10
Grieg, Edvard
Quartet: strings, G minor, Op. 27
Gubaidulina, Sophia
Quartets: strings, No. 1 (1971); No. 2 (1987); No. 3 (1987); No. 4 (1993)
Haydn, Franz Joseph
Quartets: strings, Op. 1, Op. 2, Op. 3 (spurious), Op. 9; Op. 17; Op. 20; Op. 33; Op. 50; Op. 51, *Seven Last Words of Christ on the Cross;* Opp. 54, 55, 64, *Tost Quartets;* Opp. 71, 74, *Apponyi Quartets;* Op. 76, *Erdödy Quartets;* Op. 77, *Lobkowitz Quartets*
Hindemith, Paul
Quartet: clarinet, violin, piano, cello (1938)
Quartets: strings, No. 1 (1915); No. 2 (1918); No. 3 (1920); No. 4 (1921); No. 5 (1923); No. 6 (1943); No. 7 (1945)
Husa, Karel
Quartet: Variations, piano, violin, viola, cello
Quartets: strings, Op. 2 (1943) "Nulty"; No. 1 (1948); No. 2 (1953); No. 3 (1967); No. 4, *Poems* (1989)
Ives, Charles
Prelude on "Eventide," baritone/trombone, two violins, organ

Quartets: strings, No. 1 (1909); No. 2 (1915); Practice for String Quartet; Scherzo

Janáček, Leoš

Quartets: No. 1, *The Kreuzer Sonata;* No. 2, *Intimate Letters*

Kirchner, Leon

Quartets: strings, No. 1 (1949); No. 2 (1958); No. 3 (1966)

Kódaly, Zoltán

Quartets: strings, No. 1, Op. 2 (1909); No. 2, Op. 10 (1918)

Kraft, William

Quartets: percussion, Theme and Variations (1956); Quartet (1988)

Lansky, Paul

As If, violin, viola, cello, electronics

Quartets: strings, No. 1 (1967); No. 2 (1971)

Ligeti, György

Quartet: strings, No. 1, *Metamorphoses nocturnes;* No. 2 (1968)

Lutoslawski, Witold

Quartet: strings, No. 1, (1964)

Mendelssohn, Felix

Quartets: piano, strings, Op. 1, C minor; Op. 2, F minor; Op. 3, B minor

Quartets: strings, E-flat, WoO; E-flat major, Op. 12; A-minor, Op. 13; D-major, Op. 44, no. 1; E-minor, Op. 44, no. 2; E-flat major, Op. 44, no. 3; F-minor, Op. 80; E major, Op. 81

Mendelssohn-Bartholdy-Hensel, Fanny Cäcile

Quartet: piano, strings, A-flat (1823)

Messiaen, Olivier

Quatuor pour la fin du temps, clarinet, violin, cello, piano

Mozart, Wolfgang Amadeus

Quartets: flute, strings, D major, K. 285; G major, K. 285a; C major, K. 285b; A major, K. 298

Quartet: oboe, violin, viola, cello, F major, K. 368b

Quartets: strings, K. 80, 155–160, 168–173; Op. 10: K. 387, 421, 428, 458, 464, 465; K. 499, *Hoffmeister Quartet;* K. 575, 589, 590, *Prussian Quartets*

Nielsen, Carl

Quartets: strings, F minor, Op. 5; G minor, Op. 13; E-flat, Op. 14; F major, Op. 44

Penderecki, Krzysztof

Quartet: clarinet, violin, viola, cello

Quartets: strings, No. 1 (1960); No. 2 (1968)

Prokofiev, Serge

Quartets: strings, B minor, No. 1, Op. 50 (1930); F major, No. 2, Op. 92 (1941)

Ravel, Maurice

Quartet: strings, F major

Reich, Steve

Violin Phase, 1 player, three recorded tracks

Rheinberger, Joseph

Quartets: strings, C minor, Op. 89; G minor, Op. 93; F major, Op. 147

Rimsky-Korsakoff, Nikolai
String Quartet on Russian Themes
Saint-Saëns, Camille
Quartet: piano, strings, B-flat major, Op. 41
Quartets: strings, E minor, Op. 112; G minor, Op. 153
Scarlatti, Alessandro
Sonatas: Quattro sonate a quattro, F minor, C minor, G minor, D minor
Schnittke, Alfred
Quartets: strings, No. 1 (1966); No. 2 (1980); No. 3 (1983); No. 4 (1989)
Schoenberg (Schönberg), Arnold
Quartets: strings, D major (1897); Op. 7 (1905); Op. 10 (1908); Op. 30 (1927); Op. 37 (1936)
Schubert, Franz Peter
Quartets: strings: D. 18; D. 32; D. 36; D. 46; D. 68; D. 74; D. 94; D. 112; D. 173; D. 87; A minor, Op. 29, no. 1, D. 804; D minor, *Der Tod und das Mädchen* (death and the maiden), D. 810; D. Fragment in C minor, D. 703; G major, D. 887
Schumann, Robert
Quartets: piano, strings, C minor (1829); E-flat, Op. 47
Quartets: strings, Op. 41, Nos. 1–3 A minor, F major, A major
Schütz, Heinrich
"In te, Domine, speravi," *Symphoniae sacrae*, vol. 1, SWV 259, alto, violin, bassoon, basso continuo
"Jubilate Deo omnis terra," *Symphoniae sacrae*, vol. 1, SWV 262, bass, two recorders, basso continuo
Shebalin, Vissarion
Quartets: strings
Shostakovich, Dmitri Dmitriyevich
Quartets: strings, No. 2, A major, Op. 68; No. 3, F major, Op. 73; No. 4, D major, Op. 83; No. 5, B-flat major, Op. 92; No. 8, C minor, Op. 110; No. 11, F minor, Op. 122; No. 12, D-flat major, Op. 133; No. 13, B-flat minor, Op. 138; No. 14, F-sharp major, Op. 142; No. 15, E-flat minor, Op. 144
Sibelius, Jean
Quartets: strings, A minor (1889); B-flat, Op. 4; D minor, *Voces intimæ*, Op. 56; *Andante festivo*
Smetana, Bedřich
Quartets: strings, No. 1 in E minor, "From My Life"; No. 2 in D major
Spohr, Louis
Quartets: strings, C major, Op. 29; Op. 45; Op. 58; A major, Op. 93; E-flat, Op. 152
Tschaikovsky, Pyotr Ilyich
Quartets: strings, D major, Op. 11; F major, Op. 22; E-flat minor, Op. 30
Vaughan Williams, Ralph
Quartets: strings, G minor, No. 1; A minor, No. 2; *Household Music*
Webern, Anton
Five movements for string quartet, Op. 5 (1909)
Quartet: clarinet, tenor saxophone, violin, piano, Op. 22 (1930)

Quartet: strings, Op. 28 (1938)
Six bagatelles for string quartet, Op. 9 (1913)
Three folksongs for soprano, clarinet, bass clarinet/violin, viola, Op. 17 (1925)

FIVE PERFORMERS

Bassett, Leslie
Quintet: brass (1988)
Beach, Amy
Quintet: flute, string quartet, Theme and [6] Variations, Op. 80
Quintet: piano, strings, F-sharp minor, Op. 67
Bernstein, Leonard
Quintet: brass, *Dance Suite* (1990; optional percussion)
Brahms, Johannes
Quintet: piano, strings, F minor, Op. 34
Quintet: clarinet, strings, B minor, Op. 115
Quintet: strings, F major, Op. 88; G major, Op. 111
Britten, Benjamin
Quintet: strings, F minor
Buxtehude, Dieterich
O dulcis Jesu, BuxWV 83, two sopranos, two violins, basso continuo
Cambini, Giuseppe Maria Gioacchino
Trois quintetti, Livre 1
Chadwick, George Whitefield
Quintet: piano, strings, E-flat
Danzi, Franz
Quintets: flute, oboe, clarinet, horn, bassoon, Op. 56, Nos. 1–3; Op. 67, Nos. 1–3; Op. 68, Nos. 1–3
Davidovsky, Mario
Synchronisms: flute, clarinet, violin, cello, electronics, No. 2
Davies, Peter Maxwell
Quintets: brass, 1981; Two Motets; *Pole Star*
Denisov, Edison
Quintet: clarinet, strings
Quintet: piano, strings
Quintet: wind
Romantische Musik, oboe, violin, viola, cello, harp
Druckman, Jacob
Other Voices, brass quintet
Dvořák, Antonín
Quintets: strings, A minor, B7 (1861); G major, Op. 77 B49 (1875; 2 violins, viola, cello, double bass); E-flat, Op. 97, B180 (1893)
Quintet: piano, strings, A major, Op. 81, B155 (1887)
Farrenc, Louise
Quintets: piano, violin, viola, cello, double bass, A minor, Op. 30; E major, Op. 31

Fauré, Gabriel
　　Quintets: piano, strings, D major, Op. 89; C major, Op. 115
Foote, Arthur
　　Quintet: Nocturne and Scherzo, flute, string quartet
　　Quintet: piano, strings, A minor
Franck, César
　　Quintet: piano, strings, F minor
Friedrich Christian Ludwig, Prince of Prussia
　　Larghetto variée, piano, violin, viola, cello, double bass
　　Quintet: piano, strings, C minor, Op. 1
Harrison, Lou
　　Suite: percussion (1942), 5 players
Hindemith, Paul
　　Quintet: clarinet, strings (1923; rev. 1954)
Husa, Karel
　　Divertimento, brass quintet, optional percussion
Ives, Charles
　　"The Gong on the Hook and Ladder," string quartet or quintet, piano
　　Quintet: piano, strings, "Largo risoluto" Nos. 1 and 2; "Halloween" (opt. percussion); "In Re con moto et al"
Lansky, Paul
　　Crossworks, flute, clarinet, violin, cello, piano
Leeuv, Ton de
　　"And They Shall Reign Forever," mezzo-soprano, clarinet, French horn, piano, percussion
Ligeti, György
　　Six Bagatelles, wind quintet
　　Ten Pieces, wind quintet
Mendelssohn, Felix
　　Quintets: strings, A major, Op. 18; B-flat major, Op. 87
Messiaen, Olivier
　　Quintet: *Pièce,* piano, strings
Mozart, Wolfgang Amadeus
　　Adagio and Fugue, K. 546, piano 4 hands; string quartet, double bass
　　Quintet: clarinet, strings, A major, K. 581
　　Quintet: horn, strings, double bass, K. 386c
　　Quintet: piano, oboe, clarinet, horn, bassoon, K. 452
　　Quintets: strings, K. 174; K. 406; K. 515; K. 516; K. 614
Nielsen, Carl
　　Quintet: strings, G minor
　　Quintet: wind, Op. 43
　　"Serenata in vano," clarinet, bassoon, horn, cello, double bass
　　Ved en ung kunstners Baare, string quartet, double bass
Prokofiev, Serge
　　Quintet: oboe, clarinet, violin, viola, double bass, G minor, Op. 39 (1924)
Reicha, Anton
　　Quintets: flute, oboe, clarinet, horn, bassoon, Op. 88, Nos. 1–6; Op. 91, Nos. 1–6; Op. 99, Nos. 1–6; Op. 100, Nos. 1–6

Rheinberger, Joseph
  Quintet: strings, A minor, Op. 82
Rimsky-Korsakov, Nikolai
  Quintet: flute, clarinet, horn, bassoon, piano, B-flat
Rorem, Ned
  Quintet: brass, Diversions (1989)
Saint-Saëns, Camille
  Quintet: piano, strings, A minor, Op. 14
Schnittke, Alfred
  Quintet: piano, strings (1976)
  Serenade, clarinet, violin, double bass, percussion, piano
Schoenberg (Schönberg), Arnold
  Ode to Napoleon, string quartet, reciter, Op. 41 (1945)
  Quintet: winds, Op. 26 (1924)
Schubert, Franz Peter
  Adagio and Rondo Concertante, piano, strings, D. 487
  Quintet: piano, violin, viola, cello, double bass, Op. 114, *Trout*
Schumann, Robert
  Quintet: piano, strings, E-flat, Op. 44
Schütz, Heinrich
  "Anima mea liquefacta est," *Symphoniae sacrae*, vol. 1, SWV 263–264, two tenors, two cornettos, basso continuo
  Seven Words, S, A, T, B soli, basso continuo
Shostakovich, Dmitri Dmitriyevich
  Quintet: piano, strings, G minor, Op. 57
Sibelius, Jean
  Quintet: piano, strings, G minor (1890)
Spohr, Louis
  Quintet: piano, flute, clarinet, horn, bassoon, C minor, Op. 52
Stradella, Alessandro
  "Lasciate ch'io respiri, ombre gradite" G. 1.4-12, soprano, bass, two violins, basso continuo
Vaughan Williams, Ralph
  Phantasy Quintet, strings
Webern, Anton
  Six songs with Four Instruments (soprano, clarinet, E-flat clarinet, bass clarinet, violin, cello), Op. 14 (1923)

SIX PERFORMERS

Brahms, Johannes
  Sextet: strings, B-flat major, Op. 18
Britten, Benjamin
  Sextet: winds
Cage, John
  First Construction in Metal, 6 percussionists
Chou Wen-chung
  Ceremonial, three trumpets, three trombones

Eternal Pine, flute, clarinet, violin, cello, piano, percussion (one player) bass drum, four tom-toms, two dome cymbals, two crash cymbals, cncerro, bell
Suite: harp, wind quintet
Twilight Colors, flute/alto flute, oboe/English horn, clarinet/bass clarinet, violin, viola, cello

Davidovsky, Mario
Synchronisms: wind quintet, electronics, No. 8

Denisov, Edison
Three Pictures after Paul Klee, oboe, horn, piano, vibraphone, viola, double bass

Druckman, Jacob
Delizie contente che l'alme beate, wind quintet, electronic sounds

Dvořák, Antonín
Sextet: strings, A major, Op. 48, B80

Gubaidulina, Sophia
Sextet: Meditation on the Bach Chorale "Vor deinem Thron tret ich hiermit" harpsichord, string quintet

Haydn, Franz Joseph
Echo Sonata, Hob. II/39 (2, 2, 2)
Divertimentos: Hob. II/21; II/22; II/41; II/42; II/43; II/44; II/45; II/46; F7

Husa, Karel
Divertimento, brass quintet, optional percussion

Ives, Charles
"From the Steeples and the Mountains," trumpet, trombone, four sets of bells

Janáček, Leoš
Sextet: winds, *Youth*

Messiaen, Olivier
Fête des belles eaux, six ondes Martenot

Mozart, Wolfgang Amadeus
Divertimento: K. 113; F major, K. 247; E-flat, K. 563

Penderecki, Krzysztof
Sextet: clarinet, horn, string trio, piano

Poulenc, Francis
Sextet: piano, wind quintet (1939)

Read, Gardner
Los Dioses Aztecas, Op. 107, six percussionists

Rimsky-Korsakov, Nikolai
Sextet: strings, A major

Schoenberg (Schönberg), Arnold
Sextet: strings, *Verklärte Nacht*, Op. 4

Schütz, Heinrich
"Attendite, populе meus," *Symphoniae sacrae*, vol. 1, SWV 270, bass, four trombones, basso continuo
"Domine, labia mea aperies," *Symphoniae sacrae*, vol. 1, SWV 271, soprano, tenor, cornetto, trombone, bassoon, basso continuo
"Fili mi, Absalon," *Symphoniae sacrae*, vol. 1, SWV 269, bass, four trombones, basso continuo

"In lectulo per noctes," *Symphoniae sacrae*, vol. 1, SWV 272–273, soprano, alto, three bassoons, basso continuo

Tschaikovsky, Pyotr Ilyich

Sextet: strings, *Souvenir de Florence*

Webern, Anton

Five songs with five instruments (voice, flute, clarinet/bass clarinet, trumpet, harp, violin/viola), Op. 15 (1922)

SEVEN PERFORMERS

Adams, John

Shaker Loops, three violins, viola, two celli, double bass

Beethoven, Ludwig van

Septet: Op. 20, clarinet, horn, bassoon, violin, viola, cello, double bass

Boulez, Pierre

Le marteau sans maître, alto voice, alto flute (i.e., G), guitar, vibraphone, xylorimba, percussion, viola

Cohn, James

Concerto *da camera* for violin, piano, woodwind quintet, Op. 60

Friedrich Christian Ludwig, Prince of Prussia

Notturno, flute, violin, viola, cello, piano, two horns, Op. 8

Ives, Charles

"An Old Song Deranged," clarinet/English horn, harp/guitar, violin/viola, viola, two celli

Ravel, Maurice

Introduction and Allegro, flute, clarinet, harp, string quartet

Scarlatti, Alessandro

Su le sponde del Tebro, soprano, trumpet, strings, continuo

Schoenberg (Schönberg), Arnold

Pierrot lunaire, flute/piccolo, clarinet/bass clarinet, violin/viola, cello, piano, speaking voice

Suite: 2 clarinets, bass clarinet, violin, viola, cello, piano, Op. 29

Schütz, Heinrich

"O Jesu süß, wer dein gedenkt," *Symphoniae sacrae* vol. 3, SWV 406, 2 sopranos, 2 tenors, 2 violins, basso continuo

Spohr, Louis

Septet: flute, clarinet, bassoon, horn, violin, cello, piano, A minor, Op. 147

Stravinsky, Igor

Septet: clarinet, horn, bassoon, piano, violin, viola, cello

EIGHT OR MORE PERFORMERS

Bach, Johann Sebastian

Ich habe genug, S. 82, basso, oboe, strings, basso continuo

Jauchzet Gott in allen Landen, S. 51, soprano, trumpet, strings, basso continuo

Boulez, Pierre

Sur incises, three pianos, three harps, three percussionists, vibraphones, marimba, steel drums, crotales, glockenspiel, timpani, tubular bells

Chou Wen-chung

Yü Ko, violin, alto flute, English horn, bass clarinet, trombone, bass trombone, piano, two percussionists

Gubaidulina, Sophia

Hommage à T. S. Eliot, soprano, clarinet, bassoon, horn, violins 1, 2, viola, cello, double bass

Seven Words, cello, bayan, strings

Hindemith, Paul

Octet: clarinet, bassoon, horn, violin, two violas, cello, double bass (1958)

Ives, Charles

"Scherzo: Over the Pavements" (1910; rev. 1927) piccolo, clarinet, bassoon/baritone saxophone, trumpet, three trombones, cymbals, bass drum, piano

Keuris, Tristan

Divertimento, violin, piano, woodwind quintet, double bass

Kraft, William

Encounters, eleven percussion pieces, various scorings including tape, trumpet, trombone, saxophone, English horn, violin, cello, roto-toms

Momentum, eight percussionists

Quartets: percussion, Theme and Variations (1956); Quartet (1988)

Lansky, Paul

Values of Time, wind quintet, string quartet, electronic sounds

Mendelssohn, Felix

Octet: strings, E-flat, Op. 20

Reich, Steve

Octet: flute/piccolo, clarinet/bass clarinet, two pianos, two violins, viola, cello

Rheinberger, Joseph

Nonet: flute, oboe, clarinet, bassoon, horn, violin, viola, cello, double bass, A major, Op. 139

Roldan, Amadeo

Rítmicas

Saint-Saëns, Camille

La carnaval des animaux, 2 pianos, 2 violins, viola, cello, double bass, flute, clarinet, harmonium, xylophone

Schoenberg (Schönberg), Arnold

Serenade: clarinet, bass clarinet, mandolin, guitar, violin, viola, cello, bass voice, Op. 24 (1923)

Schubert, Franz Peter

Octet: strings, double bass, F major, Op. 166, D. 803

Spohr, Louis

Double-quartets: strings, D minor, Op. 65; E-flat major, Op. 77; E minor, Op. 87; G minor, Op. 136

Nonet: violin, viola, cello, double bass, flute, oboe, clarinet, bassoon, horn, F major, Op. 31.

Octet: violin, two violas, cello, double bass, clarinet, two horns, E major, Op. 32.

Stravinsky, Igor

Octet: flute, clarinet, bassoons 1, 2, trumpets 1, 2 (C and A), trombones 1, 2 (tenor bass)

Varèse, Edgard

Octandre, flute (piccolo), clarinet (E-flat clarinet), oboe, bassoon, horn, trumpet, trombone, double bass

Notes

INTRODUCTION

1. These figures are totals for the Bronx, Brooklyn, Manhattan, Queens, and Staten Island excluding present-day Nassau County and Westchester County.

2. These figures are based on seating capacities given in Michael Forsyth, *Buildings for Music: The Architect, the Musician, and the Listener from the Seventeenth Century to the Present* (Cambridge, Mass.: MIT Press, 1985), appendix: "Chronological Table of Concert Halls and Opera Houses," 329–31.

CHAPTER 1

1. For additional information on early instruments, see Sibyl Marceuse, *Musical Instruments: A Comprehensive Dictionary* (New York: Norton, 1975).

2. But see Helen Hewitt, ed., *Harmonice Musices Odhecaton A* (Cambridge, Mass.: Mediaeval Academy of America, 1946), 31–42.

3. John Stevens, ed., *Musica Britanica*, vol. 18, *Music at the Court of Henry VIII* (London: Stainer and Bell, 1962). Stevens observes: "We have . . . in Henry VIII's Book the earliest substantial collection of part-music in England for instruments alone" (p. xix).

4. A modern edition has been published by Stainer and Bell (London, 1964).

5. The term "broken musick" refers to the breaking up of long note values into smaller values; in other words, the music as it is written is freely ornamented by the performers. Contemporary scholars sometimes use the term "mixed" consort rather than "broken" consort to avoid confusion.

6. John Irving, "Consort Playing in Mid-17th-Century Worcester," *Early Music* 12 (August 1984), 340–44, argues that the full string consort was "semi-broken" by the mid-seventeenth century, a transitional period when the violin family was gradually replacing the viol as the preferred stringed instrument. Irving's findings show that violins were sometimes used for the treble parts with viols on the lower voices

7. Eleanor Selfridge Field traces the evolution of the *canzona* in northern Italy

in *Venetian Instrumental Music from Gabrieli to Vivaldi* (New York: Praeger, 1975), 88–95, 102–18. Though Selfridge Field's title suggests otherwise, the development of the canzona in Brescia, one of the centers for its cultivation, is nicely documented and illuminated with musical examples.

8. Florentio Maschera, *Libro primo de canzoni* (Brescia: Vincenzo Sabbio, 1584).

9. Adriano Banchieri, *Canzoni* (Venice: Ricciardo Amadino, 1596); Florio Canale, *Canzoni* (Venice: Giacomo Vincenti, 1600); Tarquinio Merula, *Il primo libro delle canzoni* (Venice: Gardano, 1615); Maurizio Cazzati, *Canzoni a 3* (Venice: Bartolomeo Magni, 1642). A modern edition of Banchieri's collection has been made by Leland Bartholomew (Madison, Wis.: A-R Editions, 1975).

10. Imogen Horsley, *Fugue: History and Practice* (New York: Free Press, 1966), 135.

11. Concerning the *inganno* and its use by Frescobaldi, see Roland Jackson, "On Frescobaldi's Chromaticism and Its Background," *Musical Quarterly* 57 (1971), 255–69; John Harper, "Frescobaldi's Early *inganni* and Their Background," *Proceedings of the Royal Musical Association* 105 (1978–79), 1–12; and Gene S. Trantham, "An Analytical Approach to Seventeenth-Century Music: Exploring *inganni* in *Fantasia seconda* (1607) by Girolamo Frescobaldi," *College Music Symposium* 33–34 (1993–94), 70–92.

12. Robert Donington and Gustav Reese discovered the source of the melody simultaneously but independently. See Robert Donington and Thurston Dart, "The Origin of the *In nomine*," *Music and Letters* 30 (1949), 101; and Gustav Reese, "The Origin of the English *In nomine*," *Journal of the American Musicological Society* 2 (1949), 7.

13. For details of instrumentation, see Sandra Mangsen, "Instrumental Duos and Trios in Italian Printed Sources: 1600–1675," Ph.D. diss., Cornell University, 1989, 1:ii. For a general history of the trio sonata, see Peter Allsop, *The Italian "Trio" Sonata* (New York: Oxford University Press, 1992).

14. Exactly where sonatas were used in the Roman Catholic Mass is not clear. See Stephen Bonta, "The Uses of the Sonata *da chiesa*," *Journal of the American Musicological Society* 22 (1969), 54–84.

15. Abram Loft, *Violin and Keyboard: The Duo Repertoire*, 2 vols. (New York: Grossman, 1973), is indispensable in studying this literature. Loft's study begins with the early seventeenth century and continues through the 1960s.

16. Throughout the Baroque era, key signatures in the minor mode were frequently incomplete. In particular, the status of the sixth scale degree was not always indicated. Apparently, the Dorian mode, with its characteristic major sixth above the *finalis*, was regarded as the basic scale from which the minor mode was derived. [Michel?] de St. Lambert's treatise *Les principes du clavecin* (Paris: Christophe Ballard, 1702) was the first to advocate key signatures showing lowered third, sixth, and seventh scale degrees in minor.

17. Sonatas with obbligato keyboard parts include most movements in the six Sonatas for violin and harpsichord, BWV 1014–1019a, the Sonata for violin and harpsichord, BWV 1022, the three Sonatas for gamba and harpsichord, BWV 1027–29, and the three Sonatas for transverse flute and harpsichord, BWV 1030–32. Sonatas with basso continuo parts include the two Sonatas for violin and

continuo, BWV 1021, and 1023, the three Sonatas for transverse flute and continuo, BWV 1033–35, and the Sonata for two flutes and continuo, BWV 1039. This last sonata was reworked as the Sonata for gamba and harpsichord, BWV 1027, cited above. Sonatas of doubtful authenticity (i.e., BWV 1020, 1024, 1025, 1026, 1036, 1037, and 1038) have not been considered, nor has the special case of the sonata within Bach's *Musikalisches Opfer*, BWV 1079. It is not my intention to suggest that Bach introduced the sonata with obbligato keyboard, or that he set a trend of any sort. On the contrary, Bach was notoriously conservative, and his chamber sonatas were circulated only in a limited number of manuscript copies. For additional information regarding Bach's sonatas and further observations about the changing role of the keyboard in the music of this period, see Hans Hering, "Das Klavier in der Kammermusik des 18. Jahrhunderts," *Die Musikforschung* 23 (January–March 1970), 22–37.

18. Carolyn Gianturco, *Alessandro Stradella 1639–1682: His Life and Music* (New York: Clarendon Press, 1994), 96, 35. The G-numbers here refer to Gianturco's thematic catalog of Stradella's works (Stuyvesant, N.Y.: Pendragon Press, 1991).

19. Denis Arnold, "The Second Venetian Visit of Heinrich Schütz," *Musical Quarterly* 71 (Fall 1985), 362.

20. Ibid., 368.

21. See Kerala J. Snyder, *Dieterich Buxtehude, Organist in Lübeck*, rev. ed. (Rochester, N.Y.: University of Rochester Press, 2007).

22. Kerala J. Snyder, notes for *Dieterich Buxtehude, Vocal Music*, vol. 1 (Copenhagen: Dacapo / Marco Polo, 1996), 8.

23. Alfred Dürr, *Die Kantaten von Johann Sebastian Bach* (Kassel: Bärenreiter, 1971), 2:543.

24. Ibid., 445.

25. Ibid., 446.

CHAPTER 2

1. William S. Newman, *The Sonata in the Classic Era*, 3rd ed. (New York: Norton, 1983), 148.

2. Leopold Kotzeluch, *Trois sonatas pour le clavecin ou le forte-piano avec accompagnement d'un violon et violoncelle* (Paris: Boyer, n.d.).

3. Trans. William J. Mitchell as C. P. E. Bach, *Essay on the True Art of Playing Keyboard Instruments* (New York: Norton, 1949).

4. Trans. Edward R. Reilly as Johann Joachim Quantz, *On Playing the Flute* (New York: Free Press, 1966).

5. Trans. Editha Knocker as Leopold Mozart, *Treatise on the Fundamental Principles of Violin Playing*, 2nd ed. (New York: Oxford University Press, 1951).

6. Quoted and translated in Dora Wilson, "Löhlein's *Klavierschule:* Toward an Understanding of the *Galant* Style," *International Review of the Æsthetics and Sociology of Music* 12 (1981), 106.

7. Franz Joseph Haydn, *Trois sonates pour le forte piano composés et dediées a son altesse Madam la Princesse Marie Esterhazy* (Munich: Falter, 1797). This publication was Senenfelder's eighth lithographic work and apparently the first use of lithography for reproduction of music.

8. See my article, "Haydn and His Publishers: A Brief Survey of the Composer's Publishing Activities," *Music Review* 44 (May 1983), 87–94.

9. Johann Schobert, *Sonatas pour le clavecin qui peuvent jouer avec l'accompagnement de violon* (Paris: Bailleux[?], n.d.).

10. Bayon and her works are discussed in Deborah Hayes, "Marie-Emmanuelle Bayon, Later Madame Louis, and Music in Late Eighteenth-Century France," *College Music Symposium: Journal of the College Music Society* 30 (Spring 1990), 14–33. Additional information is contained in Hayes's introduction to the facsimile reprint (New York: Da Capo Press, 1990) of Bayon's sonatas.

11. For a detailed discussion of this complex issue, see David Fuller, "Accompanied Keyboard Music," *Musical Quarterly* 60 (January 1974), 222–45. Especially helpful is the information found on pp. 227–31.

12. Jacopo Gotifredo Ferrari, *Trois sonates pour clavecin ou forte-piano avec violon obligé et basse ad libitum . . . œuvre Iim* (Paris: Sieber; also issued in Vienna: Artaria. Pl. no. 476).

13. Ronald R. Kidd, "The Emergence of Chamber Music with Obbligato Keyboard in England," *Acta musicologica* 44 (1972), 122.

14. A précis of terminological considerations is included in Fuller's article, "Accompanied Keyboard Music," 223–24.

15. A general discussion of the form of later eighteenth-century sonatas is contained in Newman, *Sonata in Classic Era*, 112–66. The three-movement sonata plan in the tempo sequence fast-slow-fast exists as a standard only in music appreciation texts. Sonatas were commonly written as single movements, paired movements, and cycles of three or four movements throughout the eighteenth century. Only Mozart fastened onto the three-movement plan as a sine qua non of sonata composition—and this only in his solo keyboard sonatas.

16. Kidd, "Emergence of Chamber Music," 143. Kidd suggests that orchestral models inspired Schobert's style, as does Michael Broyles, "The Two Instrumental Styles of Classicism," *Journal of the American Musicological Society* 36 (Summer 1983), 226–29.

17. Gotifredo Jacopo Ferrari, *Trois grandes sonates pour harpe avec accompagnement de violon et basse* (Paris: Pleyel. Pl. no. 80; also by Sieber. Pl. no. 71.)

18. Rameau's title suggests that when a violin is used for the obbligato treble, a cello (i.e., *deuxieme violon*) should be used for the bass line; conversely, flute obbligato should be paired with a bass viol.

19. K. 6, 7, 8, 9 10, 11, 12, 13, 14, 15, 26, 27, 28, 29, 30, 31, 55, 56, 57, 58, 59, 60, 61, 296, 301, 302, 303, 304, 305, 306, 372 (only one surviving movement), 376, 377, 378, 379, 380, 402, 403, 404, 454, 481, 526, 547, and two sets of variations, K. 359 and 360.

20. The subject is explored in Boris Schwarz, "Violinists around Mozart," in *Music in the Classic Period: Essays in Honor of Barry S. Brook*, ed. Allan W. Atlas (New York: Pendragon, 1985), 233–48.

21. Loft, *Violin and Keyboard*, 230–31.

22. James Webster argues that Austria was "remarkably isolated from North and West European musical culture" up to about the year 1780. See his "Towards a History of Viennese Chamber Music in the Early Classical Period," *Journal of the American Musicological Society* 27 (1974), 212–47, especially 214–15.

23. See Loft, *Violin and Keyboard*, 228–303.

24. Webster, "Viennese Chamber Music," 246.

25. Terminology relating to mid-eighteenth-century styles was highlighted in a terse article by Charles L. Cudworth, "Baroque, Rococo, Galant, Classic," *Monthly Musical Record* 3 (September 1953), 172–75. A précis of the divergent styles of music in western Europe during the second half of the eighteenth century is contained in Jens Peter Larsen, "Some Observations of the Development and Characteristics of Vienna Classical Instrumental Music," *Studia musicologica Academiae Scientiarum Hungaricae* 9 (1967), 115–39. Important information regarding the *style galant* can be found in Ernst Bücken, "Der galante Stil: Eine Skizze seiner Entwicklung," *Zeitschrift für Musikwissenschaft* 6 (1924), 418–30; David A. Sheldon, "The Galant Style Revisited and Re-evaluated," *Acta musicologica* 47 (1975), 240–69; Sheldon, "The Concept *Galant* in the 18th Century," *Journal of Musicological Research* 9 (1989), 89–108; Lothar Hoffmann-Erbrecht, "Der 'Galante Stil' in der Musik des 18. Jahrhunderts: Zur Problematik des Begriffs," in *Studien zur Musikwissenschaft* 25 (Graz: Hermann Böhlaus, 1962), 252–60; and Mark A. Radice, "The Nature of the Style galant: Evidence from the Repertoire," *Musical Quarterly* 83 (Winter 1999), 607–47. The origin and history of the term *Sturm und Drang* is traced by William E. Grim, in "The Musical *Sturm und Drang:* Analysis of a Controversy," *Ars musica Denver* 3 (Fall 1990), 1–13.

26. Hoboken lists additional string trios of questionable authenticity; nevertheless, the typical scoring even in these is for two violins and bass. Anthony van Hoboken, *Joseph Haydn: Thematisch-bibliographisches Werkeverzeichnis*, 3 vols. (Mainz: B. Schott's Söhne, 1957).

27. Some important recent studies providing an overview of the origins, history, and development of this genre are Ludwig Finscher, *Studien zur Geschichte des Streichquartetts* (Kassel: Bärenreiter, 1974); and Paul Griffiths, *The String Quartet* (New York: Thames and Hudson, 1983).

28. For a discussion of the Allegri work, see Eaglefield Hull, "The Earliest Known String-Quartet," *Musical Quarterly* 15 (1929), 72–76; and Ruth Halle Rowen, *Early Chamber Music* (New York, 1949; reprint New York: Da Capo Press, 1974), 83–84. The Scarlatti pieces are discussed in Griffiths, *The String Quartet*, 7–8.

29. *La reine de Chypre:* Airs arrangés en quatuor pour 2 violons, alto et basse en 3 suites par Richard Wagner, Musique de F. Halévy (Paris: M. Schlesinger, 1842).

30. *Einzeldrücke vor 1800*, series A of *Repertoire internationale des sources musicales* (London, 1971–81).

31. For an overview of the later eighteenth-century Viennese string quartet, see Roger Heckman, "The Flowering of th Viennese String Quartet in the Late Eighteenth Century," *Music Review* 50 (August–November 1989), 157–80, which comments on the quartets of lesser composers including Ignaz Pleyel, F. A. Hoffmeister, Adalbert Gyrowetz, Franz Krommer, Anton Wranizky, and F. A. Förster.

32. Alan Tyson and H. C. Robbins Landon, "Who Composed Haydn's Op. 3?" *Musical Times* 105 (July 1964), 506.

33. Ibid., 507.

34. Ibid.

35. Hoboken, *Joseph Haydn*, 1:378, suggests that these quartets were composed

before 1769; Griffiths (*The String Quartet*, 19) contends that they were likely composed in 1769–70.

36. Griffiths, *The String Quartet*, 19–20.

37. Donald Francis Tovey, "Haydn," *Cobbett's Cyclopedic Survey of Chamber Music* (London: Oxford Universty Press, 1929), 533.

38. Andreas Ließ, "Fux, Johann Joseph," *Die Musik in Geschichte und Gegenwart*, vol. 4, col. 1172. An English translation of the portion of Fux's treatise devoted to counterpoint has been made by Alfred Mann under the title *The Study of Counterpoint* (New York: Norton, 1965).

39. Forbes, *Thayer's Life of Beethoven*, appendix C, 1062. Beethoven's studies in counterpoint with Haydn, which were based on Fux, are reproduced in facsimile with commentary in Alfred Mann, *The Great Composer as Teacher and Student: Theory and Practice of Composition* (reprinted New York: Dover, 1994).

40. Finscher goes too far in asserting, "Neither earlier nor later did Haydn write string quartets that were so dark and unapproachable, in which so many spheres confusedly obstruct one another as here." *Geschichte des Streichquartetts*, 218.

41. Ibid., 265.

42. Ibid., 242.

43. Eric Weimer, *"Opera Seria" and the Evolution of Classical Style: 1755–1772* (Ann Arbor, Mich.: UMI Research Press, 1984), 47.

44. Ibid., 48.

45. See Kathi Meyer and Inger M. Christensen, "Artaria Plate Numbers," *Notes* 15 (1942), 1–22.

46. *The Collected Correspondence and London Notebooks of Joseph Haydn*, ed. H. C. Robbins Landon (Fairlawn, N.J.: Essential Books, 1959), 24–25.

47. K. 80, 155, 156, 157, 158, 159, 160.

48. The Serenade in C minor for Wind Octet, K. 388, dates from ca. 1782 or 1783. In many ways, its string quintet version is an apt companion for the G-minor Quintet owing to the serenade's "driving energy and consistent intensity . . . its chromatic writing, its strikingly unorthodox phrase structure, its pulsating inner parts and its vigorous sforzandos." Stanley Sadie, *The New Grove Mozart* (New York: Norton, 1982), 98–99. The contrapuntal complexity of the serenade is apparent in the trio, for example, which makes extensive use of subject inversion, a device largely alien to eighteenth-century music for wind ensemble.

49. Howard Chandler Robbins Landon, quoted in Neal Zaslaw, ed., with William Cowdery, *The Compleat Mozart: A Guide to the Musical Works of Wolfgang Amadeus Mozart* (New York: Norton, 1990), 255.

50. Ibid. Leopold died on 28 May.

51. See Robert L. Marshall in his article "Bach and Mozart: Styles of Musical Genius," *Bach: The Journal of the Riemenschneider Bach Institute* 22 (Spring–Summer 1991), 16–32.

52. For Haydn's own account, see *Collected Correspondence and London Notebooks*.

53. Concerning the nationalistic origins and applications of Haydn's tune, see Paul Nettl, *National Anthems*, trans. Alexander Gode (New York: Storm, 1952). Nettl, following the lead of Alfred Heuss, provides a programmatic exegesis of all four movements of the quartet. See pp. 64–65.

CHAPTER 3

1. See James Webster, "The Scoring of Mozart's Chamber Music for Strings," in *Music in the Classic Period: Essays in Honor of Barry S. Brook*, ed. Allan W. Atlas (New York: Pendragon, 1985), 264–65, who indicates that "The Mozarts . . . appear to have made more consistent distinctions in terminology for the various genres. One genre that clearly is orchestral (and for which there was no counterpart in Vienna) comprises the Salzburg works that we call 'serenades' today, such as the 'Haffner' (K. 250, 1776) and the 'Posthorn' (K. 320, 1779)." He states further that "for the very large serenades of the Finalmusik type, the Mozarts customary title was at first 'Cassatio' (K. 63, 99, 100); for the later ones, 'Serenata' (K. 185, 203, 204, 250, [320?]). None bore the title 'Divertimento.'"

2. Ibid., 276.

3. The proper instrumentation of serenades was first explained by Carl Bär, "Zum Begriff des 'Basso' in Mozarts Serenaden," *Mozart-Jahrbuch* (1960–61), 133–55. Note the illustrations facing p. 136 and on p. 143, which show the standing double bassist. A summary of Bär's arguments can be found in Albert Dunning's edition of Mozart's *Ensemblemusik für größere Solobesetzungen, Divertimenti für 5–7 Streich- und Bläsinstrumente* (Kassel: Bärenreiter, 1976), xvi–xviii. The table on pp. 284–93 of Webster, "Scoring of Mozart's Chamber Music," indicates, among other things, the scoring, title, manner of performance, and instrument of the bass part.

4. Mozart, *Ensemblemusik für größere Solobesetzungen*, 23–27.

5. Bär, "Zum Begriff des 'Basso,'" 135.

6. See A. Hyatt King, *Mozart Chamber Music* (Seattle: University of Washington Press, 1968), 15, for the former hypothesis, and Sadie, *The New Grove Mozart*, 55, for the latter.

7. Homer Ulrich, *Chamber Music*, 2nd ed. (New York: Columbia University Press, 1966), 197.

8. Alfred Einstein, *Mozart: His Character, His Work* (New York: Oxford University Press, 1945), 178–79.

9. Sadie, *New Grove Mozart*, 119.

10. For a more detailed discussion, see Wolfgang Amadeus Mozart, *Kammermusik: Quintette mit Bläsern*, ed. Ernst Fritz Schmid (Kassel: Bärenreiter, 1958), viii.

11. See Jiri Kratochvíl, "Betrachtungen über die ursprüngliche Fassung des Konzerts für Klarinette und des Quintetts für Klarinette und Streicher von W. A. Mozart," *Referat auf der Internationalen Mozart-Tagung in Prag* (June 1956). See also George Dezeley, "The Original Text of Mozart's Clarinet Concerto," *Music Review* 9 (1948), 166–72.

12. Since the horn part is designated as "second horn" (*corno secondo*), it is unlikely that Leutgeb, who characteristically played the higher, first-horn parts, was involved. The score of this three-movement quintet was completed on 30 March 1784. Mozart praised it in a letter to Leopold as "the finest piece I have written to date."

13. No autograph manuscript of Hob. II/41–46 (ca. 1782–84) survives. Some contemporary sources of these works use the designation *divertimento* while *Feldparthien* (field suite) is the nomenclature in others.

CHAPTER 4

1. All are discussed in Joseph Kerman, *The Beethoven Quartets* (New York: Alfred A. Knopf, 1967), 394. A seventeenth string quartet is his own transcription of the Piano Sonata, Op. 14, No. 1 in E major. In making the transcription (1802) Beethoven transposed the piece to F major. His remarks concerning this transcription are cited in Elliot Forbes, ed. *Thayer's Life of Beethoven* (Princeton, N.J.: Princeton University Press, 1967), 301.

2. Quoted in Forbes, *Thayer's Life of Beethoven*, 54.

3. Kerman discusses the harmonic structure in detail in *The Beethoven Quartets*, 76–84.

4. Griffiths, *String Quartet*, 86.

5. Douglass M. Green, *Form in Tonal Music: An Introduction to Analysis*, 2nd ed. (New York: Holt, Rinehart and Winston, 1979), 231–32.

6. Some scholars—including Vincent d'Indy—consider this coda a miscalculation on Beethoven's part; however, examination of its pitch content and melodic gestures reveals links with the preceding movements. For a detailed discussion, see Ernest Livingstone, "The Final Coda in Beethoven's String Quartet in F Minor, Op. 95," in *Essays on Music for Charles Warren Fox*, ed. Jerald C. Graue (Rochester, N.Y.: Eastman School of Music Press, 1979), 132–44.

7. The Peters firm was founded in 1801 when Franz Anton Hoffmeister and Ambrosius Kühnel merged to form this publishing house, one that set a model for all others of the day.

8. These dates are based on Forbes, *Thayer's Life of Beethoven*, 970; Kerman (*The Beethoven Quartets*, 224) accepts this information.

9. Beethoven's association with Schlesinger began in 1819, when Moritz Schlesinger visited Vienna to enroll Beethoven on the company's roster with the intention of becoming Beethoven's principal publisher. The firm issued the *Scottische Lieder*, Op. 108, the solo piano Sonatas Opp. 109, 110, and 111, as well as the Opp. 132 and 135 Quartets.

10. Quoted in Forbes, *Thayer's Life of Beethoven*, 940. The players were Ignaz Schuppanzigh (1776–1830), violin 1, Franz Weiß (1778–1830), violin 2, Karl Holz (1799–1858), viola, and Joseph Linke (?), cello.

11. Ibid., 940–41.

12. Aldous Huxley, *Point Counter Point* (New York: Harper and Row, 1928), 425–28. Huxley's novel, as the title suggests, is about contradictions; during the course of Beethoven's heavenly music, three assassins knock at the door and murder one of the listeners!

13. See my article "Bartók's Parodies of Beethoven," *Music Review* 42 (August–November 1981), 252–60. The German heading written at the beginning of the movement is in Beethoven's handwriting; the Italian heading (i.e., *Canzona di ringraziamento offerta alla divinita da un guarito, in modo lidico*) was by someone else.

14. Kerman, *The Beethoven Quartets*, 225–29.

15. In the present discussion, I will consider the Più allegro section following the fourth movement (Alla marcia, assai vivace) as an introduction to and part of the finale; thus, measure numbers indicated here for the "last" movement include the twenty-two-measure introduction.

16. Basil Smallman's book *The Piano Trio: Its History, Technique, and Repertoire* (Oxford: Clarendon Press, 1990) provides a concise overview of this genre.

17. King, *Mozart Chamber Music,* 37.

18. Hans Christoph Worbs, jacket notes for *W. A. Mozart, Complete Trios for Piano, Violin, and Cello,* Beaux Arts Trio (Philips LP 6768-032, 1978).

19. Einstein, *Mozart,* 252, 263.

20. A. Craig Bell, "An Introduction to Haydn's Piano Trios," *Music Review* 16 (1955), 193.

21. William Mann, brochure for *Beethoven: Ten Trios for Piano, Violin and Cello,* Borodin Trio, (Chandos CD recording CHAN 8352/3/4/5, 1987).

22. Oscar G. Sonnek, *Beethoven: Impressions by His Contemporaries* (1926; New York: Dover, 1967), 48–49.

23. Bach, *Essay on the True Art.*

24. "During the . . . summer [1809], Beethoven was busy selecting and copying in order extracts from the theoretical works of C. P. E. Bach, Türk, Kirnberger, Fux and Albrechtsberger, for subsequent use in the instruction of Archduke Rudolph." Forbes, *Thayer's Life of Beethoven,* 467.

25. For the full text of the agreement, see ibid., 457.

CHAPTER 5

1. Anthony Baines, "Harmonie, Harmonie-musik," in *The New Oxford Companion to Music,* ed. Denis Arnold (New York: Oxford University Press, 1983), 1:813.

2. Anthony Baines, *Woodwind Instruments and Their History,* rev. ed. (New York: Norton, 1963), 312, 314.

3. Ralph P. Locke, "Paris: Centre of Intellectual Ferment," in *The Early Romantic Era: Between Revolutions, 1789 and 1848 in Music and Society,* ed. Alexander Ringer (Englewood Cliffs, N.J.: Prentice Hall, 1991), 33.

4. Ibid., 37.

5. A fine recording of the set has been made by the Avalon Wind Quintet (HNH International, Naxos CD 8.553410, 1996).

6. The most comprehensive study of the wind quintet and its repertoire during this formative period is Udo Sirker, *Die Entwicklung des Bläserquintetts in der ersten Hälfte des 19. Jahrhunderts* (Regensburg: Bosse, 1968). See also Roy Houser, *Catalogue of Chamber Music for Woodwind Instruments* (1962; reprint New York: Da Capo, 1973); Harry B. Peters, *The Literature of the Woodwind Quintet* (Metuchen, N.J.: Scarecrow Press, 1971); and Himie Voxman and Lyle Merriman, *Woodwind Ensemble Music Guide* (Evanston, Ill.: Instrumentalist, [1973]). For recent literature for wind quintet, the ongoing series entitled "Quintessence" in *The Clarinet* is useful.

7. Forbes, *Thayer's Life of Beethoven,* 96. Reicha arrived in Vienna in 1802 and remained there until 1808. During this time, he also renewed acquaintances with Haydn, whom he had met when the older composer visited Bonn.

8. The metronome markings associated with Reicha's quintets were actually supplied by Dauprat after the composer's death.

9. Gerhard Pätzig, "Who Was Anton Reicha?" notes for *Anton Reicha: Sämtliche Bläserquintette,* Albert-Schweitzer-Quintett, Classic Produktion Osnabrück 999 024, vols. 1–3 (1987). Regarding early performances of Reicha's works, see Jeffrey

Cooper, *The Rise of Instrumental Music and Concert Series in Paris: 1828–1871* (Ann Arbor, Mich.: UMI Research Press, 1983).

10. Boris Schwartz, *French Instrumental Music between the Revolutions: 1789–1830* (New York, 1950; reprint New York: Da Capo, 1987), 267.

11. Louis Spohr, *Louis Spohr's Autobiography* (London: Longman, Green, Longman, Roberts, and Green, 1865), 2:131.

12. Klaus Burmeister, ed., *Danzi: Neun Bläserquintette*, Opp. 56, 67, 68, 3 vols. (Leipzig: Edition Peters, 1982), 1:151.

CHAPTER 6

1. Ernst Hilmar, *Schubert in His Time*, trans. Reinhard G. Pauly (Portland, Ore.: Amadeus Press, 1988), 16.

2. The terms "progressive tonality" and "dramatic key symbolism" are also used to indicate directional tonality. Schubert's use of the technique fairly common, particularly in his early works.

3. Hans Moldenhauer, *Duo-Pianism* (Chicago: Chicago Musical College Press, 1950), 400.

4. See Ernest Lubin, *The Piano Duet: A Guide for Pianists* (New York: Grossman, 1970), 221.

5. Lubin, *The Piano Duet*, 51–52.

6. Ernst Hilmar, "Schubert and the Publishers," in *Schubert in His Time*, 33–43.

7. Dietrich Fischer-Dieskau, *Schubert: A Biographical Study of His Songs*, trans. Kenneth S. Whitton (London: Cassell, 1976), 283.

8. Otto Erich Deutsch, *Schubert: Memoirs by His Contemporaries* (New York: Macmillan, 1958), 115.

9. Franz Peter Schubert, *Neue Ausgabe sämtlicher Werke* (Kassel: Bärenreiter, 1964–), series 6, vol. 7.

10. Ibid., 115.

11. Robert Schumann, *On Music and Musicians*, ed. Konrad Wolff and trans. Paul Rosenfeld (New York: Norton, 1969), 121.

12. Griffiths, *The String Quartet*, 96.

13. Werner P. Friederich, *An Outline-History of German Literature*, 2nd ed. (New York: Barnes and Noble, 1961), 87.

14. Quoted in Deutsch, *Schubert*, 289.

15. Ibid., 372.

CHAPTER 7

1. Robert Schumann, *Gesammelte Schriften über Musik und Musiker*, ed. Martin Kreisig (Leipzig: Breitkopf und Härtel, 1914), 1:248.

2. Louis Ferdinand, *Musikalische Werke*, 8 vols. (Leipzig: Breitkopf und Härtel, 1915–17). The complete works of the prince are available in a six-disc set issued by Thorofon Schallplatten (76. 30834).

3. See Basil Smallman, *The Piano Quartet and Quintet: Style, Structure, Scoring* (Oxford: Clarendon Press, 1994), 196.

4. Recorded on the Desmar label (DSM 1025G, 1980). The present commentary on the life and works of Prince Louis Ferdinand is based in part on my jacket notes for that recording.

5. Spohr's account in his *Selbstbiographie von Louis Spohr* (Kassel: Georg H. Wigand, 1860) ended in June 1838, but was continued by Spohr's widow. For a reprint of the original German version, see Eugen Schmitz, ed., *Selbstbiographie* (Kassel: Bärenreiter, 1954). The full English translation, *Louis Spohr's Autobiography* (Longman, Green, Longman, Roberts, and Green, reprinted New York: Da Capo Press, 1969), contains numerous errors. Henry Pleasants's translation includes only those portions of the *Selbstbiographie* relating to "the account of Spohr's travels as a young virtuoso, composer, and conductor" (viii). See his *Musical Journeys of Louis Spohr* (Norman: University of Oklahoma Press, 1961).

6. This tally excludes the two string quartets of 1856–57 listed in Folker Göthel, *Thematisch-Bibliographisches Verzeichnis der Werke von Louis Spohr* (Tutzing: Hans Schneider, 1981), among the works without opus number: WoO 41, 42, pp. 300–302. In his thematic catalogue, Göthel includes Spohr's original tempo indications, which were given from about 1816 according to Gottfried Weber's method of using a pendulum. Spohr indicates the pendulum length in Rhenish inches. During the 1820s and until the end of his career, he used Mäzel's metronome indications.

7. Regarding Spohr's work at Brunswick, see Clive Brown, *Louis Spohr: A Critical Biography* (New York: Cambridge University Press, 1984), 9–34. For information relating specifically to Carl Wilhelm's character and musical interests, see pp. 9f. Note also Brown's essay "The Chamber Music of Spohr and Weber," in *Nineteenth-Century Chamber Music*, ed. Stephen E. Hefling (New York: Schirmer, 1998), 147–69. The early chamber works are discussed in Martin Wulfhorst, "Louis Spohr's Early Chamber Music (1796–1812): A Contribution to the History of Nineteenth-Century Genres," Ph.D. diss., City University of New York, 1995.

8. Brown, *Louis Spohr*, 11.

9. Ibid., 15, 27.

10. See Göthel, *Thematisch-Bibliographisches Verzeichnis*, 151. Concerning the Müller Quartet, Homer Ulrich notes: "The four Mueller brothers (b. 1797–1809, d. 1855–75) began their quartet playing in 1830. Confining themselves to Haydn, Mozart, and Beethoven and traveling in all parts of western Europe (and Russia in 1845), they did much to create interst in and to set standards for chamber-music playing." *Chamber Music*, 3n.

11. Brown, *Louis Spohr*, 37.

12. Spohr, *Autobiography*, 96.

13. Brown, "Chamber Music of Spohr and Weber," 151.

14. Clive Brown, ed., *Louis Spohr: Chamber Music with Piano* (New York: Garland, 1987), 10:viii.

15. For a complete listing of Spohr's quartets, see Göthel, *Thematisch-Bibliographisches Verzeichnis*. Quartets bearing the descriptors "grand" or "brillant" are invariably single pieces rather than sets. In his memoirs, Spohr did not always use the terminology found in the publications, and he apparently used "solo-quartet" and "quatuor brillant" interchangeably. See Brown, "Chamber Music of Spohr and Weber," 151.

16. A sampling of the string quartets can be found in Clive Brown, ed., *Chamber Music for Strings*, vol. 9, pt. 1, in *Selected Works of Louis Spohr* (New York: Garland, 1987).

17. See Göthel, *Thematisch-Bibliographisches Verzeichnis*, 104, Anmerkung. The complete string quartets of Spohr have been recorded by the New Budapest Quartet on the Marco Polo label.

18. Folker Göthel, notes for *Spohr: Double-Quartet in E minor, Op. 87*, trans. Alice Dixon (Decca Record, London Stereo Treasury Series, STS 15074, 1967).

19. Forsyth, *Buildings for Music*, 203.

CHAPTER 8

1. John Horton, *Mendelssohn Chamber Music* (Seattle: University of Washington Press, 1972), 29.

2. Eric Werner, *Mendelssohn: A New Image of the Composer and His Age*, trans. Dika Newlin (London: Free Press of Glencoe, 1963), viii.

3. Regarding the status of Bach music in the Romantic era, see Christoph Wolff, *The New Bach Reader* (New York: Norton, 1998), 485–526.

4. Werner, *Mendelssohn*, 19–20.

5. Op. 72 was Mendelssohn's last composition published during his lifetime. Opus numbers above 72 appeared after his death, and they do not reflect the chronology of composition.

6. The Sonata has been issued in a practical edition by VEB Deutscher Verlag für Musik (Leipzig, 1966). It is also included in the *Leipziger Ausgabe der Werke Felix Mendelssohn Bartholdys*, also published by VEB, in series 2, vol. 4.

7. (New York: C. F. Peters, 1953). Menuhin suggests a performance time of nineteen minutes. In the foreword, he observes that the piece "is an example of [Mendelssohn's] full maturity, bearing all the unmistakable qualities of his period and of his own personal style."

8. The first performance of the Ninth Symphony took place in 1824, only one year before Mendelssohn's completion of the Octet; the thematic similarities may, therefore, be purely coincidental.

9. Werner, *Mendelssohn*, 60.

10. Score and parts ed. Reiner Zimmermann (Leipzig: VEB Deutscher Verlag für Musik, 1986). Another edition is by Patrick Kast (Adliswil, Switzerland: Kunzelmann, 2000).

11. The Quartet has been published in a practical edition and in a study score by Ries und Erler (Berlin, 1969).

12. Werner, *Mendelssohn*, 22.

13. Ibid., 258–59.

14. Schumann, *On Music and Musicians*, 227.

15. Griffiths, *The String Quartet*, 119.

16. Concerning Fanny Mendelssohn/Hensel, see M. J. Citron, "Felix Mendelssohn's Influence on Fanny Hensel as a Composer," *Current Musicology* 37–38 (1984), 9–17; Sebastian Hensel, *The Mendelssohn Family: 1729–1847* (New York: Greenwood Press, 1968); Sarah Rothenberg, "Thus Far, but No Farther:

Fanny Mendelssohn Hensel's Unfinished Journey," *Musical Quarterly* 77 (Winter 1993), 689–708; Victoria Sirota, "The Life and Works of Fanny Mendelssohn Hensell," D.M.A. diss., Boston University School for the Arts, 1981; and Jack Werner, "Felix and Fanny Mendelssohn," *Music and Letters* 28 (October 1947), 303–37.

17. He was assisted in this task by Conrad Schleinitz, Ferdinand David, Ignaz Moscheles, Moritz Hauptmann, and Julius Rietz. Werner, *Mendelssohn*, 493.

18. Horton, *Mendelssohn Chamber Music*, 50.

19. Smallman, *Piano Trio*, 101–5.

20. Peter F. Ostwald, *Schumann: The Inner Voices of a Musical Genius* (Boston: Northeastern University Press, 1985), 118.

21. Ibid., 119–20.

22. In German usage, the letter H is used to represent B-natural, and B to represent B-flat.

23. May 1855. Quoted in Ostwald, *Schumann*, 290.

24. Ibid., 139.

25. Griffiths, *The String Quartet*, 121.

26. Ostwald, *Schumann*, 173.

27. Griffiths, *The String Quartet*, 121.

28. Smallman, *Piano Trio*, 105.

29. See, for example, Griffiths, *The String Quartet*, 122.

30. See Smallman, *Piano Trio*, 105–16.

31. Ostwald, *Schumann*, 175.

32. John Gardner, "The Chamber Music," in *Robert Schumann: The Man and His Music*, ed. Alan Walker (New York: Harper and Row, 1974), 222.

33. For details of specific tours and programs, see Joan Chissell, *Clara Schumann: A Dedicated Spirit* (New York: Taplinger, 1983).

34. Ibid., 127.

35. The final statement of the refrain begins in the subdominant, but terminates in the tonic minor key.

36. Schumann was aware that his piano cycles of the 1830s caused confusion among listeners; but in these works and his programmatic chamber pieces, definite organizational precepts are employed. Explanation of aesthetic principles behind such cycles is given in John Daverio, "Reading Schumann by Way of Jean Paul and His Contemporaries," *College Music Symposium: Journal of the College Music Society* 32 (Fall 1990), 28–45. Franz Brendel, Schumann's successor as the editor of the *Neue Zeitschrift für Musik*, was alarmed by the realization that "Schumann had changed direction after 1840 with works such as the First Symphony, the String Quartets, the Piano Quintet, and Piano Quartet. He saw these compositions as Schumann's attempts to present his ideas now through the objectivity of classical forms; he viewed them as an antithesis . . . to Schumann's former mode of creation." Jurgen Thym, "Schumann in Brendel's *Neue Zeitschrift für Musik* from 1845 to 1856," in *Mendelssohn and Schumann: Essays on Their Music and Its Context*, ed. Jon W. Finson and R. Larry Todd (Durham, N.C.: Duke University Press, 1984), 23.

37. Malcolm MacDonald, *Brahms* (New York: Schirmer, 1990), 15.

38. Thym, "Schumann in Brendel's *Neue Zeitschrift für Musik*," 30.

39. MacDonald, *Brahms*, 10.

40. Karl Geiringer, "Brahms as a Musicologist," *Musical Quarterly* 69 (Fall 1983), 464–65.

41. Ibid., 465.

42. Ibid., 468.

43. Robert Pascall, "Ruminations on Brahms's Chamber Music," *Musical Times* 116 (August 1975), 699.

44. Daniel Gregory Mason, *The Chamber Music of Brahms* (New York: Macmillan, 1933), 3–4.

45. Quoted in Theodore Thomas, *Theodore Thomas: A Musical Autobiography*, ed. George P. Upton (Chicago, 1905; reprint New York: Da Capo, 1964), 39–40 n. 1.

46. The original version of the Trio was published by Breitkopf und Härtel with the plate number 8995. The revised edition was issued in 1891 by Simrock, Brahms's principal publisher, with the plate number 9510. Both versions are contained in the complete-works edition assembled by the Gesellschaft der Musikfreunde (Leipzig: Breitkopf und Härtel; reprinted Ann Arbor, Mich.: J. W. Edwards, 1949), vol. 9.

47. MacDonald, *Brahms*, 74.

48. Mason, *Chamber Music of Brahms*, 6–7.

49. Eric Sams, "Brahms and His Clara Themes," *Musical Times* 112 (1971), 433.

50. Ibid.

51. Ibid., 434.

52. Concerning the Piano Quartet and its revision, see Karl Geiringer, *Brahms: His Life and Work*, 2nd ed. (New York: Oxford University Press, 1947), 227–28.

53. The priority of versions is unclear in this case. In the German preface to the Eulenberg score of the Sextet, Wilhelm Altmann states that Clara Schumann already knew "die Variationen in d, die Brahms ihr in der vielleicht ursprünglichen Klavier-Fassung zugesandt hatte" (iv). The botched English translation states that she already knew "the Variations in D which Brahms may have sent her in the original Piano form." Malcolm MacDonald (*Brahms*, 158 n. 1) states that "Brahms . . . made a solo piano version . . . at Clara Schumann's request."

54. Donald N. Ferguson, *Image and Structure in Chamber Music* (Minneapolis: University of Minnesota Press, 1964), 215.

55. Edwin M. Good, *Giraffes, Black Dragons, and Other Pianos* (Stanford, Calif.: Stanford University Press, 1982), 202.

56. Ibid.

57. Malcolm MacDonald, *Brahms*, 165, speaks of "a work full of tension and shadowed by minor-key conflict, magnificent in utterance but often sombre or thunderous in its moods."

58. Nora Bickley, *Letters from and to Joseph Joachim* (1914; New York: Vienna House, 1972), 307.

59. Brahms performed this version with the pianist Carl Tausig in 1864. He wrote to Clara Schumann about Tausig and the impending performance in his letter of 4 April of that year. See Berthold Litzmann, ed., *The Letters of Clara Schumann and Johannes Brahms: 1853–1896* (New York, 1927; reprint New York: Vienna House, 1971), 1:165–66.

60. The dates of composition and premiere have been botched on numerous occasions. In his biography of Brahms, MacDonald states that "its conception" took place "in the highly poetic surroundings of the Black Forest around Baden in 1864" (175). Smallman, in his study *The Piano Trio*, states unequivocally that the piece dates from 1868 (128). In the preface to the Eulenburg study score of the Trio (London: Ernst Eulenburg, n.d.), Wilhelm Altmann indicates the date of the premiere as 7 December; Melvin Berger gives the date as 5 December in his *Guide to Chamber Music* (New York: Dodd, Mead, 1985), 97.

61. *Letters of Clara Schumann and Brahms*, 1:171–72.

62. Ibid., 176.

63. Ibid., 179.

64. Ethel Mary Smyth (1858–1944) heard the Trio in Utrecht while a student at the Leipzig Conservatory. See the postscript of Elisabet von Herzogenberg in the letter of 4 October 1878 in *Johannes Brahms: The Herzogenberg Correspondence*, ed. Max Kalbeck, trans. Hannah Bryant (New York: Vienna House, 1971), 67. The Utrecht performance probably came about through Professor Wilhelm Engelmann, a resident of that city, to whom Brahms dedicated his Third String Quartet. In 1879, Theodor Billroth wrote to Brahms on 5 January from Vienna indicating that his "Horn Trio had an enormous success recently. I might scarcely have expected it with this very deeply felt music, especially since before that, the public didn't feel like listening attentively. How curious those changes in the audiences are." See *Johannes Brahms and Theodor Billroth: Letters from a Musical Friendship*, trans. and ed. Hans Barkan (Norman: University of Oklahoma Press, 1957), 77.

65. Barkan, *Johannes Brahms and Theodor Billroth*, 21 n. 1.

66. MacDonald, *Brahms*, 139.

67. Ibid., 210.

68. MacDonald, *Brahms*, 225, states that "what we know as the Scherzo may in fact have been the original Finale—a drastically curtailed but certainly 'passionate' one (a plausible thesis, since op. 60's Scherzo, most unusually, has no formal Trio)."

69. Geiringer, *Brahms*, 234.

70. See Barkan, *Johannes Brahms and Theodor Billroth*, 40.

71. Walter Frisch, *Brahms and the Principle of Developing Variation* (Berkeley: University of California Press, 1984), 160; MacDonald, *Brahms*, 251.

72. Brahms was working on two trios during the summer of 1880: one in C major—eventually published as Op. 87—and another in E-flat, which he abandoned. The Trio of this movement may well be the place where the two pieces merged into one. See MacDonald, *Brahms*, 282, for remarks by Brahms to his publisher about this piece.

73. See his letter to her in *Brahms: The Herzogenberg Correspondence*, 167. Elisabet responded on 6 August 1882 with a perceptive discussion of the first two movements, illuminated with numerous musical examples that she apparently recalled from memory. She could not comment on the last movement since she did not get to study it sufficiently before returning the score. For the text of her letter, see 167–73.

74. Geiringer, *Brahms*, 238.

75. Geiringer, "Brahms as Musicologist," 465.

76. MacDonald, *Brahms*, 146–47.

77. In her letter of 4 November 1886 to Brahms, Clara Schumann requested copies of Opp. 99 and 100, so that she might begin preparing them for performances with Hugo Becker and Joseph Joachim respectively. See *Letters of Clara Schumann and Brahms*, 2:108.

78. MacDonald, *Brahms*, 336.

79. Ibid., 342.

80. See Barkan, *Johannes Brahms and Theodor Billroth*, 220 n. 2.

81. Geiringer, *Brahms*, 242–43.

82. Barkan, *Johannes Brahms and Theodore Billroth*, 218 n. 1.

83. Bickley, *Letters from and to Joseph Joachim*, 448–49. Piatti was the cellist.

84. *Letters of Clara Schumann and Brahms*, 2:191.

85. Ibid., 2:196. Brahms must have been in earnest about the inadequate skills of solo wind players, since he subsequently urged the Vienna Tonkünstlerverein to organize a competition for the advancement of wind music. He himself contributed to the cash award to be offered. For details, see Pamela Weston, *Clarinet Virtuosi of the Past* (London: Robert Hale, 1971), 227.

86. Beethoven's Clarinet Trio of 1805 is excluded from the discussion since it actually was an arrangement, albeit by the composer himself, of his Septet in E-flat, Op. 20. Subsequent to Brahms, Alexander Zemlinsky wrote a Trio in D minor, Op. 3, for this ensemble.

87. Geiringer, *Brahms*, 244.

88. The significance of both the theme per se and the key of F-sharp minor is discussed in Frisch, *Brahms*, 147–50.

CHAPTER 9

1. Joël-Marie Fauquet, "Chamber Music in France from Luigi Cherubini to Claude Debussy," in Hefling, *Nineteenth-Century Chamber Music*, 287–88.

2. Alan Walker, *Franz Liszt*, vol. 1, *The Virtuoso Years, 1811–1847* (New York: Alfred A. Knopf, 1983), 227.

3. Ibid., 183. Katharine Ellis notes that for many French critics, including Francois-Joseph Fétis and Henri Blanchard, Beethoven's late style period "remained incomprehensible." See *Music Criticism in Nineteenth-Century France: "La revue et gazette musicale de Paris", 1834–80* (New York: Cambridge University Press, 1995), 112–16.

4. Walker, *Franz Liszt: The Virtuoso Years*, 227.

5. Vincent d'Indy, *César Franck*, trans. Rosa Newmarch (London, 1910; reprinted New York: Dover, [1965], 111.

6. Quoted in James Harding, *Saint-Saëns and His Circle* (London: Chapman and Hall, 1965), 109.

7. Quoted in Harding, *Saint-Saëns*, 110.

8. Elaine Brody, *Paris: The Musical Kaleidoscope, 1870–1925* (London: Robson, 1987), 18. The first Société concert took place on 25 November 1875. By the onset of World War I, the society had sponsored over four hundred concerts. Temporarily suspended during the war, the concerts resumed on 10 November 1917. Among its members were Georges Bizet, Ernest Guiraud, Jules Massenet,

Théodore Dubois, and Charles-Marie Widor. See Brody, 17–18. The original group of thirty who joined the society in 1871 had, by 1877, increased to two hundred (Harding, *Saint-Saëns,* 151). Despite the society's constant and dramatic growth, "at no time during its existence did the Société have a permanent home and it depended on the generosity of the Pleyel and Erard piano companies for the use of a hall. The performers gave their services free and the programmes were lithographed to save printing charges." Harding, *Saint-Saëns,* 120.

9. Farrenc was professor of piano at the Paris Conservatory from 1842 to 1873. In addition to the quintets, she also wrote two piano trios, various sonatas and pieces for violin and piano, a sextet, and a nonet. Like Franck, she had been a composition pupil of Reicha's.

10. Norman Demuth, *César Franck* (London: Dennis Dobson, 1949), 36.

11. d'Indy, *César Franck,* 186–88.

12. Ibid., 193.

13. Ibid., 55.

14. See Smallman, *Piano Trio,* 161–62. The reconstruction was made by Ellwood Derr.

15. Fauquet, "Chamber Music in France, 310.

16. The Russian influence is discussed in Arthur Wenk, *Claude Debussy and Twentieth-Century Music* (Boston: Twayne's Music Series, 1983), 53–54.

17. Abram Loft, *Ensemble! A Rehearsal Guide to Thirty Great Works of Chamber Music* (Portland, Ore.: Amadeus Press, 1992), 279.

18. James McCalla, *Twentieth-Century Chamber Music* (New York: Schirmer, 1996), 174.

19. See Robert Orledge, *Gabriel Fauré* (London: Eulenberg, 1979), 235–52; Charles Koechlin, *Gabriel Fauré: 1845–1924* (New York: AMS Press, 1976), 62–63; and James C. Kidd, "Louis Niedermeyer's System for Gregorian Chant Accompaniment as a Compositional Source for Gabriel Fauré," Ph.D. diss., University of Chicago, 1973. This last study takes as its point of departure Niedermeyer's treatise of 1856, *Traité theorétique et pratique de l'accompagnement du plainchant.*

20. Melvin Berger, *Guide to Chamber Music,* gives the violinist as Gabriel Willaume. See p. 347.

CHAPTER 10

1. Jarmil Burghauser, notes for *Antonín Dvořák: The String Quartets,* Prague String Quartet (DGG 2740177, 1977).

2. See Derek Katz and Michael Beckerman, "Chamber Music of Smetana and Dvořák," in *Nineteenth-Century Chamber Music* (New York: Schirmer, 1998), 324.

3. Jarmil Burghauser, *Antonín Dvořák: Thematik Katalog* (Prague: Supraphon, 1996), 843.

4. David Beveridge, "Dvořák and Brahms: A Chronicle, and Interpretation," in *Dvořák and His World,* ed. Michael Beckerman (Princeton University Press, 1993), 59.

5. Ibid., 66.

6. Ibid., 72.

7. Ibid., 68.

8. Otakar Dvořák, *Antonín Dvořák, My Father* (Spillville, Iowa: Czech Historical Research Center, 1993), 60.

9. Beveridge, "Dvořák and Brahms," 71–72.

10. See Klaus Henning Oelmann, *The Unfinished Chamber Music of Edvard Grieg* (Middleton, Wis.: A-R Editions, 2002).

11. The addition of another player to render the piccolo part in November 1924 ought not to be taken as a performance requirement; in May 1926, Leoš Janáček supervised a performance of *Youth* in London, and six players—with flute doubling on piccolo—participated. See the photograph of the ensemble in Ian Horsbrugh, *Leoš Janáček: The Field That Prospered* (New York: Charles Scribner's Sons, 1982), [181].

12. Kamila was married to David Stössl, an antique dealer, at the time Janáček met her. Perhaps the programmatic element of his First String Quartet was a sublimanal outworking of his relationship with Kamila and her husband. Kamila's photograph appears on [p. 179] of Horsbrugh, *Leoš Janáček.*

13. Ibid., 234.

14. Dohnányi's chamber music includes two piano quintets (1895, 1914) and three string quartets (1899, 1906, 1926).

15. For details about the Parry Collection and Bartók's work with it, see Halsey Stevens, *The Life and Music of Béla Bartók* (New York: Oxford University Press, 1953), 93–95, 338.

16. Bartók later arranged the Sonata for Two Pianos and Percussion for Two Pianos and Orchestra of 2.2.2.2.–4.2.3.0–celesta–strings.

17. This type of pizzicato—generally called "Bartók pizzacto"—was probably what Claudio Monteverdi had in mind in his 1624 score of "Il combattimento di Tancredi e Clorinda," where he instructed: "Qui si lascia l'arco e strappano le cordi con dui ditti" (At this point, put down the bow, and twang the string with two fingers).

18. Further concerning Ives's aesthetics in J. Peter Burkholder, *Charles Ives: The Ideas behind the Music* (New Haven: Yale University Press, 1985), especially "Ives and Transcendentalism: A Second Look," 20–32.

19. The Fourth Sonata—the earliest of the four despite its number—originally had four movements. It appeared this way in the lithographic printing of ca. 1915; however, "Ives tore the 4th movement out of almost all copies." John Kirkpatrick, "A Temporary Mimeographed Catalogue of the Music Manuscripts and Related Materials of Charles Edward Ives, 1874–1954," Yale University, 1960, 73.

20. Sonatas and movements designated here as I/i, I/ii, etc. Hymns given by "Tune Name" and ("First line of text"). I/i, "Shining Shore" ("My days are gliding swiftly by"), "Bringing in the Sheaves" ("Sowing in the morning"); I/ii, "Work Song" ("Work, for night is coming"); I/iii, "Watchman" ("Watchman, tell us of the night"); II/i, "Autumn" ("Mighty God, while angels bless Thee"), II/iii "Nettleton" ("Come, Thou fount of every blessing"); III/i, "Need" ("I need Thee every hour"), "Beulah Land" ("I've reached the land of corn and wine"), III/ii, "There'll Be No Dark Valley" ("There'll be no more sorrow when Jesus comes"), "Happy Day" ("O happy day that fixed my choice"), III/iii "Need" (as III/i) and "Happy Day" (as

III/ii); IV/i "Old, Old Story" ("Tell me the old, old story"), IV/ii, "Jesus Loves Me" ("Jesus loves me"), IV/iii, "Beautiful River" ("Shall we gather at the river?"). Quotations are identified in Kirkpatrick, "Music Manuscripts of Ives." For a comprehensive catalog of texts and tunes used in Ives's works, see Clayton W. Henderson, *The Charles Ives Tunebook* (Warren, Mich.: Harmonie Park Press, 1990), 292.

21. John H. Baron, *Intimate Music: A History of the Idea of Chamber Music* (Stuyvesant, N.Y.: Pendragon Press, 1998), 410.

22. David Drew, "American Chamber Music," *Chamber Music* (London: Penguin, 1957), 323.

23. Ralph Waldo Emerson, *Essays by Ralph Waldo Emerson* (New York: T. Y. Crowell, 1951), 247.

CHAPTER 11

1. Joseph Rufer, "Hommage à Schoenberg," in *Arnold Schoenberg Correspondence: A Collection of Translated and Annotated Letters Exchanged with Guido Adler, Pablo Casals, Emanuel Feuermann, and Olin Downes*, ed. Egbert M. Ennulat (Metuchen, N.J.: Scarecrow Press, 1991), 3.

2. Ibid., 2.

3. Arnold Schoenberg, letter of 7 September 1912 in *Arnold Schoenberg Correspondence*, 95.

4. Arnold Schoenberg, "National Music (2)," in *Style and Idea: Selected Writings of Arnold Schoenberg*, ed. Leonard Stein, trans. Leo Black (New York: St. Martin's Press, 1975), 173–74. In this context he lists the precise musical techniques he acquired from each composer.

5. H. H. Stuckenschmidt, *Schoenberg: His Life, World, and Work*, trans. Humphrey Searle (New York: Schirmer, 1978), 370.

6. Discussions appear in Reinhold Brinkmann and Christoph Wolff, eds., *Music of My Future: The Schoenberg Quartets and Trio* (Cambridge, Mass.: Harvard University Press, 2000), 192

7. Walter B. Bailey, *Programmatic Elements in the Works of Schoenberg* (Ann Arbor, Mich.: UMI Research Press, 1984), 28.

8. The German text and its translation appear in ibid., 28–30.

9. Stuckenschmidt, *Schoenberg*, 78.

10. For details, see Radice, *Concert Music of the Twentieth Century: Its Personalities, Institutions, and Techniques* (Englewood Cliffs, N.J.: Prentice Hall, 2003), 102.

11. Arnold Schoenberg, "Twelve-Tone Composition," in *Style and Idea*, 207–8.

12. In these pieces, one player is needed for each instrument listed.

13. The Petrarch sonnet is actually no. 256, "Far potess' io vendetta di coeli / che guardando et parlando mi distrugge, / et per più doglia poi s'asconde et fugge, / celando li occhi a me sí dolci et rei. | Cosí li afflicti et stanchi spirti mei/a poco a poco consumando sugge, / e'n sul cor quasi fiero leon rugge / la notte allor quand'io posar devrei. | L'alma, cui Morte del suo albergo caccia/da me si parte, et di tal nodo sciolta, / vassene pur a lei che la minaccia. | Meravigliomi ben s'alcuna volta, / mentre le parla et piange et poi l'abbraccia, / non rompe il sonno suo, s'ella l'ascolta."

14. The last two tones of the final statement are in the viola and violin parts.

15. Concerning Coolidge, see Cyrilla Barr, *Elizabeth Sprague Coolidge: American Patron of Music* (New York: Schirmer, 1998), 436.

16. Bailey, *Programmatic Elements in Schoenberg*, 151.

17. The complete essay and various accounts by persons in the Schoenberg circle appear in Bailey, *Programmatic Elements in Schoenberg*, 152–57.

18. Michael Cherlin examines these features in illuminating detail in "Memory and Rhetorical Trope in Schoenberg's String Trio," *Journal of the American Musicological Society* 51 (Fall 1998), 559–602.

19. Leonard Stein, "A Note on the Genesis of the *Ode to Napoleon*," *Journal of the Arnold Schoenberg Institute* 2 (October 1977), 53.

20. These are listed in appendix 1 of Hans and Rosaleen Moldenhauer, *Anton von Webern: A Chronicle of His Life and Work* (New York: Alfred A. Knopf, 1979), 697–705.

21. Reinhold Brinkmann, "Schoenberg's Quartets and the Viennese Tradition," in Brinkmann and Wolff, *Music of My Future*, 9–12.

22. Moldenhauer and Moldenhauer, *Anton von Webern*, 248.

23. Ibid., 326.

24. Moldenhauer and Moldenhauer suggest the possibility that the title originated with Emil Hertzka, the editorial director of Universal Edition at the time. Moldenhauer and Moldenhauer, *Anton von Webern*, 193.

25. Quoted in ibid., 194.

26. Moldenhauer and Moldehauer give a fascinating description of Webern's use of magic squares (i.e., charts showing all forty-eight versions of a given row) during the compositional process. See ibid., 321.

27. For Webern's report to Schoenberg, see Moldenhauer, *Anton von Webern*, 324.

28. Webern admired the work, had it in his repertoire, and conducted it on at least one occasion, albeit after the composition of Op. 22. This was on 28 September 1933. It is probable that Webern had the finale of this symphony in mind when composing his own Passacaglia, Op. 1 as well.

29. These details are explained in an essay that Webern wrote to Erwin Stein in the summer of 1939. An English translation by Zoltan Roman of this essay is included as appendix 2 in Moldenhauer, *Anton von Webern*, 751–56.

30. Berg explains this to Schoenberg in his letter of 8 September 1914, written just days before the latter's fortieth birthday on 13 September. The work that ultimately became the dedication score is the set of Three Pieces, Op. 6 (1915) for large orchestra.

31. Mosco Carner, *Alban Berg: The Man and the Work* (London: Duckworth, 1975), 108.

32. These are discussed in William DeFotis, "Berg's Op. 5: Rehearsal Instructions," *Perspectives of New Music* 17 (Fall–Winter 1978), 131–37.

33. Carner, *Alban Berg*, 109. The desire for structural integrity has also been noted by Kathryn Bailey, who argues that in his application of musical materials, "Berg took the step to a more regimented way of composing, where many things were predetermined, ahead of [Schoenberg and Webern]. See her "Berg's Aphoristic Pieces," in *Cambridge Companion to Berg*, ed. Anthony Pople (New York: Cam-

bridge University Press, 1997), 100. For the entire discussion of Op. 5, see pp. 95–110.

34. See the chart in Carner, *Alban Berg*, 110. Berg's first asthma attack occurred on 23 July (year unknown). Geoffrey Poole suggests that Berg had also consulted his natal astrological chart in which the number twenty-three figures prominently. See Poole's "Alban Berg and the Fateful Number," *Tempo* 179 (December 1991), 2–7.

35. Perle recounts his adventure in the three-part article "The Secret Programme of the *Lyric Suite*," *Musical Times* 118 (August, September, October 1977), 629–32, 709–13, 809–13. Perle also points out many structural details of the score while explaining their programmatic significance.

36. The evolution of the motif is examined in Douglass Green, "The Allegro misterioso of Berg's *Lyric Suite:* Iso- and Retrorhythms," *Journal of the American Musicological Society* 30 (Fall 1977), 507–16.

37. Joseph Straus, "*Tristan* and Berg's *Lyric Suite*," *In Theory Only* 8 (October 1984), 40–41.

CHAPTER 12

1. Carl Nielsen, *My Childhood*, trans. R. Spink (Copenhagen: Hansen, [1972]), 152.

2. Ibid., 19, 53, 117–20, 129. Nielsen's particular admiration for Mozart's music was reiterated in his collection of essays *Living Music*, trans. R. Spink (Copenhagen: Hansen, [1968]), 72.

3. This was with the score of the String Quartet in F minor, Op. 5, which had its first performance in 1892. See Povl Hamburger, "Orchestral Works and Chamber Music," in *Carl Nielsen Centenary Essays*, ed. Jürgen Balzer (Copenhagen: Nyt Nordisk Forlag, 1965), 21.

4. The early string quartets in D minor and F major (1883, 1887) were not published during Nielsen's lifetime. They will be included in series 2, vol. 11, of the Nielsen edition currently being issued by Wilhelm Hansen, Copenhagen. Both "Ved en ung kunstners Baare" and "Serenata in vano" were published in Copenhagen by Skandinavisk Musikforlag, 1942. The String Quintet was published by Samfundet Til Udgivelse Af Dansk Musik, Copenhagen, 1965. These last three pieces will appear in the Hansen edition as series 2, vol. 10. Works for up to three instruments will be included in series 2, vol. 12.

5. A detailed discussion appears in Charles M. Joseph, "Structural Pacing in Nielsen String Quartets," in *The Nielsen Companion*, ed. Mina F. Miller (Portland, Ore.: Amadeus, 1995), 460–88.

6. Joel Lester, "Continuity and Form in the Sonatas for Violin and Piano," in Miller, *The Nielsen Companion*, 513.

7. Ibid., 523.

8. Wilhelm Lanzky-Otto, notes for *Horn & Piano: Music for Horn and Piano by Schumann, Mendelssohn, Mozart, Bentzon, Heise, Nielsen* (Djursholm, Sweden: Grammofon AB BIS, 1982), BIS LP 204.

9. Data here and in the remainder of the discussion are based on Glenda Dawn Goss, "Chronology of the Works of Jean Sibelius," *Sibelius Companion* (Westport, Conn.: Greenwood Press, 1996), 323–91.

10. He owned instruments by Guadagnini, Guarneri del Gesù, and Stradivarius. For details, see W. W. Cobbett, "Chamber Music Life: The Instruments," in *Cobbett's Cyclopedic Survey of Chamber Music*, 2nd ed. (New York: Oxford University Press, 1963), 1:259.

11. W. W. Cobbett, "Cobbett Competitions and Commissions," *Cobbett's Cyclopedic Survey*, 1:284–85.

12. Founded in 1931 by Isolde Marie Menges.

13. Michael Kennedy, *The Works of Ralph Vaughan Williams* (New York: Oxford University Press, 1964), 261.

14. Quoted in ibid., 260.

15. Many youthful works are now available from the Boosey & Hawkes or Faber catalogs.

16. Parts for the Sextet are available from Faber Music.

17. Bridge's most important chamber music connected with Mrs. Coolidge—either as a result of personal commissions, Coolidge Foundation commissions, or dedications to Mrs. Coolidge—include his String Sextet No. 2 (2.2.2; 1922), String Quartet No. 3 (1927), Piano Trio (1929), Sonata (1932) for violin and piano, String Quartet No. 4 (1937), and four Divertimenti (1934) for flute, oboe, clarinet, and bassoon. This represents only a fraction of his chamber music output, which includes two earlier string quartets (No. 1 in E minor, 1906, and No. 2 in G minor, 1915), Phantasie (1905) for string quartet, *Three Idylls* (1906) for string quartet, Phantasie (1910) for piano trio, *Miniatures* (three sets of three; 1908) for violin, cello, and piano, Phantasie Piano Quartet (1910), String Sextet No. 1 (1912), Piano Quintet (1912), Sonata (1917) for cello and piano, Rhapsody (1928) for two violins and viola, and *Oration* (1930) for cello and piano. Numerous miniatures and larger unpublished works also survive. For details see Paul Hindmarsh, *Frank Bridge: A Thematic Catalogue, 1900–1941* (London: Faber Music, 1983); or Karen R. Little, *Frank Bridge: A Bio-Bibliography* (Westport, Conn.: Greenwood Press, 1991).

18. The players were William Kroll and Jack Pepper, violins; David Dawson, viola; Naoum Benditzky, cello.

19. See Esti Sheinberg, *Satire, Parody, and Grotesque in the Music of Shostakovich* (Aldershot: Ashgate, 2001); and Steven Baur, "Ravel's 'Russian' Period: Octatonicism in His Early Works, 1893–1908," *Journal of the American Musicological Society* 52 (Fall 1999), 531–92.

20. Rheinberger's numerous chamber works include his Nonet for flute oboe clarinet, bassoon, horn, violin, viola, cello, and double bass, Op. 139, the String Quintet in A minor, Op. 82; three string quartets (C minor, Op. 89, G minor, Op. 93, and F, Op. 147) the Piano Quintet in C, Op. 114, the Piano Quartet in E, Op. 38; four piano trios (D minor, Op. 34, A, Op. 112, B, Op. 121, and F, Op. 191a), the sonatas in E, Op. 77, and E-minor, Op. 105 for violin and piano, and the Sonata in C, Op. 92, for cello and piano.

21. Victor Fell Yellin, *Chadwick: Yankee Composer* (Washington, D.C.: Smithsonian Institution Press, 1990), 28.

22. Ibid., 40.

23. Samplings of these and other reviews are reproduced with translation in Bill F. Faucett, *George Whitefield Chadwick: A Bio-Bibliography* (Westport, Conn.: Greenwood Press, 1998). See the discussion "Chamber Music," 89–100.

24. For an anecdotal biographical account of the years 1914 to 1920, see Allan Lincoln Langley, "Chadwick and the New England Conservatory," *Musical Quarterly* 21 (1935), 39–52.

25. The score was found by David Kelleher and subsequently acquired by the Boston Public Library. I thank Steven Ledbetter for this information.

26. Quoted in Jeanell Wise Brown, *Amy Beach and Her Chamber Music: Biography, Documents, Style* (Metuchen, N.J.: Scarecrow Press, 1994), 40. Also in Adrienne Fried Block, *Amy Beach, Passionate Victorian* (New York: Oxford University Press, 1998), 103.

27. Details of her concert programs are preserved in correspondence with her principal publisher, the Boston firm of Arthur P. Schmidt. See Brown, *Amy Beach*, 51–57.

28. Ibid., 57.

29. *New York Evening Post* review of 17 March 1915. Quoted in ibid., 64. Similar criticism by Henry Krehbiel and Henry T. Finck is quoted in Block, *Amy Beach, Passionate Victorian*, 121.

30. Franz Boas, *The Central Eskimo*, reprinted with an introduction by Henry B. Collins. (Washington, D.C., 1888; Lincoln: University of Nebraska Press [1964]). The tunes and their texts are also in Block, *Amy Beach, Passionate Victorian*, [239].

31. The duration of the Quartet is from Beach. See her letter to the Arthur P. Schmidt Co. dated 12 March 1930, quoted in Brown, *Amy Beach*, 276. The performance by the Crescent Quartet on Leonarda CD LE336 (New York, 1994) is 14:44.

32. For details, see Block, *Amy Beach, Passionate Victorian*, 238.

33. An edition with an introduction has been made by Adrienne Fried Block (Madison, Wis.: A-R Editions, 1994.)

CHAPTER 13

1. St. Petersburg was called *Petrograd* from 1914 to 1924, then *Leningrad* from February 1924 until July 1991, when the name was changed back to St. Petersburg. Throughout this discussion, the city will be designated as St. Petersburg.

Shostakovich joined the faculty of the conservatory there in 1937 to teach instrumentation and composition. In 1939, he achieved the rank of professor. The siege of the city during World War II interrupted his teaching from 1941 until 1943. When he resumed his pedagogical work, it was at the Moscow Conservatory. In 1947, he resumed his duties at St. Petersburg briefly, but his fall from favor in 1948 forced him to leave his post. From 1961 until 1966, he taught postgraduate students at St. Petersburg Conservatory.

2. See Dethlef Arnemann, *Dmitri Schostakowitsch und das jüdische musicliashe Erbe* (Berlin: Kuhn, 2001), 354; Joachim Braun, "The Double Meaning of Jewish Elements in Dimitri Shostakovich's Music," *Musical Quarterly* 71 (Spring 1985), 68–80; Timothy L. Jackson, "Dmitry Shostakovich: The Composer as Jew," in *Shostakovich Reconsidered*, ed. Allan B. Ho and Dmitry Feofanov (London: Toccata Press, 1998), 597–640.

3. Dmitri Shostakovich, *Testimony: The Memoirs of Dmitri Shostakovich*, ed. Solomon Volkov, trans. Antonia W. Bouis (New York: Harper and Row, 1979), 289.

The accuracy of these memoirs has been questioned by Laurel Fay, "Shostakovich versus Volkov: Whose *Testimony*," *Russian Review* 39 (October 1980), 484–93; and by Richard Taruskin, "The Peculiar Martyrdom of Dmitri Shostakovich: The Opera and the Dictator," *New Republic*, 20 March 1989, 34–40. Allan B. Ho and Dmitry Feofanov have defended the accuracy of *Testimony* in "Shostakovich's *Testimony:* Reply to an Unjust Criticism," in Ho and Feofanov, *Shostakovich Reconsidered*, 33–311.

4. The principal chamber works of Serge Prokofiev (1891–1953) are his Quintet, Op. 39 (1924) for oboe, clarinet, violin, viola, and double bass; String Quartet No. 1, Op. 50 (1930), Sonata, Op. 80 (1946) for violin and piano; String Quartet No. 2, Op. 92 (1941), Sonata, Op. 94 (1944) for flute and piano; and Sonata, Op. 119 (1949) for cello and piano.

5. Regarding the episode, see Radice, *Concert Music*, 28–29.

6. Quoted in Elizabeth Wilson, *Shostakovich: A Life Remembered* (Princeton, N.J.: Princeton University Press, 1994), 104–5. Shostakovich's preference for very fast tempos was remarked by others including Nikolai Malko, his conducting teacher at St. Petersburg Conservatory, who noted that "his tempi were constantly too fast" (quoted in Wilson, 48), and the cellist Valentin Berlinsky (Wilson, 244).

7. Shostakovich stated this plainly to the cellist of the Glazunoff Quartet. See ibid., 132.

8. Quoted in Laurel Fay, *Shostakovich* (New York: Oxford University Press, 2000), 141.

9. The personal and public meanings of the Trio are examined in Patrick McCreless, "The Cycle of Structure and the Cycle of Meaning: The Piano Trio in E Minor, Op. 67," in *Shostakovich Studies*, ed. David Fanning (New York: Cambridge University Press, 1995), 113–36.

10. Jackson, "Dmitry Shostakovich," 598–99.

11. Shostakovich was well informed on the characteristics of Jewish folk music in Russia: Moshe Beregovsky compiled and published the collection *Yiddische Volks-Lieder* in 1938; he completed his Ph.D. thesis on Jewish folk music at the Moscow Conservatory in 1946, and Shostakovich was his examiner. See Wilson, *Shostakovich*, 234.

12. McCreless, "Cycle of Structure," 125.

13. Ibid., 126.

14. When the violist Borisovsky retired in 1964, he was replaced by Fyodor Druzhinin. The second violinist, Vasily Shirinsky, died in 1965 and was repalced by Nikolai Zabavnikov. Regarding the first eight quartets, see Colin M. Mason, "Form in Shostakovich's Quartets," *Musical Times* 103 (1962), 531.

15. Khrenninkov is known less for his compositions than for the fact that from 1948 until its dissolution in December 1991, he was elected forty-three times consecutively to the highly influential post of secretary of the Union of Soviet Composers.

16. Quoted in Fay, *Shostakovich*, 217.

17. Corresponding to the pitches D, E-flat, C, B-natural, taken from the letters in the German transliteration of the composer's name: D. Schostakowitsch.

18. The recording of Op. 134 with Oistrakh accompanied by Shostakovich is currently available from Eclectra Records, CD no. 2046 (© August 2000).

19. A recording of Op. 134 with Oistrakh accompanied by Shostakovich is currently available from Eclectra Records, CD no. 2046 (August 2000).

20. In their reminiscences of Shostakovich, both Denisov and Gubaidulina throw bricks along with bouquets. As a world-renowned personality, the composer was seen by Party officials as a useful vehicle for propaganda. For reasons that remain unclear, Shostakovich, in September 1960, became a candidate for membership in the Communist Party. He moved to full membership in the following year. Apparently he became complacent about statements attributed to him by the Communist Party and failed to speak out against such abuses, which often had negative impacts on other composers, performers, and creative artists. See Wilson, *Shostakovich*, 305–7 (Gubaidulina), 432–34 (Denisov).

21. His works are published primarily by Leduc, Universal, and Sikorski. The Romantishe Music was issued by Universal [1970]; the Trio by Sikorski [1985].

22. (Hamburg: Sikorski, 1989). In 1986, Denisov made an arrangement of the same piece for viola, flute, oboe, celesta, and string quintet.

23. Philip Walters, "A Survey of Soviet Religious Policy," in *Religious Policy in the Soviet Union* (New York: Cambridge University Press, 1993), 13.

24. Ibid., 13.

25. Quoted in Vera Lukomsky, "'The Eucharist in My Fantasy': An Interview with Sofia Gubaidulina," *Tempo* 206 (October 1998), 125. See also Gubaidulina's discussion of "sacred" and "religion" in *Composers on Music*, ed. Josiah Fisk, 2nd ed. (Boston: Northeastern University Press, 1997), 461.

26. Bayan is a chromatic, push-button accordion. This score and others cited in the following discussion are available from G. Schirmer.

27. Nicholas Slonimsky, ed., "Gubaidulina, Sofia," in *Baker's Biographical Dictionary of Musicians*, 8th ed. (New York: Schirmer, 1990), 679–80.

28. *Stimmen: Tagebuch, Novellen, Gedichte* (Voices: diary, tales, and poems) (Cologne: Hermansen Verlag, 1979). In addition to Gubaidulina, John Cage, Edison Denisov, and Alfred Schnittke have set Tanzer's writings. Significant chamber works that have resulted include Dennisov's *Wishing Well* for soprano, clarinet, viola, and piano (Hamburg: Sikorski, 1996); and Schnittke's *Three Madrigals* for soprano, vibraphone, harpsichord, violin, viola, and double bass (Hamburg: Sikorski, 1981). Gubaidulina has written other works inspired by Tanzer including her twelve-movement symphony *Stimmen . . . verstummen . . .* (Voices . . . growing silent . . . ; 1986) for details see Radice, *Concert Music*, 210–11.

29. BBC-Music / Profiles–Sofia Gubaidulina (website). "Music: Artist Profiles" (14 January 2004), http://www.bbc.co.uk/music/profiles/gubaidulina.shtml.

30. For Schnittke's opinion of Gershkovich see "In Memory of Filip Moiseevich Gershkovich," in *A Schnittke Reader*, ed. Alexander Ivashkin (Bloomington: Indiana University Press, 2002), 70–71.

31. At its simplest, polystylism is a musical collage. In complex applications, it may involve (1) direct quotation of specific works or, (2) paraphrase or pseudoquotation, (3) microelements of historical styles, such as phrase shapes, cadence patterns, ornamentation, etc., (4) allusion, or (5) adaptation (i.e., transformation of established musical scores into different musical idioms). These elements influence the choice of forms, rhythms, textures, and other parameters. They may appear successively, simultaneously, or both within the context of a new composition.

Schnittke notes that "a composer often plans a polystylistic effect in advance, whether it be the shock effect of a clashing collage of music from different times, a flexible glide through phases of musical history, or the use of allusions so subtle that they seem accidental." References to "flexible glide" and "allusions" suggest a new modulatory process to complement traditional concepts of tonal modulation and the more recently developed notion of metric modulation. The process of stylistic modulation, however, is unexplored territory in music theoretical literature. For more on polystylism, see Alfred Schnittke, "Polystylistic Tendencies in Modern Music," in Ivashkin, *A Schnittke Reader*, 87–90.

32. As a Bohemian Jew, Mahler's alienation from Austro-German society was twofold. Schnittke's situation paralleled Mahler's quite closely: "I don't have any Russian blood [yet] I am tied to Russia . . . but I am not Russian. . . . My Jewish half gives me no peace: I know none of the Jewish languages, but I look like a typical Jew." Quoted in Ivashkin, *A Schnittke Reader*, [xiii].

33. Berg had used his name as a motif in his String Quartet No. 2, the *Lyric Suite*.

34. Further on Lutoslawski in Steven Stucky, *Lutoslawski and His Music* (New York: Cambridge University Press, 1981), 252.

35. Further on Penderecki in *The Music of Krzysztof Penderecki: Poetics and Reception*, ed. Mieczyslaw Tomaszewski (Kraców: Akademia Muzyczna w Krakowie, 1995), 196; Wolfram Schwinger, *Krzysztof Penderecki: His Life and Work*, trans. William Mann (London: Schott, 1989), 290.

CHAPTER 14

1. Ligeti noted that the Hungarian is not quite right: In German, *Aue* means "meadow," but the Hungarian *liget* actually means "thicket." See Paul Griffiths, *György Ligeti* (London: Robson Books, 1983), 16.

2. Ibid., 24.

3. Gyögry Ligeti, "Rhapsodische, unausgewogene Gedanken über Musik, besonders über meine eigenen Kompositionen," *Neue Zeitschrift für Musik* (January 1993), 24. "Bei ihm [Ockeghem] gibt es stagnierended Strukturen, da sich die Einzelstimmen stets überlappen, ähnlich den sich überschlagenden Wellen.

4. I am grateful to Amy Sanchez for pointing out details of Ligeti's writing for a valved horn in the manner of a natural horn.

5. For details on Husa's life and works, see Mark A. Radice, ed., *Karel Husa: A Composer's Life in Essays and Documents* (Lewiston, N.Y.: Edwin Mellen Press, 2002). The chamber works are listed (along with page references of the concomittent discussions) in the "Chronological Listing of Husa's Works and Index of Works Discussed," 211–13.

6. The so-called String Quartet No. 1 was actually Husa's second; the "first," now known as the Quartet No. 0, was written in 1942–43 during Husa's student years at the Prague Conservatory. The piece was not performed until the Apollon Quartet gave the permiere in Prague on 23 February 2000, in the Lichtenstein Palace, at the concert sponsored by the Society for Contemporary Music (*Přitomnost*). It is Husa's first composition, but he did not reckon it as "Op. 1," conferring that designation instead on his Sonatina for piano solo despite the fact that it was

composed *after* the string quartet and should bear the designation "Op. 2." The opus numbers were, therefore, reversed, the String Quartet No. 0 becoming Op. 2.

7. Jacob Hardesty, "The Saxophone Music of Karel Husa," in Radice, *Karel Husa*, 98.

8. Karel Husa, quoted in ibid., 99.

9. Husa orchestrated *Élégie et rondeau*, and on 6 May 1962, Rasher gave the first performance of the orchestral version with Husa directing the Cornell University Symphony Orchestra.

10. Stephen G. Jones, Review of Karel Husa's *Landscapes* for Brass Quintet (New York: Associated Music Publishers, 1984), *International Trumpet Guild Journal* 21 (December 1997), 56–57.

11. John Rockwell, *New York Times*, 2 April 1974.

12. Earl George, "Colorado Quartet Gives Grand Performance," *Syracuse Herald Journal*, 25 November 1991.

CHAPTER 15

1. The tonal design of the Sinfonia is examined in Ethan Haimo, "Problems of Hierarchy in Stravinsky's Octet," *Perspectives on Stravinsky* (Lincoln: University of Nebraska Press, 1987), 36–54.

2. The octatonic scale had been used in the mid-nineteenth century by Franz Liszt; however, its extensive cultivation within the context of chromatic harmony was the doing of Nikolai Rimsky-Korsakov, who even referred to it as the Russian scale. This symmetrical configuration of half and whole tones was subsequently exploited by Maurice Ravel, Olivier Messiaen (in whose theoretical writings it is identified as the second mode of limited transposition), and other French composers. Stravinsky, who studed with Rimsky from 1905 until 1908, knew the scale and its potential before going to France in 1910.

3. Milton Babbitt, "Edgard Varèse: A Few Observations of His Music," *Perspectives of New Music* 4 (Spring–Summer, 1966), 14. Varèse's given name was "Edgard," but he published his music under the name "Edgar." Sometime around 1940, he reverted to the original form of the name.

4. Jonathan W. Bernard, "Pitch/Register in the Music of Edgard Varèse," *Music Theory Spectrum* 3 (Spring 1981), 5. Correspondingly, inversional equivalence is also rejected since the size of a given interval is an integral rather than coincidental element of any sonority.

5. But see the corrected edition with critical commentary by Chou Wen-chung (New York: Colfranc Music Publishing, 1980), 26 and vi.

6. In his commentary on the piece that was published in the *Baseler National Zeitung*, 13 January 1938, Bartók refers to the commission as having come "last summer"; however, Stevens, *Life and Music of Béla Bartók*, rev. ed. (New York: Oxford University Press, 1964), 83, explains that while the composition of the piece took place during July and August, the commission actually came in May.

7. For Sacher's account of the rehearsals and premiere, see Stevens, *Bartók*, rev. ed., 83. In June, the Bartóks played the piece in Luxembourg and at the London ISCM conference. In the former performance, the percussionists numbered four!

8. David Osmond-Smith kindly informed me in a communication of 4 July 2004 that a year or so before Berio's death, he suggested the compilation of a dictionary of twentieth-century composers, in which the main entries would be written by living composers and performers who felt a particular affinity for their subject. The only composer on whom he wished to write was Bartók.

9. Olivier Messiaen, *Quatuor pour la fine du temps* (Paris: Durand, n.d.), preface.

10. In the preface to the score, Messiaen cites this text in French and goes on to remark concerning the piece, "Il a été directement inspiré par cette citation de l'Apocalypse. Son langage musical est essentiellement immatériel, spirituel, catholique" (it was inspired directly from this citation from the Apocalypse. Its musical language is essentially ephemeral, spiritual, catholic).

11. Claude Samuel, *Conversations with Olivier Messiaen*, trans. Felix Aprahamian (London: Stainer and Bell, 1976), 2.

12. Ibid., 7.

13. Ibid., 10. The birdsongs used by Messiaen are cataloged in Robert Sherlaw Johnson, *Messiaen* (Berkeley: University of California Press, 1975).

14. Samuel, *Conversations*, 11.

15. Paul Griffiths, notes for *Messiaen: Quatuor pour la fin du temps*, DGG CD 423-247-2, p. 3.

16. Pierre Boulez, "Sound and Word," in *Notes of an Apprenticeship*, trans. Herbert Weinstock (New York: Alfred A. Knopf, 1968), 54.

17. Ibid.

18. Ibid., 55.

19. David Osmond-Smith, *Berio* (New York: Oxford University Press, 1991), 6. In particular, he notes that Berio has constructed his row using motifs that will remain distinctive in their serial permutations. Likewise, rows are combined in ways that facilitate convergence upon common pithches. See ibid., 7–8.

20. FURIOUS CRAFTSMEN

the red caravan at the edge of the prison
and corpse in the basket
and workhorses on horseshoes
I dream the head on the point of my knife

BEAUTIFUL BUILDING AND THE PREMONITIONS

I hear marching in my legs
the dead sea waves over my head
child the savage boardwalk
man the imitated illusion
of pure eyes in the forest
weeping and seeking a habitable head
hangmen of solitude
the step is distant, the marcher is gone
on the dial of limitation
the scale thrusts its load of granite reflex

21. Pierre Boulez, "Speaking, Playing, Singing," in *Orientations*, ed. Jean-Jacques Nattiez, trans. Martin Cooper (Cambridge: Harvard University Press, 1986), 339–40.

22. Ibid., 340.

23. Pierre Boulez, preface to *Le marteau sans maître* (Vienna: Universal, 1957). This preface is a variant translation of the earlier-cited essay, "Speaking, Playing, Singing."

24. Regarding synthesizers and the place of the Buchla synthesizer in their history, see Radice, *Concert Music*, 248–52.

25. Leon Kirchner, prefatory notes for String Quartet No. 3 for Strings and Electronic Tape (New York: Associated Music Publishers, 1971). The piece has been recorded by the Boston Composers' String Quartet on *Leon Kirchner: The Complete String Quartets* (Albany Records CD Troy 137, 1994), [6].

26. Don Gillespie, ed., *George Crumb: Profile of a Composer* (New York: C. F. Peters, 1986), 17.

27. See Chou's essay "*Ionisation:* The Function of Timbre in its Formal and Temporal Organization," in *The New World of Edgard Varèse: A Symposium*, ed. Sherman Van Solkema (New York: Institute for Studies in American Music, 1979), 27–74.

28. Chou Wen-chung, *Echoes from the Gorge* (New York: C. F. Peters, n.d. [1994]).

29. Chou's "Notes on Instruments" states that "many of the standard instruments called for in this score may be substituted by non-Western instruments with similar sound characteristics and appropriate size (i.e., pitch level)." In particular, the following equivalencies are indicated: claves = Chinese *bangzi* or Japanese *hyoshigi;* wood blocks = Chinese *nanbangzi;* temple blocks = Chinese *muyu;* high and low Chinese small tom-tom = *xiaogu;* tenor drum = Chinese *tanggu* or *dagu;* finger bells = *xing* (*ling* or *pengzhong*); Chinese cymbal s= *xiaoba;* Chinese cymbals = *nao* and *daba;* low gong = Chinese *shenboluo* or *gaobianluo.* Chou's "Notes on Instruments" includes the cryptic observation that "only 'authentic' instruments are to be used."

30. For a brief analysis of *Echoes*, see Kenneth Kwan, "Chou Wen-chung's *Echoes from the Gorge* (1989)," *Chinese Music* 18, nos. 3 and 4 (1995), 56–58, 74–78. Kwan has recently completed a more detailed analysis of *Echoes* that will appear in a collection of essays currently being edited by Mark A. Radice and Mary I. Arlin, forthcoming. Concerning the concept of "transethnicism," see David Nicholls, "Transethnicism and the American Experimental Tradition," *Musical Quarterly* 80 (Winter 1996), 569–94.

31. The information in this paragraph is derived in part from Peter M. Chang, *Chou Wen-chung: The Life and Work of a Contemporary Chinese-Born American Composer* (Lanham, Md.: Scarecrow Press, 2006), 120.

32. The *Tao-te ching* (Pinyin *Dao de ching*) "first emerged in a period of Chinese history called the Warring States (570–221 B.C.E.)." Livia Kohn and Michael LaFargue, eds., *Lao-tzu and the Tao-te-ching* (Albany: State University of New York Press, 1998), 3. Some scholars have argued that the *Tao-te ching* is not the work of a single author; moreover, the very identity of the historical Lao-tzu has been questioned. See A[ngus] C[harles] Graham, "The Origins of the Legend of Lao Tan" and Livia Kohn, "The Lao-tzu Myth," in Kohn and LaFargue, 23–40, 41–62. English spellings vary: Lao-tzu, Laozi, Laotse, Lao-zu, and Lao-tsu—in that order—are the most common.

33. Laozi, *Dao de jing: The Book of the Way*, based on the trans. with commentary by Moss Roberts (Berkeley: University of California Press, 2001), 116.

34. Roberts, ibid., 60.

35. Roberts, ibid., 117.

36. Roberts, ibid.

37. In fact, the note values are not at all "arbitrarily selected"; a comparison of meter signatures across the four percussionists' parts will show that they, too, are chosen for their structural significance.

38. Measure numbers are also continuous.

39. Kwan, "Chou Wen-chung's *Echoes from the Gorge*," 75.

40. This is a slightly different presentation of the material explained by Kwan, ibid., 76.

41. Chang, *Chou Wen-chung*, 152, actually states that the first movement "can stand alone as a separate quartet." This was never Chou's intention (phone conversation, 8 October 2010).

42. See Eric C. Lai, *The Music of Chou Wen Chung* (Burlington, Vt.: Ashgate, 2009), 65–72.

43. Chou Wen-chung, String Quartet No. 2, Streams ([New York]: Spiralis Archival Editions, 2003), v. Chou's compositions bear the Spiralis imprint until—after rehearsals, performances, and corrections—he is satisfied that the music is in final form and ready to be issued by C. F. Peters, which has been his publisher throughout his career.

Index

Family names including particles (e.g., de, dei, des, la, van, von) will be listed under the principal word in the name (e.g., Rue, Pierre de la). Umlauts are not reckoned in alphabetization, which is letter-by-letter. Page numbers in italics contain relevant musical examples.